A HISTORY OF ASHINGDON

& SOUTH FAMBRIDGE

Ian Yearsley

Published by Ian Yearsley 2023
Publishing Partner: Paragon Publishing, Rothersthorpe

© Ian Yearsley 2023

The rights of Ian Yearsley to be identified as the author of this work have been asserted by him in accordance with the Copyright, Designs and Patents Act of 1988.
All rights reserved; no part of this publication may be reproduced, stored in a retrieval system, or transmitted in any form or by any means, electronic, mechanical, photocopying, recording or otherwise without the prior written consent of the publisher or a licence permitting copying in the UK issued by the Copyright Licensing Agency Ltd. www.cla.co.uk

ISBN 978-1-78222-977-3

Book design, layout and production management by Into Print
www.intoprint.net
+44 (0)1604 832149

Contents

ACKNOWLEDGEMENTS 5

PREFACE 6

INTRODUCTION.. 8

THE PREHISTORIC PERIOD 11

ROMAN ASHINGDON 12

SAXON SIGNIFICANCE – Saxon Settlement, Saxon Ashingdon, The Battle of "Assandun" (1016), Canute's Minster Church (1020) 13

LAND OWNERSHIP & MANORS – The Domesday Book (1086), Post-Domesday Landowners & Manors, Woodlands 22

MANOR HOUSES – Ashingdon Hall, Beckney, South Fambridge Hall 34

MEDIEVAL CHURCHES – St Andrew Ashingdon, Beckney, All Saints South Fambridge 38

VILLAGE LIFE BEFORE 1700 – The Bold Love Adventure, Early Wills, Ashingdon Parish Registers, Court Records, The Hearth Tax, Ashingdon Rectors.. 48

VILLAGE LIFE IN THE 18TH CENTURY – Parish Officials, More Court Records, Witchcraft. 61

CHAPMAN & ANDRÉ'S MAP OF ESSEX (1777) – Smith's, Rouncefall, Moon's, South Fambridge Parsonage & Ministers, South Fambridge Parish Registers, Brick House Farm aka Forsters, The Ferry House. 64

THE POOR. 75

ASHINGDON PARISH MAP (1787/1808) – Ashingdon Church, Ashingdon Rectory, Ashingdon Hall, Chamberlain's, Rouncefall, Moon's, Moon's Cottages, Beckney, Smith's, Holloucks Farm, South Fambridge Hall, South Fambridge Church, South Fambridge Parsonage, South Fambridge Riverside, Lower Road & Greensward Lane, New Hall, Pulpits 76

VILLAGE LIFE 1800-1840 – Parish Registers, Poor Law Returns, Parish Officials, Local Activities, A Railway Scheme, Property Ownership, The Union Workhouse. 90

THE TITHE AWARDS – The Tithe Commutation Act 1836, Ashingdon, South Fambridge 103

THE VICTORIAN ERA – Village Life, More Railway Schemes, Potash, Flooding, Mid-Century, South Fambridge New Town, Rectory Farm, Property Ownership, Education, Last Quarter, Property Ownership, Local Activities, 1st Edition Ordnance Survey Map, The Railway Arrives in Rochford, United Benefice, Local Government Reorganisation, 2nd Edition Ordnance Survey Map, Thomas Hollick's Engineering Factory, Village Life in the 1890s, Population Trends. 109

THE EDWARDIAN ERA – Development, Village Life, Free Church Mission Hall, The Fambridge Colony, South Fambridge Airfield, The 1911 Coronation, *The Anchor Inn*, Education, The First World War.. 145

THE PERIOD BETWEEN THE WARS – Property Development and Ownership, The Ashingdon Park Estate, 3rd Edition Ordnance Survey Map, Village Life, The Ashingdon Hall Estate, Leisure & Entertainment, Education, Ashingdon Parish Council, South Fambridge Parish Council, Parish Boundary Review, King George V Silver Jubilee, Playing Fields, Street Lighting, A River Crouch Bridge, Speed Limits, Fire Protection, Flying Fleas, Cycling Problems, Police Issues, King George VI Coronation, The Late 1930s, A Village Hall, The Fambridge Ferry 160

THE SECOND WORLD WAR – Defence, Incidents, Plane Crash, Victory Looms. 201

THE POST-WAR PERIOD – A New Council, Village Life, Property Ownership, Education, A New Decade, The Restoration of St Andrew's Church, The Great Tide, The 1953 Coronation, The End of the Ferry, Roads, The Mid-Fifties, Education, Property Ownership, Constitutional Crisis, Development, The Late 1950s, More Issues/More Councillors, Increased Schooling Provision, The Church, The 1960s, The Memorial Hall, The End of the Decade, The Early 1970s, Maplin Airport, School Centenary, Local Government Reorganisation, The Mid-1970s, Queen Elizabeth II Silver Jubilee, A Radical Plan, The Late 1970s/Early 1980s, The District Plan, South Fambridge Village Plan, Ashingdon Youth Club, Boundary Changes, A Bypass for Ashingdon, The Late 1980s, Village Signs, The 1990s, Ashingdon School, Residential Development 213

THE 21ST CENTURY 297

CONCLUSION . .. .303

BIBLIOGRAPHY – Documentary Sources, Websites, Films. 304

INDEX 311

ACKNOWLEDGEMENTS

The following illustrations are reproduced by courtesy of those named: 1, Dr. Jayne Carroll from the English Place-Name Society/University of Nottingham; 4-6, Anna Powell-Smith, Professor John Palmer and George Slater from opendomesday.org; 19, 32-4, 36-8, 47, 51, 53, 70, 80, 82, 85-6 and 92 are reproduced by courtesy of the Essex Record Office; 44-5 & 63 have been reproduced under a Creative Commons Attribution-NonCommercial-ShareAlike 4.0 International (CC-BY-NC-SA) licence with the permission of the National Library of Scotland; 54 is from the archive of Fred Spalding and is believed to be out of copyright; 55 is a photograph of an original picture, so it has not been possible to trace the copyright owner for it; 77 is from *The Illustrated Sporting and Dramatic News* and is believed to be out of copyright; 87-8 are reproduced by permission of the *Essex Chronicle/Reach PLC*; 90 is copyright The Francis Frith Collection and has been reproduced with their permission; and 96 has been reproduced by permission of the RPS Group. I have tried unsuccessfully to track down the copyright holders of several other illustrations, including picture 7 from https://www.luminarium.org/, 80 which is copyright D. Troughton, 82 & 92 which are copyright George Robinson, 86 whose copyright owner is unknown and 104 which is copyright Belinda M.J. Daly and has been reproduced from her PhD thesis on *Direct Action Environmental Protest in Britain: A Critique of Radical Environmentalism and Environmental Ethics* (2005). All other illustrations are from my own collection. If I have unwittingly reproduced anything which is in copyright I apologise for this and will happily correct it at the earliest opportunity.

In addition to the illustration acknowledgements, I would also like to thank the following for their help with this book: staff at the Essex Record Office in Chelmsford; Dr. Keith Briggs for information about Roman roads in the area; Maria Medlycott of Essex County Council for sharing her report on *Ashingdon: Historic Settlement Assessment*; Simon Ford, David Huskisson and Malcom Jones for information about Ashingdon United Free Church and its associations with Ashingdon School; Peter C. Brown for the provision of information about local aviation pioneers; Michael Barker for information about Moon's Cottage; Mrs. S. Wheeler regarding Greensward Academy dates; Karen Boyce of Ashingdon Parish Council for assistance with council history; Ellie Broad at Southend Museums Service for help with my queries about the early history of the area; and the congregations at St Andrew's and All Saints' churches. I would also like to thank my wife, Alison, for accompanying me on several trips around the area and for providing advice and support regarding the book's content.

PREFACE

I have been interested in the history of Ashingdon since I discovered as an 18-year-old in 1983 that it was probably the site of a major battle which was fought between Saxons and Vikings, led by Edmund Ironside and King Cnut (Canute) respectively, in 1016. I wrote a poem about it in 1991 as a competition entry for an anthology about the Rochford Hundred which was being produced by Lily Jerram-Burrows. She was a leading light in the Rochford Hundred Historical Society and the author of a series of history booklets based on the notes of the great 19th-century local historian, Philip Benton (1815-98). Benton wrote the landmark work *The History of the Rochford Hundred* in two volumes between 1867 and 1888. Mrs. Jerram-Burrows kindly accepted my submission and it duly appeared in her book, *Smuggler's Moon: An Anthology of the Rochford Hundred*, in 1993.

I always intended my poem to be the first verse of a much longer work – an epic poem of the kind written in the Saxon period to commemorate a battle – but due to other writing commitments it took me until 2006 to complete it. I published the completed poem of 12 verses in booklet form that year, but when I set about publicising it, I was surprised to learn that a) comparatively few local people knew about the battle and b) it might not have taken place in Ashingdon after all, as Ashdon in north-west Essex was touted as an alternative location. This, and the sudden realisation that it was only 10 years until the 1,000th anniversary of the battle, set me on a quest to find out more about it and to publicise my findings. I launched a campaign through the press to spread awareness and seek the support of like-minded individuals and I still maintain a website about it on Facebook: https://www.facebook.com/battleofassandun/.

These activities brought me into close contact with the Ashingdon community and I had the opportunity to speak to long-standing Ashingdon residents and to work closely with Ashingdon Parish Council. I fell in love with Ashingdon and its people and I like to feel that I am a surrogate member of the community (I live in Eastwood, so not far away). I was delighted in the battle's millennium year to be asked by Ashingdon Parish Council to write a commemorative history booklet and the text for an information board at St Andrew's church, as well as to be asked to open the 2016 Ashingdon Flower Festival there, which featured displays based on stanzas from my poem. I felt truly honoured to be asked to be involved in these activities.

The doubts about whether the 1016 battle was fought in Ashingdon or Ashdon continue to bug me, 16 years after I first started to research them. I have tried unsuccessfully to get the TV series *Time Team*, TV historian Neil Oliver and Essex County Council to carry out a two-site archaeological dig, which I believe is the only way that the mystery will ever be solved. I have also worked closely with historians and others in both Ashingdon and

Ashdon to try to get to the bottom of it. In 2016 the millennium of the battle was celebrated in both places, which was hardly ideal. In 2022, however, my colleagues in Ashdon managed to get The Battlefields Trust involved and we are now collectively working together on trying to identify the battle site once and for all.

Ashingdon, of course, is so much more than a battle, and as I have got to know the community and to explore the location, I have been keen to research and write a full history of the place. Benton's was the last of these, and that was in 1867. I also learned during my research that the histories of Ashingdon and South Fambridge have been intertwined in many ways, so my original idea for a history of one parish quickly doubled into a history of two.

I have tried to be comprehensive without going too much into the minutiae of daily life. Having said that, however, I have deliberately retained a lot of the detail to give a flavour for what it has been like to live in Ashingdon at various periods. The minutes of Ashingdon Parish Council and its Ashingdon and South Fambridge predecessors have been particularly useful in helping me to see and understand the daily workings of a small community and the issues, large and small, that it has faced over the decades. I have also been deliberately parochial – this is a book about life in Ashingdon and South Fambridge, not the wider Rochford District – though I have paid heed to wider developments which have affected the two villages, such as the closure of Rochford Hospital and the increasing development encroachment from Rochford, Hawkwell and Hockley.

In 1020 Canute erected a minster church of "stone and lime" at the site of the Battle of Assandun to commemorate its dead, so 2020 seemed to me to be the ideal time to bring the community's whole story up to date. I had planned to publish the book in that year, but the coronavirus pandemic put paid to that. So, two years later than planned, here is my history of Ashingdon and South Fambridge. I hope you enjoy reading it as much as I have enjoyed researching and writing it.

INTRODUCTION

Ashingdon is a historic community of around 3,500 people which is situated some 30 miles east of London in the county of Essex, within the district of Rochford. The modern parish incorporates the historically separate parishes of Ashingdon, which was in three parts, and South Fambridge. As the two settlements' stories – and boundaries – are intertwined, their histories will both be discussed throughout this narrative.

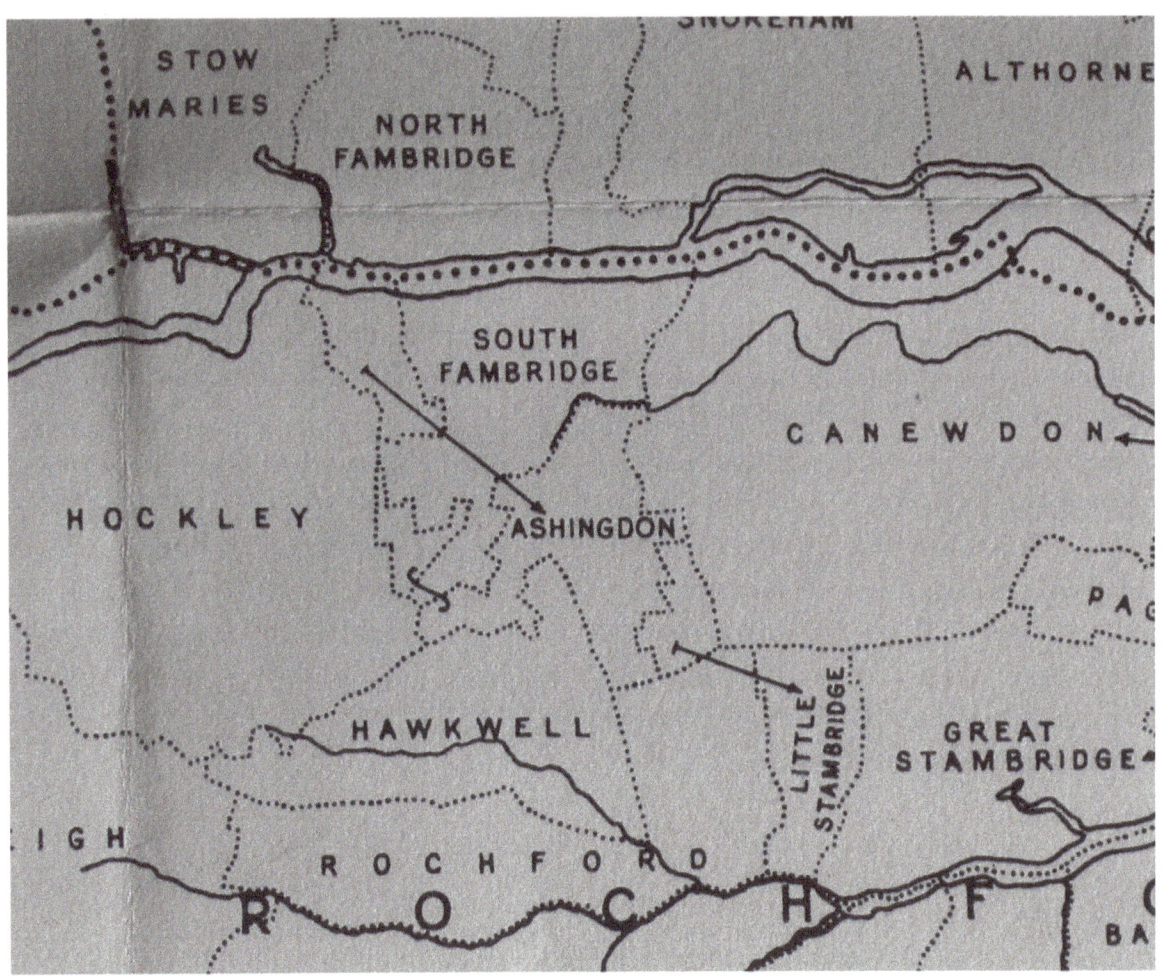

Figure 1: Map showing the historic parishes of Ashingdon and South Fambridge with arrows linking Ashingdon to its two detached parts [1]

---

1   The map is from *The Place-Names of Essex* by Dr. P.H. Reaney. It is also published by the Essex Record Office.

The map above shows the historic boundaries of the two parishes. Ashingdon, unusually, had two detached parts; the arrows linking them to the main part of Ashingdon parish can be seen on the map. Nearby Little Stambridge had a similar detached portion. Given that the two detached sections of Ashingdon parish lay on the opposite side of South Fambridge to the main part of the parish, and the boundaries between all these areas of land were very irregular and interlocking, it is not surprising that they have come to be considered as one in modern times. An explanation of how this evolved administratively is given in the text which follows.

The map shows that the conglomeration of Ashingdon and South Fambridge was historically bordered on the north by the River Crouch, on the east by Canewdon parish and the detached part of Little Stambridge, on the south by Rochford parish and on the west by Hawkwell and Hockley parishes. The boundary between Ashingdon and Rochford parishes is the western end of what is now Brays Lane; the long straight boundary northward from there between Ashingdon and Hawkwell parishes is Ashingdon Road, the main through-route in this part of the county. This road forms the whole of Hawkwell's eastern boundary.

The name "Ashingdon", which has been through a number of variations in spelling over the centuries, including in particular "Assingdon" and "Assington", has been variously interpreted to mean "the hill of the ash trees", "the hill of the asses" or "the hill belonging to Assa" (a Saxon landowner). The latter two appear to have gained the most credence in modern academic sources and are favoured by Dr. P.H. Reaney in his landmark book, *The Place-names of Essex* (1969). According to Reaney, the name "Fambridge" means "marsh bridge" or "fen bridge" – a bridge over the marsh or fen – but other historians, including Colchester-based Philip Morant, in his 1768 book *The History & Antiquities of the County of Essex (Vol. I)*, suggest that "fam" derives from "foam". The "South" prefix is used to distinguish this parish from North Fambridge, a parish on the opposite bank of the Crouch which was once home to the other end of a now lost bridge or causeway between the two. The notable foaminess of the river here, according to Morant, was occasioned by the pillars of the said bridge being in place and obstructing its natural flow. Morant writes that "the bridge that gave [its] name to this and the opposite parish, hath been down many years, but here is a noted ferry at which a very bold love adventure is said to have happened". More information about this bold love adventure will be given later.

Philip Benton observes in his *The History of the Rochford Hundred* (Vol. I, 1867) that: "Although the old historians do not narrate the circumstance, it seems probable that there were two bridges – North and South Fambridge – as in all the old maps, such as [John] Speed's [of 1610], [John] Norden's [of 1594] and others, an island is laid down in the centre of the stream, precisely in the track of the present ferry, so that the old road probably passed through it. In the course of time, after the marshes were enclosed, the velocity of the water being greater, it would soon carry away and undermine an island, whose only resistance to the current consisted of mud banks."

Speed's and Norden's maps do indeed show an island where Benton describes it. Low-lying marshland islands like this are common around the Essex coast, including Bridgemarsh Island in the River Crouch only a couple of miles to the east of the Fambridges, but none exists between them now.

The above name derivations alone for Ashingdon and South Fambridge reveal that the former is on a hill and the latter is on the flat. The highest point of Ashingdon parish is over 50 metres above sea level; South Fambridge barely gets above 10 metres anywhere. Benton, a farmer by profession, wrote of the latter that "the aspect of the parish is not very inviting, either as regards its soil or scenery; the ground is flat and lies low".

THE PREHISTORIC PERIOD

A *Historic Environment Characterisation Project* for Rochford District, which was sponsored by the District Council in 2006, records evidence of human occupation in the area dating back 450,000 years. Some of the oldest local evidence comes from South Fambridge in the Mesolithic (Middle Stone Age) period, with finds here and elsewhere along the River Crouch dating from *c.*8,000-6,800 BC.

T.J. Wilkinson and Peter Murphy, who carried out investigations on the River Crouch as part of a survey of 'Hullbridge Basin' in the 1980s and 1990s, found evidence of worked flint tools, pottery, fired clay and charcoal in the South Fambridge area, all dating from *c.*10,000-2001 BC.

Apart from that there is little documented evidence of prehistoric activity in the area, although the geography is typical of prehistoric settlement patterns, providing access to fresh water, good drainage, the availability of flint, ease of land clearance and a vantage or defensive position high up on Ashingdon Hill.

ROMAN ASHINGDON

Evidence of Roman occupation of the area is also sketchy.

The *Royal Commission on Historic Monuments* (Essex, Vol. IV, 1923) records the presence of so-called 'Red Hills' in both Ashingdon and South Fambridge. These are small mounds of reddish earth which provide evidence of the distillation of salt from seawater, a common Roman salt-making process practised all round the coast of south-east Essex. Ashingdon parish church contains reused Roman bricks in its walls.

Perhaps most intriguingly, the long, straight section of Ashingdon Road which forms the western boundaries of both Ashingdon and Rochford parishes with neighbouring Hawkwell (see the map in the Introduction), is cited in some sources as being Roman, though there is not a great deal of evidence to support this. It does not appear on the Ordnance Survey's map of *Roman Britain*, but it does appear on the maps of Dr. Keith Briggs, a visiting lecturer in mathematics at the University of Oxford who uses computer software to generate maps for illustrating documents on place-names. Dr. Briggs has informed the author that: "In general, it's probably not meaningful to say whether a specific minor road is Roman or not. It may have been in use in the Roman period, but not built to the standards of the major highways." He also notes that it was not categorised as a Roman road by a prominent 20th-century historian, Ivan Margary, who specialised in identifying and cataloguing them.

SAXON SIGNIFICANCE

Saxon Settlement

After the Romans left Britain in 410 AD, waves of Germanic tribes such as the Angles, Saxons and Jutes began to invade the country from the east. What was to become Essex was settled by the Saxons. The county's name derives from the Kingdom of the East Saxons, which once incorporated not just what is now Essex but also parts of what are now Hertfordshire, Middlesex and Kent. It was founded in the sixth century, possibly as early as the 520s. It seems likely that the settlement of some parts of the south-east corner of the county took place around this time and that the area became increasingly settled over the next 150 years. The nationally significant grave of the so-called "Saxon King", which was discovered at Prittlewell in the neighbouring Borough of Southend in 2003, has been dated to the late-6th or early-7th century.

Place-name and archaeological evidence suggests that settlement probably started in the east, around the estuaries of the Rivers Crouch, Roach and Thames, most likely in the Wakering area. It then moved westwards, as Saxon settlers first colonised the easily accessible coastal plains before moving further inland and up into the wooded hillsides to the east of Rayleigh as more settlers arrived and more land was required to accommodate them. The parishes in this part of the county were grouped into a larger administrative unit called the "Rochford Hundred". The bulk of this forms the basis of Rochford District today.

Professor Stephen Rippon, who has researched the historic landscape character of south-east Essex, has suggested that the Rochford Hundred was probably one entire administrative area in the 5th-7th centuries. Rippon writes in his report entitled 'Stonebridge: An Initial Assessment of its Historic Landscape Character' (2011) that: "In the Early Saxon period (5th to 7th centuries), the whole of South-East Essex, south of the Crouch Estuary, appears to have formed a single district – probably known at the time as a 'regio' (district) – that became the 'Hundred' of Rochford extending from South Shoebury, up to Canewdon, and across to Rawreth, Rayleigh and Hadleigh. The place-names 'Canewdon' and 'Canvey' may both contain the personal name 'Cana', making this the region of Cana's people." [2]

Leonard Helliwell, a former Southend Museum curator, writes in his book *South-east Essex in the Saxon Period* (1971, p.12), that "there can be little doubt… that the pattern of village settlement of the area had been completed during the height of East Saxon influence and probably by the end of the third quarter of the 7th century". This pattern evolved from the 8th to 12th centuries into the parish structure, which is shown in the map in the Introduction, and parish churches began to appear as religious focal points for local communities.

---

[2] Stephen Rippon, 'Stonebridge: An Initial Assessment of its Historic Landscape Character', p.7

Saxon Ashingdon

As explained in the Introduction, "Ashingdon" and "Fambridge" are both descriptive names. According to Helliwell, this places them as coming into existence sometime in the sixth century, though whether they were settled then, or were just identifiable/important local hill and bridge landmarks respectively, is open to question.

Ashingdon sits on an outcrop at the north-eastern end of the Rayleigh Hills, a ridge of high land which is unusual in this part of the country. Only the standalone hill of Canewdon, two miles to the east-north-east of it, lies beyond. Low-lying South Fambridge, on the southern bank of the River Crouch to the north, would have been easily accessible by boat, and it is easy to envisage early settlers potentially coming ashore at this location and creating the forerunners of what are now Fambridge Road and the northern end of Ashingdon Road to lead them from the river up to the top of the hill where St Andrew's church now stands. This latter location would have offered a great vantage point for observation and defence – the view today from here towards the River Crouch is one of the best in the District. If Ashingdon Road is Roman (see earlier discussion), then it could be that it and Fambridge Road together formed a Roman route to a river crossing on the Crouch long before the Saxons arrived and potentially reused it.

Saxon Ashingdon appears to have remained relatively quiet in terms of the national stage until 1016 when it came to the fore with one of its main claims to fame as its possible location as the site of the Battle of "Assandun". The next section of this book has been adapted from a booklet which the author wrote for Ashingdon Parish Council in 2016.

The Battle of Assandun (1016)

The Battle of Assandun (sometimes spelt "Assandune") was fought in the Essex countryside on 18 October 1016 between the armies of Edmund Ironside, King of England, and Cnut (usually rendered as "Canute" in English), King of Denmark. The location is disputed, with both Ashingdon and Ashdon in north-west Essex making a claim.

The political situation in England at the time of the battle was complex. Vikings from Denmark and other Scandinavian countries had been launching attacks on the independent Anglo-Saxon kingdoms which existed at the time since the late 8th century. From the mid-9th century, they had begun to settle. An agreement had been reached in the last quarter of the 9th century under Alfred the Great, King of Wessex, the most powerful kingdom, through which the eastern half of the country was ceded to the Danes under an arrangement known as "Danelaw", while the western half was retained by the Wessex-led Anglo-Saxons. Over the following century, however, Alfred's son Edward and grandson Athelstan both worked to reclaim the ceded lands and force the Danes out. This led in the 10th century to Danish defeat and the political unification of all the formerly independent Anglo-Saxon kingdoms into the country of England, with Athelstan as its first king.

After a brief period of peace, with Anglo-Saxon and Dane living side-by-side, trouble flared up again in the late 10th century and Danish invasions recommenced. In December 1013 Swein Forkbeard, King of Denmark, succeeded in deposing the then English king, Ethelred the Unready (ill-advised). However, Swein died in February 1014 and Ethelred retook the throne. When Ethelred himself died in April 1016, rival factions in a weakened nation threw their support behind Ethelred's son, Edmund Ironside, and Swein's son, Canute. Thus, the scene was set for a series of battles for the Crown which would culminate in October at "Assandun".

There are only a handful of contemporary sources in which the basic facts of the battle are recorded. Foremost of these is *The Anglo-Saxon Chronicle*, which is a collection of texts dating from the 9th to the 12th centuries which were probably all produced from one original document and have been moulded into a single narrative by modern historians. These texts were written as an attempt to trace the heritage of the English people from the beginning of the first century and they record events on an annual basis.

The entry for 1016 states that Canute, who had been in England previously with his father, re-invaded the country early in the year and began to plunder it. He was preparing to attack London, the seat of power, when Ethelred died there. The *Chronicle*, reviewing Ethelred's reign, reports that he "held his kingdom in much tribulation and difficulty as long as his life continued". Edmund, his estranged son, succeeded to the throne but was forced to lead his army in a succession of battles against Canute and the latter's right-hand man, Edric or Eadric Streona. The *Chronicle* records that there were five major battles during the year, with Edmund largely in the ascendancy. By the autumn, he had the Danes holed up on the Isle of Sheppey in Kent.

Edric Streona had previously served with Edmund's father, Ethelred, who had been sympathetic towards the Danes in a failed attempt to maintain a lasting peace with them. He had then deserted Edmund for Canute, but now went back to Edmund, whose forces appeared to have the upper hand. Edmund inexplicably trusted Edric, a major miscalculation as Edric would again turn traitor. Another contemporary source, the *Encomium Emmae Reginae* (c.1041-2) – a political tract in praise of Queen Emma, wife of both Ethelred and Canute – describes Edric as "a man skilful in counsel but treacherous in guile".

The *Chronicle* records what happened next, as Canute took his troops on a raid from Sheppey into Mercia, a formerly independent kingdom to the north-west of Essex, and Edmund and Edric acted to intercept them on their way back:

"The enemy, meanwhile, returned into Essex, and advanced into Mercia, destroying all that he overtook. When the king understood that the army was up, then collected he the fifth time all the English nation, and went behind them, and overtook them in Essex, on the hill called Assandun; where they fiercely came together. Then did Alderman Edric as he often did before [changed sides]… and so betrayed his natural lord and all the people of England. There had Canute the victory and won himself all England."

Numerous leading members of the English nobility were killed. Edmund himself escaped and retreated to Gloucestershire with his surviving forces. Canute followed him there. Both sides' armies had been ravaged by the various battles and the two kings met to agree a peace treaty which would ultimately see them rule half the country each. Edmund ruled the south and west, and Canute the north and east, much like the Danelaw arrangement brokered by Alfred two centuries earlier. Edmund, however, had been worn out by battle and died shortly afterwards on St Andrew's Day, 30 November 1016. Canute then became King of England and took the politically astute step of marrying Ethelred's widow, Emma, to help with the unification of the kingdom. He also had Edric executed, on the grounds that he could not be trusted. Canute was a strong and popular ruler until his death in 1035.

It is impossible to know exactly what happened during the battle or precisely where it took place because the surviving source material is vague and the archaeological evidence sketchy. The *Chronicle* states that Edmund's forces "overtook" Canute's "on the hill called Assandun". This suggests that the encounter took place right on the hillside, as Canute's troops were returning from raids on Mercia to their base on Sheppey and that Edmund's troops intercepted them, probably en route from London. William Camden, author of *Britannia* (1586), a major historical and topographical survey of Great Britain and Ireland, was the first to equate Assandun with Ashingdon. Scholars have been discussing this ever since. Those who appear to favour Ashingdon include Kenneth Neale, who has written in his book *Essex in History* (1977) that "much erudition has been devoted to the respective claims of Ashdon, near Saffron Walden, and Ashingdon, which commands most support, on the River Crouch". Reaney, the aforementioned place-name expert, states that "The identification of *Assandun* with Ashingdon is, on the whole, consistent with the later developments of the name. *Assandun* cannot lie behind the forms of Ashdon… with which it has alternatively been identified." Other historians argue against this.

Modern accounts from those who favour Ashingdon as the location have Edmund's forces camped on Ashingdon Hill and Canute's forces camped on Canewdon Hill, visible two miles to the east-north-east. This may in part be due to the similarity of the names "Canute" and "Canewdon", but Reaney has the latter's name derivation as the "hill of Cana's people", with no connection to Canute.

According to the *Encomium*, whose author met Canute, the battle took place shortly after dawn, "in the ninth hour of the day". If Edmund's forces did catch up with Canute's at Ashingdon Hill, it is feasible that this took place the previous evening and that Canute hastily withdrew to Canewdon, giving the two sides time overnight to ready themselves for a full-on confrontation.

The idea of the possible role of Canewdon Hill in the battle originates from the work of Professor E.A. Freeman, author of *The History of the Norman Conquest of England* (1867-79). Freeman states in Volume I of his history that "the Danes meanwhile sailed along the coast of Essex and entered the estuary of the Crouch. There they left their ships, while the army went on a plundering expedition into Mercia… After this they returned towards their ships, the latter part of their course leading them along the high ground which lies south of the Crouch. Along these heights Edmund followed them, and at last overtook and engaged them…". Freeman does not, unfortunately, explain where he got this detail from, but he then goes on to place the battle as he sees it in the context of the local terrain: "At the extremity of the range [of high ground], two hills of slight positive elevation, but which seem of considerable height in the low country in the East of England, look down on the swampy plain watered by the tidal river. Between the hills and this lowest ground lies a considerable level at an intermediate height, which seems to have been the actual site of the battle."

The theory of Canewdon Hill's involvement was taken further by Lt. Col. Alfred H. Burne in his 1952 book *More Battlefields of England*. Burne writes that: "Canute sailed with a portion of his host and disembarked in the River Crouch, near the modern Burnham [but on the south side]. From here, true to form, he carried out yet another raid, this time over Southern Mercia…". After the raid, writes Burne, Canute "fell back hastily" before Edmund's army, "intent on getting his booty safely on-board ship, and thence to his Sheppey base. The Dane was a cautious general and… prepared a defensive bridgehead. This was on the high ground at Canewdon."

Burne's case for the Crouch being Canute's anchorage is based on a number of factors: its proximity to Sheppey; the ease of the estuary for landing in compared to the gently shelving mudflats of the Thames; the fact that it had not been used before by Danish raiders (and consequently offered access to an as yet un-raided part of the mainland via the lands of an unprepared local populace); and the opportunity it provided to raid north-westwards without having to pass too close to the Anglo-Saxon stronghold of London. His case for Canewdon as the location of Canute's bridgehead is that it offered the best defensive hilltop vantage point close to the river.

Burne admits that his description of the battle, embellished from his working assumptions into the narrative above, is "necessarily conjectural", adding that "we have only five sources from which it is safe to take any details, and even in these sources the story is so encrusted with mythical details beloved of the medieval scribe, that there is very little that can be accepted as absolute fact".

If the locations above are correct, the battle must either have taken place on the hill at Ashingdon or in the flat valley bottom between Ashingdon and Canewdon. Burne has Canute's troops cornered in a defensive position on Canewdon Hill, with the river behind them, and Edmund ready to attack from nearby Ashingdon Hill. Edmund's troops launch the attack by descending into the valley bottom and Canute's troops then edge westwards along the ridge to the west of where Canewdon church is and then slowly descend that ridge to face them, the actual clash essentially taking place on the Canewdon side, below that ridge. Burne also suggests that what is now Hyde Wood may have been used strategically by Edric Streona to influence the outcome of the battle. If Burne's theory is correct, Edmund took his troops to the left of the wood and Edric took his to the right, but as Edric was a traitor, he held his troops at the wood instead of reappearing on the Canewdon side of it and simply "remained a cold spectator of the fight" as Edmund fought on alone. The *Encomium* states that Edric "had promised this [his deception] secretly to the Danes in return for some favour", though some later sources suggest it might have been a decision made in the heat of the moment, as the Danes appeared to be gaining the upper hand.

Edmund, who was outflanked and outnumbered by Edric's deception, would have known in that moment that the battle was lost, although it lasted into the evening according to the *Encomium*. Canute's troops advanced and slaughtered everyone they could lay their hands on. Edmund withdrew his surviving troops from the battlefield under the cover of night and sought sanctuary in the West Country. Canute's troops, less familiar with the terrain, remained on the battlefield overnight to recuperate. The *Encomium* states that the Danes buried their dead on the battlefield but left the bodies of the Anglo-Saxons "to the beasts and the birds".

Figure 2: The Battle of Assandun interpretation board at St Andrew's church

A detailed archaeological excavation would be essential in proving or disproving Burne's "necessary conjecture". As the 19th-century local historian, Duffield William Coller, observes in his book *The People's History of Essex* (1861): "There is not… a trace of the conflict either on the surface of the soil or in the records of the parish." Local farmers have expressed similar views to the current author, who is working with The Battlefields Trust and representatives from north-west Essex to try to identify its location once and for all.

The Battle of Assandun was a major event in England's history. It resulted in Canute becoming King and many of the Anglo-Saxon nobility meeting their deaths. It also led to a period of relative stability in a war-torn era which enabled Anglo-Saxon and Danish people and culture to become more integrated. Canute's period of rule gave what was still a young country a brief period of respite from monarchical struggle, until fifty years later when another foreigner, William the Conqueror, set his sights on invasion.

Canute's Minster Church (1020)

Four years after the battle, in 1020, Canute had a church built of "stone and lime" on the site of the battlefield in commemoration of those who died. The *Chronicle* records that "in this year the King went to Assandun, and Archbishop Wulfstan and Earl Thorkell, and with them many bishops; and they consecrated the minster at Assandun". (A minster is a church which has its origins in a monastic establishment; the root of the word is the same as that of "monastery".) It seems likely that the church was erected either where the battle was fought or where the dead of the battle were buried.

Stigand (d.1072), who was Canute's personal priest, was appointed to the living at Assandun. Little is known about Stigand's life before this appointment, but it is thought that he may have hailed from Norwich. After Canute's death, he served as an advisor to Canute's widow, Emma, to Canute's sons and successors, Kings Harold Harefoot and Harthacanute, and to their successor, King Edward the Confessor. He may also have been advisor to the next King, Harold Godwinson. Ecclesiastically, he became Bishop of Elmham, Bishop of Winchester and Archbishop of Canterbury. He also appeared on the Bayeux Tapestry.

Stigand appears to have had a bit of a chequered career, being accused of extortion and being excommunicated by various Popes for holding the Winchester and Canterbury bishoprics simultaneously (holding only one such living at a time was permitted). He was deposed in 1070 and his lands were confiscated by the then King, William the Conqueror, with whom he appears to have had an uneasy relationship. He was imprisoned at Winchester, where Canute was buried, and died there himself two years later.

Churches from the Saxon period were usually simple rectangular structures. Ashingdon church guidebooks for what is now St Andrew's parish church suggest that the original building on the site probably comprised simply what is now the chancel and perhaps a lost eastern extension to it whose foundations were uncovered during later grave-digging. The extension may have collapsed due to movement in the clay beneath it. The south wall of the chancel, which contains even earlier Roman bricks, may be original. One of the guidebooks refers to it somewhat speculatively as "probably genuine Canute". Anne Savage, who edited a modern book version of the *Chronicle*, expresses the view that "the south wall at the east end is part of Canute's building". Most of the structure that exists today was built or rebuilt in the 14th century or later. It is larger than the original church, having been extended to the west and north.

An apparently unique silver penny depicting Canute on one side and Earl Godwine on the other was discovered in the churchyard in 1928 by gravedigger, F.C. (Fred) Ewing. It is believed to have been minted by Godwine (inscribed as "Goddine" on the coin) at Oxford during Canute's reign as King of England (1016-35). It is thought currently to be in storage at Southend Central Museum, though the author has been unable to obtain access to it there.

Depictions of Canute and the battle loom large on the village signs of Canewdon and Ashingdon.

Figure 3: The village sign for Ashingdon, showing representations of a battle participant and the minster church

LAND OWNERSHIP & MANORS

The Domesday Book (1086)

The next fifty years in Ashingdon appear to have passed uneventfully.

In 1066 the Saxons were replaced by the Normans, following the Battle of Hastings and the Norman Conquest led by William the Conqueror. Twenty years later the latter commissioned the Domesday Book, a taxation book which records landholdings throughout the country both at the time of the Norman Conquest and in 1086. This sheds the next bit of light on Ashingdon's history and lists the settlement under yet another name – "Nesenduna".

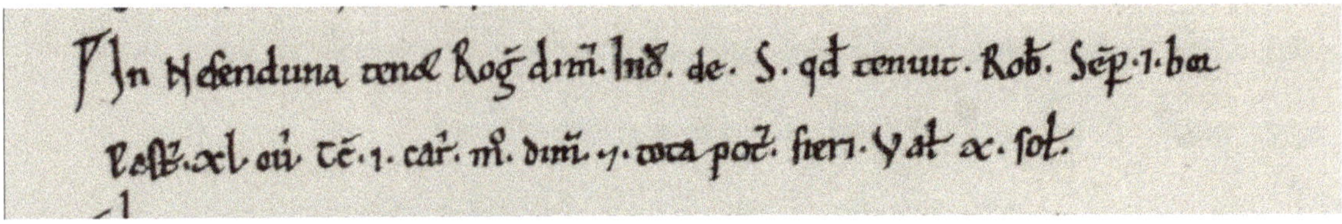

Figure 4: The Domesday book entry for Nesenduna (Ashingdon); the entries were recorded in heavily abbreviated Latin [3]

Of the 27 places listed in the Rochford Hundred in the Domesday Book, Ashingdon paid the lowest amount of tax and had the lowest number of households – just one. It must be remembered though that this was a feudal society and many of its members had no rights and did not count in official records. The householder was described as a "smallholder" (alternatively recorded as a "bordar"). Smallholders or bordars were part of the second largest group amongst the peasantry and represented about a third of the recorded population. There was pasture for 40 sheep in Nesenduna in 1086 and "half a plough" was in operation, though "a whole one [is] possible" (a whole one was recorded for 1066). (Clearly it wasn't literally half a plough. It probably means that one plough was shared between two landholdings as they were each too small to warrant their own, much like a combine harvester is shared between neighbouring farms today.)

In 1066 Nesenduna was held by Robert FitzWimarc (d. c.1075), who was a relative of both Edward the Confessor and William the Conqueror. It passed on his death to his son, Swein (sometimes spelt "Sweyn"), who is shown as its owner in 1086, though it was then let to someone called "Roger". Both Robert and Swein were major landowners in Essex.

South Fambridge was the fifth lowest contributor to taxation of the 27 places named in the Rochford Hundred and had the fifth lowest number of households – eight. It is

---

3   *The images from the Domesday Book in this section have been reproduced with permission from opendomesday.org.*

recorded as "Phenbruge" and its entry contains a crossing out by the person who wrote it down, presumably to remove a mistake.

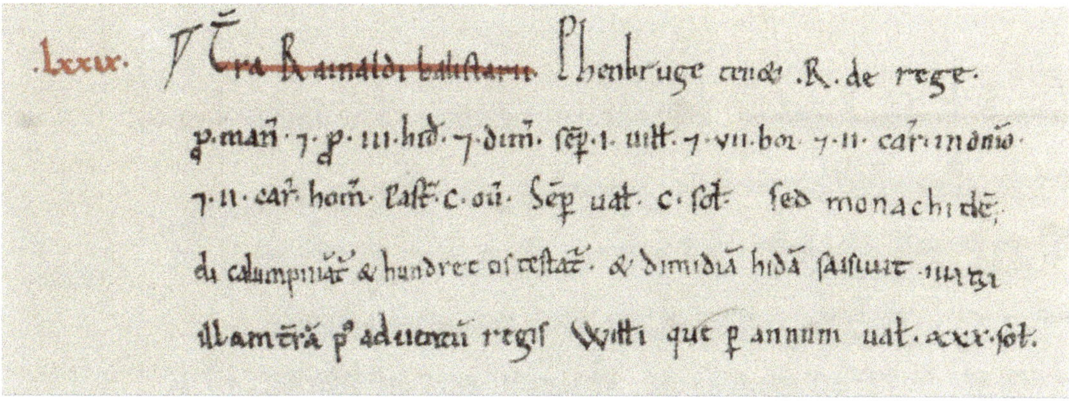

Figure 5: The Domesday book entry for Phenbruge (South Fambridge)

    The eight householders here were one villager and seven smallholders. Villagers (or "villeins") comprised the largest group of the peasantry, about 40% of the recorded population. They had more rights and larger landholdings than the smallholders. There were four ploughs in operation in Phenbruge and there was pasture for 100 sheep. The 1066 landowner is not mentioned but in 1086 Phenbruge was owned by the King and tenanted by "Reginald the Bowman" (sometimes shown as "Reginald Gunner"). It was the only place Reginald is recorded as holding. The Book adds that "the monks of Ely lay claim to it [the taxation payment for South Fambridge, which would usually go to the King] and the Hundred testifies for them". Coller states that South Fambridge "was given in Edward the Confessor's reign [1042-66] to the monks of Ely". However, Lily Jerram-Burrows, in her book, *The History of South Fambridge in the County of Essex* (1985), dates this grant to c.1022-29, citing a 12th-century chronicle called *Liber Eliensis* which states that "Fambridge" was given to the monks by Lady Godiva (of naked riding fame) at that time. An online version of the *Liber Eliensis* on the website entitled "Prosopography of Anglo-Saxon England" agrees that Godiva (Saxon name "Godgifu") made the grant c.1020-29.[4] Morant suspects that "probably it had been taken from the monks on account of their harbouring William's enemies in 1071", a reference to an anti-Norman Anglo-Saxon resistance movement led by Hereward the Wake (c.1035-72), which had its headquarters in Ely.

    The *Victoria County History of the County of Cambridgeshire and the Isle of Ely, Vol. II* (1948) also records a connection between Ashingdon and Ely: "Ælsi, the second abbot, by permission of King Ethelred translated the body of St. Wendred from the church of

---

4   The Prosopography of Anglo-Saxon England:
http://www.pase.ac.uk/jsp/DisplayPerson.jsp?personKey=-20221&pr2=1#pr2

March to be enshrined at Ely. The shrine with St. Wendred's relics was carried by monks of Ely with the army of Edmund Ironside in 1016 to the disastrous field of Ashingdon, where the monks were slain and the relics fell into the hands of King Cnut, who later gave them to the church of Canterbury. As some compensation the monks of Ely stole the body of Ædnoth, Bishop of Dorchester and formerly first Abbot of Ramsey, who had been killed at Ashingdon, when it was lodged for the night in the church of Ely on its way to Ramsey." It also connects Canute's priest, Stigand, to Ely: "It is added that Stigand, to palliate his robbery of the church [there], was very liberal of gifts of ornaments to those monasteries he held any considerable time in his hands: 'as particularly to that of Ely, he gave largely both in Gold and Silver plate for the service of the Altar; and divers ornaments to the church, a large Crucifix overlaid with silver with the image of our Lord as big as life; and the images of the Virgin Mary and St. John of brass; besides several Vestments esteemed the richest and most costly in the kingdom.'"

There is a third entry in the Domesday Book which concerns us, as the place named is now part of Ashingdon parish. That place is Beckney, whose name means "low-lying land of Becca [a personal name]" according to Reaney. It is recorded in the Domesday Book as "Bacheneia" and is documented as containing two separate parts for taxation purposes. Those two parts are the two detached portions of Ashingdon parish which are shown in the map in the Introduction. Bacheneia was second lowest in the taxation list and second lowest for the number of householders – two.

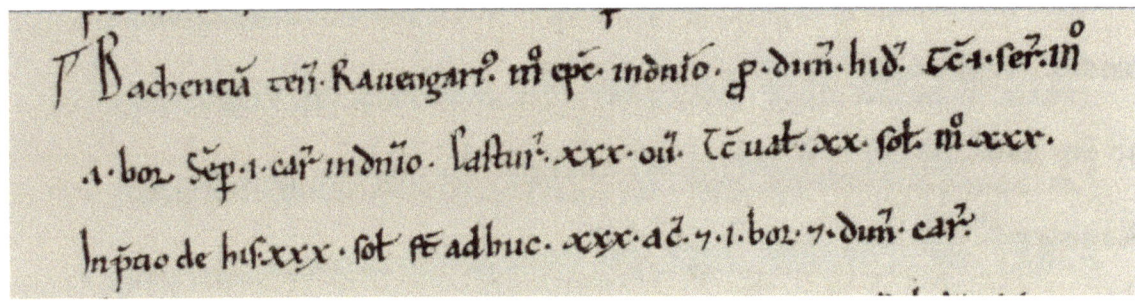

Figure 6: The Domesday book entry for Bacheneia (Beckney)

The two householders in 1086 were smallholders, but in 1066 the record shows that there was one smallholder and one slave (or "serf"). Slaves or serfs occupied the lowest rung of the social and economic feudal hierarchy, with no rights or resources of their own. There were one-and-a-half ploughs across the two parts of the Bacheneia landholding and pasture for 30 sheep. In 1066 it was held by Ravengar, his sole landowning. In 1086 it was held by Odo (c.1030-97), Bishop of Bayeux and Earl of Kent, and an important Norman figure who was the half-brother of William the Conqueror.

The Bayeux Tapestry on which both Stigand and Odo appear was probably commissioned by Odo and he was granted considerable lands in southern and eastern England after the Conquest, including at nearby Hockley. Like Stigand, Odo had a chequered career, acting as regent and therefore becoming the most powerful man in England when William was out of the country, but falling out of favour following a trial for fraud in 1076 and then facing imprisonment for planning a questionable military expedition to Italy in 1082. He spent five years in jail because of the latter and had his lands and his title of Earl of Kent confiscated. After his release from prison, and after William had died, he joined the First Crusade to Palestine, but he died on the way there in 1097 in the town of Palermo on the Italian island of Sicily. He is buried in Palermo Cathedral.

The above Domesday Book entries suggest that South Fambridge was the most important of the three places for taxation purposes in 1086, perhaps because of its pasture for sheep and its connections with Ely Abbey. They also show that all three places were relatively unimportant in the scheme of things at the time compared to virtually all the other 24 places recorded in the Rochford Hundred.

Post-Domesday Landowners & Manors

The manor of Ashingdon passed from Swein to his son Robert, who founded Prittlewell Priory in the area covered by modern Southend, and then to the latter's son, Henry de Essex (d. *c.*1170). According to contemporary sources, Henry was standard bearer to the King, Henry II, and he was accompanying the monarch on a campaign in Wales in 1157 when the English suffered a surprise attack. During the ensuing battle Henry threw down the standard and declared that the King had been killed, causing the English to panic and flee. Other noblemen rallied round, however, and it soon became clear that the King was alive and well. Henry's reputation was tarnished by this event, but he remained in favour for several more years until a personal feud with Robert de Montfort brought memory of his actions to the fore. Robert accused Henry of cowardice in the Welsh campaign and challenged him to a duel. Henry lost and ended his days in a monastery in Reading. All his estates, including Ashingdon, were forfeited to the Crown.

According to Morant – much of whose writing was based on the research notes of another Essex historian, the Rev. William Holman from Halstead (1670-1730) – the manor was then granted to the Bayouse family, about whom little is known. It then passed to the de Coggeshall and Doreward families. A later Essex historian, Thomas Wright, author of *The History & Topography of the County of Essex* (Vol. II, 1835), in which he in turn drew heavily on Morant's account of Ashingdon, states that the de Coggeshall and Doreward families, who were related by marriage, were the principal landowners in the parish from the 12th to 15th centuries until "for want of male heirs" the manor passed once again to the Crown. However, Anne Roper, who compiled a list of Ashingdon patrons from various sources for her book *The Minster at Ashingdon* (1951), has these two families as patrons of the living there for the period 1371-1513.

An entry in a manuscript for 1393 suggests that there was a windmill in Ashingdon in that year, which belonged to the recently deceased Robert de Vere, Duke of Ireland (1362-92). There is no other surviving source that references this.[5]

In 1513 the manor of Ashingdon was granted to Thomas Boteler (or Butler), 7th Earl of Ormond (1426-1515). It was inherited on his death by his daughter, Margaret (1465-1537), who married Sir William Bullen (or Boleyn) (1451-1505), and the manor descended through them to Sir Thomas Boleyn, 1st Viscount Rochford (1477-1539), father of King Henry VIII's second wife, Anne. From Thomas it passed to his eldest child, Mary (c.1499-1543), Anne's older sister, who is thought to have had an affair with the King before he turned his attentions to Anne. This topic is explored in the 2008 film, *The Other Boleyn Girl*, featuring Scarlett Johansson as Mary and Natalie Portman as Anne. Mary married twice: firstly, to William Carey, who died young (c.1500-28); and then to Sir William Stafford (c.1500-56). Her second marriage was carried out in secret in 1534, probably because she married for love at a time when she was expected to make an advantageous social marriage. The couple lived at the Boleyn family residence of Rochford Hall. Stafford was noted locally for stealing bells from churches and selling them off; according to the *Victoria County History of Essex, Vol. II* (published in 1907 and henceforth referred to as "VCH Essex II"), Ashingdon was one of the parishes which suffered this fate. Stafford also appears to have been remiss in carrying out his duty to appoint the rector at Ashingdon: Roper found that although he was patron of the living 1549-55, the appointment of Rev. John Ayer in 1549 was made by the Bishop of London "by lapse". Stafford's and Ayer's tenures were both short-lived, as the Bishop replaced Stafford as patron in 1555 and Ayer was "deprived on [Queen] Mary's accession" in the same year (Mary reigned 1553-8).

It seems likely that the manor of Ashingdon next passed to Mary Stafford's son from her first marriage, Henry Carey, Lord Hunsdon, (1526-96) who owned other land in the area, and it was then sold by him to a major Essex landowner at the time, Richard, Lord Rich (1496-1567). Rich was a shrewd lawyer and politician who frequently changed allegiances to suit his own ends. He employed a deliberate strategy of acquiring lands throughout Essex, with seats at Rochford Hall and Leez Priory (near Great Leighs). He was Lord Chancellor to Edward VI and founded Felsted School.

---

5   Essex Record Office (ERO) D/DU 23/139/1/1, p.37

Figure 7: Richard, Lord Rich, who owned land in Ashingdon in the 16th century [6]

According to Wright, the manor of Ashingdon passed through successive generations of the Rich family, later the Earls of Warwick, to Daniel Finch, 2nd Earl of Nottingham (1647-1730), one of six co-heirs, who seems likely to have acquired it c.1678. Daniel then "sold the manor, demesne lands and advowson [the right to appoint the incumbent to the parish church] to the ancestor of the Bristow family, to whom it now [1835] belongs". The Bristow family owned property and/or advowsons in other south-east Essex parishes, including Hawkwell, Hockley and Rochford. However, Wright's account conflicts with that of Benton, who states that: "William and Michael Arnold succeeded Henry St. John as patrons [owners of the advowson], by purchase, and presented in 1710; followed by Thomas Harrison and subsequently by William Wright. It [the advowson] was then sold to the Rev. John Jeremiah Brock, maternal uncle of Rev. J. [John] Nottidge, to whom he presented the living (upon the death of Angel Silke in 1791) and bequeathed him the advowson." Nottidge's tenure of the role of rector at Ashingdon is shown on the rectors' board in the porch of Ashingdon Church (see below for more on this) as commencing in 1795, so this information too does not quite tie up. Roper states that Silke died in 1794, which would make more sense.[7]

Many of the manor's owners were absentee landlords, so the manor was let to various

---

[6] The illustration is taken from the Luminarium website: https://www.luminarium.org/encyclopedia/richardrich.htm

[7] Anne Roper, *The Minster at Ashingdon*, p.43

tenants. Morant, using Holman's notes as his source, writes that Laurence de Hardell, who died in 1285, "held in Ashingdon 50 acres of arable [land] of Philip Mansell by the service of one garland of roses; and in Ashingdon and Rochford 80 acres of arable and three of wood, and 8s. rent of John de Rochford…". Hardell also had estates in Little Stambridge, Canewdon and Hockley, and had a son called Nicholas. Another tenant in the parish in 1285 was Richard le Chamberlayn. In 1340 Reginald Garrey or Garry held lands and tenements in Ashingdon. Sir Robert Tibetot, who died in 1372, held 80 acres of arable land in the parish. Tibetot had three daughters: Margaret, Millicent and Elizabeth.

After that, Morant could find no mention of the manor of Ashingdon in the historical records until King Henry VIII's time when "a considerable estate is mentioned here under the name of Beckney". This, of course, is Bacheneia from the Domesday Book. Morant says that both Ashingdon and Beckney manors "extend into some of the adjoining parishes"; this may account for the irregular, intricate course of the boundary of the historic Ashingdon parish and the two detached parts of it. Richard Allen, who died in 1517, had a house, 300 acres of pasture and 200 acres of marshland, collectively "called Beckney, in Ashingdon, Hockley and South Fambridge, of the Prior of Colne by fealty [a pledge of loyalty from a feudal tenant to his lord]". Colne Priory was a Benedictine Priory at Earls Colne in north Essex. The Essex Record Office (ERO) in Chelmsford holds documents connecting Ashingdon and Beckney to the Priory as far back as 1260, when there was an agreement between Hugh de Vere, Earl of Oxford, and the Prior "concerning the light which Hugh endowed to burn day and night before the image of the Blessed Virgin Mary in the Church of St. Mary at Colne, and which the monks are bound to maintain on penalty of distraint. Hugh grants to the monks in free alms a rent of 40s. which the heirs of Lawrence de Plumberwe pay at Michaelmas [29 September] for the marsh of Bekenney, and for tenements at Ashingdon and Great Sutton".[8]

Richard Allen had a son called John, who may well have succeeded him as tenant. In 1555, however, William Harris "held the manor of Beckney, with appurtenances, in Ashingdon, South Fambridge, Hockley and Sutton, of the Lord Rich". Harris's son, also called William, inherited the tenancy of Beckney from his father when the latter died in the above year. It then passed through other members of the Harris family until at least 1634 when "this manor, capital messuage [house] or farm, known by the name of Beckney" was tenanted by Sir William Harris and owned by Robert, 2nd Earl of Warwick (1587-1658), one of Richard, Lord Rich's descendants. Christopher Harris, who died in 1570, held Beckney "and also Crystal Hall in this parish". It has not been possible to determine where this latter property was. The Ashingdon parish registers record the burial in October 1693 of

---

8   ERO D/DPr 136

Elizbeth Sayer, daughter of John and Hannah Sayer, "of Beckney".[9]

Morant concludes that "from the Earl of Warwick this estate came to Henry, Viscount Bolingbroke, and was purchased of him by Richard, Lord Viscount Castlemain[e], afterwards Earl Tilney". Bolingbroke (1678-1751) was a leading politician and philosopher; Tilney (more commonly spelt "Tylney"), who was Bolingbroke's almost exact contemporary (1680-1750), was also a politician and he built the once-famous but now-lost Palladian mansion of Wanstead House in south-west Essex. A Mr. Reynolds paid the rate assessment for Beckney in 1730. The parish registers for Ashingdon record the burial on 10 May 1751 of "a stranger" who "worked for Mr. Carr at Beckney". In 1773 a Miss Laurence "died at Beckney".[10]

Around 1800 Beckney was in the ownership of Sir H. Featherstone. In 1807 James Digby owned it.[11] In 1835 it belonged to the Honourable and exotically named William Pole-Tylney-Long-Wellesley (1788-1857), an MP and a nephew of the Duke of Wellington, who had married Catherine Tylney-Long (1789-1825), an extremely wealthy descendant of Castlemaine. William, who owned other lands in Essex, spent much of Catherine's money and built up huge debts. The property appears to have been tenanted by the locally prominent Mew family under all these owners. In 1846 John Fane was Lord of the Manor of Ashingdon.[12]

As for South Fambridge, there was only one manor. Morant, again using Holman's notes, found that the monks of Ely, who appear to have been ousted from South Fambridge land ownership at the time of the Domesday Book, had re-taken possession of the manor by 1166, at which time Reginald de Fambridge was its tenant "under Nigel, Bishop of Ely" (c.1100-69). During the reign of Henry III (which ran from 1216 to 1272) the tenancy was taken over by the de Brianzon family of West Thurrock. In 1286 South Fambridge, then referred to as "Little Fambridge", was tenanted by Bartholomew de Brianzon. His son, William, inherited the tenancy, though the manor was still owned by the monks of Ely. William died in 1310 and his widow, Alianor (perhaps a version of "Eleanor"), remarried. Her second husband was John Bluet and she took the tenancy of Fambridge into this marriage as her dowry. Her son, John, from her first marriage, confirmed that she and John Bluet could continue to hold the tenancy there until they died. Alianor died in 1348.

By 1360 the manor of South Fambridge was in the tenancy of William de Bohun, 1st Earl of Northampton (c.1312-60), though it was still in the ownership of the monks of Ely. William was a descendant of King Edward I and a staunch supporter of the then King,

---

9   ERO TS 709/1
10   Ibid.
11   ERO D/P 89/8/2
12   ERO Q/RUm 2/53

Edward III, for whom he served as both a soldier and a diplomat. He owned other properties in Essex, including at Wix, near Harwich.

In 1396, according to *VCH Essex II*, the manor of South Fambridge was granted by Royal licence to Pleshey College, just north of Chelmsford. This establishment had been founded in 1394 as a college of nine chaplains inside Pleshey Church. The licence for founding it was granted by the then King, Richard II, to Thomas, 1st Duke of Gloucester (1355-97), the youngest child of King Edward III, the owner of Pleshey Castle and husband of Eleanor de Bohun. Eleanor (*c.*1366-99) was the grand-daughter of William de Bohun, the former tenant of South Fambridge manor. By this time, the manor was owned by the King, who had evidently re-acquired it from Ely Abbey for the Crown.

Things go quiet in the South Fambridge records for the next 150 years until the Dissolution of the Monasteries and the suppression of religious houses in the 1530s and 1540s. According to *VCH Essex II*, "The King on 29 October 1546 gave authority to Thomas Josselyn and others to receive the surrender of the college" at Pleshey. In December that year the manor of South Fambridge was consequently removed from College ownership and granted instead to Sir John Gates. Gates' ownership of the manor was, however, short-lived: Morant writes that "His estates becoming forfeited, upon his arraignment and condemnation [on] 19 August 1553, for espousing the Lady Jane Grey's interest [her claim to the throne], this, among the rest, came again to the Crown". It remained there until 1560 when the then monarch, Queen Elizabeth I, granted it, with the advowson of the parish church, to Peter Osborne (1521-92), Keeper of the Privy Purse to her brother and predecessor, King Edward VI. Morant describes Osborne as "a man of great understanding, and very active and zealous for the Reformation", a movement which challenged the dominance of the Catholic Church and led to the establishment of the Church of England by Elizabeth's and Edward's father, King Henry VIII. Elizabeth made Osborne Lord Treasurer's Remembrancer in the Exchequer and no doubt granted him the manor of South Fambridge in return for his loyal service. His memorial, which was destroyed in the Great Fire of London (1666), described him as "a man of integrity and prudence" and recorded that he and his wife Anna (died 1615) had 22 children! One of these, Sir John Osborne (*c.*1554-1628), succeeded his father in the role of Remembrancer. Sir John's son, Francis (1593-1659), was an author, whose best-remembered work, *Advice to a Son*, was published in two parts in 1656 and 1658.

The Osborne family were originally from "the north" but had connections with Purleigh and Latchingdon in Essex from *c.*1442. They retained the manor of South Fambridge until *c.*1740 when Sir Danvers Osborne (1715-53, named in some sources without the final 'e') sold it to the Stephenson family. By 1846 the manor and advowson of South Fambridge church were owned by William Walter Stephenson, a descendant of the above.[13] It remained in the family until *c.*1880. Some sources give the date as 1881, but W.F. Noble, writing in the *Essex Weekly News* in 1882 states that "It continued in the family until submitted to auction on October 6th 1879". Noble adds that "The estate came more prominently before the public a short time since as being the first farm proposed and taken in hand by the 'First Mutual Co-operative Farming Association (Limited)', to supply the public direct from the farm with produce".[14]

Woodlands

Woodlands were historically important for humans, as they provided productive resources such as timber for construction, raw material for charcoal and foraging opportunities for domesticated pigs. Although no woodlands are mentioned in the Domesday Book entries for Ashingdon, Beckney or South Fambridge, it is apparent from the documentary evidence relating to Laurence Hardell (above) that at least one wood was in existence "in Ashingdon and Rochford" by or before 1285. Oliver Rackham, who wrote a landmark book for Rochford District Council entitled *The Woods of South-East Essex* (1986), found two ancient woodlands in the area which have been in existence continuously since before 1600.

The first of these was Beckney Wood, which stands in what was originally the southern detached part of Ashingdon parish. Rackham found that a survey of Beckney in 1517 revealed 300 acres of pasture and 200 of woodland. He describes Beckney Wood as follows:

"It is a detached portion of the manor of Beckney, which itself is an exclave of Ashingdon parish. The wood is surrounded by parish boundaries on all sides except the south, including its curious northern peninsula [Hockley parish is to the west of this; South Fambridge parish is to the north and east]. Its history is little known; by the nineteenth century a third of it had somehow been acquired by the parish of Kew [see later for more information]. It has a massive but incomplete boundary bank (Period II [i.e. dating from somewhere between the Roman period and 1300]) and two mysterious eroded internal banks of Period I [Roman or earlier]… The wood is surrounded by secondary woodland and plotland."

The internal woodbanks, says Rackham, "indicate a more complex early history than the present simple perimeter suggests", while the secondary woodland "more than doubles its area". He theorises that the original wood may have conformed to a planned grid-shaped landscape. The existing wood was 31.4 acres in size in 1980 and must be on a similar scale now.

---

13   Ibid.
14   ERO T/P 204/3

Figure 8: One of the raised internal woodbanks in Beckney Wood

The wood slopes downwards from south to north, with the "curious northern peninsula" extending into the plain like a finger from the north-west corner of the main, largely square, part of the wood. A public bridleway forms a circuit inside the latter, with access paths to the south, west and north-east.

The second surviving ancient wood identified by Rackham, which he describes as "almost undocumented" historically, is Trinity Wood in South Fambridge parish. This can be accessed, on foot only, either via the private Trinity Wood Road or via the northern branch of The Chase (which used to be known as "Red Lane"). This wood, says Rackham, which is mostly of hornbeam, includes woodbanks from the 18th or possibly 17th century which form the whole boundary of the wood. A short stretch of older woodbank lies inside the wood near its north-west corner.

Rackham notes that "in the 1930s a house was built in the SW corner [of the wood]; about a quarter of the wood has been destroyed by enlargements of its garden". In 1980 Trinity Wood was 8.35 acres in size and is probably a similar size now. A public footpath connecting the above two roads passes along its southern edge.

Figure 9: The entrance to Trinity Wood, from Trinity Wood Road

Both woodlands provide important habitats for wildlife in 21st-century Ashingdon and South Fambridge.

MANOR HOUSES

Ashingdon Hall

Ashingdon's manor house, Ashingdon Hall, stands at the junction of Ashingdon Road with Church Road, an important site on the main road, close to the parish church, on the hilltop which overlooks the farmland to the north towards the River Crouch. The current building, which is Grade II-listed, dates from *c.*1700. It is described by the British Listed Buildings website as follows:

"House. C17/C18 red brick, of earlier timber framed origin, re-fronted early C19 in red brick. Red plain-tiled double-range roof, the left return with double-moulded Dutch gables, the right return hipped. Off centre right red brick chimney stack. 2 storeys. Eaves band. Of 4 bays, pilasters to right and left of the 2 central bays. 1:2:1 window range of vertically sliding sashes, gauged brick arches, tripartite ground floor windows. Off centre left C19 hipped and part-glazed porch. C19 3-panel 2-light door, moulded surround, flat canopy."

Figure 10: Ashingdon Hall

The Heritage Gateway website, which holds documentary records of England's local and national heritage, describes it as follows: "The present structure is 17th century, but it appears to incorporate some portions of an earlier timber-framed structure. It is thought that it occupies the same site of the medieval manorial hall. The current structure on this site is 17th-18th century in date, of timber-framed construction. It is Listed Grade II."

In 1808 it was owned and/or occupied by Benjamin Palmer. However, by the 1860s Benton was writing that: "Ashingdon Hall (part of which extends into Little Stambridge) was at one time the property of the late Mr. John Dowler, who resided upon the spot, and farmed it. It now belongs to his nephew, Mr. Alfred White, F.S.A., of West Drayton, Middlesex…"

The building is now a registered care home for convalescence, and long and short stay residential care.

Beckney

The manor house for Beckney stood in the northern detached part of Ashingdon parish, where Beckney Farm is now, north of Lower Road in the north-west corner of the parish. In the mid-19th century, Lower Road was known as "Beckney Lane". The site for the manor house was evidently chosen because it sits on slightly raised ground above the surrounding marshland.

Figure 11: Beckney Farm, viewed from Fambridge Road in South Fambridge

South Fambridge Hall

The manor house for South Fambridge was South Fambridge Hall, which also stood on rising ground, about half a mile north of the parish church and approximately the same distance south of the river. As at Beckney, the original manor house has been demolished, but the current one occupies essentially the same site. The ERO holds a document showing that in 1711 Thomas Sly from Canewdon leased South Fambridge Hall from John

Osborne for a 14-year period.[15] In 1787 Richard Peacock Ely was living there.[16]

Figure 12: South Fambridge Hall

As stated above, the manor of South Fambridge was in the ownership of the Stephenson family until c.1880. Jerram-Burrows, in her 1985 book on South Fambridge, records that in that year "Dean Swift and Charles Rice purchased the Hall, 'Splash' or South Fambridge Hall Wood, together with the gift of the living of this parish from Major Stephenson". They then granted a 99-year lease to the aforementioned "Mutual Co-operative Farming Association", known as Rice and Company. South Fambridge Hall was pulled down during their tenure "and the present Hall was built in the front garden". Splash Wood, also known as Coomb Hill Wood, was in Rochford parish, on the edge of Hockley Woods. Rackham records that it was "grubbed" (chopped down) between 1954 and 1986 and replaced by arable farmland.

Rice and Company were succeeded at South Fambridge by a Scottish farmer called Hugh Crawford. Then, in 1916, when Crawford died, his son, James, took over; James was released from war service in France to return home to manage the farm, following a petition to the authorities by his father-in-law, William Bentall, of Southchurch Wick Farm in nearby Southend. James managed the farm until his own death in 1949, after which

15   ERO D/DMj T13
16   ERO D/DB 172

his widow, Phyllis, worked it. Phyllis then sold it to Gibbons, a farm company from Great Bentley in north-east Essex, who also operate Beckney Farm.

South Fambridge Hall appears on Rochford District Council's list of locally important historic buildings. It is described on that as follows:

"Large two-storey building dating back to the late 1920s or early 1930s; red-tiled, hipped roof with red ridge tiles; cornice with modillions painted white; red brickwork to the ground floor; pebble dashed façade to the first floor; possibly replacement windows; two storey bay windows to the right side; ground floor bay window to the left; red brick chimney stacks."

The justification for its inclusion on the Local List is that "This building is of local interest and is a good example from this period".

MEDIEVAL CHURCHES

St Andrew, Ashingdon

As noted earlier, most of the current Grade II*-listed Ashingdon church was built or rebuilt in or after the 14th century, the original building having been extended westwards and northwards at this time. The eminent architectural historian, Sir Nikolaus Pevsner, in his volume on Essex in his landmark book series, *The Buildings of England* (1954), dates the nave and the chancel to *c.*1300, citing a window with decorative tracery on the north side of the nave and the remains of an otherwise lost chancel arch as evidence for this. The building's small, handsome tower is topped by an attractive pyramid-cum-saddle-back roof. This also dates from the 14th-century enlargement but appears to have been planned only to accommodate the width of the earlier building, as it is only half the width of the current one. A 'scratch dial' (an early sundial) on the buttress to the right of the porch may well be 14th-century or earlier.

Figure 13: St Andrew's church, Ashingdon

The walls of the building, which is quite small at around 55 feet in length and 20 feet in width, comprise a varied mixture of ragstone, flint rubble, septaria, Roman tiles and brick material, and different architectural styles, reflecting lots of change.

Some of the funding for the rebuilding may have come from an apparently lucrative period in the early 14th century when an image in the church with allegedly miraculous powers attracted thousands of pilgrims and caused such a furore that the Bishop of London, Ralph Baldock (Bishop 1304-13), sent a commission comprising the Archdeacon of Essex and the Vicar of Prittlewell to investigate. This bizarre circumstance was recorded by an early Essex historian, Richard Newcourt (d.1716), in Volume II of his *Repertorium Ecclesiasticum Parochiale Londinense, which was published in 1710.*

> Upon a Report of Miracles done by an Image in this Church, which drew a great Concourse of People thither daily, excited thereto, rather by the Imposition of those Miracles, than by orderly Devotion, *Ralph (Baldock)* B. of *London*, that the People might not be cheated in their Devotions, granted his Commission to the Official of the Archdeacon of *Essex*, and to the Vicar of *Prittlewell*, to go to this Church, and to search into the Form and Quality of this Image, and to inquire diligently among the Clergy and Laity of Credit, about the Imposition of these Miracles, and how they came first to be divulg'd, and into the Cause of such a sudden Confluence of the People thither, and into other Circumstances of the Fact, strictly inhibiting, under Pain of Excommunication and Interdiction, that no Man circumvent the People by any false Inventions, about the Premisses, or induce 'em to a new Worship, by this or any other like Occasion, till the Worship be approv'd by their Superior on better Information, sequestring in the mean time, whatever Oblations had been made to it ; but I have not found any return made of this Commission.

Figure 14: From Newcourt's "Repertorium" (1710)

Later variations of this tale record that many pilgrims, especially childless women, could regularly be seen crawling up Ashingdon Hill on their hands and knees, presumably in the hope of being granted some special favour by the miraculous image, thought to have been a statue of the Virgin Mary. The reference to childless women seems to imply that fertility was one of the blessings the image was believed to bestow. An increase in the number of marriages there was also noted. Benton observes laconically that the name "Asses' Hill", potentially the original name of this location from which the word "Ashingdon" may be derived, "seems to have been well applied" in this period. He also describes the above as a "scene of gross superstition and imposture".

In 1429 a later Bishop of London, William Grey (Bishop 1425-31), united the benefice of Ashingdon with that of neighbouring Hawkwell. This was done, according to Newcourt, with the consent of John Doreward, patron of the living of both churches, "by reason of the smallness of each living", suggesting a decline in fortune (literally) since the heyday of the previous century. However, in 1457, on the death of the incumbent minister, Rev. John

Cherylbury, the two were separated again and Doreward presented Rev. Henry Hayton or Huyton to the living at Hawkwell and Rev. David Green(e) to the living at Ashingdon.

From the 14th century onwards, many alterations have been made to the fabric of the church. Pevsner dates the brick east wall of the chancel to *c.*1500, basing his dating on the black diaper work – a decorative pattern using glazed bricks – visible on the exterior. He dates the south porch and a brick, two-light window on the north side of the chancel to same period. The porch contains the rectors' board – an unusual but easily accessible location for such a thing, although there are several gaps on it.[17] A small window on the south side of the chancel, which may once have been a leper squint (a glassless window through which a leper could watch services from outside the church without infecting the congregation), is now dedicated to Stigand, Canute's priest. This window contains some fragments of 13th-century French or Belgian glass which were found in the churchyard.

Pevsner dates the roofs of the nave and chancel to the 15th and 16th centuries respectively and a brick south window in the nave to the 18th century. The latter is the same date as the current Ashingdon Hall and it is thought that some of the bricks left over from the construction of that were used to patch up this window. The *Royal Commission* agrees with these dates and notes that the church was restored in the 18th century and the south-east angle of the nave was rebuilt at this time. The roof of the nave is supported on the north side by oak posts, suggesting that the foundations supporting the north wall are poor. The church site is known for the continued movement of the clay beneath it, and the building has numerous buttresses, structures erected to support the walls. The remains of the lost arch between the nave and the chancel, which local tradition states collapsed *c.*1700, can still be seen inside it on the north side. This arch had evidently gone by Holman's day (*c.*1720), for he refers to its loss in his notes.[18]

---

17 The rectors' board would benefit from a complete review. A full list of Ashingdon rectors was compiled by Roper from various sources for her book *The Minster at Ashingdon*. It fills in all the gaps on the board and lists all the patrons of the living.
18 ERO T/P 195/5/8

Figure 15: The interior of Ashingdon church, showing on the left the white stone pillars from the lost chancel arch and the wooden oak post erected to provide additional support

The Royal Arms of King James II, dating from 1685, can be seen inside the church, hanging on the north wall of the nave directly opposite the south porch entrance. The *Royal Commission* dates the nearby font to the early 16th century, though its lid is modern. The church has one bell, dating from 1791.

The church possesses a communion cup, or chalice, dating from either 1563 or 1564, and a Bible from 1683. The parish registers, most of which are now in the ERO, go back to the 1560s.

The building's dedication is interesting. Morant and a later Essex historian, Henry William ('H.W.') King (1816-93), writing in 1846, both record it as "St Michael", but Benton (1867) records it as "St Andrew".[19] Benton acknowledges Morant's finding, writing that St Michael "probably was the original patron, as churches dedicated to that archangel are invariably on a hill". He accounts for the change by stating that "fresh dedications occasionally occur (for example at a rebuilding)". The architectural evidence, however, suggests that there was no significant rebuilding of Ashingdon church between King's visit to it in 1846 and Benton's published history of Ashingdon in 1867, so the name-change must be

---

19   ERO T/P 196/2

attributable to some other reason. It was on St Andrew's Day (30th November) in 1016 that King Edmund, who lost the Battle of Assandun, died. Is there a connection between these two things? Was the new dedication made to mark a connection with the battle?

King was quite scathing about the church's appearance, writing that "the whole building has been most shamefully neglected and barbarised, and the chancel has been largely repaired with red brick in a very rude manner".[20] Early photographs of the building show its tower covered in greenery. Benton records that this was "a small and delicate fern, Wall Spleenwort (*Asplenium Trichomanes*)". He then refers to "the amusement of fern collecting", which was evidently a popular pastime at the time. Benton was a friend of the Southchurch naturalist, Christopher Parsons, so the latter may have been the source of this botanical information. Benton also records that a "horseblock" (a short flight of steps used for mounting a horse) formerly existed on the west side of the churchyard fence.

In 1873 a parish meeting resolved to "take steps to remedy the defect in the buttress at the south side of the church".[21]

Figure 16: One of several early-20th-century photos of Ashingdon church which shows greenery growing up the tower

---

20   Ibid.
21   ERO D/P 89/8/4

King and Benton were members of the Essex Archaeological Society and they both went on a Society outing to St Andrew's in 1879, along with fellow members who included the Chelmsford architect, Frederick Chancellor, the Shopland vicar, Rev. F. Thackeray, and a well-known south Essex landowner, Major Spitty, from Billericay. The *Essex Weekly News* recorded that there was disagreement during their visit about whether or not the building dated from Canute's day, summarising wryly that "the question as to the probable age of the church was somewhat warmly debated"![22]

Changes continued to be made to St Andrew's into the 20th century. The vestry on the north side of the nave was built in 1906 and the clock on the church tower was erected in 1910 to mark the passing of King Edward VII, who died in that year. The clock is unusual in not having numerals, but in having letters spelling out the king's name in Latin. The V, VII and X all fall in the correct places for the numerals. The clock face was restored in 2001. David Brewer, who has written several church guidebooks to St Andrew's, states that "The mark across it is a flaw in the slate".

Author Marcus Crouch, who visited Ashingdon for his 1969 book *Essex*, writes that: "It would be pleasant to believe that the church is pre-Conquest, but all the visible evidence is to the contrary. It may nevertheless be accepted that this is the successor on the same site… to the minster built 'of stone and lime' by order of Canute at the scene of his greatest victory."

King wrote of Ashingdon church as standing within an "earthwork".[23] The original churchyard, which stopped by the steps on the main path to the north-east of the building, can be seen to have an earthwork bank in that vicinity. The land to the north of this is an extension to the original churchyard. Aerial views confirm the distinction between the two areas, as they show that the orientation of the graves in the extended part of the churchyard is different from that of those in the original part.

Beckney

No evidence of a parish church has been found at Beckney. It is presumed that this is because Beckney was part of Ashingdon parish for ecclesiastical purposes.

All Saints, South Fambridge

At South Fambridge the original medieval parish church was replaced in 1846 by the current building. Little information appears to have survived about the original structure. Jerram-Burrows found evidence of a chantry there in 1481 and of poor maintenance and adherence to accepted religious practice in the 17th century. She also states that the 1846 building was "the fifth successive church to have been erected in this parish", though

---

22   ERO T/P 204/8
23   ERO T/P 196/2

where she got that information from is unclear.[24]

The rectors' board at Hawkwell church suggests that, as happened at Ashingdon, South Fambridge's benefice may have been united with Hawkwell's at one stage, as Rev. Nicholas Wardall (Hawkwell rector 1564-87) has the words "with S. Fambridge" next to his name. A former South Fambridge minister, Rev. Matthew Kay, was buried there on 21 October 1782, having died at Rochford.[25]

Morant (1768) writes that: "The church, dedicated to All Saints, is little and low, and stands in a bottom about half a mile from the creek and a ferry. Both church and chancel are of one pace, tiled. At the west end there is a little wooden turret, but no bell." Benton records that the old church was demolished "on account of the insecurity of the foundations, much to the regret of those who admire church architecture; and the present edifice was erected, with the same dedication… There was no monument in it, but [Nathaniel] Salmon [1675-1742, an early Essex historian] says there was one in the churchyard, erected to Henry Palfrey, yeoman, who died in 1685". Salmon probably got this information from Holman, whose handwritten manuscript recording the inscription on Palfrey's grave was almost certainly acquired by Salmon and is now in the ERO. King also saw Palfrey's headstone.[26] It may still be there, but the oldest headstones in the graveyard are now too weathered to read.

As early as 1838 there were clearly significant problems with the previous church. On 24 August that year, the Rural Dean, Rev. Charles Chisholm, visited the building and wrote in the parish records that: "The Archdeacon's order for [some apparently earlier] work [should] be completed as soon as possible. I have recommended a font basin to be obtained and the communion rails to be replaced." He also made a point of noting that he had written his comment in pencil because the church had run out of ink![27]

Rev. Chisholm returned on 13 May 1840 and was disappointed to find that: "the order made by the Archdeacon has not been completed, neither has my own recommendation of August 24th 1838 been attended to. Mr. Potter [the churchwarden], however, has promised to attend to these matters forthwith. The chancel is in a sad state. Recommend that an experiment be made on a small patch of the wall with Parker's cement."[28]

On 23 July 1841 Rev. Chisholm returned and found that the experiment with the Parker's cement had been tried on the north wall of the chancel "apparently with good effect". He felt that a larger portion, measuring two or three square-yards, should be tried next. He also found that "the church with the furniture and appurtenances are in good

---

24 L.E. Jerram-Burrows, *The History of South Fambridge in the County of Essex*
25 ERO TS 710/5
26 ERO T/P 196/14
27 ERO D/P 90/8
28 Ibid.

order, and that the drains have been made round the church which is a great improvement". The reference to the drains suggests that dampness was the root cause of the building's problems. This is confirmed by his next visit on 28 September 1842, on which he wrote that, despite the early promise of the Parker's cement experiment, "I found this church very damp, and I fear it cannot be repaired, the walls giving way from the sinking of the foundation". Outside, Rev. Chisholm found that "The fences of the churchyard are in a very bad state and must be made good, and horses are allowed to feed – which I desire may be immediately put a stop to". He also requested the provision of a new surplice.[29]

By 1843 it was apparent to everyone that the church needed replacing. On his visit of 23 September that year, Rev. Chisholm wrote that it was "in a state of dilapidation and must be rebuilt". He asked the churchwarden to look after the books, utensils and furniture.[30]

In the same year, a parish meeting "Resolved that the inhabitants agree to raise by oath 100£ [sic] towards rebuilding the parish church of S. Fambridge provided the Rev. J.G. Fawcett [the then incumbent, probably as curate] can raise a sufficient sum to defray the extra expenses, that is to say if the cost be 400£ if Mr. Fawcett can provide 300£". Rev. Fawcett chaired the meeting, so was clearly a party to this proposal.[31]

A second meeting in 1844, which had Rev. Charles Penny in the chair, "Resolved that it is the opinion of this meeting that it is necessary to rebuild the entire church". Penny was presumably another curate at South Fambridge.[32]

On 1 May 1846, the parish officials accepted a tender from Mr. Carter of Rochford for £235 for the church's rebuilding and resolved to seek funding towards it from the Church Building Society. They wanted the new church to be completed by 29 September 1846, giving Mr. Carter just under five months to carry out the work! The church bears the date "1846" high up on the west wall, so he evidently accomplished it in time![33]

The new church was built in yellow brick (common in south-east Essex at this period). The rector paid £100 of this, the parish vestry (forerunner of the parish council) contributed another £100, and the rest was raised by subscription.[34] It has a porch and a small bellcote at the west end.

---

29   Ibid.
30   Ibid.
31   Ibid.
32   Ibid.
33   Ibid.
34   ERO T/P 196/5

Figure 17: All Saints church, South Fambridge, in the early 20th century

When Rev. Charles Chisholm visited the new building on 1 October 1847 he must have been very relieved to write that he "found the church together with the books in excellent condition". The churchyard fence was still down, however, which he asked to be made good "as soon as convenient". It was still down on his next visit on 4 October 1848 though! Everything else was thankfully in order, "with the exception of the plate for the communion table which ought to be replaced by silver". Chisholm's successor as Rural Dean, the Rev. Edward Cockey, found that the fence was still down on 4 May 1849, "but arrangements are being made for the speedy execution of this work". One gets the sense that there was a battle of wills going on here between the parishioners and the visiting senior clergyman, but on the other hand the parishioners had had to have their church rebuilt, so they probably took the view that the repair of the fence was of comparatively low priority![35]

King was not impressed with the architecture of the new building, lamenting the loss of the old church and describing its replacement as a "paltry and unsightly structure" and a "barbarous edifice". "It is impossible," he wrote, after a visit to South Fambridge in 1869, "that such a wretched structure can be of long duration and the sooner it follows the fate of its ancient predecessor, the better". He liked the remains of an Early English font

---

[35]   ERO D/P 90/8

basin which he saw there, though, and he also got to view the church plate, which was evidently still in storage at the churchwarden's house. "I called at a small roadside cottage," he wrote, "to see the altar vessels, which were brought forth from an old chest of drawers among linen. A small, silver-gilt paten obtained by Mr. Salter, the present rector, and by him presented to the church, is reputed to have belonged to Glastonbury Abbey… All else was of pewter."[36]

All Saints church is not nationally listed, but it appears on Rochford District Council's list of locally important buildings. The justification for this is that it "is locally distinctive… is of good quality and is architecturally significant in the local area". There is little else inside, although a modern hatchment on the north wall is of interest in continuing an old tradition. The 17th-century communion cup and paten (or plate) which the church once possessed have been transferred to St Andrew's.

The churchyard was ringed by tall elm trees until Dutch Elm Disease took them out in the early 1970s.

Figure 18: The font in All Saints which probably came from an earlier church

---

36   ERO T/P 196/5

VILLAGE LIFE BEFORE 1700

What was village life like in early Ashingdon and South Fambridge? It is difficult to be certain of the details, though the population was undoubtedly small – no more than a few hundred – and most people were probably employed working the land.

The Bold Love Adventure

Details of the "bold love adventure" hinted at by Morant (see earlier) were provided by a servant of Sir Robert Rich (2nd Baron Rich, c.1537-81), a gentleman by the name of Mr. Malden, who lived in Rayne. Rich was apparently travelling from his seat at Leez Priory to his other seat at Rochford Hall with an attendant, Captain Thomas Cammock(e) (1545-1602), who was courting his daughter, Lady Frances Rich (c.1560-c.1602), evidently against his wishes. During the latter part of this journey, the captain fled on horseback with Rich's daughter to the Fambridge ferry. The fates, however, were not on their side, as the ferry was on the northern bank of the river and the water was choppy. The lovers, who had been pursued, were trapped on the South Fambridge riverbank and had no choice but to try to swim across on horseback. They were halfway across when Rich and his coterie arrived behind them on the South Fambridge side. Rich's horse neighed and the lovers' horse, on hearing it, turned around. They managed to keep their horse under control though and successfully crossed the river and headed for Maldon, where they quickly got married. Despite his opposition to their union, Rich was ultimately forgiving, acknowledging that his daughter must have been deeply in love with Cammock as she had been prepared to risk her life for him. Cammock's father, Robert (1518-86), owned considerable property in Essex and his grandfather, John (1497-1546), was from Layer Marney. The captain died in 1602 and was buried in All Saints church in Maldon – there's a monument to him there, showing him with both Frances and his first wife, Ursula. Judging from the ages of the participants in this story the event must have taken place c.1580.

We know from the above that the ferry had replaced the bridge by the late-16th century. It was certainly there in 1594 as it is mentioned in some surviving deeds from that year which are held at the ERO.[37] The bridge is still mentioned in some 1632 land sales documentation, however, perhaps as a result of old text being carried forward into new documentation and the wording not being updated.[38]

Early Wills

Other surviving documentary evidence held at the ERO sheds some light on early life in the two parishes, though only really from around 1500 onwards. Early wills, for example,

---

37   ERO D/DU 253/2
38   ERO T/B 390/1

reveal the surnames, and sometimes the occupations, of Ashingdon people. Amongst the earliest surviving are those of Richard Darawont (1482), Robert Sayer (1504), John Vyns (1540), James Underwode ("priest", 1549 – named on St Andrew's rectors' board as rector 1530-49), Nicholas Stoolyman (1571), Bridget Everod (1571 – a rare female will), Nicholas Prat (husbandman, 1572/3) and Richard Packer (yeoman, 1594).[39] Surviving early wills from South Fambridge include those for John Roo (1492), Henry Coke (1535), John Stamer (1547), Robert Barrett (1554), Owen Gerart (1556), John Barrett (1559), Thomas Pullen (1567), Robert Byshoppe (husbandman, 1569), Nicholas Perryn (mariner, 1580), Richard Whale (husbandman, 1584) and Robert Gadd (a "seafaring man", 1593).[40]

Ashingdon Parish Registers

The Ashingdon parish registers, which date back to the 1560s, also provide some early names. The first baptism recorded in those was that of Margaret Arkesden, daughter of Thomas Arkesden, who was baptised on 22 April 1566. The first burial recorded was that of Thomas Semer, on 19 March 1563/4. (Dates between January and March usually span two years at this period, as England was still using the Julian calendar, while most of Europe had adopted the Gregorian one.) Other local surnames in the period 1566-79 were Ax(e)den, Bonham, Browne, Byrde, Cannon, Choneke, Cooke, Dakewood, England/Ingland(e), Everod(e), Gylbert, Higatte, Hobster, Horsenayle, Ollyn, Peper, Parkewood, Prat(t), Sawkyns, Shoricke, Stechard, Stellyman/Stollyman/Stoolyman, Taber, Thomas, Tunbridge, Wasser and Wise. The most common local surnames from the 1560s to the 1780s (five or more different individuals either baptised or buried) were Byrde (Rev. John Byrde was rector of Ashingdon *c.*1566-92), Clarke, England/Ingland(e), Harris, Hayward, Huson, Jennings, Leake (Rev. John Leake was rector of Ashingdon 1602-14), Reynolds, Richardson, Sayer, Spencer, Stone, Terrel/Terrill, Till, Wright/Right and Young.[41]

The baptismal registers shed a bit of light on day-to-day life in the two parishes. For example, Sarah Smith, who was baptised at Ashingdon on 3 December 1649, was the daughter of "Joane & a soldier", her mother being "a poor travelling woman". Sarah's father probably fought in the Civil War, which was raging at the time. Luke Spencer, who was baptised at Ashingdon on 12 January 1656/7, was the child of Grace Spencer, a "vagrant born [at] S. Fambridge". Meanwhile, the Ashingdon burial registers list several stillborn children in the period 1614-1630.[42] Poor Grace had been in trouble at the Quarter Sessions

---

39   ERO D/AER 2/52/3, D/AER 6/151, D/ABW 38/164, D/ABW 34/124, D/ABW 13/84, D/ABW 28/332 and D/ABW 29/200 respectively
40   ERO D/AER 1/149/3, D/AER 4/214/2, D/AER 5/96/2, D/AER 5/174/3, D/AEW 3/77, D/AER 10/3/1, D/ABW 28/266, D/ABW 4/253, D/AEW 7/252 and D/AEW 8/159 respectively
41   ERO TS 709/1
42   Ibid.

at Midsummer 1650 for begging, "wandering about as a rogue" instead of taking a job as a servant, and for stealing milk from "the cows of Mr. Samuel Keble", the then rector. She was jailed as a result.[43] She was still refusing to go into service in 1656.[44]

The burial registers also shed some light on local employment and land ownership. For example, Anne Harrington, who was buried on 1 January 1628/9, is described as a servant to Thomas Hayward "of Beckney". William Reynolds, who was buried on 12 September 1648, is recorded to have "lived at Beckney", as is James Hagber, who died aged 36 on 24 May 1653. Robert Crisspe, a "servant to Ezekial England… of Beckney", was buried on 2 February 1657/8, followed far too soon by Ezekial himself on 13 August 1658. On 6 July 1686, the burial took place of John Cadge, "farmer of Beckney". Elsewhere, Rev. John Gibson, "Rector otp [of this parish, 1644-9]", was buried on 7 April 1649, less than two years after his young son, also called John, was "buried in the chancel" of Ashingdon church. Richard Spitty, who was buried at Ashingdon on 17 January 1632/3, was recorded as being a carpenter from South Fambridge. Conversely, Elizabeth Bennit of Ashingdon was buried at South Fambridge on 2 February 1677/8, having been "drowned at the ferry".[45]

Court Records

Amongst the best sources of information for day-to-day activities are the records of the courts of the Assizes and the Quarter Sessions. The Assizes can be traced back to the 12th century. They met twice a year and were run by professional judges who tended to deal with serious cases such as treason, riot, murder and burglary with violence. The Quarter Sessions, which were held once a quarter, were established in the 14th century and dealt with comparatively more minor crimes. Both types of court were abolished by the Courts Act 1971.

An Essex County Council publication, *Medieval Essex* (1976), compiled by K.C. Newton, contains a photograph of a document from the "Essex Sessions of the Peace" in 1351 recording the indictment of Peter de Barentone, his three brothers and John de Takelegh for robbing the rector of South Fambridge and for stealing a horse at Dunton. Meanwhile, records from the Vagrants Roll of the Quarter Sessions of May 1564 tell us that there was a parish constable operating in Ashingdon and South Fambridge at that time.[46] These were the local law enforcement officers before the advent of modern policing in the 19th century.

Other examples of cases that the courts had to deal with include the indictment at the Assizes in Chelmsford in March 1577 of Walter Rule, a husbandman at Ashingdon,

---

43   ERO Q/SR 345/123
44   ERO Q/SR 367/29
45   ERO TS 709/1
46   ERO Q/SR 11A/2 & Q/SR 11A/6

who was found guilty of stealing sixteen sheep from John Wrayghte, a "gentleman".[47] A similar case was heard at the Assizes in July 1587 when Thomas French, a husbandman from Great Waltham, and Robert Baules, a South Fambridge local, where found guilty of stealing a lamb worth 2s.6d. from Thomas Camper.[48] Sheep-stealing in the area was evidently rife at this period, as the July 1592 Assizes heard the case of Robert Bragge, Josh Wade and William Blakes, all South Fambridge labourers, who were found guilty of stealing three lambs worth 11d., "the property of an unknown person".[49]

The Quarter Sessions at Midsummer 1594 heard a complex paternity case involving South Fambridge residents John Brewer and Margaret Brainwoode, the latter being a servant to the rector there, Richard Bond. Margaret had given birth to an illegitimate child and the court judged from the available evidence that Brewer was the father. Brewer, who was evidently considerably wealthier than Margaret – so this was perhaps a classic case of a male member of the gentry taking advantage of a female servant – was ordered to provide for the child until it turned 16. Margaret was also taken to task, as she had "bene wrought to cover and conceale as muche as she cane the trewthe of this cause". The judges therefore ordered that if she revealed the name of the father within 20 days she would suffer no punishment, but if she failed to do that "she shall be set in the stocks at South Fambridge in the usual place there for one hour, during which time the constable shall prepare a horse and cart, and then she shall be tied to the cart's tail and whipped forwards from the place where she was imprisoned". Brewer claimed to have witnesses who had not yet been examined, so the case was referred for re-examination later.[50] This case reveals that there were both stocks and a prison in South Fambridge, the latter probably a small, single-roomed lock-up, similar to the one which survives at nearby Canewdon. It also demonstrates that the use of stocks and the whipping of prisoners were considered acceptable punishments and it give details of the constable's role in this activity.

A follow-up session in January 1595 records that: "John Brewer [now] of Great Burstead was found to be the reputed father of the child begotten on the body of Margaret Braynwood, and was to discharge the parish of South Fambridge from keeping the same, since which time the said Brewer and all his goods are conveyed away so that the parish is likely to be charged with keeping the said child; It is therefore ordered that the persons suspected of conveying away the said Brewer or his goods shall be coveted [brought] before the said Justices who are to examine them, and if they shall find any such

---

47   ERO T/A 418/28/30
48   ERO T/A 418/47/56
49   ERO T/A 418/56/42
50   ERO Q/SR 128/68

conveyers then they shall take order for discharging the said parish, and if the conveyers refuse to stand to their order then they shall bind them over to appear and answer".[51] The reference to "discharging the parish" is because the parish would have to pay for the upbringing of an illegitimate child if the father could not be identified or had absconded. The judges were keen to bring Brewer to book to avoid South Fambridge parish having to pay maintenance when he should be doing so, and he had clearly used his previous trial postponement to flee the area. The case rolled on into the summer, when Brewer's son-in-law, Robert Fuller, a Coggeshall clothier, was charged with bringing Brewer to the next Quarter Sessions "to discharge the parish of South Fambridge of a bastard child".[52]

The Assizes at Brentwood in March 1602 heard a case for the indictment of a Springfield labourer, John Gray, who was accused of stealing "an yron wedge" worth 4d. from John Kempe at Ashingdon. Gray pleaded not guilty and the court found in his favour.[53] Meanwhile, at the Midsummer 1603 Quarter Sessions, the court heard the case of William Bull, a South Fambridge yeoman, who was indicted "for not securing his ditch abutting upon the highway there on the south side and leading thence towards Hackwell [Hawkwell] common, and also that he has divers trees growing and overhanging the said highway, by reason whereof the said highway is become very noisome".[54]

Keeping the highway clear was a recurring issue. In the early days of highway maintenance, the repair of each stretch of road was the responsibility of the landowner whose property it bordered. Not all landowners took this responsibility seriously and roads were consequently often poorly maintained. The Highways Act 1555 sought to resolve this by removing the responsibility for the upkeep of roads from such landowners and introducing instead the concept of all local people being responsible for the upkeep of local roads. Each parish had to elect two highway surveyors to monitor the condition of local roads and every family had either to pay for labourers to carry out any necessary repairs or do the work themselves. As wheeled vehicles became increasingly common this became quite a burdensome task.

At the Quarter Sessions in January 1610 it was reported that "the King's highway" at South Fambridge, immediately south of the sea wall, leading to the ferry, was "in great ruin [and] decay"; the parish was called upon to repair it forthwith.[55] This was still an issue at Easter that year, however, when the landowners of both North Fambridge and South Fambridge were taken to task for failing to maintain the routes to the ferry.[56] The

---

51   ERO Q/SR 129/65
52   ERO Q/SR 130/2-3
53   ERO T/A 418/70/29
54   ERO Q/SR 163/99
55   ERO Q/SR 189/103
56   ERO Q/SR 190/56

ferryman, William Wakes of South Fambridge, was also in trouble. At Michaelmas 1604 he was summoned to the Quarter Sessions for failing to repair the causeway next to the ferry and for failing to maintain and repair his boats "accordinge to their ancient customes wherby the Kinges people maye safelye pass".[57] He was in court again in January 1610 for failing to maintain the route to the ferry, which had become impassable.[58] One year later he was back in court for failing to maintain a sufficient number of boats for ferry passengers.[59] By September 1611 Wakes had been replaced as ferryman by John Ellis, also of South Fambridge, perhaps having been relieved of his duties. We know this because Ellis himself appeared in court and was bound over with two other South Fambridge residents, Christopher Crampe and John Longe, to keep the peace towards Thomas Whitfield, a husbandman from North Fambridge, and presumably an actual or potential ferry passenger.[60]

All the above, and many subsequent similar cases, suggest that the ferry was well-used at this period and that the authorities recognised the importance of keeping it accessible and open. When ferry prices were illegally raised in 1625, both at South Fambridge and further down the coast between Wallasea Island and Creeksea, an aggrieved party, Thomas Hawes from Great Stambridge, took his complaint to the Quarter Sessions, where the following was reported:

"Whereas time out of mind there hath been a ferry one side whereof lieth in Dengie Hundred and the other in Rochford Hundred, called 'Crixie Ferry', always time out of mind kept and maintained with horse boats and foot boats fitting for the carrying of passengers to and fro, and that footmen for 1d. a man at a time and horsemen at 2d. a man and his horse at a time, now the said Hawes doth present of his own certain knowledge that within this month one Thomas Cannus ferryman there on Rochford Hundred side and one William Parr ferryman on 'Crixie' side have raised this 'ferriage' for footmen from 1d. to 2d. and horseman from 2d. to 3d. and so purpose to hold it to the great damage and wrong of the country, for redress whereof the whole country desires the aid of the court. He doth also present that the like wrong hath been done to the country of late years by the ferry at Fambridge South and North (a footman 1d. and a horseman the full due there) having raised the 'ferriage' to double the value and so holds it more than of ancient custom and time out of mind usually hath been, for redress whereof the whole country desires the aid of the Court."[61]

The outcome of the case is unclear, but the tone of the report suggests that Hawes'

---

57 ERO Q/SR 169/73
58 ERO Q/SR 189/88
59 ERO Q/SR 193/23
60 ERO Q/SR 196/54
61 ERO Q/SR 249/33

complaint is likely to have been upheld.

Cases involving illegitimate children continued to occur. At Midsummer 1619 Allan Mayot, a gentleman, and John Davye, a tailor, both of South Fambridge, were summoned to the Quarter Sessions with Thomas Clement of Bradwell-juxta-Mare, a yeoman, regarding a charge that Mayot had to answer concerning "the sitting of a woman delivered of a base [illegitimate] child within the parish of South Fambridge".[62] In January the following year Thomas Ewstace and Thomazine Pepperton were summoned to the Sessions "concerning a base child begotten on Thomazine Pepperton of South Fambridge… [by] Thomas Ewstace [who] has stood charged to be the reputed father of the said child, which fact has been confessed by the said parties". The justices "therefore order that the said parties (being both of them willing to marry each other) shall be settled in the town of South Fambridge, the said Ewstace paying the rent of the house".[63] In 1626 a Benfleet labourer, Joseph Harris, was summoned to court "for the unlawful begetting of a child upon A. Ladley of Ashingdon, widow".[64]

All kinds of other cases were heard by the courts, often regarding local disagreements. For example, in 1621 Mary Mayott and Sarah Cranford from South Fambridge were bound over at the Midsummer Quarter Sessions to keep the peace towards one another. Documentation connected with this case suggests that Mary was probably related to Allan Mayot, referred to above.[65] In July 1623 Thomas Warren of Rayleigh was summoned to the Sessions to explain why he had not paid wages to Ashingdon man Richard Tyll. In 1625 Mary Spittie, a South Benfleet native and the wife of a South Fambridge carpenter, Richard Spittie, was bound over to keep the peace towards John Robinson, a South Benfleet shoemaker.[66]

Cases of unlicensed drinking and gambling also came to court. In 1627 the Quarter Sessions heard the case of "the widow Cranford in South Fambridge [possibly the above Sarah or a relative], the widow Priscilla Somes and Mary Harvey widow, both in Chelmsford, for victualling without licence and keeping ill order".[67] At the Sessions in 1629 Richard Thorndon of Prittlewell, John Wisdome and Thomas Cranaway of Great Wakering, John Butcher of South Fambridge and Robert Clarke of Rayleigh were all indicted "for suffering play at unlawful games and for keeping disorder in their alehouses".[68] At the March 1631 Assizes Eustace Tirrell and Robert Clarke of Ashingdon were both indicted for keeping

---

62   ERO Q/SR 225/72
63   ERO Q/SR 227/98
64   ERO Q/SR 255/94
65   ERO Q/SR 233/94 & ERO Q/SR 233/90
66   ERO Q/SR 247/97
67   ERO Q/SR 258/26 & Q/SR 258/27
68   ERO Q/SR 267/18

"a common tiplinge house" without a licence for a month or more.[69] In 1632 the Quarter Sessions heard the case of Isaac England of Hockley, Henry Younge of South Fambridge and William Love of Canewdon, who were indicted "for selling less than a quart of beer for 1d".[70] Younge was back in court three years later when he was summoned for keeping a disordered alehouse in South Fambridge over the previous six months and for ferrying passengers across the river "in the time of divine service and sermon".[71]

At the Quarter Sessions in 1632 the residents of Ashingdon and Rochford were taken to task for failing to maintain the road between Golden Cross and Ballards Gore, which was causing "a great annoyance".[72] The same issue was back in court twelve years later.[73]

A bizarre case from the Michaelmas 1633 Quarter Sessions records the indictment of South Fambridge husbandmen William and Robert Chatley, and William's wife Aves, who "with other unknown malefactors… at Hockley, riotously assembled together and forcibly entered a messuage called 'Plumborrowes' and 240 acres of arable, meadow and pasture belonging thereto in Hockley being the free tenement of Isaac Allen esq., and in his own occupation and they disseised him therefrom for the space of two hours".[74]

In 1639 a writ of capias was issued against John Flack, a husbandman from Ashingdon, at the July Assizes, which were this time held at Chelmsford. This was essentially an arrest warrant calling Flack "to answer for contempt" for having failed to show up at an earlier trial.[75] John Ody of South Fambridge was summoned to the Quarter Sessions in January 1656 "for keeping an unlicensed alehouse and disorders in his house on the sabbath day". That same month William Jorden of Ashingdon was one of several local men who appeared in court "for being common drunkards and swearers".[76]

A variety of cases continued to occur. At the 1645 Assizes William Chapman, a Coggeshall labourer, was accused of bigamy when he married Jane Tabor of South Fambridge despite still being married to his first wife, Elizabeth. Both of Chapman's wives testified against him and he was branded with a hot iron as a punishment.[77] Two years later, at the Midsummer Quarter Sessions, a South Fambridge yeoman, Robert Upsheire, was summoned to court as a witness in a case where a Norfolk gentleman, Henry Brampton, was in trouble for allegedly "assaulting the petty constable and watchmen of Leigh and the high constable

---

69 ERO T/A 418/108/6
70 ERO Q/SR 278/20
71 ERO Q/SR 288/5
72 ERO Q/SR 280/13
73 ERO Q/SR 321/44
74 ERO Q/SR 283/21
75 ERO T/A 418/117/59
76 ERO Q/SR 367/29
77 ERO T/A 418/127/51

of Rochford and some others".[78] Meanwhile, the January 1648 Sessions records a dispute between two local fishermen, with John Tyboles of North Fambridge being bound over to keep the peace in respect of John Steptee of South Fambridge.[79] The fishing trade at this period evidently included locally-cultivated oysters.[80]

At the Midsummer Quarter Sessions in 1662, a Rochford labourer, John Hills, and his wife, Susan, were indicted for stealing a sack worth three shillings and a bushel of rye from Samuel Long at Ashingdon.[81] Meanwhile, at the Easter 1664 Sessions a Danbury labourer/shoemaker, Thomas Hayden or Hoyden, was found guilty of stealing a silver cup worth 3s. from South Fambridge carpenter, George Browne. Hayden was whipped as a punishment.[82] At the July 1684 Assizes in Chelmsford, Thomas Eve of Ashingdon was one of several people called to account for not attending church on Sundays.[83]

In 1688 George Holford from Bicknacre and William Stephens, a Leigh bricklayer, were summoned to the Midsummer Quarter Sessions to give evidence in the case of William Saffold, a prisoner in the County Gaol in Moulsham, who was accused of "stealing certain working tools of his [Stephens'] and his servants from South Fambridge Hall".[84]

At the Michaelmas Quarter Sessions in 1689 the inhabitants of South Fambridge were indicted for failing to repair the road from Ashingdon to the Fambridge ferry.[85] At the same Sessions Thomas Plasteed, a yeoman from South Fambridge and the parish's constable, was summoned to the court "To indict Joseph Sammey of Ashingdon, yeoman, for not aiding him as constable of South Fambridge in securing William Frith of South Fambridge, husbandman, (when required by him) and apprehended on a justice's warrant for committing a rape on Ann Shearbold whereby he escaped and is not to be found".[86] Sammey, Thomas Duckett, a yeoman from Hockley, and Nathaniel Sibberns, a sailor from Barking, were also summoned.[87] The outcome of the case is unclear, but Sammey was in trouble again at Easter 1690 when he was indicted by the Quarter Sessions for not scouring (clearing obstructions from) his ditches.[88] A Joseph Sammey was an overseer, one of the parish officials, in Ashingdon in 1689 and 1690; assuming it is the same man,

---

78   ERO Q/SR 333/75
79   ERO Q/SR 335/45
80   ERO T/S 345/3
81   ERO Q/SR 393/37
82   ERO Q/SR 400/29, Q/SR 400/92 & Q/SR 400/122
83   ERO T/A 418/195/11
84   ERO Q/SR 459/4 & Q/SR 459/5
85   ERO Q/SR 462/58 & Q/SR 462/59
86   ERO Q/SR 462/72
87   ERO Q/SR 462/100
88   ERO Q/SR 464/72 & Q/SR 73

his fall from grace was extremely swift.[89]

Sammey and Duckett were evidently repeat offenders, as both were summoned to the Quarter Sessions three years later, along with Richard Knight, a Rochford victualler, "to answer [to] Martha, wife of George Mayers, and to keep the peace to her".[90] The following year Knight, William Reynolds, a yeoman from Great Stambridge, and Joseph Sammey's wife, Sarah, were in trouble in Rochford, to where the Sammeys appear to have moved, for assaulting Sarah Addams.[91]

An unsavoury aspect of contemporary maritime activity – the press gangs, which forced local men involuntarily into naval service – came to the area in 1695-6 when Thomas Ockendon, a blacksmith, Thomas Barren, a butcher, and Samuel Smyth, a labourer, "all of Canewdown at South Fambridge, under colour of the office of 'pressmasters', did imprison and detain Peter Wakelin farmer, and John Walford 'waller', both of North Fambridge, to serve the King in his war on the sea against France, and took from Wakelin the sum of 37s. 6d. and from Walford the sum of 10s. for 'their freedoms'". Ockendon confessed and was fined 3s. 4d.[92] It is surprising to find that those forming the press gang in this case were not already in the navy themselves.

The Hearth Tax

Another useful source of information at this period is the records of the Hearth Tax, a graduated house tax based on the number of fireplaces within each household. This ran from 1662 to 1689 and was assessed and collected twice a year, with inspectors entering local properties and literally viewing and counting the number of hearths inside. The administration and collection of the tax was somewhat hit and miss, but the surviving records provide an overview of which individuals were assessed and the number of hearths they were assessed for.

The British Record Society is publishing a series of county-based volumes about the Hearth Tax, selecting the year in each county which has the highest quality of surviving returns. For Essex, the Society selected the returns for Michaelmas 1670 and published their volume on the county in 2012. This reveals that 65,000 chargeable hearths were identified in Essex for taxation purposes in the year in question, whilst the poorest individuals, and buildings like almshouses and hospitals, were generally exempt. Hearths in those pre-central heating days were generally found only in kitchens, halls, parlours and bed chambers. Properties with one or two hearths tended to be occupied by husbandmen, artisans and labourers. Those with three or four hearths were generally home to farmers,

---

89   ERO D/P 89/8/1
90   ERO Q/SR 476/47
91   ERO Q/SR 482/30
92   ERO Q/SR 487/29

parsons, millers and wealthier artisans. Those with five hearths or more were most often owned by the aristocracy, the gentry, innkeepers (so, public houses), substantial farmers and the wealthiest parsons.

The records in the *Essex Hearth Tax Return Michaelmas 1670* book show that the collector of the Hearth Tax for the Rochford Hundred in 1670 was a gentleman called Samuel Spicer. He visited the houses in Ashingdon and South Fambridge with the appropriate parish constable, William Byat in the former and John Jaggar in the latter. Ten houses in Ashingdon were found to be liable for the Hearth Tax, with the numbers of hearths in them ranging from one to five and an average of 3.1 hearths per chargeable household. Only five houses were found liable in South Fambridge, though the numbers of hearths in the four that are legible range from three to six and average 4.75. The numbers of hearths can be an indicator of property sizes and wealth, suggesting that in 1670, as in 1086, South Fambridge was a more significant place than Ashingdon for taxation revenue and that it had larger, if fewer, chargeable properties. South Fambridge had the fewest number of chargeable hearths in the Hundred in 1670. The small number of chargeable properties in both places is also of note, suggesting a predominantly rural, agricultural society.

Ashingdon Rectors

Documentary evidence also gives us an insight into the lives of some of the rectors who held the living in the two parishes. The *VCH Essex II* records, for example, that in 1650 commissioners were appointed to survey the state of individual churches throughout England and that at Ashingdon they found the rector, John Nogoose, to be "a hopeful young man and well approved of by the parishioners". The rectors' board at St Andrew's shows a gap at this period; this may be because England was in turmoil at the time, following the beheading of King Charles I the previous year.

King records that Rev. Samuel Keble or Keeble, whose milk was stolen by poor Grace Spencer in 1650 (see above), was rector of Ashingdon from 1649 until 1655, when he transferred to South Shoebury, where he died in 1672. He is one of several early rectors missing from the rectors' board at Ashingdon church, along with his successor, as identified by King, the Rev. John or James Fisher. The Board shows Rev. John Forward being appointed in 1662-3, presumably succeeding Fisher. King has this event taking place in 1668, but that cannot be right.[93] Anne Roper has Fisher as rector 1654-63. She also found a note in the records that stated that four successive rectors – Revs. Church, Gibson, Keeble and Fisher – "had the living in the time of the Civil Wars, but never had Institution nor Induction".[94] This could be why Keeble and Fisher do not appear on the rectors' board,

---

93   ERO T/P 196/28
94   Roper, p.42

though it would not explain why Church and Gibson do.

At Midsummer 1667, during a period of religious turmoil, both local rectors, Rev. John Forward of Ashingdon and Rev. William Pierce of South Fambridge, appeared before the Quarter Sessions themselves for not coming to officiate amongst their parishioners for six weeks and two months, respectively. The indictment entries have been tampered with to amend the rectors' titles and charges, perhaps reflecting the strength of local feeling on opposite sides of the debate.[95]

Rev. Thomas Malden succeeded Rev. Forward at Ashingdon in 1671 and he in turn was succeeded by Rev. Martin Brethon (sometimes spelt 'Brithon'), who held the post from 1683 to 1687. Rev. Brethon's writing survives in a parish account book which is held at the ERO and reveals that he was a conscientious record keeper, especially of expenses which he incurred. This includes the provision of funding for building repairs, such as thatch, windows, paving and wooden post-work in a barn. In 1686 Rev. Brethon recorded that his expenditure on his home (Ashingdon Rectory – see below) was necessary "to secure ye house from flying asunder as it began to do". The accounts include other interesting entries such as bread and wine for Easter and Christmas services, repairs to the churchyard gate and some expenses "for ye French protestants". One of the churchwardens and overseers during Brethon's incumbency was Peter Diamon(d)(s), a local farmer whose land abutted the churchyard. Brethon had a dispute with him at one point over who was responsible for maintaining the churchyard fence. Another overseer was John Jennings, who also served as parish constable. William Richmond served as surveyor.[96]

In 1687 Rev. Nehemiah Rogers was appointed as Ashingdon rector. Benton records that Rogers was the son of the rector of Great Tey, where he was born, and was the great nephew of another Nehemiah Rogers who was ejected from the living at Messing "by the Puritans". The Ashingdon rector was also descended from John Rogers (c.1505-55), a clergyman and Bible translator who was burnt at the stake in the reign of Queen Mary. Nehemiah's wife Lydia died in 1695 and was buried at Ashingdon where, in Benton's words, "several of his children sleep beneath the same sod". The Ashingdon parish registers record the burials of his sons Charles (in 1691) and Nehemiah junior (in 1693). The latter was "buried in the chancel" of St Andrew's church.[97] The former, according to King, was "buried in woollen", a reference to the Burying in Woollen Act 1666 which made such burials mandatory for all except plague victims and the poor in an effort to prop up the English wool trade which was then in decline and under threat from imports of

---

95   ERO Q/SR 413/75
96   ERO D/P 89/8/1
97   ERO TS 709/1

foreign textiles.[98] Rev. Nehemiah remarried at Canewdon in 1696 to Mrs. Elizabeth Ailiffe, a Rochford widow. A John Rogers was Lord of the Manor of Bacon & Flories in Great Tey parish in 1848.

Benton and King, who were almost exact contemporaries, exchanged notes for their histories and they use almost the same wording at times in their works. Benton writes of Nehemiah that despite the successes of the rest of his family, "the Ashingdon rector appears to have been a black sheep: he was one of the notorious 'Fleet Parsons' whose misdoings occasioned the introduction of Lord Hardwicke's marriage law" – the Marriage Act 1753 which came into force the following year. This was introduced to prevent clandestine, involuntary or invalid marriages, which had been increasing in number during the late-17th and early-18th centuries. The law required a formal marriage ceremony to take place in every case, for the avoidance of any doubt in cases where claims were made about the validity or otherwise of individual marriages. Benton writes that "there appears to have been an extraordinary number of couples united during his [Rogers'] incumbency; people coming from all parts". Rogers was "incarcerated in 1702, probably for debt", although he remained in post until his death in 1710. His signature survives, along with that of parish official John Jennings, on a printed document from the 1690s which is held at the ERO in which leading Ashingdon parishioners expressed their support for King William and their opposition to "Papists" who they feared wanted to assassinate him.[99]

King obtained information about Rogers and other aspects of parish history from the then Ashingdon rector, Rev. Septimus Nottidge, who consulted the registers and old parishioners for information. Their collective findings included details of a note found about Rogers which stated that "he is a very wicked man as [he] lives for drinking, whoring and swearing, he has struck and boxed the bridegroom in the chapple and damned like any common souldier, he marries both within and without the chapel…". The correspondence from Nottidge to King records, however, that "he may not have been quite so black as he is painted, though the Ashingdon registers seem to corroborate his matrimonial eccentricities".[100]

---

98   ERO T/P 196/28, pp.183
99   ERO Q/RRo 2/1
100 ERO T/P 196/28, pp.183

VILLAGE LIFE IN THE 18TH CENTURY

Parish Officials

By 1702 Michael and William Arnold had obtained the advowson of Ashingdon church. According to Roper they appointed Rev. Thomas Bateman as rector in 1702 and Rev. James Armstead or Armistead as Bateman's successor in 1712.[101] There are two entries for Thomas Bateman on the rectors' board at St Andrew's: one for 1710-12 and one for 1724-45. Whether these are the same individual or two different ones, and why the dates do not match Roper's dates for Bateman is unclear.

Many rectors were absent from the parish and appointed curates. The accounts books mentioned above reveal the names of several of those. From 1712 to 1715, for example, Rev. Samuel Maldon is listed as curate, when Rev. Armstead/Armistead was rector. Maldon's surname is sometimes spelt "Malden", so he could be a relative of Rev. Thomas Malden, who was rector late in the previous century. In 1731 Rev. Thomas Bateman (see above) signed the accounts books, but in 1735 they were signed by a curate, Rev. George Lumley, and from 1737-40 by another curate, Rev. Charles Morgan. Rev. Thomas Harrison was rector 1745-60. He was succeeded by Rev. John Harrison, potentially a relative, from 1760 to 1764. The latter had Rev. George Pye as his curate in 1763. Rev. Angel Silke (rector 1764-94) had Rev. Benjamin Gregson as his curate in 1775.[102] Benton has Rev. T. Bate and Rev. Joseph Wise as Silke's curates at various times, noting that "Angel Silke never resided at Ashingdon". The Ashingdon parish registers record a baptism carried out on 17 June 1787 "by Joseph Wise, Curate".[103]

The accounts books also reveal that the main officials who were running Ashingdon parish in the 17th and 18th centuries were the rector (or curate), churchwarden(s), overseer(s), parish constable and surveyor.[104] Abraham Davey was surveyor in 1787. His expenses included gravel, picks and beer for workmen. Thomas Keyes was surveyor in 1797-8 and he also served as churchwarden.[105]

Another name – and signature – that appears in the account books c.1753-66 is that of Chester Moor Hall. It is presumed that this is the same Chester Moor Hall who was born in Leigh in 1703 and died at Sutton in 1771 and invented the achromatic lens which greatly improved the viewing quality of telescopes. There is a monument to Hall in Sutton church,

---

101 Roper, p.43
102 ERO D/P 89/8/1
103 ERO TS 709/1
104 ERO D/P 89/8/1
105 ERO D/P 89/21

but his connection with Ashingdon – if this is the same man – is not widely documented. [106]

More Court Records

The court cases continued into the new century.

In 1702 Thomas Goldspring, a Canewdon victualler, was brought before the Quarter Sessions "to answer the overseers of Ashingdon touching his begetting a child of Elizabeth Cramplin of Ashingdon, singlewoman". The judge on the case was George Asser, a member of a prominent Essex family.[107]

In 1714 William Ballard of South Fambridge was brought before the Sessions "to answer the complaints of the inhabitants of North Fambridge for his bringing a poor sick woman out of South Fambridge without any order or pass of the justices, and leaving her in the highway in North Fambridge 'in a perishing condition'".[108]

Regarding ecclesiastical court matters, the *VCH Essex II* cites some archdeaconry records from 1717 in which a local man is recorded as having to do penance in Ashingdon church for marrying his deceased wife's sister.

Witchcraft

Neighbouring Canewdon parish is noted for its witchcraft history, but this is not a subject which crops up with any regularity in the records for Ashingdon and South Fambridge. Benton, however, records a case of witchcraft having occurred at the Fambridge ferry in the mid-18th century.

"It was at this ferry," writes Benton, in his South Fambridge chapter (*c.*1867), "about the middle of the last century, that a man and woman in this hundred who were suspected of witchcraft underwent the water ordeal. Captain Harriott, of Broom-hills near Rochford… alludes to this poor woman in his biography or 'Struggles Through Life'…. He tells us she lived in Rochford, at the second cottage upon entering the town from the Stambridge road, and he remembers in his school days, many were the tales told of her… He states, she 'kept constantly cropping in her garden, with the large white-headed poppy, the juice of which it was said, she carefully preserved, to treat her imps with, every full moon'." This poor woman endured merciless persecution and Harriott himself played a trick on her to satisfy himself of her innocence. "These poor people," continues Benton, "named Hart, were swum in the presence of a great concourse of people; the husband was adjudged innocent, after having been nearly drowned, but the wife being tied to a boat by a line, floated like a cork, and is believed to have been a witch by the credulous to this day." A local waterman supported these allegations of witchcraft after Mrs. Hart's funeral. He said

---

106   ERO D/P 89/8/1 and see https://www.southendtimeline.co.uk/2/southend-timeline-chester-moor-hall-history-of-southend-on-sea.html
107   ERO Q/SR 510/17
108   ERO Q/SR 560/6

that he had once seen her "swimming in the river in a bowl". She told him he would forget this incident and suddenly remember it later. He did indeed forget it and only remembered it at her funeral.

CHAPMAN & ANDRÉ'S MAP OF ESSEX (1777)

By the late 18th century, local map-making had advanced considerably since the days of Norden and Speed. Other maps of Essex had appeared in the interim, notably those of Johannes Blaeu (1645) and John Ogilby & William Morgan (1678), but it was only in 1777 that the first reasonably accurate, large-scale map of the county appeared. This was produced by John Chapman & Peter André. Their map makes it possible to see much more detail of the Ashingdon and South Fambridge area than those of their predecessors. For the first time, individual buildings are named on a local map.

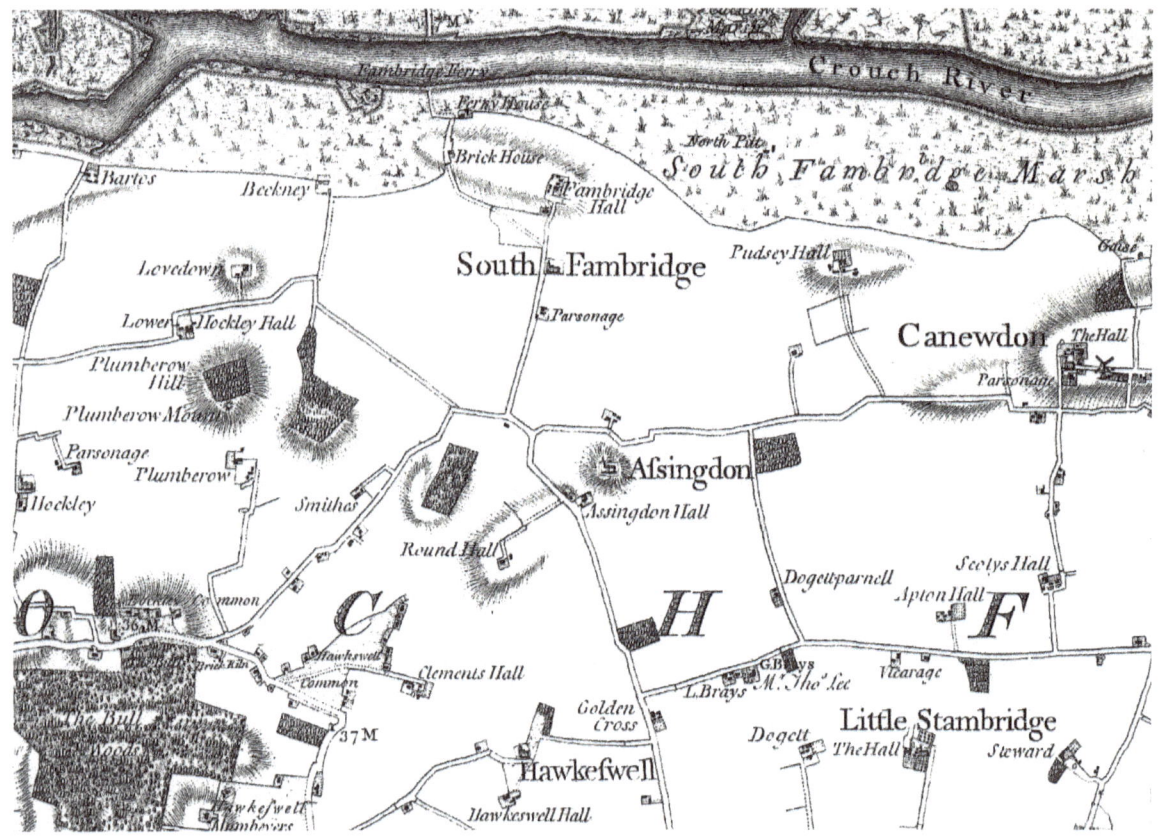

Figure 19: Chapman & André's map of Essex

In Ashingdon, "Assingdon Hall" and the parish church are both depicted on the map, as are Beckney, "Smithes" and "Round Hall", plus an unnamed building to the north of the church which we now know as Moon's. Meanwhile, in South Fambridge, the parish church, Parsonage, Fambridge Hall, Brick House, Ferry House and the Fambridge Ferry are also featured. The southern edge of South Fambridge Marsh appears to provide the limit of the building line here (except for at North Pitt, which is in Canewdon parish).

The main local road network is also visible, with what are now Ashingdon Road, Brays Lane, Hyde Wood Lane, Canewdon Road, Fambridge Road, Lower Road and Greensward Lane all clearly shown. Beckney and Trinity Woods are also shown, as is a third wood on the eastern side of Ashingdon Road just north of Brays Lane. Hyde Wood (in Canewdon parish, to the east of Hyde Wood Lane) can also be seen.

The churches and manor houses have been covered above, so this section looks at the other buildings and landscape features which appear on Chapman & André's map.

Smith's

"Smithes" was in the southern part of the detached Beckney portion of Ashingdon, to the west of Greensward Lane and roughly equidistantly placed between Beckney and Trinity Woods. The map shows that it had its own lane serving it. It would have been roughly in the vicinity of what is now the eastern arm of Malvern Road, at the top end of Harrogate Drive.

In Benton's day it was known as "Smiths" (without the 'e') and was the residence of a Mr. H. Keyes, who was probably a relative of the 1790s surveyor, Thomas Keyes. Benton states that it "was formerly known by the name of 'Snares'", which he deduces was in turn named after a 14th-century landowner called Reginald Snarry. The *Feet of Fines for Essex* (Vol. III, 1949, which lists agreements between two parties in legal disputes over land ownership) names a Richard Snarry, his wife Joan and a Robert Snarry as being "of Assyngdon" in 1373, and a John Snarry "of Hokle" [Hockley] in 1421. Reaney calls this property "Smith's and Snares Farm" and cites Reginald Snarry (1325) and John Smyth (1374) as the sources of the two names. Greensward Lane was called Greenstead Lane when Benton was writing (though he mentions that it was called Greensward Lane before that).

"A messuage called Smithes or Snares in Ashingdon and Hockley" is named in a conveyance held at the ERO which dates from 1665.[109] The property is also mentioned in a deed dating from 1772.[110]

Rouncefall

"Round Hall" on Chapman & André's map appears to be located where Rouncefall is now, at the western end of the southern branch of The Chase, off Ashingdon Hill. It could be an earlier name for that, or a mis-transcription of it. Benton writes of it as: "'Rounsefulls', otherwise Rouncefall, Rounevalls, or Cattlynsland, a farm on the hill, [which] belongs to Miss Emma Potter. It pays a quit rent to the manor of Pudsey Hall [in Canewdon parish]." Reaney has the name as "Rouncefall *alias* Rouncefields". He also found it documented as Runcyvall in some Chancery proceedings from 1579. He states that: "This was probably

---

[109] ERO D/DQ 41/10
[110] ERO D/DA T574

part of the possessions here of the Hospital of Our Lady of Rouncevale, Charing Cross [which he researched back to 1291]… but it is curious that Geoffrey de Runceual(l) was connected with Ashingdon and Hawkwell in 1254… and Katherine Runcevale with Sutton in 1305. The Hospital at Charing Cross was a cell of the Priory of St Mary of Roncesvalles in the [Spanish] Pyrenees." King also refers to connections between Ashingdon and "the Fraternity or Guild of St Mary Rouncyvall near Charing Cross".[111] According to the *Survey of London* (Vol. XVIII, 1937) the earliest known documentary reference to the Charing Cross hospital is from 18 October 1236; the day and month are the same as those of the Battle of Assandun in 1016 – is this a coincidence or is there a connection? The Ashingdon parish registers record the burial on 23 January 1646/7 of Marie Brannard, wife of Richard, who "lived at Rainsfall".[112] This is presumably another variation of the name, spelt roughly as it sounded.

Figure 20: Rouncefall, viewed from The Chase

The *Royal Commission* (1923) describes Rouncefall as follows: "House, about ½ m. W.S.W. of the church, … of one storey with attics, timber-framed and weather-boarded; the roofs are tiled. It was built in the 17th century on a rectangular plan and has an original central chimney stack, square on plan with rebated angles. Inside the building the

---

111   ERO T/P 196/14, p.69
112   ERO TS 709/1

timber-framing and ceiling-beams are exposed. Condition—Good." The building is on Rochford District Council's list of important local buildings. Documents at the ERO date it to at least 1612.[113]

Moon's

Although not named on Chapman & André's map, Moon's Farm can be seen depicted on it to the immediate north of Ashingdon church, on the northern side of Canewdon Road. A public footpath leads downhill from the church to the farm. Moon's seems to have been a significant property, as by 1808 most of the land in the parish came within its boundaries.

Figure 21: The entrance to Moon's Farm

Reaney traced the property's name to a John le Mone, who owned it in 1327. The ERO holds a document from 1314 which lists le Mone as a witness on the deeds of a property called "Blunts" in neighbouring Hockley parish.[114] King unearthed a record of a burial in 1645 of his namesake John King, who "lived at Moones".[115] The Ashingdon parish registers record a burial on 13 June 1650 of John Michell who "lived at Moons Fm". They also record

---

113   ERO D/DB T1612
114   ERO D/DU 568/1
115   ERO T/P 196/28 pp.183

the burial in April 1656/7 of poor Grace Spencer, the "vagrant born at South Fambridge", and her child (presumably Luke, who was baptised only in the January (see above)); Grace is described as having "died at Moons". Her death preceded her child's by only a matter of days.[116]

Benton writes of a William Harris of Moon's who lost his first wife Elizabeth on 13 May 1656 and had her buried at Rayleigh. William was presumably a member of the Harris family who were once tenants of the Manor of Beckney. He soon afterwards became engaged to Mary Tourney, "daughter of Mr. Robert Tourney, parson of South Fambridge". They were married on 17 October 1656 and solemnized their wedding day six days later at Hockley parsonage. The couple had two daughters, with the unusual names of "Cleer" (Clare?) and "Plary" (?). King adds that they also had two sons, William and Charles.[117] Harris's wife survived him and subsequently remarried, to Christopher Cornish of South Benfleet, in 1665. According to Benton, Rev. Tourney "conformed at the Restoration" of the monarchy under King Charles II at South Fambridge in 1660.

Benton also found a rating assessment in the churchwardens' accounts for Ashingdon parish in 1730 that listed a Christopher Hatchman as then occupying Moon's. He writes that "in the churchyard is to be seen a monument to Christopher Hatchman, son of Christian Hatchman, who died in 1749, on the 24th July, aged 16 years". Christopher Hatchman signed the Ashingdon parish account books in 1726 and a Sarah Hatchman, possibly his wife, appears in the same books several times throughout the 1750s.[118]

The Lascelles family are mentioned in property ownership documents for Moons in the late 18th century.[119] There is a Lascelles Gardens on the western side of Ashingdon Road which may take its name from the family.

South Fambridge Parsonage & Ministers

The map shows South Fambridge Parsonage standing on the east side of Fambridge Road, south of the church, somewhere in the vicinity of what are now the Rectory Farm outbuildings and The Cow Shed. No trace of the building remains. Benton writes of it (c.1867) that: "Like many of the old parsonage houses, it is altogether unsuitable to the requirements of the day, and a new house is now in the course of construction, by the present rector – the Rev. D.M. [David Mede] Salter, the builder being a Mr. Saunders". There was then, he adds, an excellent glebe land of 124 acres attached to it. The "new house" is what is now Rectory Farm (see below).

The Heritage Gateway website contains two records of the Parsonage. This is the first

---

116 ERO TS 709/1
117 ERO T/P 196/28
118 ERO D/P 89/8/1
119 ERO D/DO T790/17

one: "Medieval (C14-C15) and post medieval pottery found on the site of the old parsonage. Finds also included brick, tile and clay pipes. Large amount of tile and brick reported by Mr. J. Squier to Southend Museum lying in field S. of S. Fambridge church. Investigation by South East Essex Archaeological Society showed these to be the surface remains of a parsonage erected in the later C17. Medieval pottery indicates an earlier building on the site. There were six sherds of medieval date, one glazed, the rest unglazed."

The second record is as follows: "Post medieval pottery (C17 and C19) found on the site of the old parsonage. Also, brick, tile and clay pipes. The finds are the surface remains of the parsonage erected in the C17 and demolished in about 1870. The earliest documentary [evidence] is of 1610, when it was stated that there was a parsonage with a kitchen, barn and that there was also a church house (probably built near the church)."

We know from information already given above that Rev. Nicholas Wardall was probably parson of South Fambridge c.1564-87 and that Rev. Robert Tourney was parson there from at least 1656 to 1660. Rev. William Pierce was parson in 1667 and Rev. Matthew Kay in 1782. Rev. Edward Fawcett was parson from 1809 until at least 1835, according to Wright, though he may not have been present very often, as Benton found that he also held the living at Cockermouth in the Lake District, where he died in 1865. He is named as Rector of South Fambridge in a railway proposal document of 1846 (see below for more on this).[120] His son, Rev. James Grisdale Fawcett, served as his curate at South Fambridge and was also chaplain at the Rochford Union Workhouse. As stated above, it was Rev. J.G. Fawcett who agreed to find the majority of the funding for the rebuilding of the parish church.

Benton states that the earliest patron of the living on record at South Fambridge was John de Peyton, who presented an unnamed minister to the living in 1336. The Ashingdon parish registers show that Rev. John Horrocks, a "clerk and parson of South Fambridge", was buried locally in 1626.[121] Benton also states that the appropriately named Rev. John Vicars, who was presented to the living in 1640 by the patron, Henry Osborne, was ejected from it c.1644-5 "for [lack of] loyalty and conformity" and because "he was non-resident, kept a drunken curate, and was suspected of being a Popish priest". The churchwardens there were excommunicated in the 17th century, potentially at the same time, "for not exhibiting their presentment". According to T.W. Davids, in his book *Annals of Evangelical nonconformity in the county of Essex* (2019), depositions were taken against Vicars at Maldon on 16 April 1644.

Benton adds that Vicars was succeeded by Rev. Jackson, whose tenure must have been very short-lived, as he died in 1645 and his Christian name is not recorded. Jackson's

---

120   ERO Q/RUm 2/53
121   ERO T/P 196/28, pp.183

ministry was followed by the equally short tenure of Rev. John Hopkins, "who was dismissed for neglecting the cure" in 1646. Parishioners had set up a petition to have Hopkins ejected, as he was evidently absent and had failed to provide them with a curate. This resulted in the appointment of Rev. Robert Tourney, who began as curate and later became rector. He lived at the Parsonage until his death in 1661.

Rev. George Heriot was "presented to the rectory of South Fambridge" in 1683 and was still there in 1698, though apparently also often absent.[122] Rev. Thomas Osborne, a member of the patron's family, held the role of vicar there in 1726-7. Rev. Miles Steadman, rector of South Fambridge, is recorded as being buried in the chancel of the church there on 7 September 1794.[123] Benton writes that this burial service was performed by Rev. J. Wise; this is presumably the Rev. Joseph Wise who was curate at Ashingdon at the time.

The parish seems to have suffered from a succession of absentee rectors, perhaps because of its extremely rural nature and consequent low stipend, for Benton adds that "upon the death of Fawcett, the patronage for that time being sold, this living devolved upon the present [1867] rector, the Rev. David Mede Salter, who is at present an absentee". Salter's father was curate at Glastonbury, which explains how Salter obtained the silver-gilt paten which King saw in 1869 (see above). Rev. Salter junior gave it to South Fambridge parish "for use in the administration of the holy communion". King was not a fan of the "pluralist and non-resident rectors" with which South Fambridge had apparently been lumbered.[124]

The records show that Revs. Tourney and Heriot both lived in the Parsonage and it is presumed that the others did so too when they were in the job and present in the parish.

South Fambridge Parish Registers

The 19th-century Ashingdon rector, Rev. Septimus Nottidge, informed King, that "there are no registers [for South Fambridge] beyond the year 1765". He adds that "I have enquired among the oldest and chiefest families in the place and they have never known any registers or parochial books of older date".[125] The ERO, however, holds marriage registers for South Fambridge back to 1754; these evidently came to light later. There are indeed, however, no baptism or burial registers there which pre-date 1765. It was a legal duty to keep parish registers from the 16th century onwards in England, so it is surprising to read that this may not have been done in this parish.

The first four baptisms recorded in the South Fambridge registers are all of sons of Martin and Mary Lurring: Martin (1765); John (1767); William (1769); and Robert (1771).

---

122   ERO D/DXb 26 & D/DXb 27
123   ERO TS 710/5
124   ERO T/P 196/5
125   ERO T/P 196/28, pp.183

The Lurrings were the most populous family in South Fambridge in the period 1765-1837, with 19 baptisms and 11 burials recorded. One of the Martin Lurrings is named as attending an Ashingdon parish meeting in 1802.[126] He also regularly attended parish meetings 1803-8, almost certainly as one of the parish officials.[127]

Other early baptisms in the parish were of sisters Sarah (1770) and Ann Bragge (1773). These were the only six baptisms in the eight-year period 1765-73, suggesting a small population, a low fertility rate and slow population growth. Other 18th-century surnames recorded in the registers were Allen/Ellen, Atkins, Attridge, Beard, Bridge, Chitticks (various spellings), Clark, Cock, Cockley, Coller, Crealy, Darcey, Dawson, Gray, Hayes, Hughes (various spellings), Levith, Packman, Palmer, Rainer/Rayner, Reed, Richardson, Teaby, Terry, Thorrington, Ward and White. The most common surnames in South Fambridge in the 1765-1837 period were Allen, Cage, Chitticks, Clark, Cockley, Hughes, Lurring, Potter, Saunders and Wash.[128] In 1797 William Allen, a farmer and victualler of South Fambridge, leased land in Rochford from a Rochford maltster, John Bright.[129] John Chittick/Chittock was parish constable of South Fambridge c.1838-48.[130]

The burial registers begin 10 years later than the baptism ones. The earliest burial recorded was that of Gilbert Allen from North Fambridge on 2 November 1775. Another early record is that of the double burial of Mary Wherley, wife of George, and George Wherley, their son, on 29 March 1777. It is likely that Mary and her son, who were from Hawkwell, died while she was giving birth to him. The registers also record the burial in the 1780s of Joseph (surname not recorded) who died from smallpox, Daniel Carter, a "baseborn" child, and Thomas Pavett, "a stranger".[131]

Brick House Farm aka Forsters

Brick House (sometimes Brickhouse) Farm stands at the southern end of Fambridge village and feels like it marks the entrance to it. According to Jerram-Burrows it was previously known as "Fosters" or "Fersters". A property called "Forsters" appears regularly in the parish records; it is presumed this is one and the same as all the above.

---

126 ERO D/P 89/21
127 ERO D/CR 11
128 ERO TS 710/5
129 ERO D/DA T285
130 ERO D/P 90/8
131 ERO TS 710/5

Figure 22: Brick House Farm, once known as "Forsters"

Morant writes that: "A messuage here called Forsters, and 160 acres of arable, and 10 of marsh, belonged in 1422 to John Baud; and in 1447 to Robert Darcy…" King found that Robert Darcy Snr. obtain his rights in Forsters from Richard Valoryan.[132] Darcy or D'Arcy was a wealthy and influential Maldon lawyer who had connections with the Coggeshall and Doreward families, owners of the Manor of Ashingdon. He also enjoyed the support of Joan de Bohun (née FitzAlan, 1347-1419), whose father-in-law was tenant of the Manor of South Fambridge. He was one of the executors of her will. He died in 1448 and, like Captain Cammock, was buried in All Saints church in Maldon. He is commemorated there in the D'Arcy Chapel.

Jerram-Burrows found that in 1557 Forsters was in the ownership of John Barratt. It was still known by that name in 1718, when it had oyster layings in the Crouch.[133] Jerram-Burrows adds that the present farmhouse was built "about 250 years ago" (from 1985), making it of *c.*1735 date. Perhaps the name change was occasioned by the rebuilding? A coin depicting King George III (monarch 1760-1820) was found beneath a windowsill in the building recently to when Jerram-Burrows was writing. In Benton's day the building belonged to a Mr. J.J. Willan, whose family owned it for many years.

One of the barns on the site also dates from the 18th century, so may well have been constructed at the same time as the farmhouse. The Heritage Gateway website states

---

132   ERO T/P 196/14
133   ERO D/DCf T170

that: "The barn is poss. early C18 and has a rare stone threshing floor in the midstrey [its projecting porch]. It consists of 3 bays with a further rebuilt bay to the west and modern bay to the east… The barn was built with a queen strut roof with two rows of purlins [horizontal beams]. The tiles were torched into place without the use of pegs or nails. Mainly built in oak with some elm and softwood infill and elm weatherboarding. There… remain features of interest in the barn, showing that money was available in the early eighteenth century for farming and this farm does appear to have been an arable farm at that time. It has also seen many changes, some showing up the downturn in farming fortunes as well as the better times… The main comment would be that arable farming seems to take off [here] in the late seventeenth century as the marsh areas were drained."

Figure 23: Brick House Barn, in the background, with the black weatherboarding

In 2006 the barn, which was by then in separate ownership from the farmhouse, was converted to residential use and it is consequently now a dwelling called "Brick House Barn". [134]

The Ferry House

The Ferry House, now the Grade II-listed Old Ferry House, is at the northern end of the village, next to the entrance to the track which leads to the seawall. It is easy to see from the map why it was built where it was: it is on the northernmost promontory of dry land before the marshes.

---

[134] ERO T2360

Figure 24: The Old Ferry House

Morant writes that "Two messuages, and lands called Ferry-lands, with the passage or ferry, and Betts, belonged in 1556 to William Harris Esq. who held them of the Lord Rich". Ferry-lands may have been the Ferry House, but where Betts was is not known. Harris, of course, also held the Manor of Beckney from Lord Rich at this time. Toll payments from the ferry were shared between Ferry-lands and an equivalent farm across the river in North Fambridge.

The Ashingdon parish registers record the burial in 1678 of John D… (it is not possible to make out the surname) who is described as "landlord of the ferry house".[135] This suggests that the ferry house was a public house, probably doubling as somewhere for ferry passengers to wait and simultaneously obtain refreshment. The current building was erected in the late 18th century, so it must have superseded the previous one and been built around the time that Chapman & André's map was produced. The British Listed Buildings website states that "the C18 roof incorporates one steeply cambered tie beam with huge brace mortices, probably pre-mid C15 and many re-used sooted rafters"; the 15th-century beam and mortices may have been reused from the earlier building or sourced from elsewhere.

---

[135] ERO TS 709/1

THE POOR

According to the book *Poverty & Poor Law Reform in 19th Century Britain, 1834-1914* by David Englander, sustained population growth across the country from the mid-18th century onwards and the increasing commercialisation of agriculture led to a growing imbalance between the numbers of rural labourers and the opportunities for rural employment. The Poor Law Relief Act 1662 had been introduced to establish the parish to which a person belonged and therefore identify which parish was responsible for providing poor relief for that individual. These "laws of settlement", as they became known, had the unexpected disadvantage of preventing people from moving outside their native parishes if they did not have work. This effectively trapped unemployed agricultural labourers in locations where employment opportunities were declining, and their living standards deteriorated as a result. Ashingdon and South Fambridge were both rural communities, so were significantly adversely affected by any loss of agricultural employment at this time, with an increasing financial burden being placed on the parishes as a result. Across the country, the poor rate quadrupled in size between 1790 and 1820. For small parishes like Ashingdon and South Fambridge it must have been extremely challenging for the parish officials to meet the demands placed upon them.

From 1781 onwards the Ashingdon parish burial records begin to refer to some of the deceased as a "pauper" or "a pauper otp [of this parish]".[136] The parish account books show that poor relief was being regularly paid to widows at this period, and in 1795 there is a record of the provision of a nurse for "Widow Tillbrook".[137] These documents alone give some insight into the local "poor management" situation.

---

136 Ibid.
137 ERO D/P 89/8/1

ASHINGDON PARISH MAP (1787/1808)

In 1787, ten years after Chapman & André, a parish map of Ashingdon was produced, showing the parish boundaries, roads and properties. It was revisited and revised in 1808. The map states that the detail shown was "Perambulated 16th May 1787 and 26th May 1808" and that it was produced by "J. Wise". This is presumably the Rev. Joseph Wise mentioned above who was curate at Ashingdon around this time. The map is marked with crosses which, according to the key, "denote Boundary Posts". The original map was evidently damaged at some point, as all three copies seen by the author show the same staining marks down the middle of it, but it is fortunate to have survived at all, as such a document is incredibly rare. The one shown in the photograph below was on display at the Church Hall during a parish history exhibition.

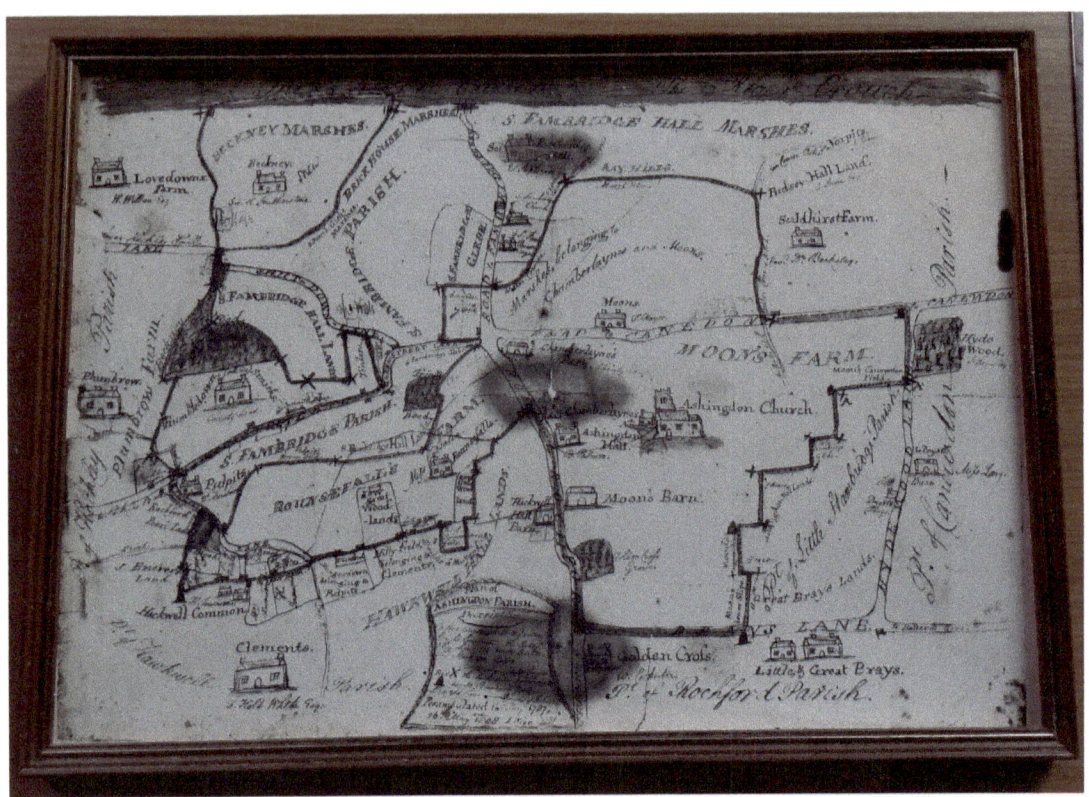

Figure 25: The 1787/1808 map of Ashingdon Parish, showing parish boundaries, boundary markers and roads

The thick black lines on the map with the crosses on them show the three separate parts of Ashingdon parish. Rouncefall and Moon's dominate the main part of the parish, while Beckney can be seen in the northern detached portion. Smith's, in the southern detached portion, has become "Rumbledown, (alias Smiths)" since Chapman & André. The interweaving of the lands of South Fambridge parish between the various Ashingdon properties can also be seen.

Parish boundaries were historically of great importance: the issuing of poor relief, the provision of schooling and the allocation of charitable funds were all administered in accordance with, and dependent upon, a person's parish of birth. They were also used to ratify a person's liability for the repair of the church, the payment of tithes or land rents and the right to be buried in the parish's churchyard. In days when maps were rare there was consequently an annual ceremony held in many parts of the country in which parishioners walked the boundaries of their parish, marking them at certain points as they went. This ceremony, which was generally led by the parish priest or another church official, was called "Beating the Bounds" and it usually took place in Rogation Week or on Ascension Day (late April or May). Prayers were said at certain parts of the route to bless the parish, its inhabitants and the harvest. The perambulation often included the whipping of small boys or the banging of their heads on certain significant posts and trees, so that they remembered as they grew up where these key markers stood. Walkers often took long sticks with them to physically "beat" the boundaries at certain points. In some cases, man-made boundary markers were erected, especially where a parish boundary was disputed. The origins of these ceremonies may well date back to the Saxon period. Several accounts of local Beating the Bounds ceremonies survive. The fact that the Ashingdon map was produced and revised in May and shows the parish boundaries and boundary markers, suggests that it was probably created for a Beating of the Bounds ceremony.

Below are descriptions of the key places on the map.

Ashingdon Church

The drawing of Ashingdon church on the map is interesting, as the tower depicted there bears no resemblance to the current tower. It may be a stylised representation of a church, but the church shown at South Fambridge is different, and it looks more like historic descriptions of it. Did Ashingdon church once have a different tower, offset to the north of the building as shown?

Ashingdon Rectory

The building to the immediate north-west of the church is named on the map in very small writing as "A [Ashingdon] Parsonage". The present rectory stands roughly in this vicinity, but the Parsonage shown on the map is a now-lost predecessor. Benton, quoting a note that he obtained, writes that "The Rectory House was removed by Gabriel Price [rector 1614-23] in 1621 from the Glebe Land near the wont way [the junction of what are now Ashingdon, Canewdon and Fambridge Roads], to the north side of the church, and…

the Right Honourable Robert Earl of Warwick contributed ten loads of timber thereto; and in 1642 Josiah Church [rector 1641-4, and sometimes recorded as 'Josias' Church] built a lean-to". He adds that "The house rebuilt by Gabriel Price still [1867] exists, within a few rods to the north of the present rectory house: the latter was erected by the Rev. Septimus Nottidge [rector 1846-79], in 1855". It seems from this evidence and that of the Heritage Gateway entries for Ashingdon, that there have been four rectories in the parish: the first, which stood by the wont way; the second, which was built by Rev. Price nearer to the church in 1621; the third, which was built by Rev. Nottidge in 1855, close to Price's building; and the current one which is obviously 20th century. Only the last of these survives, but the land by the wont way which is shown on the map as "Ashingdon Glebe" provides evidence of where the first of these four buildings stood.

Figure 26: The top end of Church Road in Ashingdon in the early 20th century, showing the 1855 rectory which was built by Rev. Septimus Nottidge

In the records of Ashingdon parish marriage banns, Rev. Septimus Nottidge wrote of the marriage of John Argent, widower, and Susan Marvin, spinster, in November 1846 that this was "my first marriage at Ashingdon as Rector".[138]

---

138   ERO D/P 89/1/7

In 1867 Benton recorded that the living and advowson of St Andrew's, Ashingdon, were both in the hands of Rev. Septimus Nottidge, who evidently inherited the right to appoint the incumbent from his father. Roper, however, found that William Wright was the patron during Rev. Septimus Nottidge's tenure (1846-79).

Ashingdon Hall

To the west of the church and parsonage, abutting Ashingdon Road (named on the map as "Road to Rochford"), stands Ashingdon Hall. This is shown as being in the occupation or ownership of "B. [Benjamin] Palmer".

Chamberlain's

To the immediate north of Ashingdon Hall stands "Chamberlaynes", and further north of that, by the wont way, is "Chamberlaynes Barn". Opposite that barn, on the other side of Ashingdon Road, south of Ashingdon Glebe, is what looks like a field with the word "Chamberlaynes" written very lightly on it.

It will be recalled from the preceding section on Post-Domesday Landowners & Manors that Richard le Chamberlayn was a tenant in Ashingdon in 1285. Reaney derives the name of the property from a Richard le Chamberlyn who owned it in 1326; this may be the same individual or one of his heirs. The records go quiet until the 16th century, when Benton found that the property was owned by the Higgate or Heygate family. Under the will of Thomas Heygate, written in 1557, the property was left to Thomas's wife, Margaret. The bequest included cows, sheep, ploughs, horses, "a little white mare", crops and some silver spoons. There were also legacies for all of Thomas's servants. The pair had at least one son and three daughters. The son, Edmond, inherited the property in due course. Benton found that his wife, Dorryly, died in 1570 and was buried in Ashingdon churchyard. His sisters were named Joanne, Margaret and Thomasine.

Benton writes that: "The double cottage upon the summit of the hill was formerly the farmhouse, and a member of the Kesterman [or Kersteman] family resided in it, in later times, who likewise held 'Smith's'. These two farms are in three parishes, Ashingdon, South Fambridge and Hockley."[139] [Richard] Woollaston, who flourished in the seventeenth century, was owner of 'Chamberlains' [which is how it was spelt by the 1860s] and probably farmed it himself, as in his will mention is made that he had twenty score of sheep on the 'Saltings'. There are seven trustees of the charity, (so named from him,) which is unconnected with the parish, except so far as they are owners of the property."

The map includes the words "Charity Land" next to Chamberlaynes Barn (and beneath Smith's, in the southern detached part of the parish). The charity was founded

---

139   Primary source documents held at the ERO state that Chamberlain's was in Ashingdon, South Fambridge and Hawkwell parishes. See, for example, ERO D/DQ 41/10 (1665) and D/DHt T8/2 (1688).

in 1689 by Richard Woollaston, a London merchant from Wormley in Hertfordshire. Its aim was to clothe the poor, on condition that they are "judged to fear God". Benton writes that there were six acres of charity land in South Fambridge in addition to those in Ashingdon.

The ERO holds documentation relating to Chamberlain's from at least 1611. This includes several indentures showing that it was in the occupation of the Attwood family in the latter part of the 17th century and that it passed from them to Woollaston c.1703. These indentures reveal that the building was alternatively known as "The White House", presumably from its exterior colour. They also refer to "the manor of Chamberlaynes", a designation which suggests that the original Ashingdon Domesday manor may have been subdivided.[140] The Ashingdon parish registers record the burial on 9 October 1650 of Elizabeth Huilson, wife of George, of Chamberlain's, who "died in childbed".[141]

Figure 27: The postcard from which this picture is taken has the words "The White House, Ashingdon" inscribed in ink on its reverse; the only historic property in the parish to have that designation was Chamberlain's, so it is presumed that, if the ink writing is correct, this is Chamberlain's Farm

---

140   ERO D/DQ 41/10-11 and D/DHt T8/1-4
141   ERO TS 709/1

In 1730 the rate assessment for Chamberlain's was paid by Thomas Sly, a wealthy local farmer and former lessee of South Fambridge Hall, who also paid the rates on Ashingdon Glebe and for part of Smith's. The farm paid rent to the Lawless Court at King's Hill in Rochford, a bizarre court, originally held at Rayleigh, at which tenants had to pay both homage and rent to the Lord of Manor in the early hours of the morning and carry out their business in whispers. Sly is regularly mentioned in Ashingdon account books in the early part of the 18th century. He is listed as overseer, one of the parish officials, in 1713.[142]

Both Chamberlain's and its barn are gone.

Rouncefall

Across the road from Chamberlain's, the western half of the main part of Ashingdon parish is dominated by "ROUNSEFALL'S FARM", which is shown on the map as being in the ownership of "Miss Godsalve". The land at Rouncefall includes two distinct areas labelled as "Kew Great Woodlands" and "Kew Little Woodlands". A small field between them is described as "Late a Grove", i.e. a wood which has recently been chopped down. A small field to the south-east of that is described as "Part of Rounsefall's". The western end of the Rouncefall lands is shown broken up into several small fields – see the section below on Pulpits for more information about that and the Kew connection.

Moon's

East of Rouncefall, the parish boundary can be seen running south from Ashingdon Hall down the centre of Ashingdon Road. Hawkwell parish and the lands of Hawkwell Hall lie to the west of this road, while the lands of "MOON's FARM" dominate the eastern side of it. Here stand "Moon's Barn" and the small wood depicted on Chapman & André's map, which is named here as "Golden Cross Grove". This wood stood immediately adjacent to the distinctive "chicane" in the Ashingdon Road, which would put it south of where Nansen Avenue is now, opposite the entrance to Lascelles Gardens, but it has long-since disappeared. Moon's Barn is also no longer there, but Moons Close has been built not far from where it stood.

At Brays Lane the parish boundary turns east and then makes its way in a staggered north-easterly direction across the fields around the southern and south-eastern edges of Moon's farmland towards Hyde Wood in Hyde Wood Lane. The left-hand side of this staggered boundary at the southern end includes the words "Moon's Lower Slipe" and "Moon's Upper Slipe". One meaning of "slipe" is a thin, narrow strip of land. The field at the top-right of this boundary, opposite Hyde Wood, is named "Moon's Canewdon Field".

The map records that the lands to the south-east of this staggered section of the boundary were "Pt. of Little Stambridge Parish" (as shown on the map in the Introduction).

---

142 ERO D/P 89/8/1

This was a detached part of that parish and it seems odd that it has been carved out here when the logical boundary line would have been where Brays Lane and Hyde Wood Lane meet. Detached parts of parishes, which are historically common locally, were usually established either to benefit from fertile marshland on local islands like Wallasea and Canvey or to benefit from the productive woodland areas around Hockley. This part fits neither description, so it has to be pure conjecture as to why this was the case, but a possible option is that because Little Stambridge was a small parish, some local agreement was reached centuries ago to provide it with additional agricultural land, and that this piece was carved out of Ashingdon. Part of the land on the Little Stambridge side of the boundary is described as "Ashingdon Hall Lands", showing that there was definitely a historic connection of some kind here between these two parishes.

Figure 28: Brays Lane, c.1930

It can be seen from the map that Brays Lane takes its name from Little and Great Brays farms, whilst Golden Cross, a building which was presumably connected in some way with the lost wood and which now gives its name to this whole area, stands to their west. The map shows that these three buildings were in "Pt. of Rochford Parish". Benton writes that: "Goulden [sic] Cross is so named from the cross formerly existing at the three-wont way, leading to Hawkwell church [the junction of Ashingdon Road with Rectory Road further south]. These crosses were set up to inspire recollection and reverence."

Having staggered its way in a north-easterly direction across the fields, the Ashingdon parish boundary reaches Hyde Wood Lane at the south-west corner of Hyde Wood. The map records that the latter and the lands around it were "Pt. of Canewdon Parish". The boundary goes northwards from here to what is described on the map as the "Road to Canewdon" – now the junction of Canewdon Road and Lark Hill Road – and turns west along the former until it reaches a "Water Course Ditch". This water course crosses under the road to the immediate west of where Three Bays Farm is now and extends into "S. FAMBRIDGE HALL MARSHES" at the top of the map.

From the cross on this water course boundary at "Pudsey Hall Land" (in Canewdon parish), the Ashingdon parish boundary then turns west along a "Marsh Ditch". It then turns south from a point just south-east of South Fambridge Hall, staying east of South Fambridge Church and Parsonage, before curving west along another "Water Course" to cross the "Road to Fambridge" (now Fambridge Road). It then encompasses a rectangular section on the south-western corner of this road which is labelled as "Ashingdon Glebe" and was the location of the earliest of the four recorded Ashingdon rectories.

Moon's farmhouse is shown as being in the occupation of "T. [Thomas] Keyes", while the land to its north is shown as "Marshes, belonging to Chamberlaynes and Moons". Thomas Keyes, who served at various times as surveyor and churchwarden, is mentioned in Ashingdon parish account books from the 1770s to the 1790s.[143] The parish registers record the baptisms of Thomas and Mary Keyes' sons, Thomas and James, on 26 March 1780. Thomas the younger was aged one year and four months at the time, while James was "b[or]n new y[ea]rs day preceding". A third son, William, was baptised in 1784.[144]

According to Benton, writing in 1867, Moon's Farm belonged then to William Keyes, but "was formerly the property of Lord Harewood". This suggests that the property may have left the Keyes family and then returned to it. There is a Harewood Avenue on the Hawkwell side of Ashingdon Road.

The east window of St Andrew's church, dating from 1910, is dedicated to the Keyes family, two generations of whom were successively churchwardens there for 77 years. Benton writes that the bell at St Andrew's has the names of Thomas Keyes and Benjamin Palmer, the then churchwardens, on it. It will be recalled that a Mr H. Keyes was resident at Smith's in Benton's day as well.

Moon's Cottages

The lightly drawn building to the east of Moon's on the map, close to the parish boundary and looking like it has been partly erased, is a building called "Moon's Cottages". This building, which was originally a row of separate dwellings, has been converted into one

---

143   ERO D/P 89/8/1 & D/P 89/21
144   ERO TS 709/1

and renamed "Moon's Cottage". It has a modern plaque on it dated "A.D. 1726", but it does not appear on Chapman & André's map of 1777. The addition of the building on the 1787/1808 map is in a different hand from that of Rev. Wise, suggesting it was added in 1808. Why the building bears a plaque of 1726 but is not on the 1777 and 1787 maps is unclear, as the property's current owner has advised the author that surviving timber-framing inside the building has been dated by an historic buildings specialist to possibly as far back as the late-16th century.

Figure 29: Moon's Cottage

The building is on Rochford District Council's Local List of important Ashingdon buildings and is described as having a "rendered and painted façade with exposed timbers; gambrel roof with red tiling and a long ridge line; rendered and painted chimney stacks; numerous catslide dormers to the frontage; original windows have been replaced". The building is on the List because it: "is of historic importance and has some group value which adds to the street scene. Although the windows are considered to detract from the character of the building, it still retains much of its historic value."

Beckney

At the top left of the map can be seen the northern detached part of Ashingdon parish, featuring "BECKNEY MARSHES" and Beckney farmhouse. The latter is shown as being in the ownership of "Sir H. Featherstone". It also has the word "Mew" written next to it. As noted above, the Mew family were tenants of Sir H. Featherstone.

Some "Cottages" are also shown in this section of the parish, lightly drawn in a different hand, as with Moon's Cottages above. This suggests that these appeared between 1787 and 1808.

Beckney Wood can be clearly seen in the southern detached part of Ashingdon parish.

Smith's

South of Beckney Wood, in the southern detached part of the parish, can be seen the words "Rumbledown, (alias) Smith's". The appearance of the alias "Rumbledown" for Smith's is a bit of a surprise, given the earlier evidence, but the Ashingdon parish registers record the burial on 1 October 1652 of Thomas Budworth who "worked at Rumbledowns" and they also mention a Thomas Turner who "lived in Rumbledown" and was buried on 8 January 1652-3.[145] There is therefore a clear evolution of the name of the property from Snares to Rumbledown to Smith's, in that order.

To the south-west of the property, beneath the "R" in "Rumbledown", can be seen a dog-leg-shaped "Brook". A small field with the word "Rumbledown" written on it can also be seen there, just outside the parish boundary, in Hockley parish, to the left of this brook. As mentioned above under Chamberlain's, the words "Charity Land" beneath Rumbledown/Smith's suggest a connection with Richard Woollaston's charity.

Some of the documents at the ERO which relate to Chamberlain's also refer to a property in Ashingdon in the 17th and 18th centuries called "Jack Heards" or "Jackheards".[146] The Ashingdon parish registers record the burial on 30 March 1651 of Nicholas Ableson of Jackheards.[147] In 1849 Henry James Keyes leased 186 acres of Chamberlain's Farm "in Ashingdon and South Fambridge" from the trustees of Woollaston's Charity for 14 years until 1863. The lease included an additional 104+ acres of "Smith's and Snare's Farm, heretofore or sometime called Jackeard's [sic] and Smith's Farm", which was described as having land in Ashingdon, South Fambridge and Hockley parishes.[148] Smith's, Snare's, Rumbledown and Jackheards were all evidently one and the same place.

Of interest, too, on the map, in this part of the parish, is the "Blacksmith Shop", which can be seen fronting Greenstreet (now Greensward) Lane just to the south-east of Smith's. A field called "Tinkers" is shown to the east of that. The Blacksmith's Shop is remembered today in a modern property called "The Old Forge" at 223 Greensward Lane and in the name of "The Blacksmith's Shop" nearby bus stop, opposite Trinity Wood Road. Smith's itself has gone.

Holloucks Farm

Documentation in the ERO refers to a place called Holloucks Farm in Ashingdon, $7/_{12}$ of

---

145   Ibid.
146   ERO D/DQ 41/10-11 & D/DA T574
147   ERO TS 709/1
148   ERO D/DJe E18

which (120 acres) was sold by Thomas Everett and Rev. John Bearblock to a Shaw King in 1781. It was in the occupation of a Mr. Harridge at the time.[149] No such farm is named on Chapman & André nor on the 1787/1808 map, so it has not been possible to establish where this farm was.

South Fambridge Hall

Because of the intertwining nature of the Ashingdon and South Fambridge parishes, the map also reveals good information about properties in the latter.

At the top of the map can be seen "S. FAMBRIDGE HALL MARSHES" and beneath that "RAY HILLS". The latter name reflects the nature of the land here and the fact that South Fambridge Hall sits on raised land. A "Water Course Ditch" runs to the east of the Hall, which is shown as being in the ownership of "Ed. Stephenson Esq.".

South Fambridge Church

To the south of the Hall stands South Fambridge church. This is probably the best illustration available of the building which preceded the current one. It appears to fit Morant's 1768 description of it as "little and low… of one pace, tiled" and with "a little wooden turret" at the west end. Again, the apparent accuracy of the depiction of All Saints calls into question the depiction of St Andrew's, with its unexpected castellated tower.

South Fambridge Parsonage

To the south of the church stands South Fambridge Parsonage and, on the opposite of the "Road to Fambridge Ferry", is "S. Fambridge Glebe". The fact that this is immediately adjacent to Ashingdon Glebe suggests some distant historic Church connection between them. "S. Famb. Glebe Marshes" can be seen away to the west by the Beckney boundary.

South Fambridge Riverside

Little is depicted of riverside South Fambridge, though this is a map of Ashingdon, and the South Fambridge additions are incidental. As stated above, Brickhouse Farm was already there and "BRICK HOUSE MARSHES" can be seen by the Beckney boundary as well.

Lower Road & Greensward Lane

Moving south-westwards to what is now Lower Road, we find that this thoroughfare is named on the map as "Shut-Down Lane". The origins of this name are unknown. Where the lane joins Greenstreet (now Greensward) Lane, there are two additional parts of South Fambridge Glebe, one on either side of the latter. The fact that Ashingdon Glebe has parts of South Fambridge Glebe on either side of it again suggests some distant historic connection between the two. Beneath Greenstreet Lane can be seen both Trinity Wood and additional lands of South Fambridge Hall.

---

149   ERO D/DC 23/8

New Hall

A lightly drawn property on the north side of Shut-Down Lane, roughly where the Hockley Market Garden Centre is now, looks to be bearing the name "New Hall". In the will of William Carr of Hackwell [Hawkwell] Hall, dating from 1772, "New Hall in Ashingdon" was left to his son Backhouse Carr and then, if Backhouse died childless, to his niece Mary Hennett, daughter of Thomas and Elizabeth Hennett.[150] There is no New Hall in Ashingdon on the highly accurate late-1830s Tithe Map, which suggests that the above building had disappeared by this time or it was wrongly referred to as being in Ashingdon, because if the building on the 1787/1808 map is named "New Hall", it would be in South Fambridge parish here, not in Ashingdon parish.

In 1867 Benton wrote under his chapter on South Fambridge that because South Fambridge Hall farm comprised nearly 800 acres "the corn from some portion (until recently), had to be carried more than two miles to the homestall [the farmhouse], but the farm is now divided, and a new house (called New-hall) and farm premises were built in Beckney Lane [now Lower Road], about the year 1840". This would appear to describe the handwritten building on the 1787/1808 map.

This location is today home to the Hockley Market Garden Centre. This garden centre has a New Hall House on its site, and a New Hall Lane to the east of it. There is also a New Hall Farm opposite the garden centre. In the 1870s the garden centre property was known as Beckney Lane Farm.[151] However, the 1st Edition Ordnance Survey Map of 1880 shows "New Hall" on the site.

It seems likely therefore that the 1772 will refers either to a now-lost property in Ashingdon parish or wrongly places South Fambridge's New Hall in Ashingdon, and that the hand-drawn addition to the 1787/1808 map shows the New Hall in South Fambridge parish and post-dates 1840. As with Moon's Cottages and the cottages at Beckney, it is drawn in a different hand from that of Rev. Wise who produced the map, which would also seem to support this supposition.

There was a planning inquiry relating to New Hall in 1977-8, which may be connected with the switch of the farm from the north side of what is now Lower Road to the south.[152]

Pulpits

The most significant additionally named South Fambridge building since Chapman & André which is shown on the 1787/1808 map is "Pulpits". It can be seen on Chapman & André's map with the beginnings of a track next to it, but it is not named on that map. On the 1787/1808 map it is clearly named and is in the ownership or occupation of what

---

150   ERO D/DNe T43/27
151   ERO D/DJe L4
152   ERO D/J 126/2/4

looks to be "T. Marsham". "Pulpits Broomfield" is shown to the east of it, beneath the words "S. FAMBRIDGE PARISH", and "Pulpit Lane" can be seen immediately to the left of the building at the very western end of the historic South Fambridge parish. The proximity of the brook to Pulpits suggests that the latter was constructed here to be close to that natural water source. The map shows that Pulpits held lands in South Fambridge, Ashingdon and Hawkwell parishes.

Figure 30: Pulpits Farm in Greensward Lane

Pulpit Lane leads on the map into the Rouncefall part of the main Ashingdon parish, where the land has been broken up into several small fields. This area is now occupied by the modern Hockley Streets of Southview Road and Southbourne Grove, while Pulpit Lane itself has become "Kangle Wood Boundary Path Bridleway" (on Google Maps, at least), with its entrance being immediately south-west of where the Greensward Surgery is. There is also a modern street called "Pulpits Close" nearby, on the other side of Greensward Lane in what was historically the Smith's part of Ashingdon parish.

Officially now 144 Greensward Lane, Pulpits is a Grade II-listed building which is described in its listing from 1985 as follows: "House. Early C18. Timber framed and roughcast. Hipped red plain tiled roof. 2 storeys. 2 window range, 3-light small paned casements to first floor, vertically sliding sashes to ground floor. C20 lean-to left forward extension with French doors. Lobby entrance plan with door to (east) rear." The Heritage Gateway entry describes it as an "early C18 timber framed house".

Reaney found it named as "Pulpitts" in 1730 and "Pokepetts Farm" in 1872. He attributes the name to its association with the family of a 14th-century owner called John Pokepet or Pukpet. This owner evidently lived in an earlier building than the current 18th-century one. The ERO has a document showing the ownership of "Pokepetts" from 1596 to 1716.[153] The property is also mentioned in a court case about highway maintenance in 1687.[154] The rate assessment for part of Pulpits in 1730 was paid by Thomas Wright.

Benton writes in his section on Pulpits that 27 acres of land in South Fambridge parish belonged in the 1860s to the vicarage of Kew, which he records as being then in the incumbency of Rev. Percy Nott. "It was bought as an endowment for that living on the 1st of March 1716," writes Benton, "with money given to Dr. Slave, by the then Bishop of Winchester, and by the Governors of Queen Anne's Bounty. This farm was held by the Rev. Mr. Colton, vicar of Kew, in 1820. He was author of a work called *Lacon, or many things in few words*. He disappeared suddenly from Kew, and was not heard of for years, but subsequently was discovered at Paris, his vicarage [at Kew] in the meantime being sequestrated." It is unknown what the connection is between this and the Kew woodlands mentioned above under Rouncefall in Ashingdon, but there must surely be one. It will be recalled from earlier information given about Beckney Wood that a section of that also belonged to Kew. Benton adds that: "The parish of Kew has nine acres twenty-six poles of woodland, and twenty-three acres three roods of arable land, formerly wood. The vicar of Kew has twenty-three acres three roods eighteen poles (Pulpits)."

The ERO documentation mentioned above appears to show that "Pokepetts" belonged in 1716 to Edward and George Downes, who bought it from William Wild Mercy, and that some of its land was used to generate revenue for poor clergymen in Kew and the chapelry of St Anne's in Kew Green. Kew resident, Sir Charles Eyre, who was an administrator with the British East India Company and one of the contributors to the founding of St Anne's Church in Kew Green in 1714, is mentioned in the documentation, as is its curate, Rev. Thomas Fogg.[155]

---

153 ERO T/B 418/1
154 ERO Q/SR 455/74
155 ERO T/B 418/1

VILLAGE LIFE 1800-1840

Parish Registers

The South Fambridge parish registers shed some light on activity in the parish around the time of the 1787/1808 map. For example, in October 1794 John Connoway, the "infant son of a militia man" from Kent was buried in the parish. Meanwhile, between 1797 and 1804, 33 people were buried there, 18 of them aged five or less.[156] This is suggestive of a disease of some kind sweeping the parish, possibly smallpox, which was prevalent in Essex at the time and mainly affected children.[157] A further eight infants died in the period 1806-10.[158]

Poor Law Returns

The Poor Law returns for 1800-17 also reveal something about life in the two parishes. These returns cover, amongst other things, the raising of money for the poor rate, the construction or repair of county gaols and bridges, the payments to wives of militia men and the repair of local highways. They were required from every parish and had to be sent to the Clerk of the Peace at Chelmsford. In Ashingdon the overseers James and William Keyes diligently completed them, but a note accompanying the last batch of returns for the Rochford Division in 1818 states that "we enclose you the remainder of the parish returns for this Division, with the exception of that for South Fambridge which the overseer Mr. Potter refuses to fill in".[159]

The Ashingdon parish vestry minutes record many payments to local poor people in the early 19th century, especially clothing for children and financial assistance for widows. Common items paid for included shirts, gowns, petticoats, shifts, smocks, aprons, coats/jackets, trousers/breeches, handkerchiefs, stockings (socks), shoes and Calico cloth. Payments were also sometimes made towards rent and the purchase of coal. Coloured cotton, doctors' bills and midwives' expenses were also paid for, the latter two showing that those services were available to Ashingdon parishioners. In 1835 the minutes included a list of the poorest families in Ashingdon. Top of the list was that of John King, who had 12 children, six of whom were under the age of 13.[160]

The parish vestry also acted swiftly against anyone who shirked their responsibilities, such as the time in 1839 when James Booty absconded from Ashingdon and left his wife and her expenses chargeable to the parish's ratepayers. The vestry decided to

---

156 ERO TS 710/5
157 J.R. Smith, *The Speckled Monster*, p.23 and Noel Beer, *Health Care in Early 19th-century Rayleigh*, p.9
158 ERO TS 710/5
159 ERO Q/CR 1/9/18
160 ERO D/P 89/8/3

put an advertisement in the *Chelmsford Chronicle* offering £2 for Booty's apprehension.[161] When he was eventually caught, the parish "Paid Coe's bill for executing [the] warrant [for] apprehending and conveying James Booty to Chelmsford Gaol".[162] Conversely, in 1828, Ashingdon natives, John and Elizabeth Chittock, and their four children, were forcibly removed back to Ashingdon under the Poor Law legislation after trying unsuccessfully to settle in Hawkwell.[163] A similar fate befell Jeremiah and Mary-Ann Emmons, and their three children, who were subject to a removal order from Horndon-on-the-Hill to South Fambridge in 1833.[164] In 1844 Barnabas Baker and family were removed from Basildon to Ashingdon. Expenses for this activity included the hire of a waggon and horses in which to transport their goods.[165]

Jerram-Burrows writes of a workhouse for the poor in South Fambridge which in 1812 was struck by a "fire-ball" during a storm. One elderly resident suffered burns to her face, arms and neck.

Parish Officials

In 1802 in Ashingdon Thomas Keyes and Benjamin Palmer were churchwardens. They were also overseers, along with John Wyatt, while William Clift was the parish constable.[166] Rev. Henry Hodge was curate at St Andrew's 1802-3, but in 1804 Rev. J. Mills and Rev. D. Humphreys were successively in the post. Some services in 1804-5 were also carried out by Rev. Edward Fawcett from South Fambridge. In 1807 and from 1813 to 1822 Rev. Miles Moor was curate, while in 1824 Rev. William Worsley was in the role.[167] The parish owned three cottages and some adjacent land in North Street, Rochford, *c.*1811, at which time Rev. Moor was Ashingdon's minister, Benjamin Palmer and William Keyes were its overseers, and Palmer was also its churchwarden.[168] Ownership of these premises and land continued until 1933 when the parish was instructed to sell them by the Ministry of Health.[169]

In 1827-30 Rev. A. Anderson held the post of curate at Ashingdon, but from 1832 until 1839 Edward Fawcett's son and curate at South Fambridge, Rev. James Grisdale Fawcett, was regularly shown in the records as "officiating minister" or curate at Ashingdon as

---

161   Ibid.
162   ERO D/P 89/12/1
163   ERO Q/SBb 494/61
164   ERO Q/SBb 511/65
165   ERO D/P 89/12/1
166   ERO D/P 89/8/2
167   ERO D/CR 11
168   ERO D/DS 439/11
169   ERO A13442 Box 5

well.[170] Rev. Anderson was simultaneously curate of Ashingdon and Hawkwell in 1829, when he completed a nil return regarding non-conformist meeting houses in both parishes.[171] John Poulton was the parish's overseer in 1828, while James Keyes, William Keyes and Richard Bowton were between them surveyors, churchwardens and overseers from 1832 to 1835.[172] Bowton was the local blacksmith.[173] He also saw service as a churchwarden and parish constable.[174] Bowton, the Keyes family and the Bright family, who lived at Rouncefall, regularly held key posts in the village throughout the 1830s.[175] James Keyes, presumably the same man as above, also served as an overseer in South Fambridge in 1843-4.[176]

The rectors' board (and Roper's list) shows Rev. John Nottidge as Ashingdon rector from 1795 to 1846, but the evidence above shows that he was often or continually absent. Benton records that Nottidge also held the living at East Hanningfield and that "he resided at the latter place fifty-one years". A letter from Rev. Nottidge to the Bishop of London survives in the ERO. In it, the rector reports his exemption from the living at Ashingdon for the two years 1813 and 1814 because he was resident at his rectory in East Hanningfield.[177]

---

170   ERO D/CR 11 & D/P 90/8
171   ERO Q/CR 3/1/11
172   ERO D/P 89/8/3
173   ERO D/CR 139
174   ERO D/P 89/8/2
175   ERO D/P 89/8/3, D/P 89/11/1 & Q/RPc 11
176   ERO D/P 90/8
177   ERO D/P 250/28/11

Figure 31: A section of the rectors' board at Ashingdon church, headed by the name of Rev. John Nottidge

In South Fambridge in 1800 Rev. W. Atkinson was curate and in 1802 James Potter was churchwarden.[178] The latter was still churchwarden c.1811-3 and was churchwarden and overseer in 1817.[179] He must also have been the overseer mentioned above who refused to fill in the parish's Poor Law return.

In 1811-2 Potter was reimbursed for expenses which included the purchase of wine for the sacrament and the costs of "cleanen the church" and "washen the serpls [surplice]". J. Wise, Benny White, George Peacock and James Keyes were the signatories who authorised this, as well as the "clark['s] sallery". Wise was presumably the Rev. Joseph Wise, who was curate at Ashingdon. In 1812-3 Rev. Jonathan Clementon was curate of South Fambridge, whilst J. Allen, G. Wyatt and George Wayland Potter were other parish officials.[180] The latter was churchwarden in 1817, 1819-21, and presumably in 1818 as well.[181] He was also overseer in 1817.[182] He was the son of James Potter, with whom he shared the churchwarden

---

178   ERO D/CR 139
179   ERO D/P 90/8 & Q/SBb 448
180   ERO D/P 90/8
181   ERO D/CR 139, Q/SBb 448 & D/P 90/8
182   ERO Q/SBb 448

and overseer roles.[183]

In 1806 the records show that Rev. Edward Fawcett was rector at South Fambridge. This conflicts with the information given above by Wright, that Fawcett was inducted there in 1809. William Lant or Sant was Fawcett's churchwarden in 1806. Fawcett's curate in 1814-8 was Rev. Isaac Smith. Smith remained as curate until 1822 when he was succeeded by Rev. W.C. Ray.[184] The latter appears to have been the incumbent at North Shoebury either at the same time or slightly afterwards, as he completed a nil return regarding non-conformist meeting houses for both parishes in 1829.[185]

Rev. James Grisdale Fawcett is named in the records as curate at South Fambridge from at least 1831 to 1839. Rev A. Anderson, almost certainly the Ashingdon curate, was "officiating minister" there on occasion during 1831-2.[186]

As well as being one of the parish officials, George Wayland Potter was a significant landowner in South Fambridge and evidently also a shrewd businessman. In his draft will of 1826 he left his leasehold farms at South Fambridge Hall and Parsonage Farm, plus "two other farms" at New Hall and Bolt Hall in Canewdon, and all other leasehold property, farming equipment and livestock, plus all the household goods at South Fambridge Hall, where he lived, to his wife, Amy. The income from this was to be used to pay his funeral expenses and to provide financial support to his father, James. Amy and their eldest son, James Swaine Potter, were appointed as trustees to manage George's affairs. He also left his copyhold ownership of the manor of Clement's Hall in Hawkwell to his son, plus £500 which came with the stipulation that James Swaine had to repay any debts he owed to his father out of this legacy. George also left £10 to his second son, Zachariah Lewis Potter, and £10 to his daughter, Louisa Pissey, wife of a Great Wakering farmer, Daniel Pissey, and he released Daniel from all debts that the latter owed him. He left £10 for his third son, also called George Wayland Potter, and stipulated that the latter was to repay his debts to him from it. He left £500 to his second daughter, Susannah Grimwood Potter, £500 to his fourth son, Jeffrey Grimwood Potter, and £500 to his third daughter and seventh child, Emma Potter. The last two of these were not yet 21 and were to inherit their legacies when they reached that age. There was also a sum of £500 left jointly to Amy and James Swaine to invest in government securities, the dividends from which were to be paid to Susannah and, after that, to any future children she might have once they attained the age of 21. George also charged Amy and James Swaine with the task of putting his two youngest children, Jeffrey and Emma, into apprenticeships, which presumably meant domestic

---

183   ERO D/DCf F180
184   ERO D/CR 139 & D/P 90/8
185   ERO Q/CR 3/1/240
186   ERO D/CR 139

service for Emma, as this was a common occupation for young women at the time. The consciously different treatments of the various children are very interesting, seemingly reflecting both their individual characters and their relationships with their father. As if all this was not enough, George left a further £10 to his "esteemed friend", William Smith of Hockley, for "a suit of mourning" and he also charged William with taking on the role of arbiter in any financial disputes between his wife and children.[187]

George's daughter Emma was presumably the same person as the owner of Rouncefall's in Ashingdon in 1867, as mentioned above by Benton. George Wayland Potter junior was present at a meeting of the South Fambridge parish vestry in 1814-5. Jeffrey Grimwood Potter and John Staines Potter, who was presumably a relative of the family, were churchwardens and overseers at South Fambridge c.1837-44. Zachariah Lewis Potter also attended vestry meetings.[188]

Major expenses for Ashingdon's parish officials at this period included an iron chest (1814), communion plates (1816), 2.25 yards of black cloth (1819) and various payments to local workmen.[189] Expenses incurred in South Fambridge at this period included a purchase of 300 tiles, presumably for the church roof (1812-3), and several yards of "Irish" (a type of cloth) with which to make a new surplice (1819).[190]

Local Activities

In 1805 in Ashingdon Lucy Keys (Keyes), daughter of Thomas, married a widower, William Bentall from Goldhanger. In 1813 James and Charlotte Keyes, and William and Susannah Keyes, were all farmers. James was also a churchwarden from then until at least 1827. By 1830 William Keyes had taken over the post. The burials of both Charles and Alfred Keyes took place in 1818. In 1813, Samuel and Martha Dennis were living at Beckney Farm, while in 1819 an unusual travelling visitor came to town in the form of William White, a "tramper-chimney sweep" of "no settled place of abode". William had his pregnant wife Ann with him and in August their newly born twins, Susannah and Sarah Ann, were baptised at St Andrew's.[191] In 1810-11 W. Vanderzee was paid some money from the rates "for Local Militia Orders".[192]

In 1805 in South Fambridge Sarah Davey married Samuel Clark of Goldhanger. There must be some connection with the Keyes-Bentall marriage described above, since it seems unlikely that two men from Goldhanger would marry local girls in the same year. In 1818

---

187 ERO D/DCf F180
188 ERO D/P 90/8
189 ERO D/P 89/5/1
190 ERO D/P 90/8
191 ERO D/CR 11
192 ERO D/P 89/8/2

Zachariah and Elizabeth Potter were farmers in South Fambridge, the former presumably being the second son of the aforementioned George Wayland Potter. In the following year Thomas Valentine was a blacksmith in South Fambridge, while Samuel Saunders was a publican, presumably at *The Ferry House*. There was a lot of call for the services of blacksmiths locally at this period because both parishes were agricultural and relied heavily on horses and ploughs and because South Fambridge had a lot of river trade and there was no doubt some work available in the maritime industry. A William Bullingbrook unfortunately died at the ferry in 1819.[193]

In 1837 Benjamin Saunders, son of Samuel, married Ann Cardern. Samuel is described in the marriage details as a "mariner", while Benjamin was living at the "Fambridge Ferry". This information seems to confirm that it was at *The Ferry House* where Samuel was a publican and it suggests that he had two jobs. Ann's father, Thomas, was also a mariner. In 1848-50 William Saunders, presumably a relative, was also a mariner in the parish.[194] In 1836 a Samuel Saunders who was a labourer was bound over at the Quarter Sessions to keep the peace in respect of Herbert Mew. It is possible this was the above publican, but again it could be another family member.[195] S. Saunders was an overseer in South Fambridge in 1838 and H. Mew held the same role in 1843, so the two men may have had some interesting conversations![196]

Another 1837 marriage took place between John Argent and Sarah Brand. It was stated in the register that John "does not know his father's name". Meanwhile, Reuben and Ann Dines were South Fambridge farmers in the same year.[197] Reuben Dines was variously a churchwarden, overseer and parish constable *c.*1837-48.[198]

In 1829 James Pilkington, "Pastor of the Particular or Calvinistic Baptist Church [in] Rayleigh", completed a return of Baptist congregations in the local area. His return included a "House at Greensward Lane, South Fambridge", which he reported as having a congregation of about 100 people.[199] This appears to conflict with the nil return for non-conformist meeting houses in South Fambridge, which was furnished by the parish's curate Rev. W.C. Ray in the same year (see above), but this is probably because the congregation was meeting in a private house. According to *VCH Essex II* the population of South Fambridge was only 91 in 1831, so unless Pilkington was making extravagant and/or inaccurate claims, the congregation must have included numerous worshippers from outside the parish.

---

193 ERO D/CR 139
194 ERO D/CR 11 & D/CR 139
195 ERO Q/SBb 523/61/2
196 ERO D/P 90/8
197 ERO D/CR 139
198 ERO D/P 90/8
199 ERO Q/CR 3/2/83

A Railway Scheme

In 1811 a proposal was put forward to construct a railway line from London to Wallasea Island, with a branch line to Mucking on the River Thames. The scheme, which was known as "The London & Essex Railway", included plans for a station at South Fambridge. With its two coastal termini and the final part of its main route hugging the south bank of the River Crouch, it was clearly aimed at increasing maritime trade. It never came to pass, however.[200]

Figure 32: The proposed route of the 1811 railway scheme at South Fambridge (faint horizontal line)

Property Ownership

As for property ownership, Thomas Keyes held Chamberlain's and Smith's in 1806, Benjamin Palmer held Ashingdon Hall and the Glebe land, and J. Bright held Rouncefall. Rev. Wise held Pulpits and some of the woodlands.[201] The ERO holds an 1808 indenture for a 99-year lease by Edward Stephenson Esq., Lord of the Manor of South Fambridge, to Rev. Wise "of Rochford" for "all that piece or parcel of land with the Cowhouse thereupon erected" and "the premises belonging to the vicarage of Kew and commonly called Pulpitts and adjoining the road commonly called Green Street Lane". A second indenture records that Rev. Wise died in 1815 and that his executor, George Davis Carr of Rochford, sold the remaining lease in the property by a public auction to Jeremiah Page of Hockley. Four months later, however, Page was convicted of "felony" at Chelmsford and

---

200   ERO Q/RUm 1/19
201   ERO D/P 89/8/2

his property was forfeited and seized by the Sheriff of Essex, Luke William Walford Esquire. Walford sold the remaining lease of the above to John Alabaster, a Rayleigh victualler, by another public auction. In 1827 what remained of the lease was sold by Alabaster to George Belcham of Rayleigh, who owned a lot of property in the local area.[202] Belcham also rented some cottages in Ashingdon in the 1830s.[203]

By 1810-11 James Keyes was at Chamberlain's and Thomas Keyes was at Moon's. In 1814 and 1834 William Keyes was at Moon's, while James held Chamberlain's and Smith's.[204] James was also renting 294 acres of land at Little Stambridge Hall Farm in the neighbouring parish of Little Stambridge at the time.[205] Thomas Keyes appears to have been sharing Moon's with William in 1814, as they both paid the rates on it. James Keyes was at Pulpits in that year, James Digby was at Beckney, J. Bright was at Rouncefall and Mr. [probably Benjamin] Palmer was at Ashingdon Hall. Richard Bowton and Thomas Freeman both owned shops in the village.[206]

In the days when the electoral franchise was limited, property ownership was an essential pre-requisite for someone to have voting rights. There was also no secret ballot. The ERO holds a document showing who was eligible to vote in the 1832 General Election for the Southern Division of Essex and which way they individually voted. In Ashingdon, there were only two eligible voters: William Keyes of Moon's and William Mew, who farmed Beckney but lived at Apton Hall in neighbouring Canewdon. In South Fambridge there were four: Rev. Edward Fawcett (whose abode is listed as Cockermouth in the Lake District), Herbert Mew (who farmed Brick House Farm and was probably a relative of William), George Wayland Potter (South Fambridge Hall) and Jeffrey Grimwood Potter (Parsonage Farm). Two MPs were elected to represent the Division: Robert Westley Hall-Dare (Tory) and Sir Thomas Barrett-Lennard (Liberal).[207] Following the Representation of the People Act 1832, also known as the Reform Act, the franchise was extended to more male voters, though not yet to female ones. However, in 1836 and 1838 the eligible property-owning voters in Ashingdon parish still amounted to just four individuals: Charles Bright (of Rouncefall), John Dowler (Ashingdon Hall), William Keyes (Moon's) and William Mew (Beckney, but still living at Apton Hall in Canewdon).[208]

In 1834 James Keyes also held some of the Kew lands. James and William also jointly held Ashingdon Hall. C. Richardson held the Glebe in that year and the Mew family was

---

202   ERO D/DJe F3
203   ERO D/P 89/12/1
204   ERO D/P 89/8/2
205   ERO D/DS 254/35
206   ERO D/P 89/5/1
207   ERO TS 299/1
208   ERO Q/RPc 11

still at Beckney.[209] William Mew was one of the parish officials *c.*1837-40 and sometimes chaired the parish vestry meetings.[210]

By 1834 Pulpits had passed to "Z. L. Potter", presumably the Zachariah Lewis Potter of South Fambridge mentioned above. Charles Bright held Rouncefall, which was then called "Hill Farm". Mr. J. Dowler held somewhere called "Moon's Hill Farm"; it is unclear which property this description refers to, but it seems likely to have been a part of Moon's Farm which was adjacent to Ashingdon Hall, as part of Moon's and Ashingdon Hall are often referred to together in parish documentation.[211] Bright was an overseer in 1838, while Dowler was a churchwarden and overseer by 1842. In the early 1840s Bright moved to Little Wheatleys Farm in Rayleigh and was succeeded as owner of Rouncefall by Emma Potter from South Fambridge. By 1845, Pulpits was in the occupation of Reuben Dines. Beckney was tenanted in the late 1840s by William Rhodes.[212] Rhodes became a parish overseer in South Fambridge in 1852.[213]

Rev. James Grisdale Fawcett of South Fambridge was chairman of Ashingdon parish vestry in 1834, presumably in Rev. John Nottidge's absence, demonstrating that there was close co-operation between the two parishes regarding the running of their affairs.[214]

In 1836 a return of local property owners was completed by Ashingdon parish. James Keyes was the occupier of charity land at Smith's and Chamberlain's, which was owned by charity trustees. William Keyes still owned and occupied Moon's. William Mew owned and occupied Beckney. Rouncefall was occupied by Charles Bright but owned by a Reverend Clarke. John Dowler owned and occupied Ashingdon Hall and some of Moon's farmland. Ashingdon's Glebe land was let to William Keyes by Rev. John Nottidge. The Vicar of Kew owned Pulpits, which was occupied by Reuben Dines. Richard Bowton still occupied his blacksmith's shop, though it was owned by William Keyes. Keyes also owned a "wheeler's shop", presumably a wheelwright's, which was occupied by Samuel "Savall" (Saville), and a house occupied by Mary Keyes. James Crick owned some land which was occupied by Peter Parker.[215] There is an entry in a surviving 1836 receipts and payments book for Ashingdon which refers to "Savall's Bill of Coffins", which suggest that Samuel Savall made coffins as well as wheels.[216] The Vicar of Kew also owned Great Brays Farm in Rochford, which is mentioned in a property return for Ashingdon in that year, as is

---

209   ERO D/P 89/8/2
210   ERO D/P 89/8/3 & D/P 90/8
211   ERO D/P 89/8/2
212   ERO D/P 89/11/1, D/P 90/8 & D/DJe T52
213   ERO D/P 90/8
214   ERO D/P 89/8/2
215   ERO D/P 89/11/1
216   ERO D/P 89/12/1

neighbouring Golden Cross Farm, which was owned by W. Cockerton, but occupied by Thomas Coolbear.[217] Although the farmhouses for these farms were not in Ashingdon parish, some of their farmland was.[218] When Great Brays Farm was put up for sale in 1870 it included a 13-acre arable plot in the parish called "Ashingdon Field".[219]

In 1838 and 1839 several additional properties were listed on Ashingdon parish's property return. These were various houses and cottages owned by William Keyes, James Keyes, William Mew and John Dowler, which were all let to tenants. It seems likely that these landowners erected these additional properties on their various landholdings. One of William Keyes tenants was the aforementioned James Booty, who the following year absconded from the parish, leaving his wife and children chargeable to the parish's ratepayers.[220]

The ownership picture in 1846 was much as it had been 10 years earlier, with John Dowler at Ashingdon Hall, William Keyes at Moon's and William Mew at Beckney, though the latter was living in Canewdon at the time. Reuben Dines was still at Pulpits and Rev. Edward Fawcett was still named as the owner of South Fambridge rectory, although he was still living in Cockermouth. Jeffrey Grimwood Potter was at Parsonage Farm. South Fambridge Hall, however, was by now in the ownership of William Walter Stephenson, whose place of residence was listed as "Florence in Tuscany".[221]

In 1848 James Keyes and William Keyes were still living at Smith's & Chamberlain's and Moon's respectively, while William Keyes junior was leasing the Glebe from Rev. Septimus Nottidge.[222] William Keyes junior served as one of the overseers in Ashingdon c.1851-79.[223] He also served as churchwarden in 1868 and waywarden (highways supervisor) c.1868-73.[224] He dropped the "junior" from his signature in the parish accounts books in 1854.[225]

Mr. C.D. Knapping occupied Ashingdon Hall in 1848 and part of Moon's, though it was in the ownership of Alfred White.[226] An Alfred White was a parish overseer and surveyor in Ashingdon c.1887-94 and a churchwarden in 1889.[227] Emma Potter owned and occupied Rouncefall. Reuben Dines still lived at Pulpits. John Whittingham occupied a house and two shops which belonged to William Keyes. William Rhodes leased Beckney from

---

217 ERO D/P 89/11/1
218 See, for example, ERO S2926 & T/B 356/1 for the landholdings of Golden Cross Farm
219 ERO D/DSa 1334/3
220 ERO D/P 89/11/1 & D/P 89/8/3
221 ERO LIB/POL 1/22
222 ERO D/P 89/11/2
223 ERO D/P 89/12/2 & D/P 89/8/4
224 ERO D/P 89/8/4
225 ERO D/P 89/12/2
226 ERO D/P 89/11/2
227 ERO D/P 89/8/4 & A13442 Box 5

John Mew, but by 1850 Beckney was owned and occupied by Henry Mew, who also owned Beckney Wood. In that year, Rouncefall was occupied by Jonathan Potter, though still owned by Emma. In 1851 Smith's and Chamberlain's was still occupied by Henry James Keyes, while Moon's was owned and occupied by "William Keyes and son". In 1852 Rouncefall was occupied by John S. Potter and Moon's was occupied by William Keyes junior. The ownership sequence for this property suggests that William Keyes senior had died by 1852 and that there was a period immediately before that where its ownership was slowly but surely being transferred to his son.[228]

As mentioned under Smith's above, Henry James Keyes, James Keyes' son, leased Smith's and Chamberlain's Farms from Woollaston's Charity Trustees for 14 years 1849-63. He was living at Little Stambridge Hall in Little Stambridge parish when the lease was taken out. Both landholdings included reclaimed marshland, which would have been particularly fertile. Keyes also leased 15+ acres of Rochford parish's charity land in Hockley 1869-83, by which time he was living in Ashingdon, probably at Smith's and Chamberlain's.[229]

There are many references in surviving Ashingdon and South Fambridge documentary evidence to properties which border the two parishes. Sometimes their owners and/or occupiers were members of the parishes' parish vestries. Property owners in Ashingdon are regularly mentioned in South Fambridge parish documents and vice versa. This all suggests that the parish boundaries were not regarded as a barrier to business, property ownership and local government.

The Union Workhouse

At the other end of the scale from the property owners were the poorest members of the parish. Up to 1835, these were the responsibility of individual parishes and payments were often made to them by the parish vestry, as outlined above.

In that year, however, a significant change was made to local poor relief arrangements, as a result of the Poor Law Amendment Act 1834, known subsequently as the New Poor Law. This transformed the original Elizabethan Poor Laws by introducing the concept of Union Workhouses, whose working conditions and physical demands on inmates were designed to discourage malingerers from claiming poor relief when they were able to work, with a view to cutting the cost of poor relief payments.

In south-east Essex, a new Rochford Hundred-wide Poor Law Union was established and a Union Workhouse was built in Rochford. Twenty-three parishes were grouped into this Union. Anyone in Ashingdon and South Fambridge who claimed to be unable to work was put into the Rochford Union Workhouse and was set to work on menial, often back-breaking tasks, such as picking oakum, which involved the unwinding of tarred strands of

---

228   ERO D/P 89/11/2
229   ERO D/Je E18

old ships' rope, which took a significant toll on the hands of the pickers.

The new Union Workhouse and the associated Poor Law arrangements were managed by a Board of Guardians. Two Guardians were elected from each of Rochford, Rayleigh and Leigh parishes, and one from each of the remaining 20 parishes. Anyone wishing to be elected as a Guardian had to have a £20 or more land or property rental qualification. Property owners and ratepayers were the only ones who could nominate or vote for Guardians (including having the ability to nominate themselves). The Board had the power to levy the poor rate. Churchwardens and overseers in the individual parishes continued to manage its collection.

Guardians were required to consider applications for poor relief, determine the kind of work to be given to paupers and examine the accounts and processes of the Union Workhouse. They could also agree loans to paupers if they felt they could be repaid and they could fund essential foodstuffs such as bread, flour and meat for workhouse inmates. The Guardians were supported by a clerk, who managed the meetings and correspondence, a treasurer, who managed the accounts, and relieving officers, who carried out an initial examination of the merits of individual applications for poor relief. The Guardians were also required to notify the local Medical Officer if any paupers fell ill, including those living in the workhouse. Relief when it was paid could be in cash or in kind (clothes, food, etc.). No-one in employment was entitled to poor relief and no-one aged 16-60 from outside the Union was eligible either.

The first meeting of the Rochford Union Board of Guardians was scheduled for 10am on 12 October 1835 at the *King's Head Inn* in Rochford.[230] The Bishop's Transcripts for South Fambridge in 1854 record the burial there of Charles Smith, whose address is given as the Union Workhouse.[231] Those for Ashingdon record the burial by Rev. Septimus Nottidge in 1867 of Thomas Brown of the Union Workhouse.[232]

---

[230] Information in this section is taken largely from ERO TS 87/1
[231] ERO D/CR 139
[232] ERO D/CR 11

THE TITHE AWARDS

The Tithe Commutation Act 1836

Historically, payments in kind were made by parishioners to local churches in the form of tithes – a tenth part of their agricultural produce and/or livestock. There are records of tithes being paid in Ashingdon in commodities such as geese and pigs.

In 1836, however, the Tithe Commutation Act replaced this system with monetary payments. As a result, every parish was assessed for the rental value of individual properties within it. A Tithe Award, listing land ownership and rental data, and an accompanying Tithe Map, showing every individual building and field, were produced for each parish. These were accurately surveyed and recorded, and they consequently provide invaluable information about the parishes at this period.

Ashingdon

The Tithe Map for Ashingdon is dated 1838 and the Tithe Award is dated 17 March 1840. These jointly show that Beckney Farm and Wood were owned and occupied at the time by William Mew.

By this stage Chamberlain's and Smith's Farms had been merged into one large landholding, the farmhouse for Chamberlain's had been demolished and Smith's farmhouse had been renamed as "Great Chamberlain's Farm" to reflect the larger landholding. This and Tinkers Field were owned by Woollaston's Charity but occupied by James Keyes. The blacksmith's shop from the 1808 map in Greensward Lane was owned by William Keyes but occupied by blacksmith Richard Bowton. The Tithe Map shows that Great Chamberlain's Farm was accessed via what is now Harrogate Drive, with the farmhouse standing to the west of the top-end of that, approximately where the eastern arm of Malvern Road is now.

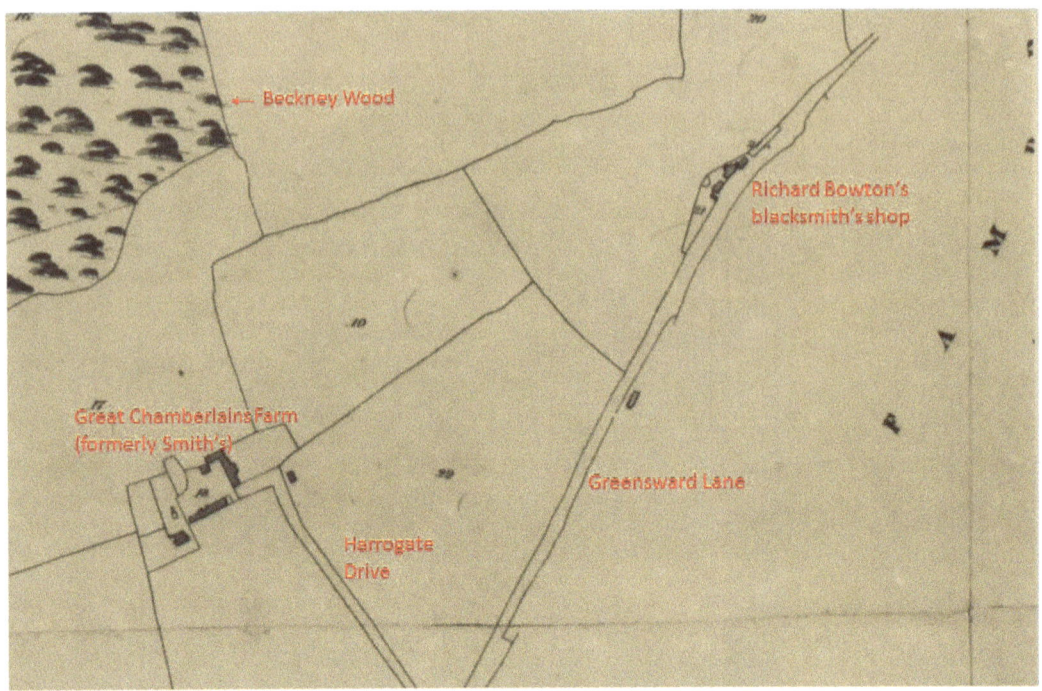

Figure 33: A section of the Ashingdon Tithe Map of 1838, annotated to show Great Chamberlain's Farm and Richard Bowton's blacksmith's shop

Ashingdon Glebe was unsurprisingly owned by Rev. John Nottidge, but "occupied" by William Keyes, presumably as pasture. A single cottage on the eastern side of Ashingdon Road, just north of Church Road, was owned by Woollaston's Charity but occupied by Joyce and Stephen Brown. South of this was an orchard, owned by the charity but tenanted by James Keyes.

Across the road, Rouncefall – named on the Tithe Award and Map as "Hill Farm" – was owned by Rev. Thomas Clark but occupied by Charles Bright. Clark may have been one of Nottidge's curates, but it seems more likely that he was from outside the parish, as a curate would not normally possess enough wealth at this period to purchase a farm of this size. Odd fields around here and elsewhere in the parish were listed as "New Parish Land (Trustees)", suggesting perhaps that the parish vestry had acquired land for some unspecified purpose. Several of Rouncefall's fields were owned by John Crick but occupied by Peter Porter or Pinter (both names are given, but it seems likely that they are the same individual). Five other fields at the western end of Rouncefall's land, where the landholdings had historically been broken up into smaller fields and where there were obvious overlaps in land ownership with South Fambridge parish, especially adjacent to Pulpits, were owned by Rev. Richard Burgh Byam but occupied by Reuben Dines. Byam may have been the successor to Rev. Joseph Wise as minister at South Fambridge. Other lands on the eastern side of Ashingdon Road, at its junction with Brays Lane, are also labelled as being part of "Hill Farm" and are shown as being owned by William Cockerton but occupied by Thomas Coolbear.

Moon's Farm and Moon's Cottage were owned and occupied by William Keyes. Obviously, he could not physically live in two places simultaneously, so it is presumed that the cottage was occupied by a family member. Moon's Barn was still there, on the eastern side of Ashingdon Road, roughly in the vicinity of where Moon's Close is now.

St Andrew's church and the rectory were unsurprisingly "owned" by Rev. John Nottidge, but they were "occupied" by (Rev.?) Marshall Hatley, who was presumably Nottidge's curate. The rectory – the one built by Rev. Gabriel Price – is shown to the north of the church. Additional Glebe land – where the current rectory, the Church Hall, the house called "The Lodge", the top section of Church Road and the houses at 40 and 42 Highcliff Crescent would later be built – was also owned by Nottidge, but "occupied", again presumably as pasture, by William Keyes. Ashingdon Hall and its accompanying farmland were owned and occupied by John Dowler.

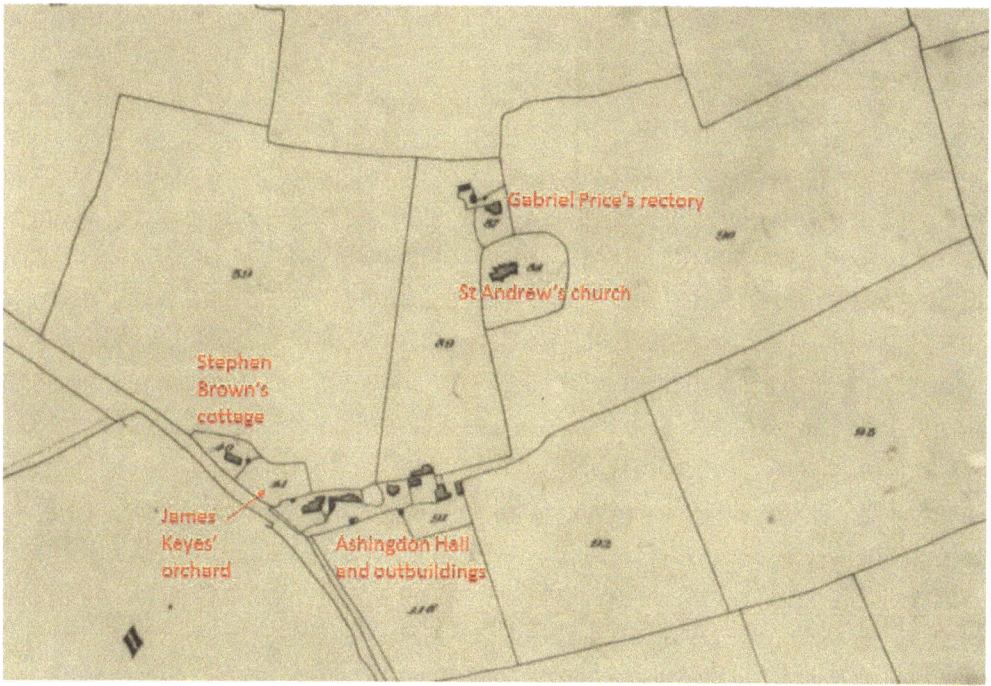

Figure 34: Ashingdon Hall and St Andrew's church, as shown on the 1838 Tithe Map. Note that Church Road does not really exist beyond the Hall's outbuildings. The field to the left of St Andrew's is glebe land where the current rectory and Church Hall would later be built

Figure 35: The entrance to Church Road in the early 20th century, showing Ashingdon Hall on the left and its associated farm buildings in the background

The most noteworthy addition since the earlier maps is the presence just north of Moon's Barn in Ashingdon Road of a "School House & Garden", which was owned by John Dowler but occupied by James Turner. Curiously, no building is shown on the relevant plot, so perhaps it was earmarked for this usage, but no premises had yet been erected. James Turner was presumably a schoolteacher. See below for further information about education in Victorian Ashingdon.

One field of Great Brays Farm is shown in Ashingdon, on the north side of Brays Lane (the aforementioned "Ashingdon Field"). This was owned by William Barker and Abel Rous Dottin, but occupied by Thomas Merryfield. The last of these was a Rochford maltster who had been leasing the land since at least 1828.[233]

Ashingdon parish vestry made a tithe payment of £250 to the rector in 1840.[234]

---

233   ERO D/DJe E5
234   ERO D/P 89/8/3

South Fambridge

The Tithe Map for South Fambridge is dated 7 June 1839 and the Tithe Award is dated 1837. By far the largest landholding at the time was that of South Fambridge Hall, named on the Award as "The Hall Farm". The main bulk of the farmland for this lay to the north and east of the Hall, running from the river in the north to All Saints church in the south. The Hall and its lands were in the ownership of William Walter Stephenson but occupied by Amy Potter, presumably the widow of George Wayland Potter.

The Ferry House and the surrounding "Fambridge Ferry Farm" were owned and occupied by Jeremiah Kersteman whose family were from Canewdon. A Thomas Kersteman was an overseer in Ashingdon in the 1750s and 1760s.[235] Brickhouse Farm was owned by William Willan, but occupied by Herbert Mew.

All Saints church and South Fambridge parsonage were both "owned" by Rev. Edward Fawcett, but "occupied" by Jeffrey Grimwood Potter.

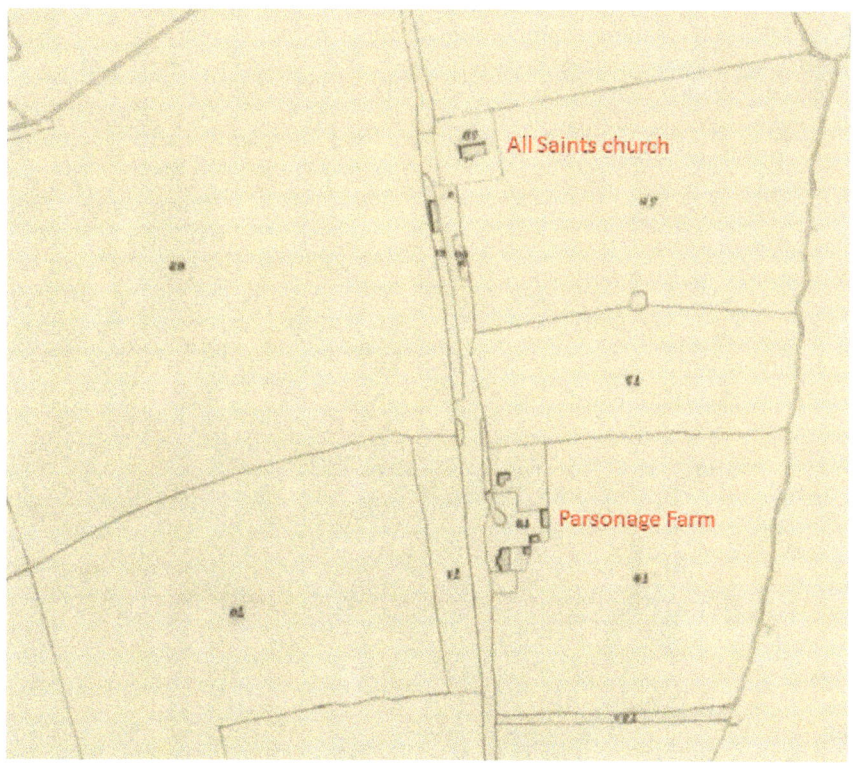

Figure 36: An extract from the Tithe Map for South Fambridge, deliberately reproduced upside-down because for some reason the original ignores convention by having north rather than south at the bottom of the page. Note the cottages on the road to the immediate south of the church

---

235   ERO D/P 89/8/1

Some land in the south of the parish belonged to Great Chamberlain's Farm. Like the land for that in Ashingdon parish, it was owned by Woollaston's Charity but occupied by James Keyes. Lower Road is named on the Award as "Beckney Lane"; it still had that name in the 1860s.

The other major farm in the parish, Pulpits, was owned, like the Pulpits' fields in Ashingdon, by Rev. Richard Burgh Byam, but occupied by Reuben Dines (wrongly shown as "Daines" on the South Fambridge Tithe Award). George Belcham's land is also shown, adjacent to Pulpits. There are also three cottages to the north of Pulpits, on the eastern side of what is now Greensward Lane, roughly opposite what is now Crouch View Crescent. A parcel of land between the cottages was owned by Richard Bowton, who had the blacksmith's shop opposite.

THE VICTORIAN ERA

Village Life

The increase in record-keeping and the advent of postal directories during the Victorian period both help shed a brighter light on daily life in the two parishes from this period onwards. According to William White's *History, Gazetteer & Directory of Essex* of 1848 (a kind of early *Yellow Pages*) James Keyes of Little Stambridge, Christopher Dale Knapping of South Shoebury, William Keyes of Moon's and Miss Emma Potter were all farmers in Ashingdon that year. John Whittingham was a blacksmith and beer seller. Rev. John Nottidge was still the patron of St Andrew's church and his son, Rev. Septimus Nottidge, was still the incumbent. The latter lived for a while at Little Brays Farm in neighbouring Rochford parish, perhaps because the rectory (which he replaced in 1855) was not to his liking.[236]

The principal farmers in South Fambridge were Reuben Dines at Pulpits, James Keyes (as above), John Mew of Canewdon and John Potter of South Fambridge Hall. The latter was presumably a member of the Potter family who had served as churchwardens and overseers in the parish and was related to Emma. A Mrs. Lawrence was a victualler at *The Ferry Inn*. Mr. E. Stephenson was Lord of the Manor and patron of the living of All Saints church. Nottidge was curate at South Fambridge at times during the period 1849-68.[237] He also served as curate at South Fambridge in 1847. H.J. (presumably Henry James) Keyes was tenant of South Fambridge Glebe in the same year and served as one of the churchwardens and overseers *c.*1848-68.[238] Nathaniel Meeres was "officiating minister" at Ashingdon in December 1849, when he performed the burial service for Richenda Lee, "the child of a gipsy".[239]

The main parish vestry posts in Ashingdon at this period continued to be occupied by the principal land and property owners, who had to face all kinds of daily challenges. In 1842, for example, due to the "depreciation of the value of land", the parishioners in Ashingdon banded together to ask for a rate reduction. Their request was accepted and their rents were reduced by 10%.[240]

In some cases, responsibilities passed down the family, for example when William Keyes was succeeded by his son, William Keyes junior, in some of the parish vestry posts. William junior and Henry James Keyes, who lived initially at Little Stambridge Hall and then at

---

236   ERO Q/RPc 11
237   ERO D/CR 139
238   ERO D/P 90/8 & D/P 89/12/2
239   ERO D/CR 11
240   ERO D/P 89/8/3

Smith's and Chamberlain's, were Ashingdon's two overseers in 1852-9. Alfred White of Ashingdon Hall appeared on the voters' roll in 1850; he lived in Middlesex at the time. George Raven, who also owned land at the Hall, was added to the voters' roll in 1859.[241] John Whittingham was the parish constable for Ashingdon in 1857.[242] William Rhodes was still tenant at Beckney in 1859.[243] The voters' rolls are a useful source of information for local history and have been used extensively to inform the following sections of this book.

The eligible voters in 1848-9 in Ashingdon were William Keyes of Moon's and the Rev. Septimus Nottidge, who lived at Little Brays. Meanwhile, in South Fambridge, the eligible voters were Reuben Dines (who lived at Pulpits), Rev. Edward Fawcett (who lived in Cockermouth), Henry James Keyes (who lived in Little Stambridge but leased Parsonage Farm), William Walter Stephenson (who lived in Tuscany but owned South Fambridge Hall) and William Willan (who lived in London but owned Brick House Farm and leased it to John Mew).[244] The number of South Fambridge voters being greater than those of Ashingdon suggests that the former was probably still regarded as the more important of the two places at this period.

In 1858 the Ashingdon parish vestry agreed to fund repairs to the west end of the church and obtained an estimate from Mr. Carter for the purpose.[245] Additional payments were made to Mr. Carter for repairs to the church in 1867.[246] He was clearly a regular go-to tradesman for Ashingdon's parish officials, as he often crops up in the accounts books, such as in 1850 and 1858 when he carried out repairs to parish-owned cottages.[247] This was presumably the same Mr. Carter who had been awarded the contract for the construction of the new South Fambridge parish church in 1846.

More Railway Schemes

In 1844 a plan was put forward to construct a railway line between Maldon and Southend. This was planned to cross the Crouch at South Fambridge, passing just east of South Fambridge Hall and Ashingdon church.[248] Nothing came of it, however.

---

241 ERO Q/RPc 11
242 ERO D/P 89/8/3
243 ERO Q/RPc 11
244 ERO LIB/POL 1/24
245 ERO D/P 89/8/3
246 ERO D/P 89/5/1
247 ERO D/P 89/12/2
248 ERO A12774 Box 1 Bundle 2

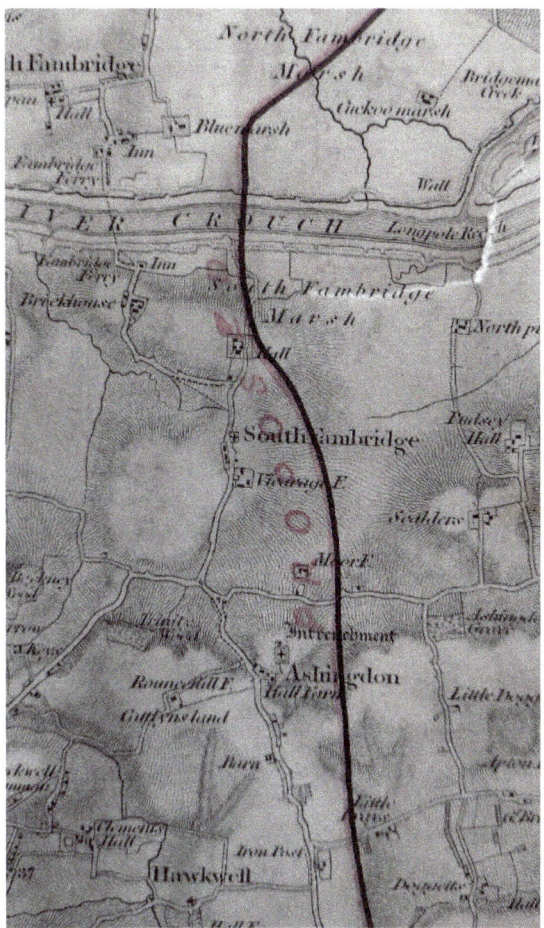

Figure 37: The proposed route of the 1844 railway scheme from Maldon to Southend

Two years later another railway scheme was proposed for the area: the "London & Blackwall Extension Railway to the River Crouch". The main line for this was planned to go from London to Wallasea Island, with branches to Tilbury and Southend; it was to run west-to-east across Fambridge Road, cutting through the old Parsonage Farm (shown as "Vicarage Farm" on the accompanying map). The branch to Southend was due to start near the western end of what is now Lower Road, about mid-way between Beckney Farm and Beckney Wood, and to curve southwards to the east of Trinity Wood and Rouncefall, keeping to the west of Ashingdon Road.[249] The gradient of Ashingdon Hill here would have been a real challenge and once again the plan did not come to fruition.

---

249   ERO Q/RUm 2/53

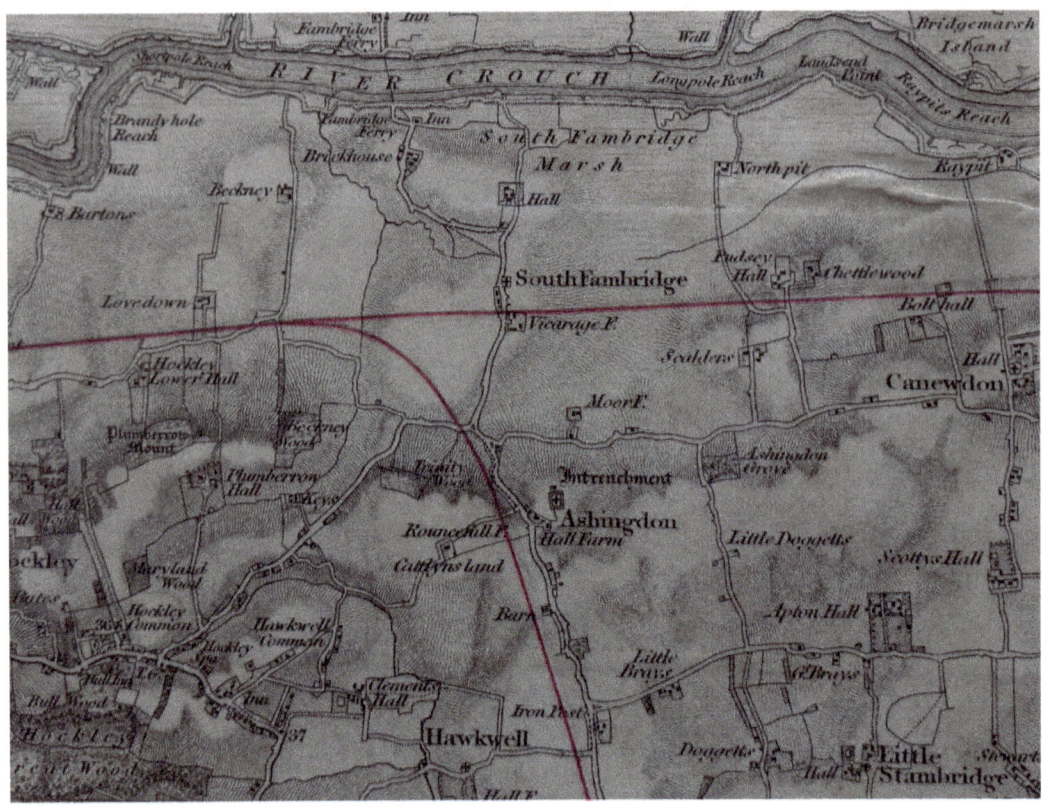

Figure 38: The proposed route of the 1846 railway scheme from London

The above map reveals some local building changes over previous ones. It shows, for example, that in South Fambridge there are two buildings on Fambridge Road opposite Brick House Farm and another on that road at the junction of the lane to South Fambridge Hall. There also looks to be at least one more building on the road between All Saints church and Vicarage (Parsonage) Farm. In Ashingdon, Moon's Cottages have arrived, whilst Moon's Farm is wrongly shown as "Moor F.". Great Chamberlain's Farm (formerly Smith's) is shown as "Keys", presumably due to its connections with the Keyes family. There are more/different buildings in Greensward Lane. The "Intrenchment" at Ashingdon church is probably the churchyard boundary (pre-20th-century extension), which some have suggested follows the line of the embanked walls of King Edmund Ironside's supposed camp there before the Battle of Assandun in 1016.

Potash

The *VCH Essex II* (1907) has an article in it by Henry Laver entitled "The Making of Potash". Laver writes the following: "Until about sixty or seventy years ago [so, early 1840s], the MAKING OF POTASH from the ashes of burnt wood, weeds, and other vegetable matter was a common rural industry, and was carried on (as it had been, doubtless, for centuries) in most parishes in the county. The 'potash' (potassium carbonate) was used in washing clothes, soap-making, dyeing, linen-bleaching, glass-making, and in many other ways – in fact, for nearly all purposes for which soda (sodium carbonate) is now commonly used." Laver adds that "Personally, I can recollect only two Essex 'potashes'", one of which "(worked by Barnabas Townsend) [was] on the east side of the road from Fambridge Ferry to Rochford, close to the spot (known as 'Potash Corner') at which the road from Ballard's Gore joins it…". This would presumably be the Ashingdon Road/Brays Lane junction.

Flooding

One of the constant challenges facing local farmers at this period seems to have been the adequate maintenance of the seawalls. The ERO holds some correspondence between Henry Mew of Rochford and a Mr. H. Crawter of Bedford Row in Middlesex (his agent) about repairs to gutters and seawalls which were carried out by a Mr. D. Gardner of Burnham at Brick House and Beckney Farms over the winter of 1855-6.[250] Other documents held there include writs, affidavits, legal briefs and correspondence relating to a lawsuit in the Exchequer of Pleas in 1873 between, on the one hand, Henry Wolton of Colchester and a widow, Ann Winmill of Shopland, who were lessees of Beckney Farm (which was owned by Henry Mew), and, on the other, George James Potter of Bolt Hall, Canewdon, who was lessee of Brick House Farm, and Frank Willan of Whitchurch in Oxfordshire, who by that time was its owner. Wolton and Winmill claimed compensation against damage caused to Beckney Farm by flooding in 1872 due to a breach in the seawall at Brick House Farm while it was in the process of being repaired by Thomas Whitwell of Canewdon. This appears to have been caused by Whitwell's employers not providing him with sufficient pipework.[251] Wolton and Winmill were awarded substantial damages.[252] Damages were also awarded to a Rochford bank manager, Edward Trotter Jackson, who was the lessee of two fields of glebe land from the then South Fambridge rector, Rev. Percival Alfred Fothergill. These fields were repeatedly flooded by every tide from the end of October 1872 until March 1873, when the seawall at Brick House Farm was finally repaired. Jackson had invested a considerable sum into preparing the fields for wheat, but they were instead severely damaged by seawater and taken over by "luxuriant" crab grass which was costly and time consuming to remove.[253] Edward Trotter Jackson held posts on both Ashingdon and South Fambridge parish vestries c.1877-89. A G.J. Potter was one of South Fambridge's parish officials c.1861-75.[254]

---

250   ERO D/DJe L3
251   ERO D/DJe L4 & L5
252   ERO D/DJe L5 & L6
253   ERO D/DJe L7 & L8
254   ERO D/P 89/8/4 & D/P 90/8 for Ashingdon and South Fambridge respectively

Mid-Century

As the century wore on, the main properties continued to be in the ownership and occupation of the same few families. Smith's & Chamberlain's, though still owned by Woollaston's Charity, continued to be occupied by Henry James Keyes from at least 1854 to 1868.[255] Keyes was an overseer and churchwarden c.1868-70.[256] Meanwhile, William Keyes junior still owned and occupied Moon's during this period and Henry Mew owned Beckney Farm and Beckney Wood. The former was leased to William Rhodes until 1859, when William Keyes junior took over the tenancy. Keyes was succeeded as tenant in 1868 by Ann Wolton. Alfred White owned Ashingdon Hall and part of Moon's, leasing it initially to Dale Knapping, who had made his fortune from brick manufacture in Southend, and then briefly to George Raven (1858-9), before passing on the tenancy to Benjamin Moss from at least late 1861.[257] Moss was a parish overseer c.1862-87, churchwarden c.1872-87, waywarden in 1875-81, surveyor c.1882-6 and assessor c.1884-6.[258] He continued to own Ashingdon Hall until at least 1894.[259]

Rouncefall was still owned by Emma Potter, but leased to John S. Potter, who evidently died late in 1861, for the tenancy was in the hands of his executors then. Louisa Crick had taken on the tenancy by 1865. Pulpits was still owned by the Vicar of Kew and occupied by Reuben Dines in 1854, but from 1855 onwards it was tenanted by William Keyes junior, who was evidently building up a significant local farming enterprise. He also owned two shops in Ashingdon, one of which, a blacksmith's, was tenanted from 1854 to c.1862 by John Whittingham, and the other, its use unspecified, by William Whittingham, who was presumably a relative and was its tenant for a similar period. Edward Brown took over the tenancy of the blacksmith's shop in 1863, while James Hart took over the tenancy of the other shop in late 1862.[260] Hart still had a shop in the parish in 1880.[261] Brown served as a parish overseer in Ashingdon for much of the period c.1871-91 and also as an assessor c.1881-7.[262]

Golden Cross Farm in Rochford, whose lands extended into Ashingdon and Hawkwell parishes, was owned by William Cockerton in 1854 and leased to James S. Cockerton, presumably a relative, possibly William's son.[263] However, in 1858 it was put up for sale

---

255 ERO D/P 89/11/3
256 ERO D/P 89/8/4
257 ERO D/P 89/11/3
258 ERO D/P 89/8/3, D/P 89/8/4, D/P 89/12/2, G/Ro N90 & Q/RPc 11
259 ERO C/E 1/7/4-6
260 ERO D/P 89/11/3
261 ERO G/Ro N63
262 ERO D/P 89/8/4 & A13442 Box 5
263 ERO D/P 89/11/3

by auction by the trustees of William Cockerton, who had evidently died by this point. James S. Cockerton held a 14-year lease which had commenced in September 1850. The "compact freehold estate" included a bailiff's cottage, stable, barn, hen house, implement shed, garden and orchard.[264] It was owned from at least 1861 onwards by W.H. Rankin, a member of a notable Rochford farming family who presumably bought it at the auction, with James S. Cockerton still its tenant. Neighbouring Great Brays Farm was tenanted by W.T. Meason (Meeson) from at least 1854 to 1894.[265] Ashingdon's part of the latter became incorporated into the Great Doggetts farm estate in Rochford by 1881.[266]

The leading inhabitants of Ashingdon according to William White's 1863 *Directory* were: Benjamin Moss at Ashingdon Hall; Henry James Keyes at Chamberlain's; William Keyes at Moon's Farm; Miss Emma Potter at Hill Farm (Rouncefall). Rev. Septimus Nottidge was the rector, George Brown was the parish clerk, John Whittington was a blacksmith, John Mead was a farm bailiff and Sarah Turner was a schoolmistress. Benjamin Moss and his wife, Annie, were farmers in Ashingdon from at least 1862. They lived at Ashingdon Hall from c.1864-77.[267] Eva Moss of Ashingdon Hall died in 1877 aged just two years and 16 days. Meanwhile, a John and Ann Lindsell lived at Hill Farm (Rouncefall) c.1865-70, presumably having taken over there from Emma Potter.[268] The leading inhabitants of South Fambridge were: William Potter and Miss Emma Potter, farmers at New Hall; George James Potter, farmer at Brick House Farm; William Rhodes, farmer; James Andrews, a coal merchant and victualler at *The Ferry Inn*; Isaac Cox, a marine store dealer; and John Chittocks, the parish clerk. The larger number of prominent inhabitants at Ashingdon compared with South Fambridge suggests that, for the first time, the former was becoming the more dominant settlement of the two, though the existence of a marine store dealer shows that the river still played an important role in South Fambridge parish life. Rev. Septimus Nottidge of Ashingdon was in the role of curate at South Fambridge in the absence of Rev. Edward Fawcett. Later, in 1866, Rev. John Pick was curate at South Fambridge, while Rev. William Henry Wardell occupied the role in 1867-8. Rev. Nottidge, was back in the role in 1868-70.[269]

In 1865 "Fambridge Ferry Farm" was leased by John Waylett Stallibrass of Eastwood to James Andrews of South Fambridge. The lease included the rights to operate the ferry, some pasture, the seawall and a wharf, as well as the village's public house (the Ferry House/*The Ferry Inn*), which had by this time been renamed *The Anchor*. Andrews was

---

264   ERO T/B 356/1 & S2926
265   ERO D/P 89/11/3, D/DSa 1334/3, Q/RPr 2/22, G/Ro N63 & C/E 1/7/1-6
266   ERO SALE/B4068
267   ERO D/CR 11
268   ERO D/CR 11
269   ERO D/CR 139

resident at *The Anchor* at the time, showing in conjunction with the above 1863 list that there was a continuation of occupation of the establishment by him but a change of name for it which has to have happened c.1863-5.[270]

Notable Ashingdon parish expenses at this period included a "pair of steel handcuffs for the constable" (1857), "Jackson's bill [for] planning [the] boundaries of [the] Parish properly" (1861) and "fire insurance on [a] house belonging to [the] parish" (1863).[271] Meanwhile, the Sacramental Alms books for Ashingdon and South Fambridge record some of the causes that money raised by the churches' congregations went to at this period. In Ashingdon, for example, George Brown was given 2s 6d in 1863 because he was "ill and could not work". Mrs. Newman was given 4s because she was "Dying of consumption and not allowed [a] nurse". Mrs. Twin was given 2s because she and her children were "suffering from daily attacks of ague" (fever). Other parishioners were given money in the 1860s to tide them over while they recovered from measles or fractured/broken bones, or for poor relief while incapacitated "from working during harvest" or being "out of the Union [Workhouse] for a short time". One woman was given 3s in 1868 because her "youngest child [was] seriously hurt by falling on the fire". Others were given cold weather payments, blankets and funding for medicines, maternity payments or trips to hospital in London.[272]

In 1867 the vaccination of children against smallpox was made mandatory across the country, but some local people were evidently slow to comply with the law. J.R. Smith, who wrote a book about the disease, found that four years later, on 5 December 1871, three children of Mr. W.A. Potter of South Fambridge had not been vaccinated and that the local authorities took steps to ensure that this was carried out. Eighteen months later, in July 1873, George Potter, a South Fambridge farmer and presumably a relative of the above, was summoned to court for neglecting to have his daughter, Ethel (born 4 August 1872), vaccinated.

South Fambridge New Town

In the mid-19th century South Fambridge was surprisingly identified as the potential location for a daring but short-lived scheme for the creation of a New Town. The ERO holds a newspaper article from 1866 in which it was reported that a London gentleman had purchased a large tract of land on the marshes with the intention of erecting an ironworks there. He placed a large order for bricks for 50 cottages for employees, but the whole scheme fell through.[273]

---

270 ERO D/DS 254/47
271 ERO D/P 89/12/2
272 ERO D/P 89/5/2
273 ERO T/P 181/5/11

Rectory Farm

As noted above, the old South Fambridge Parsonage was demolished in the late 1860s and replaced by a new one by the then incumbent, Rev. David Mede Salter. This was the Rectory, now Rectory Farm, which stands on the other side of the road. It was built in 1869 on part of the old South Fambridge glebe land.

Rectory Farm appears on Rochford District Council's Local List of important historic buildings, where it is described as follows: "Two storey red brick building; replacement plastic windows to the ground floor; vertical sliding sash windows to the first floor with prominent gable above and white bargeboard; grey slate gable roof with red ridge tiles; interesting gothic turret style roof to the frontage."

The justification for its inclusion on the list is that: "This building is of local architectural significance. It is a distinctive building which has an interesting roof style."

Figure 39: South Fambridge Rectory, now Rectory Farm

Property Ownership

The voters' roll for 1868-9 shows that Henry James Keyes still occupied Smith's & Chamberlain's at this time and was living at Smith's.[274] He also leased two fields of glebe land in South Fambridge from Rev. Salter.[275] William Keyes (junior) still owned and occu-

---

274 ERO Q/RPr 2/1
275 ERO D/DJe L7

pied Moon's.²⁷⁶ In 1870 he made a payment of £5,250 to James Burness in respect of Prittlewell Priory.²⁷⁷ The Priory was owned by Burness, a London merchant, with Keyes being the tenant farmer.²⁷⁸ This gives some idea of Keyes' wealth and social status locally.

Henry Mew owned Beckney but was living in Rochford. Ashingdon Hall was still owned by Alfred White, though he was still living in Middlesex and leasing it to Benjamin Moss. Rev. Septimus Nottidge was living at Ashingdon Rectory. Rev. Percy Wemyss Nott, who lived in, and was vicar of, Kew, qualified to vote through his ownership of Pulpits. The Kew connections with the area have been covered above, but again there is evidence in the surviving documentation of a bit of a blurring of the geographical boundaries at this period, as the voters' roll which mentions Nott was for Ashingdon parish, but the land at Pulpits that he occupied was in South Fambridge. Apart from the above property owners, there were also two "voters qualified in respect of the occupation of premises by The Representation of the People Act, 1867" in Ashingdon. This Act, sometimes called the Second Reform Act, built on the provisions of the 1832 Representation of the People Act (the first Reform Act) by enfranchising part of the urban male working class for the first time, doubling the number of people who were able to vote from one million to two million. The beneficiaries of this legislation in Ashingdon were Edward Brown, at the blacksmith's, and Jonathan Rose of Hawkwell, who occupied some of the other Kew-owned lands in the parish. Meanwhile, in South Fambridge, George James Potter owned and occupied Brick House Farm, while William Arthur Potter occupied South Fambridge Hall. He was leasing this from William Walter Stephenson, who was described as "travelling abroad". Ferry Farm was owned by Stephen Allen, who lived in Wiltshire, and occupied by James Andrews, who also held the licence to run the ferry. Rev. Salter, whose place of abode was given as London, "occupied" the Rectory.²⁷⁹ Allen was originally from Eastwood. His daughter, Mary, married John Waylett Stallibrass, the Eastwood farmer who leased Fambridge Ferry Farm. John and Mary (d.1866) had a son called Allen Stallibrass, who married Middlesex spinster, Catherine Emma Somervail *c*.1883.²⁸⁰

All the above property ownership was the same on the voter's roll for 1870, except that Rose had been removed from it, which suggests that he had relinquished his occupation of the Kew lands.²⁸¹ In 1871 William Keyes (junior) still owned Moon's but was living at Prittlewell Priory. Rev. Nott still held Pulpits. Edward Brown was still at the blacksmith's shop in "Greenstead" (Greensward) Lane. He may have taken over the premises from

---

276   ERO Q/RPr 2/1
277   ERO D/DSc/T15
278   Southend Museums Service, *A Short History of Prittlewell Priory*, p.28
279   ERO Q/RPr 2/1
280   ERO D/DGs/F7
281   ERO Q/RPr 2/4

Richard Bowton. Brown was also an overseer for Ashingdon in that year.[282] All other property ownership remained the same in 1871, except that Rev. Salter had been removed from the voter's roll for South Fambridge, suggesting that he had left his post as rector by then. Rev. Septimus Nottidge was still the incumbent at Ashingdon in both the above years.[283]

Property ownership was consistent throughout 1872-3, with William Keyes at Moon's, Henry Mew at Beckney, Alfred White owning Ashingdon Hall but leasing it to Benjamin Moss, Rev. Septimus Nottidge at Ashingdon Rectory, Rev. Percy Wemyss Nott owning Pulpits, Edward Brown owning the blacksmith's shop, Stephen Allen owning Ferry Farm but leasing it and the ferry to James Andrews, William Walter Stephenson owning South Fambridge Hall but leasing it to William Arthur Potter, and George James Potter occupying Brick House Farm.[284] By 1874 John Morris Hamilton, who lived in Hull, had taken over the ownership of South Fambridge Hall and James Andrews had relinquished his occupancy of Ferry Farm, but everything else was the same in both parishes.[285]

Education

Formal education seems first to have made itself felt in Ashingdon in the early years of the 19th century. Jerram-Burrows writes that local children were taught in 1808 at one of three schools in neighbouring Hockley.

In 1818 the *Digest of Parochial Returns* from the *Select Committee on Education of the Poor* recorded the following education position in Ashingdon parish: "The clerk teaches about 20 boys in the summer and about 7 during the winter, in the church before service begins. All the poor children of the parish have the privilege of attending the Rochford national school." There was no school in South Fambridge though and the Committee found that the poor there were "without sufficient means of education and are desirous of possessing them".

By 1833, however, according to House of Commons papers, there was one Daily School in Ashingdon "containing 7 males and 9 females, and One Sunday School of 16 males and 23 females: both Schools (commenced 1833) are supported by the Rector and Curate of Ashingdon and South Fambridge, and are for the inhabitants of those places jointly".

In 1839 a return of schools information in Ashingdon to the London Diocesan Board of Education recorded that there was one day school and Sunday school in the parish. Both schools had been established seven years earlier and were both free to attend. The day school had capacity for 30 pupils but there were only 20 pupils on the books. Regular

---

282 ERO Q/RPc 11
283 ERO Q/RPr 2/7
284 ERO Q/RPr 2/10 & Q/RPr 2/13
285 ERO Q/RPr 2/16

attendance was just 15, comprising nine boys and six girls. The Sunday school, which was taught in the chancel of the parish church, had capacity for 60 pupils. There were only 35 on the books, though, and the regular attendance was just 26. The two schools, which cost about £14-£15 per year to run, were funded by the ministers of Ashingdon and South Fambridge and were managed by Rev. James Grisdale Fawcett, who completed the return and described himself on it as "curate of Ashingdon and South Fambridge". Girls were provided with new frocks and boys with new smocks. The maximum distance travelled to school by any pupil from the two parishes was two miles and "every child is educated who is old enough to attend". This covered children from age four to 14 or 15 for the Sunday school and four to 10 for boys and four to 12 for girls for the day school. There were no libraries, lectures, adult schools or evening tuition and there were no keeping-in-touch arrangements for ex-pupils once they had left. The population of Ashingdon was given by Rev. Fawcett as 170, but it is unclear whether this included South Fambridge as well. It seems likely that it did, as the return covered pupils from both parishes and the combined population figure for the two at this time was similar to this number (see below).[286]

As discussed above, the Tithe Map and Award for Ashingdon c.1838-40 describe a plot of land in Ashingdon Road which was in the occupation of James Turner as a "School House & Garden". It is possible that this was for the Day School or had some connection with it.

Despite the above efforts, the educational situation in the two parishes was still very poor in comparison with other local parishes. A new Education Act of 1870 required every parish to have a school and, if no school existed, it gave powers to local ratepayers to elect a School Board to raise the money to build one. The School Board could also enforce compulsory attendance. Evidently as a result of this, the Rochford Rural Deanery commissioned a report of church schools within that administrative area and found that Ashingdon had a Dame's School, but no grant for a church school, nor any likelihood of the Church providing one or of raising a rate to finance it. The 11 existing schools in the Deanery were rated in four categories from "Best" to "Very Poor": Ashingdon was the only one in the latter category. South Fambridge did not have a school at all and it was noted that children from that parish attended the Dame's School in Ashingdon.[287]

Parishioners must have acted quickly to address the above deficiencies, as the ERO holds plans for a new school which date from 1870 and show that a brand-new school building was planned to be erected at the junction of Ashingdon and Fambridge Roads and to accommodate 40 children, with a separate outbuilding for boys' and girls' toilets. The site chosen for it was the historic Ashingdon parish glebe (Church) land, in a central,

---

286 ERO TS 45/2
287 ERO TS 323/1

accessible location for pupils from both parishes.[288] The Ashingdon & South Fambridge National School was duly constructed and was a significant step towards improving education provision within the parishes. It opened in 1873, with Miss Rosina Aylett as its first mistress.

Figure 40: Ashingdon School in 1931

Children were often absent from school in the early days, as their labour was required for key local events such as helping with the harvest. Bad weather and epidemics also regularly caused poor attendance, as did activities such as blackberrying or attending local fairs. Most children walked to school in those days, often across the fields, though some were lucky enough to be able to get a ride on a horse and cart.

By 1882, according to *Kelly's Directory* (the most long-running of the local postal directories), the school was accommodating 60 children and Miss Harriett Lethbridge held the role of mistress.

Last Quarter

In 1874 the *Post Office Directory of Essex* listed the following as the leading local inhabitants of Ashingdon: George Brown, parish clerk; Miss R.H. Aylett, mistress at the National

---

288 ERO E/P 2/1

School; Rev. Septimus Nottidge, B.A., rector; Edward Brown, blacksmith; William Keyes, farmer; and Benjamin Moss, farmer. At South Fambridge, the following were listed: George James Potter, farmer, New Hall; Charles Sorrell, farm bailiff; William Clark, *Anchor PH* and coal merchant, and William Potter, farmer, South Fambridge Hall. Sorrell was farm bailiff at Beckney, where he and his wife Mary Ann had been living since at least 1868. The couple were living at Brick House Farm at the time of their deaths, which took place within a few weeks of one another in 1877.[289] It is strange that the Beckney (Ashingdon) bailiff is listed in the South Fambridge part of the *Directory*, but Beckney is listed under the South Fambridge Bishop's Transcripts in 1862 as well, so there was evidently some cross over between Ashingdon and South Fambridge by this stage regarding this strange, detached part of Ashingdon parish.[290]

Property Ownership

By 1876 there were a number of changes in property ownership. In Ashingdon, William Taylor Meeson was registered on the voters' roll through his ownership of Brays Farm, part of which was in the parish. It is surprising that he does not appear on earlier rolls. William Keyes had moved from Prittlewell Priory to Southchurch Hall. Frank Willan was tenant of Beckney, and Henry Winmill, from Rochford, was tenant of some woodland either at or adjacent to Beckney Wood. The names "Willan" and "Winmill" will be familiar from the 1872-3 flood information given above, but 1876 is the first year in which they appear on the voters' roll for either parish. In South Fambridge, George James Potter had relinquished his tenancy of Brick House Farm and moved to farm South Fambridge Hall alongside William Arthur Potter. No owner of Brick House Farm was given on the voters' roll and there was no listing for either ownership or occupation of Ferry Farm. Rev. Fothergill still "occupied" South Fambridge Rectory, though his address was given as Whitbread's in Hockley.[291]

In 1877 Frank Willan was listed as owner of Brick House Farm on the voters' roll, so he had evidently transferred his voting rights to there from Beckney. This is a bit bizarre, as he was clearly the occupant of Brick House Farm in 1872-3 and there is evidence given earlier that it had previously been in the Willan family's ownership, so perhaps he moved his ownership/voting rights around, or the family relinquished ownership of Brick House Farm and then regained it?[292] The former seems more likely, as he appears as occupant of Brick House Farm on the voters' roll for 1881, occupant of Beckney Farm in 1882-3 and owner of Beckney Farm in 1884-7, having taken over there from Henry Mew, who

---

289   ERO D/CR 11
290   ERO D/CR 139
291   ERO Q/RPr 2/22
292   ERO Q/RPr 2/25

last appeared on the voters' roll for Beckney in 1882.[293] Willan was assessed for the poor rate for Beckney Farm *c.*1877-90, so he clearly owned and/or occupied it throughout this period.[294] He also appears at Beckney Farm on the voters' rolls for 1888-94, plus at Brick House Farm in 1889.[295]

The remaining South Fambridge property ownership in 1877 was the same as in 1876. Meanwhile, in Ashingdon, H. Mill was claiming voting rights for his occupancy of Beckney Wood. The similarity of the names "H. Mill" and "H. Winmill", and their dual simultaneous occupancy of Beckney Wood, sounds suspiciously like they might be the same person, but they are listed separately in the 1887 voters' roll, so it has to be presumed that they are different individuals. Elsewhere, Edward Trotter Jackson had taken over the ownership of Smith's and Chamberlain's.[296] He was assessed for the poor rates on the property from *c.*1877-90.[297] Curiously, Jackson, who lived in Rochford, is shown as a "lodger" at "Smith's Farm" on the 1886 and 1887 voters' rolls, occupying "Two sitting rooms and a bedroom, furnished".[298] He appears on the voters' rolls for Smith's and Chamberlain's in 1889-94.[299] The freehold belonged to Alfred Gardiner from *c.*1888 to 1894.[300]

There was no change in property ownership in the parish in 1878.[301] In 1879, however, William Keyes disappeared from the Ashingdon voters' roll and no-one else was shown as owning or occupying Moon's.[302] Keyes continued to be assessed for the poor rate on Moon's, however, until at least 1880. He was also assessed for the poor rate on Pulpits Farm in 1877, suggesting the farmland there was in his occupation.[303] His last appearance on the voters' roll for Ashingdon was in 1881, when he qualified as a voter under the 1867 Act for his occupation (farming) of the glebe land in the parish.[304]

In South Fambridge in 1879, the Potters also disappeared from the voters' roll. The disappearances of the Keyes and Potter families from the voters' rolls/property ownership lists in the late 1870s provides evidence of the changing of the guard, as those two hitherto dominant farming families began to relinquish their long-standing local control.[305]

---

293 ERO Q/RPr 2/37, Q/RPr 2/40, Q/RPr 2/43, Q/RPr 2/46, Q/RPr 2/49, Q/RPr 3/8 & Q/RPr 3/16
294 ERO G/Ro N63
295 ERO Q/RPr 3/24 & C/E 1/7/1-6
296 ERO Q/RPr 2/25. See also Q/RPr 2/37, Q/RPr 2/40, Q/RPr 2/43, Q/RPr 2/46 & Q/RPr 2/49 (1881-5).
297 ERO G/Ro N63
298 ERO Q/RPr 3/8 & Q/RPr 3/16
299 ERO C/E 1/7/1-6
300 ERO Q/RPr 3/24 & C/E 1/7/1-6
301 ERO Q/RPr 2/28
302 ERO Q/RPr 2/34
303 ERO G/Ro N63
304 ERO Q/RPr 2/37
305 ERO Q/RPr 2/31

Elsewhere in South Fambridge, Ferry Farm was in the occupation of William Lazell Clark from Rochford. Edward Trotter Jackson was occupying The Glebe.[306] Clark himself disappeared from the South Fambridge voters' roll in 1880. New voters then appearing, under the 1867 Act, were Burnham residents John Rogers and John Smith, who were both owners of apparently new oyster grounds in the parish.[307] They probably worked for the Burnham River Company, which was assessed for poor rates for oyster layings in South Fambridge in c.1877-90.[308] Smith appears periodically on the voters' rolls for South Fambridge as late as 1894.[309]

There were no changes of property ownership indicated by the voters' roll for Ashingdon in 1880.[310] Edward Brown, however, was assessed for the poor rate on Pulpits in that year, and also in 1890, suggesting that he had taken over its tenancy, although it was still in the ownership of the Vicar of Kew.[311] Brown is also listed as being the occupant of Pulpits on the voters' roll for Ashingdon in 1882.[312] He was still being assessed for property valuation purposes on the blacksmith's in 1888.[313] The voters' rolls for 1888-92 show him living in Greensward Lane.[314] James Sorrell is listed as being resident at Pulpits in 1892 and 1894.[315]

Henry Mew still owned Beckney Wood in 1880, despite having evidently relinquished his ownership of Beckney Farm to Frank Willan.[316] However, by 1889 Beckney Wood was in the ownership of Colonel Huntley Bacon, ending Henry Mew's long tenure of land and property in the area. Bacon continued to own it until at least 1894.[317]

The Golden Cross lands in Ashingdon were in the ownership of Dr. Thomas King in 1877, 1880 and 1886 but occupied (farmed) by Benjamin Moss. In 1890 they were still owned by King but occupied by Samuel Scraggs Matthews.[318] King had evidently succeeded W.H. Rankin as owner. These lands were put up for sale in 1898 and the farm's field in Ashingdon, which measured just under 35 acres, was sold as a separate lot. It was leased by Mr. W. Bishop at the time.[319]

---

306 Ibid.
307 ERO Q/RPr 2/34
308 ERO G/Ro N63
309 ERO Q/RPr 2/37, Q/RPr 2/40, Q/RPr 2/43, Q/RPr 2/46, Q/RPr 2/49 & C/E 1/7/1-6
310 ERO Q/RPr 2/34
311 ERO G/Ro N63
312 ERO Q/RPr 2/40
313 ERO G/Ro N90
314 ERO Q/RPr 3/24 & C/E 1/7/1-4
315 ERO C/E 1/7/4-6
316 ERO G/Ro N63
317 ERO C/E 1/7/1-6
318 ERO G/Ro N63 & G/Ro N90
319 ERO SALE/B2374

At Rouncefall, Emma Potter was owner and Louisa Crick tenant in 1877, but by 1880 both roles had been taken over by Susan Pissey. By 1890, however, the land at Rouncefall had been carved up into a number of owners. A place called "Crick's Land" was found by Reaney to be in existence in 1534. It is possible that Louisa Crick was a descendant of the original owner of this. It was in the ownership of a Mr. Harvey in 1877 and 1880 but occupied by J.P. Williams. By 1890, however, it was in the ownership of George Frederick Browne.[320]

The blacksmith's in Greensward Lane was still tenanted by Edward Brown in 1877-80 but ownership of it passed from William Keyes to Thomas Keyes during that period. The main owners of rental properties in Ashingdon in 1877 were William Keyes, Frank Willan, Alfred White and the Woollaston Charity Trustees.[321]

Rev. Septimus Nottidge died on Christmas Eve 1879 and was buried next to the south wall of St Andrew's church. He was succeeded as rector of Ashingdon in 1880 by Rev. Ernest Henry Fothergill.[322] Fothergill appears in the parish vestry minutes from 1881 to 1892, often in the role of meeting chairman.[323] He is also listed as owner of the freehold benefice of Ashingdon Rectory on the voters' rolls for 1881-92. It seems likely that he was related to the above-mentioned Rev. Percival Alfred Fothergill, rector of South Fambridge. The latter appears on the voters' rolls for South Fambridge in 1881-8, suggesting with the above flood information that he was in the role of rector there from at least 1872 to 1888.[324]

---

320 ERO G/Ro N63
321 Ibid.
322 ERO D/P 89/1/7
323 ERO D/P 89/8/4 & A13442 Box 5
324 ERO Q/RPr 2/37, Q/RPr 2/40, Q/RPr 2/43, Q/RPr 2/46, Q/RPr 2/49, Q/RPr 3/8, Q/RPr 3/16, Q/RPr 3/24 & C/E 1/7/1-4

Figure 41: The grave of Rev. Septimus Nottidge, Ashingdon rector 1846-79

John Morris Hamilton, owner of South Fambridge Hall, last appears on the voters' roll for South Fambridge in 1881. He was replaced from 1883 onwards by Charles Rice and Dean Swift of 21 Union Bank Buildings, Holborn Viaduct, London. This joint ownership and the London office address are redolent of the company takeover which gave birth to the aforementioned Rice and Company mutual farming co-operative and reflect the beginnings of a transition from the old individual to new corporate ownership of local land.[325] In 1885 Rice and Swift were living in South Fambridge. However, neither is on the voters' roll for 1886 and only Swift was on it in 1887.[326] In 1893 South Fambridge Hall was occupied by George Harrington.[327]

A new name on the 1882 voters' roll for Ashingdon was Charles Edward Rashleigh, owner of Moon's. He disappears from the roll in 1883-4.[328] However, he is shown as owner of Moon's on the Ashingdon Poor Rate Valuation list for 1890. Ellen Jolly was then its

---

325 ERO Q/RPr 2/40, Q/RPr 2/43 & Q/RPr 2/46
326 ERO Q/RPr 2/49, Q/RPr 3/8 & Q/RPr 3/16
327 ERO C/E 1/7/5
328 ERO Q/RPr 2/40, Q/RPr 2/43 & Q/RPr 2/46

tenant.[329] Frederick Emberson was listed on the voters' roll for Moon's in 1889.[330] John Jolly, who was presumably a relative of Ellen's, was listed on the voters' rolls for the property in 1891-4.[331] There is a grave just inside the gate of All Saints churchyard to Hector MacDonald Jolly of Rectory Farm, and his wife, Mary. In 1893-4 Charles Edward Rashleigh of Sydenham and Henry Burvill Rashleigh of Dartford were shown on the voters' rolls as freeholders for Moon's, along with William Tristam of Lancashire. Clearly all three co-owners, the first two of whom were presumably related, were absentee landlords.[332]

Figure 42: The grave of Hector MacDonald Jolly and his wife, Mary, at South Fambridge

The Representation of the People Act 1884, sometimes called the Third Reform Act, significantly extended the voting franchise from two million to over five million (all male). The Act gave voting rights to those paying an annual rental of £10 or holding land valued at £10. It also gave those living in the countryside equivalent voting rights to those living in towns. The impact of this in Ashingdon and South Fambridge was greatly to increase the number of eligible male voters in the two parishes from nine and four respectively in 1885 to 19 and 15 respectively in 1886. The polling districts locally were also reorganised, with South Fambridge being moved out of Rochford Polling District, in which both parishes had hitherto been counted, into a new Canewdon Polling District.[333]

---

329   ERO G/Ro N63
330   ERO C/E 1/7/1
331   ERO C/E 1/7/3-6
332   ERO C/E 1/7/5-6
333   ERO Q/RPr 2/49 & Q/RPr 3/8

By 1885 Moon's in Ashingdon had been taken over by Samuel Garrard, who was living in Prittlewell Square in Southend at the time.[334] Conversely, Rev. Percy Wemyss Nott's ownership of Pulpits appears to have come to an end in 1886, the last year he is listed on the voters' roll.[335] John Brighten is listed on the 1886 voters' roll as occupying a "House on Beckney farm", but in 1887 this had changed subtly to "Beckney farm house". As Frank Willan was evidently an absent owner of Beckney Farm, it seems that Brighten was the person who was actually living there. Alfred Gardiner was living at "Smith's Farm" in 1887, with "Smith's and Chamberlain's farmhouse" being the "Description of Qualifying Property" for him to vote. It will be recalled from above that Edward Trotter Jackson was listed as a lodger at Smith's Farm at the time. The "Chamberlain's" element of the farm's name was evidently in the process of being dropped.[336] Rouncefall was in the ownership of John Lindsell c.1887-90.[337]

Meanwhile, in South Fambridge, Brick House Farm was in the occupation of Henry Carver *c.* 1886-94.[338] George Harris was occupying South Fambridge Hall, apparently alongside Dean Swift in 1887.[339] However, he was at Ferry Farm in 1888-94.[340] William Hymas was there in 1886-7.[341] The freehold for Ferry Farm was owned by Edward and Frank Stallibrass in 1890-4, who were absentee landlords.[342] In 1893 the ferry appears to have been run by Charles Potton.[343]

Thomas Shead was listed as occupying a "Cottage on Glebe farm" in 1886. It is unclear from the documentation whether this means that there was a cottage on the parish's glebe lands or whether this is another name for one of the farms, perhaps Rectory Farm.[344] E.G. Laver was listed as living at Rectory Farm on the South Fambridge voters' roll for 1892, with Hugh Woodthorpe as his lodger.[345]

In 1886-7 New Hall first appears on the voters' roll for South Fambridge, being then in the occupation of Joseph Wordley junior, one of three Wordleys on the voters' rolls at the time across the two parishes.[346] He appears at Beckney Farm on the voters' roll

---

334 ERO Q/RPr 2/49
335 ERO Q/RPr 3/8
336 ERO Q/RPr 3/8 & Q/RPr 3/16
337 ERO Q/RPr 3/8, Q/RPr 3/16, Q/RPr 3/24 & C/E 1/7/1-2
338 ERO Q/RPr 3/8, Q/RPr 3/16, Q/RPr 3/24 & C/E 1/7/1-6
339 ERO Q/RPr 3/8 & Q/RPr 3/16
340 ERO Q/RPr 3/24 & C/E 1/7/6
341 ERO Q/RPr 3/8 & Q/RPr 3/16
342 ERO C/E 1/7/2-6
343 ERO C/E 1/7/5
344 ERO Q/RPr 3/8 & Q/RPr 3/16
345 ERO C/E 1/7/4
346 ERO Q/RPr 3/8 & Q/RPr 3/16

for Ashingdon in 1888 and in a cottage on South Fambridge Hall Farm in 1893.[347] It is surprising to find that this is the first time a voter is listed for New Hall, given that, according to the evidence previously discussed, it probably came into existence c.1840-67 and that the voting franchise should have been extended sufficiently to capture its residents from 1867 onwards. Joshua Nunn and William Hammond are both listed as having connections with New Hall on the parishes voters' rolls for 1892: Nunn probably owned it but it was occupied by Hammond.[348] Joshua Nunn appears on the 1893-4 voters' rolls as a freeholder of part of Hill Farm (Rouncefall). He was living in South Fambridge at the time. William Hammond was shown as the owner of land and a tenement at New Hall in the same sources.[349]

In 1888 Ashingdon Hall was occupied by Samuel Blowers.[350] From 1889 to 1894 it was occupied by Alfred Chantler.[351] By 1898 William Henry Clark (spelt with an 'e' on the end of his surname in some documents) was at Ashingdon Hall.[352] The latter was leasing an orchard on Ashingdon Hill in 1905, presumably the one previously tenanted by James Keyes.[353]

John Dean was tenant at Beckney Farm c.1890-4.[354] By 1890 John William Perry had taken over the occupancy of some of the Kew-owned woodlands in Ashingdon from Henry Winmill.[355]

Frederick Keys [sic] is listed as a voter in Greensward Lane and then expressly at the blacksmith's forge there in 1889-94. He was living in Canterbury in the last two of those years.[356] Thomas Keyes had evidently died by 1899, as his executors were listed as owners of his blacksmith's premises in Greensward Lane in that year, where Walter Mann was apparently in residence, having succeeded Edward Brown.[357]

The 1892-3 voters' rolls list Thomas Parnell as owner and occupant of "Poultry Farm".[358] Philip Jones had replaced Parnell there by 1894.[359] It is unclear where this property was.

---

347 ERO Q/RPr 3/24 & C/E 1/7/5 respectively
348 ERO C/E 1/7/4
349 ERO C/E 1/7/5-6
350 ERO Q/RPr 3/24
351 ERO C/E 1/7/1-6
352 ERO SALE/B2374 & G/Ro N90
353 ERO D/DGs B376
354 ERO C/E 1/7/2-6
355 ERO G/Ro N63
356 ERO C/1/7/1-6
357 ERO G/Ro N90
358 ERO C/E 1/7/4-5
359 ERO C/E 1/7/6

Local Activities

A new American organ was purchased for Ashingdon Church and installed there on 5 June 1876. Contributors towards the funding for this included, for some reason, a Mr. M.B. Harrison of Braintree and several other inhabitants of that town, and Miss J. Nottidge, who was presumably a relative of the rector. Local landowner William Keyes, Benjamin Moss of Ashingdon Hall, and Rev. North, the vicar of Kew, also contributed. Further work appears to have been carried out at the church in the period 1875-8, including giving the inside walls a coat of whitewash, purchasing benches for the interior and varnishing the face of the coat-of-arms. Churches in south-east Essex were often restored or rebuilt at this period (as at South Fambridge in 1846), so activities at Ashingdon were clearly mirroring the trend.[360]

The church records for South Fambridge confirm that there was a changing of the guard *c.*1877-8, as the hitherto dominant Potter and Keyes families finally began to relinquish their hold on the various parish roles. By 1880 Edward Trotter Jackson was chairman of the parish vestry there, while George Lancaster and Edward Brown were the parish's overseers. All three still held posts on the parish vestry in 1885, while Brown continued to serve in various capacities until at least 1890.[361] Edward Trotter Jackson also served as an overseer and assessor in Ashingdon on-and-off in the period 1877-89.[362] George Lancaster lived in a "Cottage near the Church" in 1886-94.[363] This was probably one of the tenements in Church Cottages, a row of now-demolished, weatherboarded cottages which stood opposite All Saints in Fambridge Road and can be seen on some of the preceding maps.

Alfred White, who owned Ashingdon Hall, hosted a visit of the Essex Archaeological Society to the Hall in 1879, which was much appreciated by his visitors, who were on their way to view St Andrew's church. The party enjoyed the shade of the trees on the Hall's lawn on what was evidently a very hot day and helped themselves to the contents of "tables spread with appetising edibles and drinkables…". The *Essex Weekly News*, which reported on the visit, noted that "the cooling claret-cup" was "especially being largely in request". Mr. White was still living outside the area at the time but owned both Ashingdon Hall and "other property in the parish". He was also "an old member" of the Society and "an ardent archaeologist". After the refreshments, "the company were conducted through the Hall gardens to the church", an interesting description which reflects again that the approach to the church has changed since the 19th century.[364] White retained ownership

---

360	ERO D/P 89/5/1
361	ERO D/P 90/8
362	ERO D/P 89/8/4
363	ERO Q/RPr 3/8, Q/RPr 3/16 & C/E 1/7/5-6
364	ERO T/P 204/8

of Ashingdon Hall until at least 1890.[365] He may have owned it until 1894 and moved to live there after 1887, as he is named as churchwarden and overseer on Ashingdon property valuation lists from 1888 to 1894 and is shown as occupier in the parish's Poor Rate Valuation List in 1890.[366]

In 1880 William Carter Wood was appointed as a salaried assistant overseer in Ashingdon parish. He served in that capacity as rate collector until at least 1894.[367]

In the 1890s numerous "building land" entries appear in the Ashingdon parish valuation lists, along with buildings with names like "New Cottage". This suggests that the area was beginning to be seen as somewhere that could be developed and that land was being sold off and new property constructed. Two cottages on Ashingdon Hill which were owned by the Charity Trustees were pulled down in 1899, perhaps as part of this development activity. Meanwhile, some greenhouses were erected on the fields around Rouncefall, suggesting that commercial gardening was becoming prominent.[368] Residents in several cottages on Ashingdon Hill and at Ashingdon Hall, Moon's, Smith's and Chamberlain's and Beckney Farms are regularly named on the voters' rolls from 1888 onwards, as are residents in cottages in Greensward Lane and at Church Cottages in Fambridge Road.[369]

---

[365] ERO G/Ro N63
[366] ERO G/Ro N90 & G/Ro N63
[367] ERO D/P 89/8/4
[368] ERO G/RO N90
[369] ERO Q/RPr 3/24 & C/E 1/7/1-4

Figure 43: A cottage at the top of Ashingdon Hill, where some of the earliest development took place

In 1891 Thomas Warnell and William Clark Wells were appointed as parish overseers for Ashingdon, alongside Alfred White. E.H. Ruegg joined them in the role the following year. Warnell stood down shortly afterwards. Ruegg served until 1894, when he was replaced by John Jolly, who would become a very active and long-serving member of the community.[370] An Edward William Ruegg of Catford appears on the voters' rolls for Ashingdon in 1893-4 as a freehold owner of part of Hill Farm (Rouncefall) along with Joshua Nunn. William Clark Wells was owner of land and a tenement at Hill Farm in 1893-4.[371]

1st Edition Ordnance Survey Map

The 1st Edition Ordnance Survey Map of 1873 records the state of play in Ashingdon and South Fambridge at the time. This was the first large-scale, accurate map of the area since the Tithe Maps.

In South Fambridge, *The Anchor* and Rectory Farm had appeared, as had New Hall Farm. In Ashingdon, the main new arrival since the Tithe Map was the National School. The beginnings of the road through Ashingdon Hall farmyard to the church can also be seen.

---

370   ERO D/P 89/8/4
371   ERO C/E 1/7/5-6

The 1855 Rectory is there, but a building also survives on the site of the 1621 Rectory to the north of St Andrew's church. Moon's Cottages and Beckney Cottages (both unnamed) are also on the map. Meanwhile, in the southernmost of the detached Beckney parts of Ashingdon parish, the Smithy can be seen in Greensward Lane, while nearby Smith's is named on the map as "Chamberlain's".

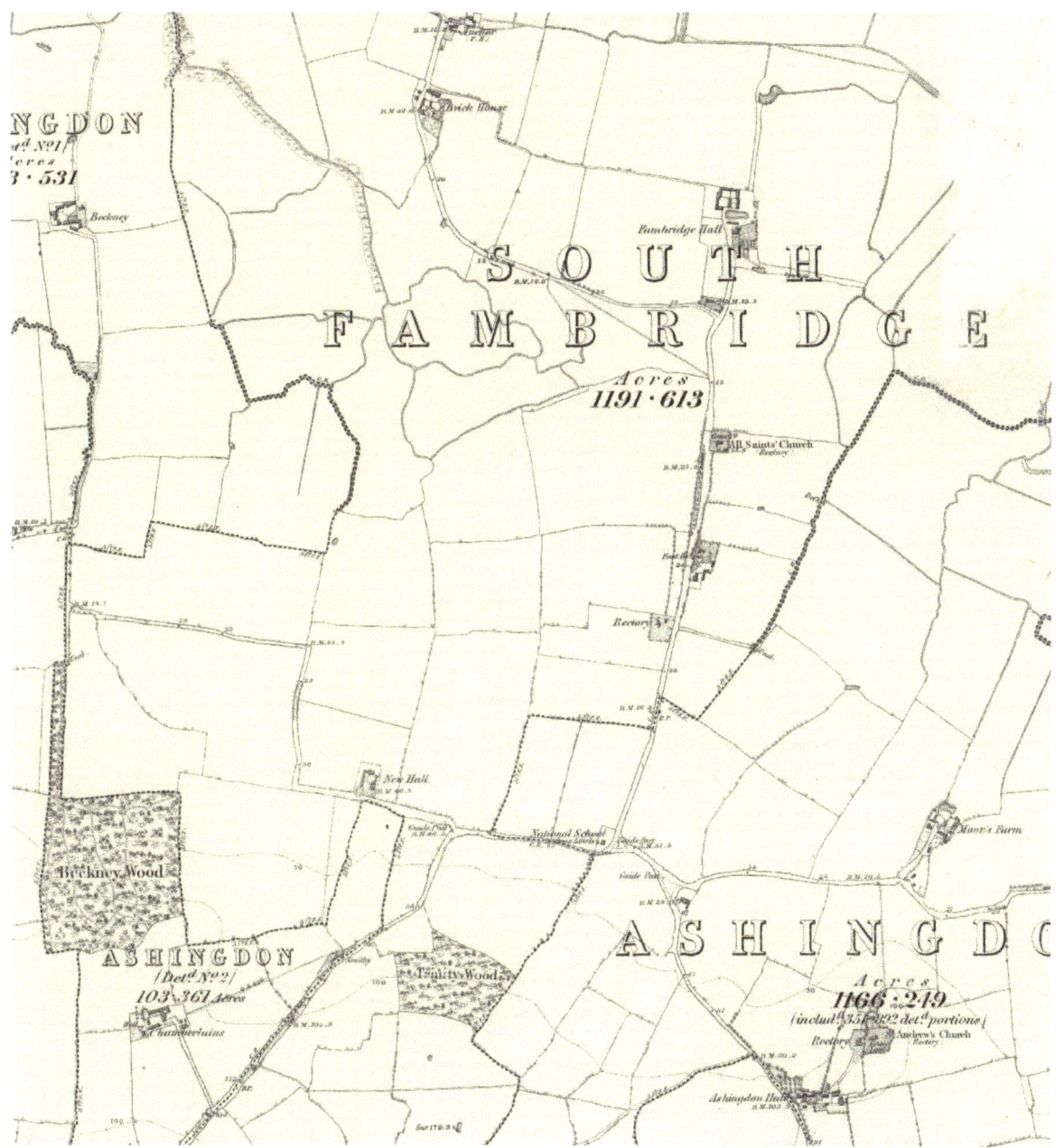

Figure 44: First edition OS Map (surveyed 1873, published 1880)

The Railway Arrives in Rochford

In 1889 the local area finally got a railway line, with the opening of what is now the Shenfield to Southend Victoria branch. The nearest station to Ashingdon and South Fambridge was at Hockley, just under a mile-and-a-half from the top of Ashingdon Hill as the crow flies and over two miles from South Fambridge village. The next nearest station was at Rochford, just under two miles from the same point in Ashingdon but over three-and-a-half miles as the crow flies from South Fambridge. Many local people have recorded their memories of walks along the then unmade roads to and from these two stations before the advent of a local bus service.

United Benefice

As rural populations began to dwindle across the country, with more individuals moving to urban areas, parishes began to join together to share their clergymen. Ashingdon and South Fambridge followed the national trend and were merged into one United Benefice for ecclesiastical purposes on 7 August 1894.[372] As rectors from each parish had already been accustomed to officiating at each other's churches, this was a logical and presumably painless development.

Rev. Ernest Fothergill was succeeded as rector of Ashingdon in 1893 by Rev. Robert Bourne.[373] The latter oversaw the uniting of the two benefices and formally became rector of the whole.[374] He appears as chairman of the parish vestry meeting in the minutes of 1894.[375] He was succeeded by Rev. Harry Campbell Bourne in 1895.[376] The latter appears on Ashingdon property valuation lists *c.*1897-1900.[377]

Local Government Reorganisation

Towards the end of the 19th century, local government was significantly reformed, beginning with the Local Government Act 1888 which introduced elected county councils, in most cases with effect from 1 April 1889. This was swiftly followed by the Local Government Act 1894 which introduced elected district and parish councils. District councils assumed responsibility for sanitary and highways measures, and Boards of Guardians were reorganised and/or replaced. Parish councils formed the lowest rung of a new three-tier structure below a brand-new Rochford Rural District Council and a still relatively new Essex County Council.

In Ashingdon and South Fambridge the centuries-old parish vestries appear to have

---

[372] ERO D/CP 1/13 & D/CPc 87
[373] ERO D/P 89/1/7
[374] ERO D/CPc 87
[375] ERO D/P 89/8/4
[376] ERO D/P 89/1/7
[377] ERO G/Ro N90

been superseded in 1894 by "Meetings of Parochial Electors". They ought to have been superseded by parish councils, but neither body had parish council status, so perhaps the vestry arrangements continued but along more formalised lines. Both organisations met for the first time on 4 December 1894. The meeting for Ashingdon was held at the National School, where it was chaired by John Jolly of Moon's Farm, while the meeting for South Fambridge was held just up the road at Rectory Farm, where it was chaired by Hugh Crawford "of Smith's Farm in Hockley" (presumably Smith's & Chamberlain's, which was actually in Ashingdon). Crawford was present at, and briefly chaired, the initial Ashingdon meeting and he was elected as one of that parish's overseers in 1896, along with John Jolly, who served as chairman and/or overseer for Ashingdon throughout the 1890s and beyond. Crawford was also elected as an overseer for South Fambridge in 1895, along with E.G. Laver. This kind of overlap of personnel between the two places is much in evidence in the minutes of both parish meetings over the years.[378]

When Jolly was not the chairman of the Ashingdon meeting (1897-8), that role was filled by W.H. Clark, who also served as an overseer during that period. South Fambridge parish meetings were held in various locations, including at All Saints church, South Fambridge Hall and Ashingdon School. One of the first topics discussed at both meetings was a proposal in 1895 for a School Board to cover the combined parishes.[379]

2nd Edition Ordnance Survey Map

The 2nd Edition Ordnance Survey Map of Ashingdon from 1898 shows very little change from the 1st Edition Map. Smith's has reverted to its previous ancient name of Smith's & Snares and has lost the Chamberlain element of the name altogether. There are a couple of new named properties in The Chase – Hillside and Rainbow Cottage – and The Chase has grown a northern arm, but other than that the only significant new arrival in the area is that of the railway through neighbouring Hockley and Hawkwell parishes to the south-west.

The detached "Beckney" parts of Ashingdon parish are clearly shown. Detached parts of parishes were removed by legislation, notably the Detached Parishes Act 1882, but this did not happen locally until the 1930s (see below).[380]

---

378   ERO D/J 126/1/1 & D/DS 313/19/1
379   Ibid.
380   Edward Higgs, *Making Sense of the Census – Revisited*, p.38 notes that this Act "stated that detached parts [of parishes] should be incorporated into the parish surrounding them". See also *VCH Essex Vol. II*, pp.342-3.

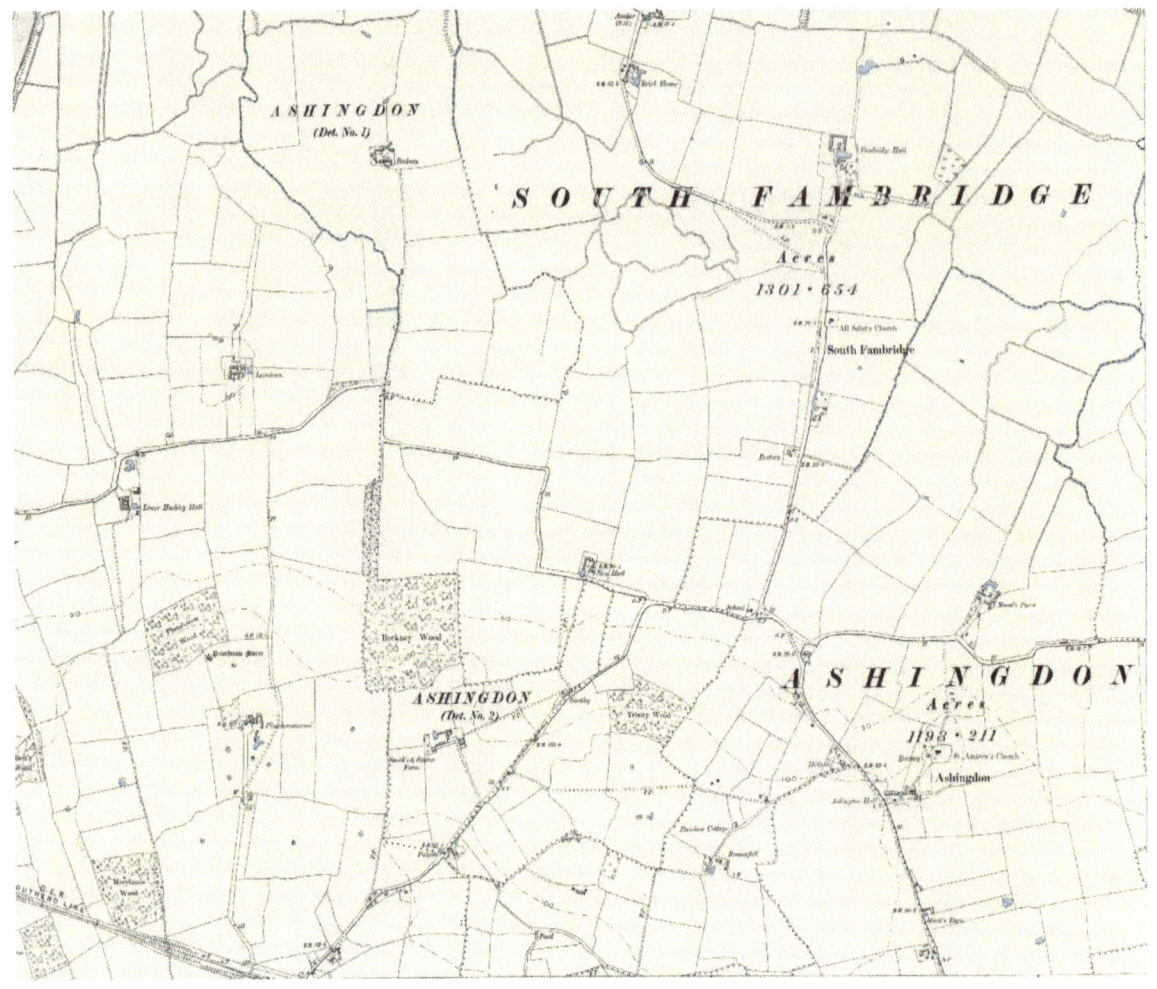

Figure 45: Second edition OS Map 1898

Another notable arrival was a public letterbox at Ashingdon Hall, which provides evidence that a postal service had reached the area by this stage. The letterbox remains in situ and is on Rochford District Council's Local List of important historic structures. It is described in the listing for it as a "Victorian cast iron wall box with 'VR' cipher and crown on top; set in a brick pillar which was rebuilt in the mid-20th Century". The justification for including it on the List is that it "is character-enhancing and of good quality".

Figure 46: The Victorian letterbox in Church Road, Ashingdon

Thomas Hollick's Engineering Factory

In 1898 a man called Thomas Hollick built an engineering factory in South Fambridge, no doubt to take advantage of the riverside location for the importation of raw materials and the exportation of manufactured goods. The factory produced electric cranes and dynamos, under the name of Wimshurst, Hollick & Company. Hollick also built two rows of workmen's cottages and a club house for factory employees. We can get a flavour of the kind of person who worked there from a surviving collection of letters to Hoffman's ball-bearing manufacturers in Chelmsford, which includes one from a Mr. A. Goodchild of South Fambridge, who was applying for a job there as a turner and had evidently worked at Hollick's. He had 12 years' experience in the trade.[381]

The Heritage Gateway website records that the two rows of cottages built by Hollick were numbers 1-20 on the east side of St Thomas Road, the first new road in the parish in modern times, and numbers 21-32 on the west side. Mr Goodchild lived at number 24. The former row, which backed onto the factory site and included a Post Office (at numbers 1-2) and a boarding house (19-20), has since been demolished and replaced with new housing. The latter row has survived, but with significant alterations to individual cottages' windows and doors in most cases. It is unclear why the name "St Thomas Road" was chosen, when the parish church was dedicated to All Saints. Perhaps Thomas Hollick named it after himself?

---

381   ERO D/F 18/1/1 - the letter is dated 27/04/1899

Figure 47: St Thomas Road, South Fambridge, pictured c.1906; the Post Office (right) burnt down during the Second World War

Thomas Hollick's scheme has echoes of the failed New Town scheme of 1866 for the erection of an ironworks in South Fambridge, as although his venture got off the ground, it was unfortunately short-lived. A newspaper article from 1905 reported as follows: "Messrs. Wimshurst and Hollick's works at South Fambridge, which have provided employment for many men in making electric cranes, etc., are to be closed. Most of the hands [employees] have already gone."[382] The factory closed in 1906 but is remembered in the name of a road that was built on its site, Crane Court Drive. One of the factory chimneys was still standing in the 1980s. A small, overgrown brick building just past the entrance to Crane Court Drive, which was the base of a water tower, appears to be the only former structure left on the site.

Village Life in the 1890s

Some other newspaper articles which are held by the ERO give a flavour of life in South Fambridge in the 1890s. For example, a court case in 1898 arose due to the shortage of

---

[382] ERO T/P 185/5/11

drinking water in the village, perhaps due to the increasing population and the influx of outsiders which was brought about by the establishment of Hollick's factory. Hannah Emmons was summoned to court for assaulting Charlotte Ward after the former deliberately spilt the latter's pail of water while she was filling it from the village pump and then assaulted her when Ward objected. Ward stated in court that the defendant thrashed her, made her nose bleed and threated to kill her. Corroborative evidence was given by witnesses. Emmons claimed in return that Ward was "piggish" and "[h]oggish" about the water, which "only ran in a drizzle" and took two hours to fill a pail. Nevertheless, she was found guilty of the assault and was fined 10s with 14s costs.[383]

In 1899 one newspaper carried an article entitled "Extension of the Public Telegraphs to South Fambridge". The article stated that the Postmaster General had received Royal Assent under the Telegraph Acts 1863-92 to place a telegraph over and along the public road from Hockley station to South Fambridge Post Office, presumably the one in St Thomas Road.[384]

Meanwhile, in Ashingdon, in 1897 a "small Tolstoyan anarchist smallholdings colony" was founded in the parish by one James Evans, according to Utopia Britannica, a website which documents British Utopian Experiments 1325-1945.[385] Evans was living in "Brotherhood Cottage" – in The Chase – as late as 1939.[386] Not much is known about this colony, which appears to have been a type of commune. It was, however, evidently home to a very colourful character who appears to have caused all sorts of mayhem locally.

Colony member, Frederick Murray Browne, sometimes named as Frederick M. Von K. Browne, was regularly in the newspapers for his unconventional activities. An artist and self-styled anarchist, Browne, 42, was sentenced in October 1897 to six months' hard labour for sending indecent postcards through the post. After behaving violently in prison, he was certified as insane and transferred to the County Lunatic Asylum at Warley, near Brentwood. On his release from the asylum, he took exception to his treatment and visited the Borough Court at Southend in June 1898 where he tried to get the ear of the town's mayor, who was presiding. His home address was given in the newspapers as "Anarchae Keep" in Ashingdon. The mayor referred him to the County Bench, as his case came under their jurisdiction. When Browne refused to go there, he was told to take up law himself so he could understand the process. He returned, with his wife, to the Southend courtroom the following month and appears to have generally disrupted proceedings. Newspapers reported that "Browne became very abusive and had to be forcibly removed

---

383 Ibid.
384 Ibid.
385 Utopia Britannica website: http://www.utopia-britannica.org.uk/pages/ESSEX.htm
386 ERO D/RR 2/2/2/3

from court… it took six policemen to eject him".[387]

He perhaps unwisely boasted that he had continued to send postcards after his release, and he duly was back in the County Court later in the month charged with sending three of them to individuals in positions of authority, including Dr. Amsden from the County Asylum, whom he described as a "scoundrel", amongst other things. This time his address was given as "Brotherhood Cottage" and he had both his wife and daughters with him. He was bailed for two lots of £50 from two sureties. He did not go quietly, however, and continued to make his case. He seemed particularly aggrieved that he was being charged with offending the rules of the realm, when his postcards contained quotations from the Bible, which was mandatory learning in schools throughout the kingdom. His daughter, Ida, even spoke up on his behalf, stating that she had been beaten in school for not attending to scripture, the implication being that the use of scripture on postcards could not therefore be inherently wrong. Browne was given another £100 bail at the end of the discussion.[388]

In October 1898, one newspaper carried the rather weary headline of "Browne the Anarchist – again" as it wrapped up the narrative of the affair. He was unsurprisingly sentenced to another nine months' hard labour at Warley. That was not the end of the matter, however, because in March 1900 the newspapers were reporting that he had escaped from the asylum and had fled to London! He must have been apprehended and returned to Essex, however, because in 1901 he was fined £1 for beating a four-year-old boy who had thrown stones at him. What a character![389]

Other notable Ashingdon activities in the 1890s included the fining of W.H. Clark of Ashingdon Hall the sum of £30 for shooting two dogs belonging to a neighbour, Beaufoi Moore, after a long-running dispute between them, and the subsequent sale of Ashingdon Hall by Mr. Clark to buyers who included Mr. Hart (who bought the Hall and its outbuildings) and Mr. Wyeth (who bought some of its land). There were also some poaching activities going on in the Ashingdon area.[390] In 1900 Charles Howard Atkinson appeared alongside the Wyeths on the property valuation list for a separate part of Ashingdon Hall.[391]

Population Trends

The population of Ashingdon remained low and fairly static throughout the 19th century, averaging just 96 in the period 1801-1901. There was, however, a gradual trend upwards

---

387   ERO T/P 181/1/11
388   Ibid.
389   Ibid.
390   Ibid.
391   ERO G/Ro N90

from 59 inhabitants in 1801 to 178 a century later – a 302% growth.

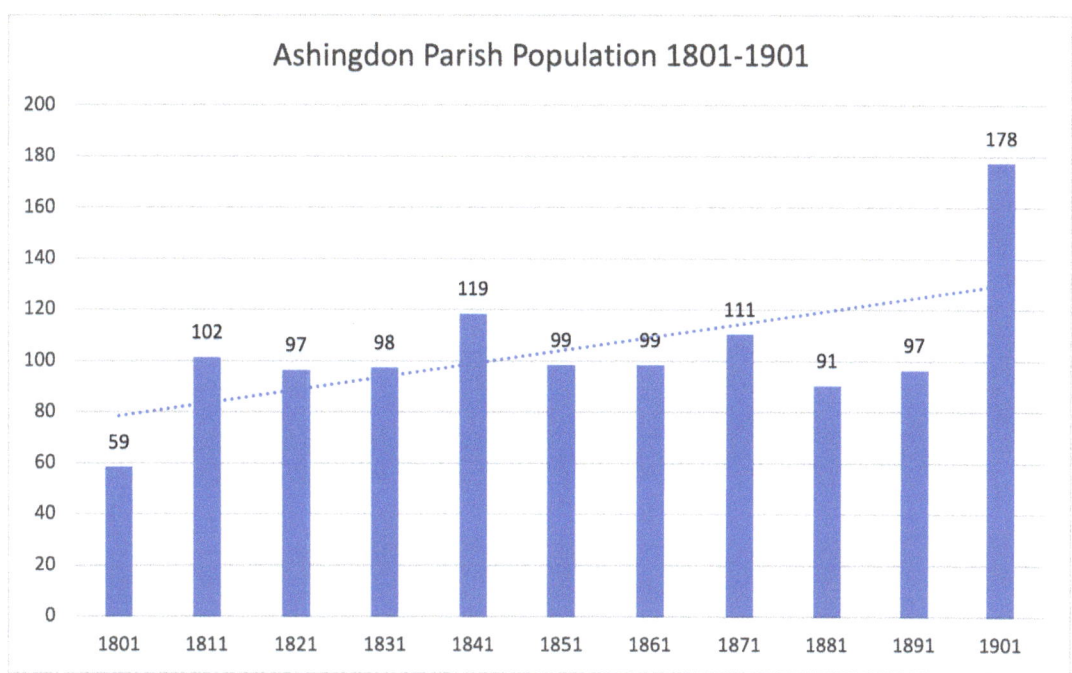

Figure 48: Ashingdon Population 1801-1901[392]

The situation in South Fambridge was not too dissimilar, with an average of 93 across the century and a 200% increase from 83 in 1801 to 166 in 1901. There was a notable jump in the final decade, with the population more than doubling from a century low point of just 79 in 1891 to 166 ten years later. This is almost certainly due to the arrival of Hollick's engineering factory, as the 1901 census includes numerous individuals who were employed there. The arrival of the factory appears to have arrested a steady decline in population numbers which began after 1871.

---

392 Figures taken from *VCH Essex II*

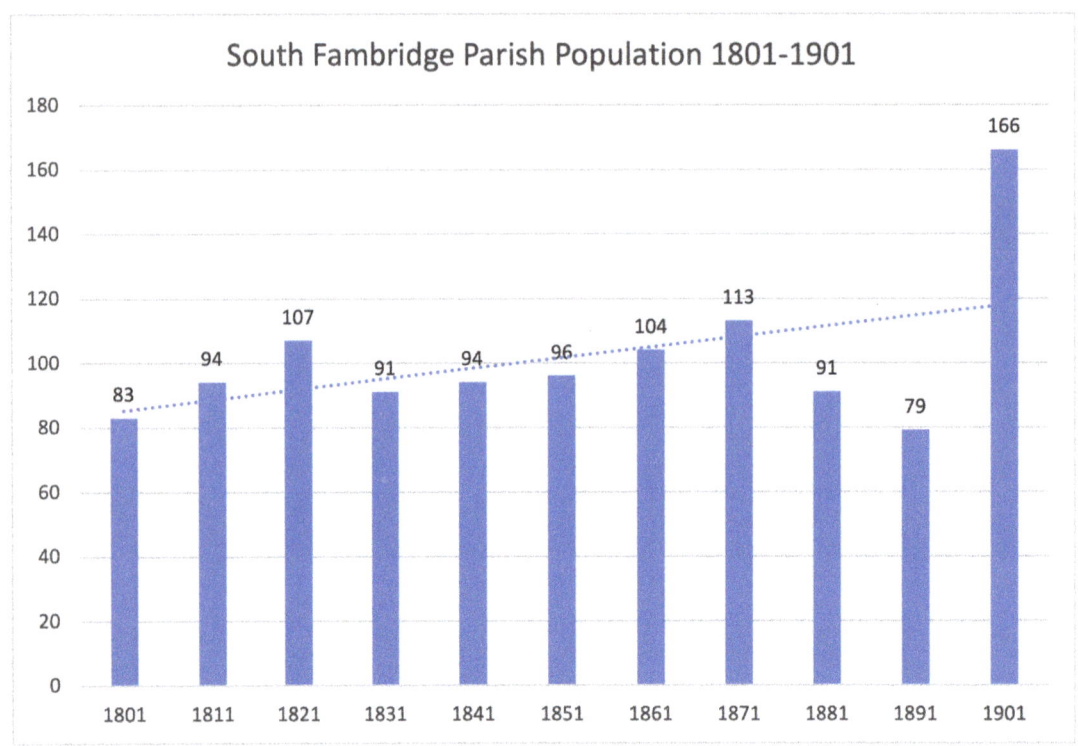

Figure 49: South Fambridge Population 1801-1901[393]

According to the 1881 census, Rochford Hundred had a population of 23,283 in that year. That means that just 0.4% of the Hundred's population lived in each of the two parishes. The average parish population in Essex at the time was 1,366, showing that Ashingdon and South Fambridge had very small populations compared to the rest of the county.

Only 17% of those born in Ashingdon parish were shown as living in Ashingdon in the 1881 census, which is the joint second-lowest percentage for the then 25 parishes in the Rochford Hundred, so there was clearly significant population migration going on. For comparison, 31% of those born in South Fambridge were living in South Fambridge parish in 1881, while the island parish of Foulness at the eastern end of the Hundred had the highest figure for what might be called "non-movers", with 63% of those born on the island living there at the time of the census. The average across all 25 parishes was 36%, with all but Ashingdon and four others falling in the 23%-50% range. The majority of in-migrants to Ashingdon came from relatively local parishes, as shown in the table below.

393   Ibid.

Parish of Residence	Parish of Birth	Number of Residents by Birthplace
Ashingdon	Ashingdon	16
Ashingdon	Hawkwell	10
Ashingdon	Hockley	7
Ashingdon	South Fambridge	5
Ashingdon	Canewdon	4
Ashingdon	Broxted	3
Ashingdon	Eastwood	3
Ashingdon	Great Stambridge	3
Ashingdon	Latchingdon	3
Ashingdon	Rochford	3

Figure 50: Most common birthplaces of individuals resident in Ashingdon in 1881

When converted to percentages, the above figures reveal that 24% of Ashingdon's residents in 1881 were born in the neighbouring parishes of Hawkwell, Hockley or South Fambridge. Similarly, 21% of South Fambridge's residents in that year came from Hawkwell, Hockley or Canewdon.

Ashingdon was, of course, an entirely agricultural parish, comprised of unmade roads, "scattered cottages few and far between" and a transient population.[394] In 1881 60% of those with a recorded occupation in the parish were farm labourers. Another 10% were farmers or farm bailiffs. Of those moving in from Hawkwell, Hockley and South Fambridge, 80% were farm labourers. The male-to-female ratio was lower than the Hundred average but higher than has been recorded in studies of parishes outside the Hundred. This all suggests that Ashingdon was attracting male farm labourers from immediately neighbouring parishes. A contributory factor could be Ashingdon's detached portions: perhaps many of those who moved in went to one of its two detached parts. It is impossible to tell from the available data.

Obviously, a significant number of Ashingdon-born individuals also moved out of the parish. This is probably because agricultural depression was at its height in Essex around this period and many, particularly young, people left agriculture for the growing sectors of manufacturing and service. In the county generally, the Essex historian, A.F.J. Brown, found that "during the depression after 1875 so many [labourers]… migrated from Essex

---

394   Colin Henry, *125 Years of Ashingdon School*

farms that those who remained were able to retain their wage increases even amid falling prices".[395] Another historian, G.E. Mingay, found that "the less productive claylands – like much of Essex – … saw rents sink to very low levels".[396] Consequently, "one of the counties [which was] most badly affected by the wet of the late 1870s was Essex, and the undrained heavy lands there were particularly difficult to let".[397] According to a major migration study by Colin Pooley and Ian Whyte, "the more rural the area [in a selection of Essex parishes that they looked at], the more likely it was to record quite high rates of out-migration".[398]

In Rochford Hundred, Benton recorded that the soil varied greatly, so that "in the present depressed time, some of it does not pay the cost of cultivation, whilst on the other hand the major part produces Corn, Mustard and Potatoes in abundance and is of great fertility". Rents were a key factor, as they had "in many instances, more than doubled or even trebled". In Benton's view, "the tithe act… is a heavy incubus on the poor soils", so that "in some extreme cases, land will be almost valueless to owners, whilst in others a great boon is conferred on agriculture".[399] Lesley Vingoe, author of a book about Hockley and Hullbridge, observed that "things were so bad that by 1871 it was said that only old people and fools were left in… Rochford Hundred".[400]

Ashingdon, which evidently had a high population turnover at this period, may have been one of those parishes which was adversely affected by soil quality. Benton observes that "the soil of Ashingdon is strong and heavy, much of it requiring under-draining". He adds that it was difficult to grow crops there and that rents were high.[401] Ashingdon also had the largest percentage of out-migrants in the Hundred, at 87%. At least 48 Ashingdon-born and 19 South Fambridge-born individuals left the Hundred completely.[402]

---

395   A.F.J. Brown, *English History from Essex Sources 1750-1900*, p.37
396   G.E. Mingay, *Rural Life in Victorian England*, p.39
397   Ibid., p.63
398   Colin G. Pooley & Ian D. Whyte, *Migrants, Emigrants and Immigrants in a Social history of Migration*, p.112
399   Philip Benton, *The History of Rochford Hundred*, pp.774-5
400   Lesley Vingoe, *Hockley, Hawkwell & Hullbridge Past*, p.38
401   Benton, p.19
402   Analysis in this section is taken from ERO T/Z 490 'Migration into, out of and within the Rochford Hundred in Essex in 1881' by Ian Yearsley (MA dissertation, 2011)

THE EDWARDIAN ERA

Development

Between 1899 and 1901 a London developer, Benjamin Albert Passant, of the *Mitre Tavern* in Holborn, began buying up land on four new building estates in south-east Essex. Two of these were in Ashingdon – the Ashingdon Road Estate and the Golden Cross Estate.[403] They were based around Canewdon View Road and Golden Cross Road respectively.[404] The other two were in Rochford and Eastwood – the Rochford Town Estate and the Prittlewell Crescent Estate. Passant's first purchases on the Golden Cross Estate were made in June 1899. His first purchases on the Ashingdon Road Estate were made in May 1900.[405] Passant died in 1911. His fellow publicans, William Benjamin Cousins and Henry Middleton, were the executors of his estate.[406]

Other significant land sales also took place at this period, including, in 1905 for what became the Harrogate Estate.[407] This occurred on 15 March 1905 and was for 297 acres of arable, grassland and grazing marsh on Smith's and Chamberlain's Farm (shown on the sales map as "Smith's and Snares Farm"). This land, which spanned the boundaries of Ashingdon, South Fambridge and Hockley parishes, but was primarily in Ashingdon, was divided into two sections, comprising a total of 15 lots. The southern section was on the western side of Greensward Lane, running north from Plumberow Avenue and including the area now occupied by Harrogate Road and the Smith's and Chamberlain's six-bedroom farmhouse, which had drawing, sitting and dining rooms, plus outbuildings for horses, cows and carts. The northern section was based around the junctions of Ashingdon, Fambridge and Canewdon Roads and included the "Wantz Barn", on the eastern side of the Ashingdon Road/Canewdon Road junction. The southern section was presumably from the original Smith's Farm and the northern section (and barn) were from the original Chamberlain's Farm.[408]

---

403   ERO D/DB T1522/1-21
404   ERO D/DB T1522/30-1
405   ERO D/DB T1522/1-21
406   ERO D/DB T1522/22-37
407   ERO T/P 181/1/1
408   ERO D/DGs B376

Figure 51: Map of the Harrogate Estate sale, 1905, shown with north at the top

Advertising for the sale, which took place at the Public Hall in Hockley, stressed the easy access to London and Southend by rail, the proximity of Rochford's golf links and the nearness of the River Crouch. There were 12,000 feet of main road frontage in the sale and the land "was in an excellent state of cultivation". The latter was described as "ripe for development" due to "the growth of the neighbourhood during the last few years and the increasing demand for houses" and was deemed suitable for residential development, small dairy and poultry farms, and horticultural properties. The growing Southend market for local produce and the picturesque views were other advertised selling points.[409] In the event, only four of the 15 lots were sold, however.[410]

The attempted sale of some freehold land next to Trinity Wood in July 1906, which was marketed as "suitable for the erection of country residences" and may have been one of the 1905 lots, appears to have been equally unsuccessful. This land reached 180 feet in altitude and was advertised as having "very extensive views of the New Hall Estate".[411] There is no significant development around New Hall, so this was evidently speculative advertising.

409	Ibid.
410	ERO SALE/A1036
411	ERO SALE/A1035

One area that did seem to gain a development foothold at this period was the land around Hillsborough and Lyndhurst Roads. Fifty-five plots here were advertised for sale in June 1907, so the roads themselves had clearly at least been laid out at the time. The district was described as "rapidly developing and becoming a favourite residential part for London businessmen and others", which gives a clue to the advertisement's target audience. It was also said to afford "a grand opportunity for investment" and was "ripe for the erection of bungalows and villa residences". The proximity of the area to local railway stations and the river were both touted as being important factors and special trains to the sale were laid on from London and Southend.[412] Other sales in this area took place in July. Lunch was laid on for prospective purchasers.[413]

Hillsborough and Lyndhurst Roads were subsequently developed, though not properly until the 1920s. It seems likely that it was the 1907 sales which secured the initial investment for them.

Village life

As the new century dawned, parish meetings in Ashingdon continued to be chaired by John Jolly, who remained in the role until 1922, having first been elected to it in 1894. He and J. Burgess were elected as overseers throughout the period 1900-7. As with his chairmanship, Jolly continued to be re-elected as overseer until 1922. Burgess was succeeded in 1908 by George Hart, who was then also repeatedly re-elected until 1922. Fred Hollick, who presumably had connections with the family behind Thomas Hollick's South Fambridge engineering works, was elected as the school manager from 1903 to 1906, when he was succeeded by Walter William Neal of New Hall, South Fambridge, who served in the post until 1917 when he left the parish. James Crawford, son of Hugh, was elected to replace him.[414]

In South Fambridge, Hugh Crawford, by now of South Fambridge Hall, continued to be re-elected as chairman of parish meetings up to and including 1916, the year he died, except for in 1908 when Neal was elected. Crawford was succeeded as chairman in 1917 by Seaman Jefferies, who remained in the role until at least 1919. All three of the above also served as parish overseers, Neal from c.1906-10, Crawford apparently continuously from 1895 to 1916, and Jefferies from 1911 to at least 1919. James Crawford also served as overseer, from 1917 until 1928. Parish business was usually of a very local nature, for example in October 1906 when £5 was authorised to be spent on the repair of footpath bridges and stiles between the ferry and "the lower Beckney road" (now Lower Road).[415]

---

412   ERO D/DTo E13
413   ERO D/DTo E14 & E15
414   ERO DJ 126/1/1
415   ERO D/DS 313/19/1

At the church in 1900 Rev. Harry Campbell Bourne was succeeded as rector of the combined parishes by Rev. John Imrie, who first appears in the parish meeting minutes for Ashingdon in 1903.[416] According to Roper, Imrie died in 1906. He was succeeded in that year by Rev. William Henry Barnes. Barnes also served a six-year incumbency, until 1912 when he was replaced by Rev. John Shaw Bryers.

The provision of mains water to Ashingdon was a key topic which cropped up in the early years of the 20th century. Villagers were presumably then using streams, wells and standpipes, as happened elsewhere. In 1906 the Ashingdon parish meeting passed a motion which was "carried by a majority of 3 that the water be laid on in the parish, the District Council first letting us know the cost". The matter rumbled on though and it was at least 1914 before mains water was provided. In that year there was a joint meeting between parish members and Southend Waterworks representatives, with an initial 3,370-yards stretch being planned from "Bishop's Farm" to Ashingdon School and a second section earmarked for The Chase.[417] It is not clear where Bishop's Farm was, but the description suggests that it was somewhere on Ashingdon Road.

The increasing amount of development led to continued population growth. In 1890 Ashingdon's Poor Rate Valuation List had just 36 property owners on it; by 1911 this number had risen to 103.[418] The 1910 Finance Act Reference Book for Ashingdon records the ownership of the key properties. Mary H. Balls owned and occupied 23 acres of land and buildings at Smith's Farm, while Seaman Jeffries occupied part of the building and Walter Henry Mann also occupied some property there which belonged to J. Pearson. John Jolly occupied 210 acres of land and buildings at Moon's Farm, which was owned by Rashleigh & Co. Pulpits was still part-owned by the Vicar of Kew, another part being owned by Jon Freeman. Seaman Jeffries occupied 23 acres there too. George J. Brown owned and occupied five acres at Crick's Land. 186 acres of land and buildings at Beckney Farm were owned by T.W. Offin junior of Clement's Hall in Hockley, but occupied by William P. Burles. Another 69 of Offin's acres at Beckney were occupied by Rick Berry. Beckney Wood was owned and "occupied" by Neville J. Hine. Ashingdon Hall was split between several owners: W.J. Meeking owned and farmed 50 acres of land there; Charles Weight owned land and buildings; Essex County Council owned part of the agricultural land; and J.W. Culver occupied another part of the property. E.W. Ruegg owned and occupied Hill Farm (Rouncefall) and was one of a number of occupiers of land there. William Meeson Taylor, who was living at Doggetts Farm in Rochford, owned 13 acres of Brays Farm in

---

416   ERO DJ 126/1/1
417   Ibid.
418   ERO G/Ro N63

Ashingdon.[419] Meeson died in 1914 and his estates were sold off. The 13 Ashingdon acres, which lay to the north of Brays Lane and east of Ashingdon Road, were described as "pasture land" in the sale particulars.[420]

Charles H. Slow occupied 25 acres at Chamberlain's, while other occupants of land there included Seaman Jeffries and W.J. Meeking. The Wantz Barn from Chamberlain's was being used by John Jolly, while other parts of Chamberlain's were described as "building land". Rev. W.H. Barnes was at Ashingdon Rectory. Part of his glebe land was let to Hugh Crawford. The Burnham Oyster Fishery Company Ltd. owned 18 acres of oyster layings in the River Crouch, presumably off Beckney. Kew Parish also still owned property in the locality.[421]

The bungalow and garden of "Assandune", one of the first modern cottages to be built in Ashingdon, were owned in 1910 by Louisa Whittingham and occupied by Jonathan Whittingham, who was presumably a relative. George Hart occupied Hollick Cottage, which was owned by T.W. Hollick, presumably of the former Fambridge factory. Various members of the Wyeth family also occupied property in the area, including a shop in Ashingdon Road. Raymond Newton owned the eponymous Newton Hall, whose site is now occupied by Newton Hall Gardens. Charles Muers had glasshouses in the parish at "Hockley Nursery".[422] Muers still owned Hockley Nurseries all the way through to at least 1939.[423] Between 1932 and 1939 the premises were recorded as being in White Hart Lane.[424] If they were, then they must have been at the north-eastern end of it, otherwise they would not have been in Ashingdon parish.[425]

James Cutting owned and occupied 32 acres at Old Oak Farm in 1910.[426] The latter was described in Jerram-Burrows history of Ashingdon School as being occupied around the same time by Mr. Jeffries and lying on the east side of Ashingdon Road, south of the church.

The above lists of property owners and occupants show how the fragmentation of the big, historic farming landholdings was underway, with multiple owners on properties that had once been in sole ownership and small plots being developed to make them affordable and bring more people into the area.

---

419 ERO A/R 2/6/28
420 ERO D/DS 526/13
421 ERO A/R 2/6/28
422 Ibid.
423 ERO G/Ro Z23, G/Ro Z24, G/Ro Z203, D/RR 2/6/1/1, D/RR 2/2/3/3, D/RR 2/2/37 & D/RR 2/2/2/3
424 ERO DRR 2/2/3/3, D/RR 2/2/3/7 & D/RR 2/2/2/3
425 ERO A/R 2/6/28
426 Ibid.

Free Church Mission Hall

In 1904 a Mission Hall was built on the eastern side of Fambridge Road at its junction with Ashingdon Road. The Hall's trustees were Alfred Poulton, a furrier, John Jolly, the farmer at Moon's Farm, Hugh Crawford, the farmer at Smith's Farm, and Charles Weight, a fruit merchant. The organisation was founded by Mr. Poulton, a free church evangelist who had come to the area in 1901 from Bethnal Green. Meetings were originally held across the road in Ashingdon School and in the club room at the engineering works at South Fambridge. However, by 1904 the group had grown so much that it needed its own premises. The land for this was donated by Hugh Crawford. The Mission Hall was built of wood, with a corrugated iron roof and a small spire, for an estimated cost of £250. It was to be a free, non-denominational church for local people.

The opening ceremony for the building was reported on in the *Southend Standard* newspaper of 21 April 1904. It was described as "neat and commodious" and took only three months to build. The weather was great and flags and banners were flying. Alfred Poulton, President of the Mission, had, according to the paper, laboured hard for three years with unbounded enthusiasm to get the organisation up-and-running. The opening address was given by George Nokes, a noted Whitechapel evangelist. This was followed by an evening tea which was so well supported "that it taxed the resources of the ladies' committee to the utmost". The building had varnished walls and ceilings and was light and cheerful inside. William Smellie made a brief speech and introduced a hymn and impressed on his audience that there was to be no "class-feeling" in the church, which would be open to people of all backgrounds. Charles Weight, the organisation's secretary, then gave a report on how the church building had come into being. Alfred Poulton gave a financial report, revealing that £80 was still required, though this was reduced to £60 by donations made during the meeting. Several other speakers gave illuminating talks.

A programme of music and songs had taken place at Ashingdon School on 21 March 1902 in connection with the Mission. Chaired by Alfred Poulton, it was billed as a social meeting and featured 22 performances from local people, including Mr. Jolly and Mrs. Wyeth. Performances included a "Nigger Sketch" and a "Nigger Song", titles of their time which would not be acceptable now.[427]

---

427   ERO D/DS 463/15

Figure 52: The Free Church Mission Hall, showing the rural nature of the area.

According to recollections in Jerram-Burrows' Ashingdon School centenary book, Hugh Crawford and his family were involved in a collision with a bus on Ashingdon Hill in 1916 and he died a few days later. He is buried at St Andrew's.

The Mission Hall continued to maintain close connections with Ashingdon School, where its community had first met. In 1923-5, for example, infant school pupils were taught in the Mission Hall due to overcrowding.

The Fambridge Colony

In 1906 what became known as "the Fambridge Colony" was set up in Thomas Hollick's redundant engineering factory buildings. This was a group of otherwise unemployed London men who had been found employment as part of a centrally funded scheme to fix some serious breaches in the sea walls across the river in North Fambridge which had been caused by a major storm in November 1897. Several former factory workers' cottages in South Fambridge were rented for the men as well. A Scot called William Wilkie Scotland was appointed as superintendent to manage the venture. He lived for the duration in what is now Aero Lodge, a bungalow in Crane Court Drive.

In March 1906 the factory premises and cottages were adapted to house 180 men. The factory buildings were converted into dormitories, a mess room, a day room and an office. There was also a kitchen and some storage space there. Each of the cottages was configured to house 12 men, with a zinc bath and water pumped from a well. One cottage was later converted into a full wash house, with extra baths. Conditions were basic – and there were complaints from some of the earliest arrivals about the domestic arrangements and food provision – but the scheme offered accommodation, employment and training for those who would otherwise have had none of those things.

By April, there were 60 men on the site. This quickly rose to around 150. They were provided with entertainment by local people and a lecture on the history of sea walls. They were also provided with a billiard table and a piano. In the summer, they were encouraged to cultivate gardens and they were given cricket facilities on rented land.

Colonists were ferried daily across the river to carry out repairs to the sea walls. Sometimes they had to walk as much as three miles to get to the repair site. They were, at least, provided with high leather boots and, in the winter, oilskin capes and leggings, but it was challenging work in tough conditions, with the ever-present threat of the next tide wiping out the work they had done.

There were also issues between the colonists and the superintendent. The latter was twice accused of hitting the men, while the colonists for their part were often unwisely tempted by the proximity of *The Anchor* inn on the South Fambridge side of the river and *The Ferry Boat* inn on the North Fambridge side. At one point the men went on strike and an inquiry was held which led to 14 of them leaving. Issues with the engineer, the contractor and a general unwillingness to get engaged with the work also dogged the project.

In January 1907, Scotland was superseded as superintendent of the works by Hubert Holland. Holland oversaw the completion of the work, which ended in mid-July. The colony was formally closed at the end of that month.

The colony project was a bit of an experiment and encountered several problems, but ultimately it succeeded in its main aims of repairing the sea wall and finding work for some of London's unemployed.[428]

Figure 53: Inside one of the colony buildings

---

428 Information in this section is taken from Beryl A. Board's article 'The Fambridge Colony: an experiment in land reclamation by unemployed Londoners, 1906-7' in *Essex Archaeology & History (Transactions)*, 3rd Series, volume xviii (1987), pp.75-87.

South Fambridge Airfield

In 1909 South Fambridge became the unlikely location for Britain's first airfield.

According to Graham Smith, author of *Essex and its Race for the Skies*, the driving force behind the venture was a multi-talented maverick called Noel Pemberton Billing, who had a varied career as an actor, author, inventor, yacht dealer, policeman and MP. He was also a leading aircraft designer and aviation pioneer at a time when flying was in its infancy. Inspired by the feats of the Wright Brothers, London-born Billing built a glider and a kite before moving to Burnham-on-Crouch in 1908 to try his hand at aircraft design. His upper-middle-class background and his family connections enabled him to finance the purchase of the abandoned factory/colony site in South Fambridge for the creation of what he called a "Colony of British Aerocraft", where he envisaged that he and fellow aviation pioneers would be able to build and test their own machines. The low, flat marshland seemed ideal for an airfield, whilst the abandoned factory buildings could be used as engineering and storage sheds. The calm, straight waters of the River Crouch also offered the opportunity for the launch of waterplanes.

Figure 54: South Fambridge from across the river, showing towards the left the curved roof of Billing's aircraft hangar and associated adjacent buildings; St Thomas Road and The Anchor Inn can also be seen (centre and right)

Billing took possession of the site by February 1909 and "The Fambridge Flight Grounds" were featured in editions of *Flight* magazine and the *Illustrated London News* that same month. Billing also founded his own aviation journal, *Aerocraft*, in March, in which to publicise and report on the activities there. He took copies of this journal and a scale model of the Colony to the first-ever Aero & Motor-Boat Exhibition at Olympia that month to help with the publicity and to discuss his project with fellow enthusiasts. Amongst those he met were Eric C. Gordon England, who became the Colony's manager, and the aviation pioneers José Weiss and Frederick Handley Page. The latter's eponymous company became a noted name in subsequent decades for its production of heavy bombers and large airliners. Billing also met Richard Lascelles, a motorcycle dealer, at Olympia. Lascelles set up a spare parts service in one of the Colony workshops at South Fambridge, identifying an obvious business opportunity, as many of the early aircraft used motorcycle engines in their design. Gerald Leake, a pilot for Weiss, and H. Seton-Karr, who had a biplane built for him by Howard T. Wright Bros. Ltd. of Battersea, were other key contacts. Billing changed the Colony's name to "The Association of British Aerocraft" and the above pioneers were joined a few months later by another early aviator, Robert Macfie, who brought a monoplane to the site.

Figure 55: A close-up of the airfield buildings

Unfortunately, however, the venture's success was very short-lived. Seton-Karr and Billing managed some short hops in their aircraft, but a wet summer and the marshy ground combined to make taxi-ing and take-off manoeuvres very challenging. There were a number of minor accidents as a result. Gradually, everyone lost faith in the project and left to try their luck elsewhere, so that by November 1909 there was only Billing left. The last *Aerocraft* journal was published in January/February 1910 and then Billing himself temporarily abandoned the pursuit of flying for a yacht-selling business in Southampton.

He was to reappear in aviation in 1914, however, when he founded a company called "Pemberton Billing Ltd" and built a "Supermarine" flying boat at Southampton. He sold the company in 1916 and it was renamed "Supermarine Aviation Works Ltd" by its new owner. Supermarine went on to make the Spitfire, one of the most iconic aircraft of the Second World War. Billing had proposed the use of aircraft for military purposes during his time at South Fambridge and he was a leading advocate of this when he was an MP during the First World War, so it was fitting that the Spitfire was produced by the company he founded.

A memorial commemorating Billing's South Fambridge airfield was unveiled in the village on 20 February 2009 by the Airfields of Britain Conservation Trust, a hundred years to the day after its first mention in *Flight* magazine. Carolyn Grace, a noted pilot, flew a Spitfire overhead during the unveiling ceremony, acknowledging Billing's connections with both South Fambridge and the Supermarine company.[429] Pemberton Field, a modern housing estate, is named after the airfield pioneer.

Figure 56: The 1909 memorial which commemorates South Fambridge airfield

---

429   A13442 Box 1

Billing's departure from South Fambridge did not quite mark the end of the story of aviation in the village. In 1913 two local boatbuilders, J.J. Talbot and W.B. Quick, who had evidently been inspired by the pioneer airman, built a waterplane in one of Billing's disused sheds with the help of a noted London engineer called Albert Pink. Their plane was launched on the River Crouch in 1914, but it was unfortunately no more successful than Billing's "Colony" venture. One man drowned during its launch and the plane was hauled out of the river and left to rot on the marshes.[430] Nevertheless, the Talbot-Quick waterplane has a proud place in local history and is remembered on the village sign for South Fambridge.

Figure 57: The launch of the Talbot-Quick waterplane at South Fambridge in 1914

The 1911 Coronation

On 22 June 1911 local people in both parishes celebrated the coronation of King George V.

It was reported in a local newspaper the following day that there had been a children's service in church and that each child had received a souvenir card bearing coloured portraits of the King, the Queen and the Prince of Wales. There was also an afternoon service for everyone, followed by sports and a tea. Proceedings concluded with a bonfire in the evening.[431]

---

430   ERO LIB/E/FAMS4
431   ERO T/P 181/1/11

The Anchor Inn

As mentioned above, the Ferry House/*The Ferry Inn* had been renamed *The Anchor* by the 1860s. It presumably survived in that capacity until the early 20th century, when a new *Anchor Inn* was built up the hill by the entrance to the village in Fambridge Road.

Vernon Clarke, writing in *Walking the Seawalls of Essex*, observes that *The Anchor* was "a surprisingly large building to find in such an isolated position". He adds that: "It was built in 1912 by brewers who had heard that a bridge was going to be built over the river here, but the bridge was never built".

It is also possible that the arrival of Hollick's engineering factory, and the growth of the village occasioned by that and the subsequent schemes of the Fambridge Colony and Noel Billing's airfield, made a new pub look an attractive proposition to those behind the venture.

Figure 58: South Fambridge, showing The Anchor Inn (right) in the early 20th century

The building was demolished *c.*2004 and its site is now occupied by the Maritime Mews apartments.

Education

In 1903 there were still just two classrooms at Ashingdon School and one of those was divided by a curtain. This arrangement must have been a challenge for pupils and teachers, as no doubt each class could hear the other's lessons. There were 50-60 pupils on the register and the headmistress was Miss Sarah Rolfe.

School attendance improved in the first decade of the 20th century and growing class sizes combined with this to require the construction of an extension to the original building. Some children were accommodated in the Mission Hall over the road while this work was going on. A wooden classroom was also built at this time.

Services to the building were still fairly basic: water was obtained from a pump; oil lamps were used for lighting; and a coal fire was used for heating. Children wrote on slates rather than on paper, though they were allowed to spend their playtimes and mealtimes in Fambridge Road, which shows how little traffic was using it in those days.

Figure 59: Ashingdon Hill, showing schoolchildren coming home from school in the early 20th century

Around 1910 the schoolchildren played cricket on a field on the eastern side of the junction of Ashingdon and Canewdon Roads. An old tithe barn there – presumably the aforementioned Wantz Barn and a survivor from the original Chamberlain's Farm – was used as a cricket pavilion.

The First World War

The First World War saw several aerial attacks on nearby Southend by Zeppelin airships and Gotha bombers. Ashingdon and South Fambridge do not appear to have suffered too badly, but many local people fought on the front line or gave their time for community service at home.

A surviving letter from "Beek", thought to be Blanche, the fiancée of Eldred Bentall, whose family had started farming in the area, gives a flavour of what it was like locally during the war. Written on embossed "Ashingdon Hall" notepaper and addressed to Miss J. Bentall at Brick House Farm in Leigh (which stood where Leigh fire station is now), the letter dates from 21 August 1917. In it, Beek writes as follows: "I thought our airmen did splendidly in keeping the raiders from London, although it was a great pity they could not keep them off Southend".[432]

There are war memorials to those who lost their lives during the war in both the chancel of St Andrew's church and in the Ashingdon & East Hawkwell Memorial Hall. Amongst those commemorated are the pilot, Captain Henry Clifford Stroud, who was killed in a mid-air collision with Captain A.B. Kynock over Shotgate, near Wickford, on 7 March 1918.

---

[432] ERO D/DS 509/14

THE PERIOD BETWEEN THE WARS

Property Development and Ownership

Land sales and property development continued after the war, at times with almost indecent haste.

In September 1919, 14 acres of land at Trinity Wood, "on the New Hall Estate", were put up for sale and were advertised, as was now common, as "affording many sites for the erection of country Villas or Bungalows which are in great demand". The land, which was being sold by Charles Futvoye Gold, had frontages to the main roads and was advertised as being pleasant and picturesque, and only a 15-minute walk to Hockley station (presumably a brisk one!). Poultry- or game-rearing were other suggested usages for it. Logs, posts and firewood were also for sale.[433] The 14 acres were evidently sold to C.W. Neville.[434] By 1928, however, Trinity Wood was in the ownership of Arthur F. Taylor.[435] He was still there in 1936.[436]

In February 1920 three plots on "the New Hall Estate in South Fambridge", in what is now Lower Road, were marketed for sale by auction at the Hotel Victoria in Southend. As with the pre-war promotion of this estate, not much building work subsequently took place, so the speculative development of it was evidently once again unsuccessful.[437] Attempts to develop it evidently lingered on, however, for by c.1928 the "New Hall Building Estate" was in the ownership of Ernest Hocking.[438]

As for the historic properties, Moon's Farm, which had been owned by C.E. Rashleigh and occupied by John Jolly in 1915, was in 1922 in the ownership of Henry Knightbridge and the occupation of William and Hugh Bentall. The latter were major farmers in the Rochford area and also farmed Chamberlain's Marshes in Ashingdon. By 1925 the Bentalls owned some of the land at Moon's, John Wall owned buildings, a shop and a dairy there, and Daisy Mercer owned land and buildings. Wall also owned Moon's Cottages.[439] By 1928 Moons Farm (farmhouse) and buildings were in the ownership and occupation of Alice E. Mercer, presumably a relative of Daisy's.[440] The farmhouse, outbuildings and 29 acres of land were offered for sale by auction in June 1931 by Mrs. E.A. Mercer. The farmhouse was described as old-fashioned and gabled, and contained four bedrooms, three reception

---

433   ERO D/F 36/5/48
434   ERO G/Ro Z55
435   ERO D/RR 2/6/1/1
436   ERO D/RR 2/2/3/7
437   ERO D/DGs B103
438   ERO D/RR 2/6/1/1
439   ERO T/P 181/1/11, G/Ro Z23, G/Ro Z24 & G/Ro Z203
440   ERO D/RR 2/6/1/1

rooms and a bathroom. Mains water was laid on, but sewage was handled via a cesspool. The outbuildings had various uses – including stables, cattle sheds and a "rabbitry" – and some of them were thatched. The land was by now characteristically advertised as being suitable for a building estate or for the use of piggeries or poultry. The property sold post-auction to Victor Oliver of Weston Road (presumably the Southend one) for £1,050, just under the reserve of £1,100.[441]

"Harrogate Farm", which was presumably what had been Smith's, was owned and occupied from at least 1915 to c.1928 by George Kipling.[442] In 1936 it was occupied by L.J. Maylin.[443] In 1939 it was occupied by Edward Walton.[444]

Pulpits was owned in 1915 by the Vicar of Kew but occupied by Seaman Jeffries. In 1922-8, however, it was in the ownership of G.E. Wardell and occupied by Herbert Henry Wardell, a development which severed the parish of Kew's long ties with the property.[445] Herbert Wardell was still the occupier in 1939.[446] The Wardells may have been related to Rev. William Wardell, curate of All Saints, South Fambridge, in the 1860s.

Beckney Farm was occupied by Edward Pratt in 1915, and owned and occupied by him in 1922-8.[447] Pratt also farmed some land at Brick House Farm in South Fambridge in 1928.[448]

Crick's Land was owned by George Frederick Brown 1915-25, while Beckney Wood was owned by Neville Joseph Hine over roughly the same period.[449] Hine sold it to Henry William Blake in 1923. Blake retained ownership until his death in 1945, often letting it to tenants, as he was not resident locally. It passed on his death, to his widow, Zillah.[450]

Ashingdon Hall was owned and occupied by William Thomas Meekings in 1915, but much of the land was let to tenant farmers. By 1919, however, it was in the ownership of Edgar Imray, with the multiple tenancies of land and buildings continuing.[451] Imray still had it c.1928.[452] He also owned the Wantz Barn, which was tenanted by Hubert Belton in 1925. John Herbert Wyeth also owned and occupied land at Ashingdon Hall, as did Charles Weight, until he was bought out by John Wall. By 1925 Imray had sold his portion of it to

---

441   ERO D/F 36/14/11
442   ERO T/P 181/1/11, G/Ro Z23, G/Ro Z24, G/Ro Z203 & D/RR 2/6/1/1
443   ERO D/RR 2/2/3/7
444   ERO D/RR 2/2/2/3
445   ERO T/P 181/1/11, G/Ro Z23, G/Ro Z24, G/Ro Z203 & D/RR 2/6/1/1
446   ERO D/RR 2/2/12/3
447   ERO T/P 181/1/11, G/Ro Z23, G/Ro Z24, G/Ro Z203 & D/RR 2/6/1/1
448   ERO D/RR 2/6/1/1
449   ERO T/P 181/1/11, G/Ro Z23, G/Ro Z24 & G/Ro Z203
450   ERO D/DTo T14
451   ERO G/Ro Z23, Z24, G/Ro Z55 & G/Ro Z203
452   ERO D/RR 2/6/1/1

Belton.[453] Eric L. Wyeth owned some land at Ashingdon Hall c.1928.[454] Thomas Smith and William Beehag are both listed (separately) as being resident at the Hall in 1932.[455]

John Wall had purchased the "Wantz Farm Field" in 1918. Imray bought the "Assandune" bungalow at the same time. He still owned it in 1925, though it was occupied by Eleanor Priestley.[456] By 1932 it was in the occupation of Frank Priestley.[457]

Rouncefall was owned and occupied by E.W. Ruegg until c.1919, but was in the ownership and occupation of Herbert Bacon by 1922.[458] The latter was still there in 1939.[459]

Old Oak Farm was still owned by James Cutting 1915-22, but let to various tenants. By 1925 it was owned by Eliza Turner, who lived there with George Franklin. Some agricultural land in Brays Lane was owned by Essex County Council but farmed by Frederick Smoothy. Reginald Gordon Bates owned and occupied part of Brays Farm, 1915-25. Hollick Cottage, later renamed "Hollick Lodge", was still owned by T.W. Hollick and occupied by George Hart until at least 1919. Hart was both owner and occupier by 1922.[460] Emily Wash had evidently purchased it from him by c.1928.[461] She was still there in 1939.[462] Hollick Lodge stood where 430 Ashingdon Road is now.[463]

In 1932-6 Walter Charles Vincent owned Beehive Farm and George Edwards owned Ashingdon Hall Poultry Farm.[464] The location of Beehive Farm is confusingly listed as Ellesmere Road in the 1932 rating and valuation returns for Ashingdon, but in Canewdon View Road for the 1936 and 1939 returns.[465] Other sources suggest it was in the latter. Walter married Emily Maidment and the couple had a small dairy herd. Their daughter, Lorna, delivered milk from the herd in a milk churn attached to the handlebars of her bicycle.[466]

It can be seen from the above that the large historic farms of Ashingdon Hall, Moon's and Rouncefall were increasingly being sub-divided and sold to multiple owners. The

---

453   ERO G/Ro Z23, Z24, G/Ro Z55 & G/Ro Z203
454   ERO D/RR 2/6/1/1
455   ERO D/RR 2/2/3/3
456   ERO T/P 181/1/11 & G/Ro Z203
457   ERO D/RR 2/2/3/3
458   ERO G/Ro Z23, G/Ro Z24 & G/Ro Z203
459   ERO D/RR 2/2/3/7 & D/RR 2/2/2/3
460   ERO G/Ro Z23, G/Ro Z24 & G/Ro Z203
461   ERO D/RR 2/6/1/1
462   ERO D/RR 2/2/2/3
463   ERO D/DS 365/1/14
464   ERO D/RR 2/2/3/3
465   ERO D/RR 2/2/3/3, D/RR 2/2/3/7 & D/RR 2/2/2/3
466   Rochford District Community Archive: Canewdon View Road, Ashingdon
http://www.rochforddistricthistory.org.uk/page_id__337.aspx

developers' dreams of creating small residences and farms in the area were fast becoming a reality.

Meanwhile, in South Fambridge, Rectory Farm was sold by Rev. Bryers in 1918 to "the present tenant", John Jolly, for £3,400.[467] Brick House Farm and 50 acres of grazing land were sold for £1,500 in the same year to John William Rollin.[468] Brick House Farm was owned and occupied *c.*1928 by James William Rollin junior. He also farmed "Rectory Marshes."[469] James Rollin was still the occupier of Brick House Farm in 1939.[470]

The Ferry House and Thomas Hollick's old factory site were owned in 1920 by Plastic Cements Ltd. The house was occupied by George Pearson, while the factory hosted a drying shed, paint shop and stores. The company also owned numbers 19-22 St Thomas Road. Another major landowner that year was Arthur Catton, who lived in Aero Lodge and owned numbers 1-18 and 23-28 St Thomas Road, and a bungalow opposite *The Anchor*. He also farmed some of the land at Ferry House and Brick House Farm. William Bentall owned a separate portion of land at Ferry House, as well as South Fambridge Hall and the cottages opposite All Saints church. James Crawford lived at the Hall and farmed Bentall's land at Ferry Farm.[471] He was still occupying both places in 1939.[472] It would appear that the historic South Fambridge Hall was replaced by the current building *c.*1920.[473]

Bentall also owned 29-32 St Thomas Road. All the St Thomas Road properties were occupied by single men, presumably workers at the factory. *The Anchor* was owned by Truman, Hanbury & Buxton, a giant in the pub trade. The landlord was Henry Balls. John Rider Jolly owned and occupied Rectory Farm, plus part of Glebe Farm. Thomas Taylor owned and lived at New Hall. Smith Brothers Ltd. operated some oyster layings in the Crouch until at least 1939.[474]

By 1924 George Robert Whybrow was living at Ferry House and the Plastic Cements company had sold this and its other landholdings. Arthur Catton and the Bentalls retained their property ownership and most of their local farming operations, while *The Anchor* was still owned by Truman's but tenanted by Harry Arnold.[475] *The Anchor* was owned in 1928 by T.W. Arnold and occupied by Henry William (presumably "Harry") Arnold from

---

467   ERO T/P 181/1/11
468   ERO T/P 181/5/11 & D/DS 313/19/1
469   ERO D/RR 2/6/1/1
470   ERO D/RR 2/2/12/3
471   ERO G/Ro Z55 & D/RR 2/2/3/3
472   ERO D/RR 2/2/12/3
473   Rochford District Community Archive: A Lost Fambridge Crawford
http://www.rochforddistricthistory.org.uk/page/a_lost_fambridge_crawford
474   ERO G/Ro Z55, D/RR 2/2/3/3, D/RR 2/2/3/7 & D/RR 2/2/3/3
475   ERO G/Ro Z55, D/RR 2/6/1/1 & D/RR 2/2/3/3

at least then until after the Second World War.[476] John Rider Jolly still owned and occupied Rectory Farm and part of Glebe Farm. Jesse Bridge owned and occupied New Hall between 1924 and 1932.[477] Robert Charles Mays was at New Hall Farm in 1936.[478] Mrs. Thomas was there in 1939.[479]

By 1928 there had been some slight changes in ownership of the properties in St Thomas Road. Arthur Catton now owned numbers 3-28, while numbers 1 and 2 were owned by John Bridge, possibly a relative of Jesse's. Bridge lived at number 1 and operated a shop from it. William Bentall still owned numbers 29-32.[480] In 1936 Ernest J. Crowley was operating the shop at 1 St Thomas Road.[481] By 1939 it had passed to John Richards.[482]

Rectory Farm was owned in 1928 by the executors of John H. Jolly and occupied by Harriet Jolly.[483] The latter was still there in 1936.[484] By 1939 it had passed to her sons.[485]

Arthur Hugo Kilner owned the South Fambridge works (factory, buildings and stores).[486] By 1932 George R.D Kilner was occupying the factory house and buildings.[487] He was still at the Factory House in 1936, but the factory itself was occupied by Mr. R. Chittock.[488]

By 1936 the Ferry House was in the occupation of Nelson J. Rowley and Aero Lodge was in the occupation of Sidney F. Brown.[489] The latter was still in situ in 1939, but Mrs. J Hayward was occupying the Ferry House.[490]

Homefield Farm is also mentioned for the first time in the 1928 Rating and Valuation Lists for both Ashingdon and South Fambridge. It was owned and occupied by William Ernest Cheek and Albert Henry Cheek.[491] They were still there in 1936.[492]

In 1928, there was also a Fairview Nursery in South Fambridge parish.[493]

---

476 ERO D/RR 2/6/1/1, D/DS 2/2/3/7, D/DS 2/2/12/3 & D/RR 2/2/12/9
477 ERO G/Ro Z55, D/RR 2/6/1/1 & D/RR 2/2/3/3
478 ERO D/RR 2/2/3/7
479 ERO D/RR 2/2/12/3
480 ERO D/RR 2/6/1/1
481 ERO D/RR 2/2/3/7
482 ERO D/RR 2/2/12/3
483 ERO D/RR 2/6/1/1
484 ERO D/RR 2/2/3/7
485 ERO D/RR 2/2/12/3
486 ERO D/RR 2/6/1/1
487 ERO D/RR 2/2/3/3
488 ERO D/RR 2/2/3/7
489 Ibid.
490 ERO D/RR 2/2/12/3
491 ERO D/RR 2/6/1/1
492 ERO D/RR 2/2/3/7
493 ERO D/RR 2/6/1/1

The Ashingdon Park Estate

Despite continuing attempts to develop the area, Ashingdon and South Fambridge remained substantially rural and undeveloped until the 1920s. Their historic cores were largely untouched and the majority of their land was agricultural and home to scattered farms. Only the school and a few odd cottages had appeared to change the local historic landscape. This began to change, however, in the interwar period with the advent of the Ashingdon Park Estate on land to the east of Fambridge Road and the north of Canewdon Road. This had been one of the unsold lots in the 1905 Smith's and Chamberlain's sale and was then remarketed on its own in the 1907 sale of land at Hillsborough and Lyndhurst Roads (see above). During the 1920s additional areas were laid out in what became Arundel, Radnor, Ulverston, Ellesmere and Ethelbert Roads. All became important sites for what was called "plotland" development.

Plotlands were one of the most significant types of development in the inter-war period in south-east England. They were small, regular-sized plots of land, often laid out in a grid pattern, which were sold by entrepreneurs who had purchased a tract of farmland relatively cheaply following late-19th century agricultural depression and were bought and developed by individuals as sites for holiday homes, country retreats or smallholdings. Cheap train tickets and free refreshments were often laid on by the vendors to attract would-be purchasers, many of whom came from London in search of the chance to enjoy rural living. Each plot was developed in a unique way by each owner and their development took place at different paces, leading to a classic overall appearance of either grass or earthen tracks sparsely populated by a variety of self-built bungalows, sheds, chalets and empty plots, which between them gradually took on the form of ruralised suburban development. The plotlands and their buildings were tolerated by local authorities until the post-war period and were at their peak in the 1920s and 1930s.

A second 1920s plotland in Ashingdon was laid out to the north of The Chase and the west of Ashingdon Road. This and the Ashingdon Park Estate both retain their classic plotland appearance.

Figure 60: Plotland development in The Chase, looking towards the bottom of Ashingdon Hill

Figure 61: The reverse view from Ashingdon Hill, showing the three buildings seen in the background in the previous picture; the building at top-left is 'Hillcrest', a now-lost but well-remembered house

Figure 62: A now-lost plotland cottage further up Ashingdon Hill, c.1926

These developments began the process of changing Ashingdon from a rural community into a suburban one. They also brought in people from outside the area. South Fambridge village, for the time being, remained largely untouched.

3rd Edition Ordnance Survey Map

The 3rd Edition Ordnance Survey Map of 1924 (surveyed 1919-20) for South Fambridge shows the "South Fambridge Works (Plastic Cement)", St Thomas Road and *The Anchor* Hotel.

In Ashingdon, the Free Church Mission Hall is shown as the "U.F. Ch." (United Free Church). The plotlands to the north of The Chase and the west of Ashingdon Hill have several houses on them, while those to the north of Canewdon Road and the east of Fambridge Road are shown in embryonic state, with the roads laid out but no properties erected. The nearby road junction of Canewdon Road and Ashingdon Road is laid out differently from how it is now and there is a building shown on the eastern side of the junction, which is probably the Wantz Barn.

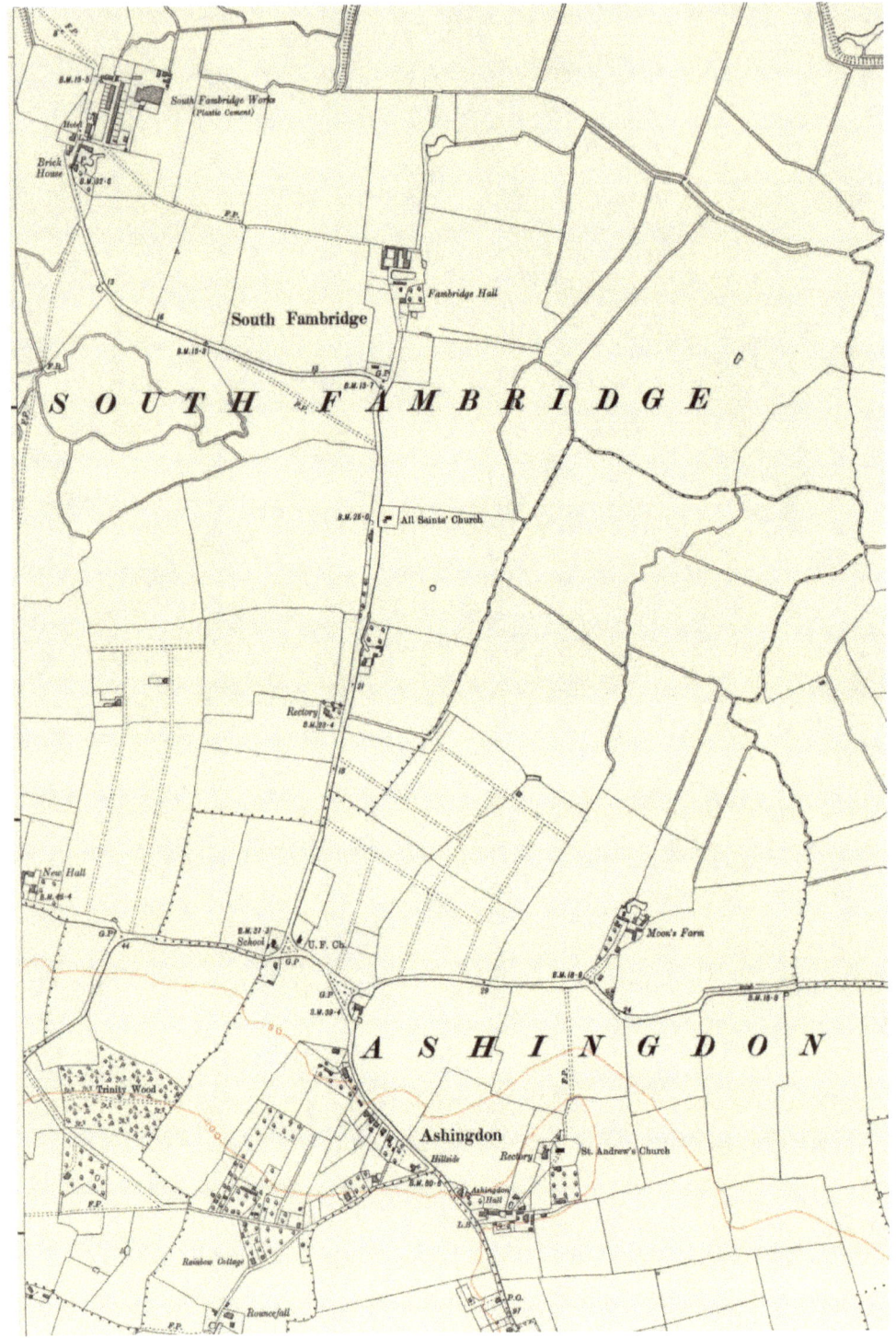

Figure 63: Third edition OS Map 1924

Village Life

In 1918 a case of spotted fever was reported in a girl who had recently been in service in Ashingdon.[494] Thankfully, this does not appear to have developed into a major event. This was just as well, because the plotlands and the other developments were between them increasing the local population, which in turn meant that more services and infrastructure were required and more was expected of the local authorities.

By 1922 the population had evidently grown sufficiently for William Price to have opened a shop, Ashingdon Stores.[495] Three years later, there were two other shops in the parish, both on the main road, one owned by Harry Croft, the other by Charles Hadley. The smithy in Greensward Lane, by now in the ownership of Frederick Payne, may also have still been operating.[496] Ashingdon Stores was being run by Henry Ford in 1932. There was also a shop at "Alma" in Canewdon Road, run by Charles Alfred Newland, and another one called "The Mascot", run by Gertrude Wagstaff, in Ashingdon Road.[497] Eric Wyeth still had a shop in the area in 1934.[498] This was probably the newsagent and sweet shop that many local people remember which stood in Ashingdon Road, just north of Canewdon View Road.[499] In 1936 W.R. Evans had a shop in Canewdon Road at "The Croft". J. Wall and G. Wall had a dairy and shop, respectively, next door to one another in Ashingdon Road in 1936.[500]

By 1932 Ashingdon was home to Stanley Garage, the village's first motor car establishment, which stood at the top of Ashingdon Hill opposite Church Road.[501] It is believed to have been built single-handedly by Eric Gregory, a civil engineer. Gregory's daughter, Elsie, married John Coolbear, and the couple ran the garage for many years. Before *The Victory Inn* and the Memorial Hall were built, it also operated as a community centre in the evenings.[502] There was another garage in Greensward Lane, South Fambridge, in 1932, run by Ernest A. Hocking.[503] Stanley Garage later morphed into Texaco, until the latter was replaced with housing.

The number of residents listed in the Poor Rate returns for Ashingdon rose from 104 in

---

494 ERO T/P 181/1/11
495 ERO G/Ro Z24
496 ERO G/Ro Z203
497 ERO D/RR 2/2/3/3
498 ERO D/J 126/1/1
499 Rochford District Community Archive: http://www.rochforddistricthistory.org.uk/page/canewdon_view_road_-_ashingdon
500 ERO D/RR 2/2/3/7
501 ERO D/RR 2/2/3/3
502 Video footage from John V. Chambers
503 ERO D/RR 2/2/3/3

1915 to 165 in 1925.[504] The figures for South Fambridge were 98 in 1920 and 109 in 1924.[505] As mentioned above, classes at the infants school had grown so much by 1923 that from then until 1925 some pupils were taught at the Mission Hall. Southend Waterworks were active in the area in the early 1920s.[506]

Figures 64 & 65: Two of the early shops in Ashingdon. Note the notice board advertising development land for sale on the left of the second picture, which dates from c.1922

---

504   ERO G/Ro Z23, G/Ro Z24 & G/Ro Z203
505   ERO G/Ro Z55
506   ERO G/Ro Z24

The 3rd Edition Ordnance Survey Map shows that a Post Office had arrived in the south of the parish by the 1920s, on the west side of Ashingdon Road. The modern Post Office survives today in the same vicinity.

On the Greensward Lane side of the parish a sub-Post Office and shop called Trinity Stores opened up. This was housed in the bungalow now called Holly House at the junction of Greensward Lane and Trinity Wood Road. It was owned *c.*1928-39 by Frederick Payne.[507] In more recent times, it was in the ownership of Gerry and Lily Massey.[508] It appears to have closed by 1981, when it was referred to as "the premises which used to be Trinity Stores".[509]

Figures 66 & 67: Trinity Stores/Holly House, then and now

---

507 ERO D/RR 2/6/1/1, D/RR 2/2/3/3, D/RR 2/2/3/7 & D/RR 2/2/2/3
508 https://www.facebook.com/groups/855872487839281/search/?q=trinity%20stores
509 ERO D/J 126/2/5

Despite the growing population, there were still not many road names in existence, with Ashingdon residents' addresses being given in the returns mostly as house names or estates.[510] This continued well into the 1930s.[511] Golden Cross Road, Nelson Road and Harrogate Road had, however, all appeared by 1925.[512] Crouch View Crescent and Harrogate Drive had both appeared by 1932. There was apparently a shop very close to the former.[513]

The South Fambridge returns of the early 1920s mention New Hall Road, Vincent Road, Cavendish Road, Arundel Road, the Ashingdon Park Estate, the Fairview Estate and Trinity Wood Road. This is the first time that many of these are mentioned in that parish's records.[514] Wellington Road is first mentioned in the Valuation Lists for the parish, c.1928.[515] Clarendon Road and New Park Roads (the latter being essentially the heart of the Fairview Estate) are recorded by 1932.[516] Granville Road had appeared by 1936.[517] As with some streets in Ashingdon, but even more so here, the ambition for the full development of many of these roads does not appear to have been realised. Clarendon and Granville Roads have hardly any development on them, while Vincent Road, which had three residences listed there in 1932, appears to have undergone un-development and is now no more than a track.[518]

Figure 68: Vincent Road has a signpost, but no real road

---

510   ERO G/Ro Z23 & G/Ro Z24
511   ERO D/RR 2/2/3/3
512   ERO G/Ro Z203
513   ERO D/RR 2/2/3/3
514   ERO G/Ro Z55
515   ERO D/RR 2/6/1/1
516   ERO D/RR 2/2/3/3
517   ERO D/RR 2/2/3/7
518   ERO D/RR 2/2/3/3

The long reign of John Jolly as chairman of the Ashingdon parish meetings came to an end in 1922, presumably due to his advancing years. The meeting minutes reveal that he died in 1928 and that his fellow parishioners sent a letter of condolence to his widow. Jolly "was a valuable worker for the Parish and will be greatly missed by many". He was succeeded as chairman in 1923 by Seaman Jeffries of Golden Manor in Ashingdon, a retired farmer who was already chairman of the South Fambridge parish meetings. Jeffries served in the role until c.1927. He also served as overseer for the same period, replacing John Jolly. John Wall, who lived at "Thorndene", replaced George Hart in 1922 as the other overseer for Ashingdon.[519] He was still in the role in 1925.[520] Charles Weight was Ashingdon's representative as school manager until his death in 1924, when he was succeeded by a Mr. Camplin.[521]

In 1927 Rochford Rural District Council invited the local parishes to send representatives to its Rating Authority. Seaman Jeffries and John Wall were appointed to represent Ashingdon. In 1928 Jeffries was superseded by Wall as chairman of the Ashingdon parish meetings and by Horace Edmund Camplin of "Shadingfield" as a Rating Authority representative. Wall was still meetings chairman in 1931.[522]

The South Fambridge parish minutes make the distinction between John Jolly (chairman until 1923) and John Rider Jolly (chairman 1924-6 and parish representative on the Rochford Rural District Rating Authority in 1927). Both were farmers who lived at Rectory Farm, so it is presumed that the latter is the former's son. As well as his long service as a South Fambridge overseer, James Crawford also served as chairman of parish meetings in 1928 and as a second parish representative on the Rating Authority 1927-8. John William Rollin of Brick House Farm replaced John Rider Jolly as Rating Authority representative in 1928. Business discussed at South Fambridge parish meetings in the 1920s included issues with public footpaths, the rejection of a housing scheme proposed by Rochford Rural District Council and a vote in favour of a water main extension.[523] The extension of the water mains in Ashingdon was approved at a meeting of that parish's representatives in 1929.[524]

In 1923 Rev. Bryers left to become rector at Bowers Gifford. He lived there until his death at the age of 70 in 1945.[525] Part of a letter from F.C. Ewing which is held at the ERO

---

519   ERO D/J 126/1/1
520   ERO G/Ro Z203
521   ERO D/J 126/1/1
522   Ibid.
523   ERO D/DS 313/19/1
524   ERO D/J 126/1/1
525   ERO D/CP 1/13 and Basildon History website:
http://www.basildon.com/history/chronology/19201929.html

states that it was Rev. Bryers who planted the trees at the top end of Church Road in Ashingdon.[526]

Bryers was succeeded as incumbent at St Andrew's by Rev. Reginald Williams, who had the task of administering to the spiritual needs of the growing, cosmopolitan population. Rev. Williams first appears in the Ashingdon parish meeting minutes in 1926.[527] A Rev. Ralph Henry Williams is listed in the Poor Rate returns for Ashingdon in 1922.[528] It is presumed that this is an incorrect entry, as "Reginald Henry" are the forenames given for the rector in the Poor Rate returns for South Fambridge in 1924 and for Ashingdon in 1925.[529]

Rev. Williams died in 1931 and was succeeded as rector of Ashingdon with South Fambridge by Rev. John Hampden Thompson. Rev. Thompson oversaw the installation of electric lighting in Ashingdon church, something which Rev. Williams had initiated. He was assisted in this by the churchwardens, Ernest Gaitskell and Henry Harris. The lighting scheme, which was implemented by the County of London Electric Supply Company Limited, was designed by the well-known architect, Sir Charles Nicholson, who lived in Southend.[530] Public electricity and gas supplies were both well-established in Ashingdon by the mid-1930s. South Fambridge had water and electricity, but no gas.[531]

In May 1931 two Ashingdon members of the Rochford-based Peculiar People sect were in trouble with the authorities, when their daughter, Ivy, aged eight, died of diphtheria. Her parents, Mr. & Mrs. Arthur G. Upson, had refused to call the doctor because medical intervention was against the principles of the sect. No action was taken against them, though it was noted that the chances of Ivy surviving would have been good had a doctor been called.[532]

According to Ashingdon Parish Council's website, a regular visitor to the area in the interwar period was the famous author, Rudyard Kipling, who used to stay with his family at a house called "Meadowside" at 185 Greensward Lane. He was presumably a relative of George Kipling, who owned nearby Harrogate Farm in the 1910s and 1920s. Meadowside was in the occupation of Charles Kipling in 1932.[533]

---

526 ERO A13543 Box 2
527 ERO D/J 126/1/1
528 ERO G/Ro Z24
529 ERO G/Ro Z55 & G/Ro Z203
530 ERO D/CF 70/3
531 ERO D/RR 2/2/3/7
532 ERO T/P 181/1/11
533 ERO D/RR 2/2/3/3

The Ashingdon Hall Estate

By the late 1920s another big area of plotlands had begun to appear south of The Chase to the west of Ashingdon Road, around what are now Stanley, Clifton, York, Alexandra and Albert Roads and Albert Close, with the southern boundary marked by what is now Public Footpath 44, which runs behind the houses in the latter two streets. This land was laid out in plots and marketed to potential purchasers perhaps as early as 1920. Again, the extensive views and the suitability of the land to market gardening, fruit growing and poultry rearing were promoted.[534] In around 1924 a Bethany Gospel Hall was erected here, in Clifton Road.[535] By 1925, J. Allen – a land and estate agent from London, whose sale board can be seen in one of the preceding shop photographs – was also promoting the easy access to water mains and bus services on Ashingdon Road.[536]

Technically, this area was – and still is – in Hawkwell parish, but it is so close to the historic centre of Ashingdon at Ashingdon Hall and church, that it feels like it is a core component of the heart of modern Ashingdon. As Ashingdon Parish Council puts it on their website:

"Some of what appears to be Ashingdon is in fact in Hawkwell Parish... The northern part of East Hawkwell is a narrow strip about 450 metres wide which juts into and is almost surrounded by Ashingdon and is as little as 250 metres (275 yards) from Ashingdon's St Andrew's Church, but is 2.5 km (1.5 miles) from Hawkwell's St Mary's Church. That part of northeast Hawkwell is called 'Ashingdon' by all who live there because it is in the village of Ashingdon, being only a few paces across the road and most of the houses and businesses in that part of Hawkwell use Ashingdon as their postal address."

---

534   ERO SALE/B4690
535   Information courtesy Geoff Durham
536   ERO D/DU 665/1/3

Figure 69: Ashingdon Road, looking south from its junction with Stanley Road, showing a sign for Hawkwell parish on the west side of the road and Ashingdon Hall on the east side

Unlike the first 1920s plotlands, the streets there were later formally adopted and regularised by Rochford District Council, a process which included the making up of the roads, the provision of pavements and the laying on of water supply and sewerage facilities. They may look like "normal" streets now, but their layout is the original plotland one. This is best appreciated on a map from above, where the five Roads can be seen to be straight and parallel and, with the exception of Clifton Road, which was opened up to connect with the later Rectory Avenue, petering out at their western ends.

One of the buildings constructed on the estate was what appears to have been Ashingdon's first public house, *The Victory Inn*, which stands on the corner of Ashingdon and Albert Roads. It was open by 1933, when Mrs. Matilda Louisa Oscroft was listed as its publican.[537]

---

537   Pub wiki: *The Victory Inn* https://pubwiki.co.uk/EssexPubs/Ashingdon/victory.shtml

Figure 70: Chapel estate agents, showing The Victory Inn at the left[538]

Leisure & Entertainment

The increasing population needed more things to do, so various activities were soon laid on to keep people entertained.

Postcards survive of Ashingdon Fete, which appears to have been held in the grounds of Ashingdon Rectory.

---

[538] ERO D/DS 483/2

Figure 71: Ashingdon Fete with, probably, Ashingdon Rectory (and a piano) on the left

An event that was often held at shows and fetes at this period, and which was evidently held at Ashingdon, was called "Bowling for the Pig". A description of the event at the parish of Littleton and Harestock in Hampshire reveals that this was essentially a game which consisted of a vertical board about two feet in height which had seven small holes in it at ground level. Each of these holes was about six inches high, numbered from one to seven, and was just wide enough to allow a wooden ball to pass through them. Participants in the game were given three balls and the aim was to roll the balls through the holes to score some points. The maximum possible score was 21 (three balls through the number seven hole). Anyone who scored this would win a live pig. There were presumably smaller prizes for those who managed to score anything else.[539]

---

539   A History of Littleton and Harestock Show: https://www.lhshow.org.uk/show-history

Figure 72: "Bowling for the Pig" at Ashingdon Fete, in front of Ashingdon Rectory

The Fete was still going in 1953, but was held at the King George V Playing Field.[540]

Ashingdon Parish Council's website lists numerous other attractions in the interwar period, including cycle racing, Ashingdon Fair and some tennis courts. Ashingdon Cycle Club had a club house and racing circuit on a large plot of land on the north-east side of the junction of Ashingdon and Canewdon View Roads, where Newton Hall Gardens is now.[541] The club ran a cycling team called "Ashingdon Adders".[542] The team was offered land at the playing field in 1950, but chose to stay at Canewdon View Road.[543]

Cycle racing around local streets also took place, often in conjunction with Ashingdon Fair, which was held at various locations until the King George V Playing Field was in existence and became its permanent home. The tennis courts were off Cavendish Road, behind Beckney Wood House.[544] The latter was owned by the Dennington family in the

---

540 South Essex District Cricket Board: 1953 – Umpires Bribed at Ashingdon
http://www.sedcb.org.uk/yesterdays-our-timeline/1953-ashingdon
541 See, for example, ERO D/RR 2/2/3/3 & D/RR 2/2/3/7
542 Rochford District Community Archive:
http://www.rochforddistricthistory.org.uk/page/canewdon_view_road_-_ashingdon
543 ERO D/J 126/1/2
544 Ashingdon Parish Council: The History of Ashingdon https://ashingdonparishcouncil.gov.uk/history/

late 1920s and 1930s.[545] Rate returns show that there were also some tennis courts on Ashingdon Road, owned by Ernest Turner, who lived in the adjacent Tennis Lodge.[546]

Education

The number of children at Ashingdon School reached 100 in the mid-1920s, another sign that the village's population was growing. Facilities were still quite basic, however, with earth closet lavatories on the other side of the playground and no mains drainage.

As pupil numbers continued to rise, the Mission Hall was used formally for the teaching of infants in the 1920s, while the school building was home to junior pupils.

The school bell was used to summon children to school in the morning and there are several accounts of dawdlers having to run to make it in time. The advent of bus services in the area in the early 1930s must have been a boon to parents, children and teachers alike.

The headmistress, Mrs. Rolfe, left the school in 1933 and was replaced by Mr., later Captain, Cecil G. Ford. There was accommodation for 136 children at the time, with 130 on the register. Jerram-Burrows writes of Mrs. Rolfe that she was "a dedicated teacher; deeply interested in the welfare of the children".

Her successor encountered a number of challenges when he first arrived, including inadequate desk space for children, their books and furniture being in a poor state, and coal fires being used for heating, except in the wooden classroom, which had a combustion stove. He went to the County Education Office to get an inspector down very shortly after taking up his role, going over the heads of the school managers, which by his own admission made him unpopular with them. Nevertheless, he oversaw a complete overhaul of school activities, including improvements to the premises, the introduction of new processes and the addition of new subjects to the curriculum.

New equipment was funded as a result of the school inspection and Mr. Ford ultimately became a popular head teacher with his pupils, introducing looms for spinning and weaving classes, which were extremely well-attended, and art sessions in the local countryside. He also used maths lessons to encourage children to produce a map of the local area. Better lavatories were also provided, as was central heating, whilst the introduction of microscopes helped children with their science studies.

In 1937 schooling in the area was reorganised. Ashingdon became a Junior Mixed and Infants School and all pupils older than 10 years and nine months were transferred to the newly built Rochford Senior School.[547]

---

545   See, for example, ERO D/RR 2/2/3/3 & D/RR 2/2/3/7
546   ERO D/RR 2/2/3/3 & D/RR 2/2/2/3
547   ERO TS 619

Ashingdon Parish Council

A parish meeting on 2 March 1931 proposed the establishment of a parish council for Ashingdon. After a postponement to allow residents to consider the issue, the decision to proceed was approved by 20 votes to zero on 24 March. Elections duly took place and there were seven candidates for five places: Frederick Payne (who lived at The Forge and owned Trinity Stores), William George Bevans, John William Brittain, Jessop Morrison, Eric Wilfred Lawson Wyeth, E.H. Mayhew and John Wall. The first five in the above list were elected. John Wall, the parish meeting chairman and a prominent local landowner, surprisingly received the fewest votes. Mr. Payne was elected as parish council chairman and served in that capacity until 1936, when he informed his fellow councillors that he was planning to leave the district (although he was still there in 1938).[548]

Early business for the new local authority, which first met on 11 August 1931, included discussions about the adoption of the Lighting and Watching Act 1833 which, amongst other things, gave parish councils the authority to pay for their own police forces and provide street lighting. An early decision was to sell the land and three cottages which the parish owned in Rochford.[549] The condition of local footpaths, roads, ditches and signposts was also discussed, along with the provision of a public post box near Ashingdon School. Ditches being blocked with rubbish and overflowing into local properties was a regular problem well into the late 1930s.[550] This was especially true on the Ashingdon Park Estate and in The Chase, where in February 1937 manhole covers were popping up due to blocked ditches and associated flooding.[551] Council meetings took place in St Andrew's Church Hall, which is first mentioned in the Valuation Lists for Ashingdon c.1928.[552]

---

548   ERO D/J 126/1/1, D/J 126/2/1 & D/J 126/4/1
549   Ibid.
550   ERO D/J 126/2/1
551   ERO D/J 126/1/1
552   ERO D/J 126/1/1 & D/RR 2/6/1/1

Figure 73: Ashingdon Church Hall

H.A. Stock was appointed as clerk to the parish council and served in that capacity until 1934. Councillors Brittain and Morrison were appointed as School Managers, but resigned in 1932 and were replaced by Councillors Bevans and Wyeth. The council regularly received correspondence from the Ashingdon and District Ratepayers Association, which had evidently been established by 1931. Post boxes, fire hydrants and playing fields were amongst the topics raised by the Association. Ashingdon Girl Guides donated a seat to the council for public use in 1932, showing that that organisation was also in existence.[553]

In 1932 the parish council discussed the provision of a water supply to properties in The Chase. The following year they received a letter about the provision of a sewerage scheme locally, but resolved to take no action. In March 1933 the dangerous state of the temporary classroom at Ashingdon School was on the agenda. Things evidently got

---

553   ERO D/J 126/2/1

quickly worse at the school, for in December it was reported as being infested by rats![554]

In 1934 all five parish councillors were required to seek re-election, having served a three-year term. Councillor Morrison stood down and replaced Mr. Stock as parish clerk with effect from 1 April. Councillors Payne and Wyeth were re-elected. Three new councillors were also elected: Sidney Price, John Joseph Gore (who lived at "Rosetta" in Arundel Road,[555] South Fambridge) and our old anarchist friend, James Evans from Brotherhood Cottage, who clearly enjoyed much local support. Councillors Payne and Evans were appointed to represent the council on the Rochford Rural District Council Rating Authority. Councillors Price and Wyeth were appointed as School Managers. Councillor Gore stepped down shortly after his election to take up the role of parish clerk in South Fambridge; he was replaced by former Councillor Brittain.[556]

The newly elected councillors' early business included writing to the Automobile Association to ask for some of their signs to be erected on Ashingdon Hill, which had been the scene of several recent accidents, and receiving a request from Rev. Thompson to install some "waste paper baskets" (litter bins) along the main road, though this request was "regretfully refused".[557] Litter complaints continued into the late 1930s.[558]

In October 1935 Councillor Payne, who was still Parish Council chairman, spoke passionately about the lack of attendance of members of the public at council meetings. This included an observation that "Councillors were not getting the support that should be given them and were getting rather sick of people who never attended meetings but were always complaining about Parish Councillors". Meanwhile, the council made its own complaint to the local bus operators, Westcliff Motor Services, about overcrowding on their vehicles and their conductors' repeated failures to change destination boards.[559]

In February 1936 councillors resolved to invite members of the main local newspaper, *The Southend Standard*, to attend their meetings to help with the general publicising of their activities.[560]

---

554 Ibid.
555 ERO D/RR 2/2/3/3
556 ERO D/J 126/2/1 & D/J 126/4/1
557 Ibid.
558 ERO D/J 126/1/1 & D/J 126/2/1
559 ERO D/J 126/2/1
560 Ibid.

Figure 74: Ashingdon, c.1926

South Fambridge Parish Council

Meanwhile, in South Fambridge, on 12 March 1934, a public meeting was held at a Mission Hall there – managed by Mrs. Gwinnell – to discuss that parish's future.[561] This building was described in 1941 as the "Mission Room at Fambridge Ferry".[562] Mr. Gregory, the Rochford Rural District Council representative, was elected as meeting chairman and "spoke at some length" on "the water question" and on a proposal to amalgamate South Fambridge with Ashingdon for governance purposes. The meeting was adjourned, to be reconvened at Ashingdon School so that parishioners "at the other end of the parish" could attend. A committee was set up in preparation for this, comprising Messrs. Arnold, Croft, Gore (the Ashingdon parish councillor), Gwinnell, Kilner and Whybrow.[563]

On 22 March 1934 a very similar second meeting was held at which Captain G.R.D. Kilner was elected as parish chairman. The meeting discussed whether to elect a parish council for South Fambridge or to amalgamate with Ashingdon. A committee was elected to consider this topic, this time comprising H.W. Arnold (*The Anchor* publican), J. Crawford,

561   ERO D/DS 313/19/1
562   ERO D/J 126/1/2
563   ERO D/DS 313/19/1

H. Croft, J.J. Gore and A.F. Taylor.[564]

In April the committee recommended that the parish elders should "apply to Essex County Council for the establishment of a separate parish council for South Fambridge". Committee members had already visited the clerk to Essex County Council to discuss the topic and were writing to various local bodies about it. They also made phone calls, showing that a telephone was now available in the parish.[565]

In May 1934 another public meeting was held at Ashingdon School, with Captain Kilner again in the chair. The attendees included Major Wedd, the district's representative on Essex County Council. It was revealed during the discussion that the parish's population had grown from 79 in 1891 to 282 in 1931, no doubt due largely to the various initiatives at Hollick's factory and the creation of the Ashingdon Park Estate, whose territories were partly in South Fambridge. A resolution was passed unanimously to form a South Fambridge Parish Council. James Crawford and Harry Croft were also elected (re-elected in Crawford's case) as the parish's representatives on Rochford Rural District Council's Rating Authority.[566]

Other topics discussed at the meeting – both somewhat off-topic – were the blocking of a footpath on the seawall by a bungalow built there by Mr. Pratt and a proposal from the County Council for a bridge over the river at South Fambridge which Major Wedd reported had been deferred because of the expected £400,000 cost of it.[567]

In July 1934 yet another meeting was convened to discuss progress on the formation of a South Fambridge Parish Council. It was reported that Essex County Council had been meeting to consider this and had agreed that, as with Ashingdon, five councillors could be elected. The names of various candidates were proposed, but it was not until August that voting took place.[568]

By then, a different list of candidates had been put forward, with those successfully elected by a show of hands being John Joseph Gore, H. Croft, Captain G.R.D. Kilner, James Crawford and G.H. Jones. Councillor Kilner was elected as Parish Council chairman and Councillor Gore was elected (unpaid) to continue in his role as parish clerk. Councillors Crawford and Croft continued in their roles as representatives on the District Council's Rating Authority.[569]

The first meeting of South Fambridge Parish Council took place on 27 August 1934. Early business included the need for a playing field in the parish and that bridge over the river.

---

564 Ibid.
565 Ibid.
566 Ibid.
567 Ibid.
568 Ibid.
569 Ibid.

Refuse collections were also discussed early on, as was the state of a footpath from the New Hall Estate to South Fambridge village and the state of the ditch behind Frederick Payne's forge. A bus stop at "Beckney Corner" – now the Ashingdon Road/Greensward Lane/Lower Road junction – was also on the agenda, as were a water supply for the New Hall Estate and the problem of cattle escaping from fenceless fields and fouling Lower Road.[570]

In January 1935 Messrs. Wyeth and Gore were respectively endorsed as Ashingdon's and South Fambridge's representatives on Rochford Rural District Council.[571]

Figure 75: A general view of South Fambridge village, showing the terraced houses of St Thomas Road and, to their right, the ancient Ferry House

Parish Boundary Review

In August 1933, Ashingdon Parish Council discussed the potential alteration of the parish boundary between Ashingdon and Hawkwell, a measure which could be applied for under the Local Government Act 1888. It was proposed "that that part of the Parish of Hawkwell which adjoins the Main Road and forms part of Ashingdon Hill may be added to the Parish of Ashingdon". The reasons given for this were as follows:

---

570   Ibid.
571   ERO D/J 126/2/1

"1) the area in question regards itself socially as part of Ashingdon

2) it trades in the name of Ashingdon, e.g. Ashingdon Post Office, Garage, etc.

3) Ashingdon provides the amenities, historic church, battlefield, views of the River Crouch, etc.

4) with this part of Hawkwell wedged into the heart of Ashingdon, the latter parish cannot develop on lines compatible with its own wishes [and]

5) Hawkwell is not so handicapped because the area in question is somewhat remote from the remainder of the parish."

The proposal was carried but did not come into effect.[572]

In September 1934 Essex County Council wrote to the parish council, asking for councillors' views about boundary revision. Councillors proposed several changes, including taking the above area covered by Stanley to Albert Roads into the parish from Hawkwell and moving "Pratt's Farm" (Beckney Farm) into South Fambridge.[573] Councillor Wyeth made what seems an eminently sensible suggestion at a public meeting to revise the boundary to run along Rectory Lane (now Road, in Hawkwell) to the railway bridge, along the railway line to Hockley station, from there up Greensward Lane to Beckney Corner (the junction with what is now Lower Road), along Ashingdon Road, past the school into Canewdon Road as far as "Hidey" (Hyde) Wood Lane, south down Hyde Wood Lane to Brays Lane, and back to Ashingdon Road and Rectory Lane. This would greatly simplify the parish boundary and do away with all the old complexities and detached components of the parish, as well as centralise everything around the main stretch of Ashingdon Road. Attendees agreed to contact Essex County Council about this. The County Council replied with some counter-proposals in March 1935, acknowledging in the process that any alterations would affect not just Ashingdon, but South Fambridge, Hawkwell and Little Stambridge parishes as well.[574]

The matter was picked up again in November 1937, with the County and Rural District Councils reported as having it under consideration. However, whereas "it was largely felt" in 1934 that the streets in East Hawkwell should be taken into Ashingdon, the view now emanating from Hawkwell Parish Council was that their members were opposed to this. This was despite the fact that "most of the residents of roads like Alexandra Road and York Road were in favour of joining with Ashingdon". The County Council was reported as being in favour of a similar scheme to that previously set out by Councillor Wyeth, i.e. moving the parts of Hawkwell that were north of Rectory Road and north-east of

---

572   ERO D/J 126/1/1
573   ERO D/J 126/2/1 & D/J 126/4/1
574   ERO D/J 126/1/1

the railway line into Ashingdon, along with the detached part of Little Stambridge, in exchange for moving a bit of Ashingdon parish into South Fambridge.[575]

Things came to a head in May 1938 when the matter went to a Public Inquiry in Rochford. Ashingdon's parish councillors had a lengthy discussion about it a few days beforehand to agree on their approach. There seems to have been some ill-feeling between Ashingdon and South Fambridge Parish Councils about this, with the former's minutes recording in respect of the Ashingdon Park Estate, which straddled the boundary between the two parishes, that "The chairman pointed out that all the way along Fambridge had wanted all it could get out of Ashingdon". This seems a little uncharitable, as there is nothing of that nature in the minutes of South Fambridge Parish Council. It was acknowledged that Ashingdon was developing more rapidly than South Fambridge, so perhaps the latter's Council wanted the Ashingdon Park Estate to help their parish to grow. It was also observed that the incorporation of the East Hawkwell streets in Ashingdon parish "should have happened 12 years ago".[576]

In August 1938 it was reported that, following the Public Inquiry, Essex County Council favoured merging Ashingdon, South Fambridge and the detached part of Little Stambridge into one parish, to be known as Ashingdon parish. There was a lot of logic to this, as it would remove the historic anomalies in the parish boundaries, although the more modern anomaly of the Ashingdon-centric Ashingdon Hall Estate streets remaining in East Hawkwell would continue. Ashingdon's parish councillors were happy with the outcome, but South Fambridge's were not.[577] The latter wrote to Essex County Council, objecting to the proposal to unite the parishes of Ashingdon and South Fambridge and "deploring the suggestion made in the report that there is ill feeling between the two parishes". A parish meeting heard that South Fambridge was a larger parish than Ashingdon, with a higher rateable value, and had witnessed much progress of late, not least with the development of its streets on the Ashingdon Park Estate, which many felt ought to be moved in its entirety into the parish. The parish council decided to write the government about it.[578]

The advent of the Second World War, however, put paid to further discussion on the topic until 1945.

King George V Silver Jubilee

On 6 May 1935 local people joined the rest of the country in celebrating the Silver Jubilee of King George V. Ashingdon and South Fambridge held a joint event featuring sports,

---

575   ERO D/J 126/2/1
576   Ibid.
577   Ibid.
578   ERO D/DS 313/19/1

entertainments and teas. A parade which included two decorated waggons set off from the foot of Ashingdon Hill to Mr. Turner's field.[579] Money for the event was raised by a house-to-house collection to avoid overtaxing the ratepayers.[580]

South Fambridge Parish Council resolved to erect a public seat and a tree at Beckney Corner to commemorate the event but by September the tree had unfortunately died. A replacement tree was planted, but that died too![581]

Playing Fields

The question of playing field provision came to the fore in 1934, with Mrs. Lovelock of Newton Hall offering some land for this purpose for a fee of £950. Councillor Evans, however, made a "vigorous protest" against the proposal and no action was taken. The matter rumbled on into 1935, with a long discussion being held about the subject in January that year. Mr. Ford, the headmaster of Ashingdon School, was in attendance and expressed the desirability of having a playing field available for schoolchildren to use. Councillor Evans was again opposed to the idea, due, it would seem, judging from a stance that he regularly took at parish council meetings, to the expected cost to parish ratepayers. He even challenged three members of the public present who were not Ashingdon voters. A vote was, however, carried 10-3, amongst those eligible to vote, to ask Rochford Rural District Council to select a site for a playing field from three that had by that stage been proposed: the one at Newton Hall and two others on land owned by Mr. Jolly and Mr. Turner. Councillor Evans remained dissatisfied, suggesting that "the motion was an illegal one".[582]

During 1936, however, the proposal for the provision of a playing field began to gain some traction. Mrs. Thring, a regular contributor to public meetings who lived in The Chase, suggested to a meeting in Ashingdon in July that year that facilities should include a running track, simple gymnastic equipment, a sand pit and an open-air school. Children should be put first, she said, as "3 children had been killed on the open road".[583] By October the parish council was corresponding with Rochford Rural District Council about the layout of a playing field in Ashingdon.[584] By March 1937 a public meeting was calling for the playing field to be opened that year.[585] It was to be named in honour of King George V, who died on 20 January 1936.

---

579 ERO D/J 126/2/1 & D/DS 313/19/1
580 ERO D/J 126/1/1
581 ERO D/DS 313/19/1
582 ERO D/J 126/2/1 & D/J 126/4/1
583 ERO D/J 126/1/1
584 ERO D/J 126/2/1
585 ERO D/J 126/1/1

Figure 76: One of the two pillars which marks the entrance to "King George's Field" (the words can just be made out); the other pillar has the words "George V A.D. 1910-1936" on it

In November 1938 South Fambridge's parishioners were entertained at a meeting by a speaker from the National Fitness Campaign, who extolled the virtues of playing fields in keeping people fit. The speaker must have been disappointed, however, when the meeting concluded that the parish "had neither population or resources enough to justify a separate playing field, especially as an expensive field had just been funded in Ashingdon".[586]

Street Lighting

The question of the provision of street lighting for Ashingdon was also gaining increased attention in the early 1930s. Councillor Wyeth had devised a scheme for this and he asked

---

586   ERO D/DS 313/19/1

to be able to put it to a public meeting.[587] This duly took place on 17 September 1934, with a 22-2 vote in favour of adopting the Lighting and Watching Act 1833 and installing street lighting in the parish. Councillor Evans again challenged non-parish attendees who were present and again opposed the move on the grounds of cost. Mr. W.A.J. Lloyd, who was evidently the other person who voted against the scheme, declared that "lights were not wanted in Ashingdon and that roads were much better without them".[588] Nevertheless, the result of this meeting led directly to the installation of the first three lamp posts in Ashingdon, all on the main road: at the school, The Chase and Lascelles Gardens (technically in Hawkwell).[589]

In South Fambridge, the inhabitants of the Fairview and New Hall Estates requested lighting in January 1935 and the parish council there resolved to contact the London Electricity Supply Company about this.[590]

Lighting in Ashingdon remained a bone of contention throughout the 1930s, with money for it constantly running short in the face of increasing demand. In July 1936 Ashingdon Parish Council resolved to form a Lighting Committee to deal with the topic, the council's first-ever committee.[591]

At a public debate in March 1937 the point was made that as most Ashingdon residents lived in side-roads, and those residents were paying rates towards the provision of services, streetlights ought to be provided in the side roads first. A motion along these lines was voted on and carried and £50 was set aside as a lighting budget up to September 1938.[592]

South Fambridge Parish Council discussed adopting the Lighting and Watching Act for that parish several times in the late 1930s, but discussion was deferred in May 1938, pending the outcome of the parish boundary review, and ended altogether with the arrival of Second World War blackout restrictions.[593]

A River Crouch Bridge

In 1934 it was reported in the local press that Mr. Hocking had proposed at a meeting of South Fambridge Parish Council that a letter be sent to Essex County Council's Highways Committee, asking them to consider the construction of a bridge across the Crouch somewhere in the vicinity of South Fambridge and to hold a joint conference with Southend

---

587   ERO D/J 126/2/1 & D/J 126/4/1
588   ERO D/J 126/1/1
589   ERO D/J 126/2/1 & D/J 126/4/1
590   ERO D/DS 313/19/1
591   ERO D/J 126/2/1
592   ERO D/J 126/1/1
593   ERO D/DS 313/19/1

and Maldon Councils. The Parish Council supported this motion.[594]

In April 1936 the council wrote to Ashingdon Parish Council to seek support for the construction of such a bridge. Ashingdon's councillors agreed to contact Essex County Council about it, although unsurprisingly Councillor Evans was opposed to this on the grounds of cost.[595] Mr. Downs of South Fambridge caused some hilarity when observing that there had been talk of a bridge being erected since he was a boy and the talk was still likely to be going on long after he was gone.[596]

Despite the pressure, Essex County Council informed South Fambridge Parish Council in July 1936 that they had too many other projects on the go at the time to be able to look into building a bridge in the village.[597]

Speed Limits

Another new initiative was a proposal in August 1935 for a 30mph speed limit on Ashingdon Road between Brays Lane and the bottom of Ashingdon Hill.[598] Ashingdon Parish Council made a formal request for this to the county council in October, but their request was rejected in February 1936 as it was not supported by either the County Surveyor or the Chief Constable. Parish councillors resolved to approach the Ministry of Transport about it instead, part of their rationale for this being that there were by now two schools abutting onto the main road.[599] One was the county council-run Ashingdon School; the other was probably the Ashingdon House School, a private school run by Henry Harris, presumably the aforementioned churchwarden.[600]

Nothing was done as a result, however, and in April 1937 the council contacted Rochford Rural District Council to seek their support in persuading the county council to establish a 30mph speed limit for the whole of Ashingdon Road. This pressure evidently paid off, for in September the parish clerk was asked to contact the county council to find out when the latter envisaged the limit coming into force.[601]

South Fambridge Parish Council had noted in 1936 that there was an increasing amount of traffic on the roads and was concerned about the lack of footpaths in Fambridge Road and Greensward Lane. In July 1937 the Council heard that there had been several accidents in "Lower Hockley Road" (Lower Road) at the right-angled bend outside Beckney Wood

---

594 ERO T/P 181/5/11
595 ERO D/J 126/2/1
596 ERO D/DS 313/19/1
597 Ibid.
598 ERO D/J 126/1/1
599 ERO D/J 126/2/1
600 ERO D/RR 2/2/3/3
601 ERO D/J 126/2/1

House.[602] Local people increasingly began to acquire cars: Mr. F. Saunders of Ashingdon, for example, purchased a Vauxhall 10 saloon in August 1938 from Woodyatt Motors of Milton Road, Southend.[603]

Fire Protection

In February 1936 a fire in Alexandra Road caused much local consternation. Ashingdon did not have its own fire-fighters or equipment and was reliant upon Rochford fire crews coming to the village. It was reported that for this fire the Rochford fire crew had been called out at 2:30pm but did not turn up until 4pm, by which time it was too late. Councillors made allegations of ineptitude against the Rochford firefighters, one of whom was reported as saying "It's only an old Army Hut so let it burn". A vote of no confidence in the Rochford fire brigade was recorded.[604]

As a result of the above, Rochford Rural District Council suggested that Ashingdon and South Fambridge should join forces and acquire their own fire-fighting equipment. Ashingdon councillors agreed with this proposal and resolved to look into purchasing some equipment and operating it on a voluntary basis.[605] At a public meeting in March attendees rejected a request from Rochford fire brigade for an amalgamation of fire-fighting services with Ashingdon because of the former's perceived incompetence with the Alexandra Road fire.[606]

In April 1936 Councillor Wyeth was elected as parish council chairman, replacing Councillor Payne. The meeting he chaired that month concluded that it would be too expensive to purchase fire-fighting equipment, so councillors resolved to contact Hockley Parish Council to ask them to use their equipment to cover Ashingdon for fire-fighting purposes.[607]

It was reported in May 1936 that Hockley Parish Council and its fire brigade representatives had agreed to use their fire-fighting equipment to cover Ashingdon parish for a small sum, on condition that Ashingdon provided a map of all the fire hydrants. Hockley had a motor fire engine with a portable pump and 1800 feet of hose. Councillor Evans, whose views were again out-of-kilter with everyone else's, abstained from a vote on whether to accept this offer and stormed out of the meeting. The other four councillors were in favour and duly signed a formal agreement about it in July.[608]

---

602 ERO D/DS 313/19/1
603 ERO S2868
604 ERO D/J 126/2/1
605 Ibid.
606 ERO D/J 126/1/1
607 ERO D/J 126/2/1
608 Ibid.

By May 1938 a national Fire Protection Bill was due in Parliament. This would give Rochford Rural District Council district-wide fire prevention responsibility locally, alleviating the individual parishes from what had evidently been a bit of a burden up until then.[609] The National Fire Service was formed in 1941, largely in response to the war.

Flying Fleas

In the 1930s the pioneering spirit of the early aviators from 1909 South Fambridge was recaptured in Ashingdon through a number of related ventures.

First of all, the Southend Flying Club, the first to be formed in Essex, according to Smith, set up home at the delightfully named "Canute Air Park", a field on Moon's Farm which lay at the junction of Canewdon Road and Hyde Wood Lane. Aircraft had moved on significantly since 1909 and planes had become more reliable and more common, so the large, flat, open field there was ideal for the purpose.

In February 1936 a celebrated Austrian glider pilot, Robert Kronfield, gave an aerial display at the Canute Air Park to members of the Aero 8 Club which had by then taken over residence of the Park from the Southend Flying Club, which in turn had moved to Rochford. The Aero 8 Club had been formed the previous year by two engineers, Mervyn Chadwick and Raymond Gordon, who were enthusiastic about a new type of plane called the "Flying Flea" and planned to further its development. The Flying Flea, which was only about 11 or 12 feet long and was cheap and easy to make, had been invented by a Frenchman, Henry Mignet, in 1933. Mignet had written a book which included a set of instructions on how to build one, so hundreds of enthusiasts across the world were able to build their own planes to his design. Consequently, in April 1936 the Aero 8 Club hosted "the greatest Flying Flea Rally ever" at the Canute Air Park, an event which was featured in *The Illustrated Sporting & Dramatic News* magazine that same month.

---

609   Ibid.

Figure 77: The Flying Flea rally at Ashingdon in April 1936[610]

Sadly, the Flying Flea was not a particularly safe vehicle and the craze for them ended after a series of fatal accidents abroad led to the UK authorities revoking authorisations to fly them here. Chadwick and Gordon went on to build a new monoplane design at Harold Wood, but that was the end of aviation in Ashingdon. The Aero 8 Club wound up its affairs on 11 November 1937 and the Canute Air Park closed the same day.

The Aero 8 Club and another organisation, the South-East Essex Flying Club, are both listed in rating and valuation returns for Ashingdon in 1936.[611]

Cycling Problems

Cycling had been gaining increasingly in popularity since the turn of the century, but with the increase in motor traffic in the interwar period it led to increasing conflict between cyclists and pedestrians, as both parties tried to stay off the roads. In 1935 a local resident, Peter Satchell, was fined five shillings for cycling on a pavement in Ashingdon. His defence was that the road was unfit for cycling on and he said he was prepared out of principle to go to prison rather than pay the fine.[612]

In July 1936, Ashingdon Parish Council resolved to request a ban on cycling on "The

---

610   The photo is from *The Illustrated Sporting and Dramatic News* (17 April 1936, p.158)
611   ERO D/RR 2/2/3/7
612   ERO T/P 181/1/11

public footpath known as The Chase". The Chase and a historic footpath extension from it south of Trinity Wood to Greensward Lane provided an important shortcut for pedestrians from Ashingdon to Hockley station.[613] Several residents reported accidents there had befallen pedestrians "owing to cyclists using the path".[614] The council's request for a ban was, however, rejected by Rochford Rural District Council on the grounds that footpaths there (and elsewhere) were already protected.[615]

Police Issues

In July 1936 Ashingdon Parish Council paid for repairs to a public seat outside Ashingdon Hall, but by February 1937 it had been damaged again. This had been caused by "a gang of youths who had uprooted the seat". This event prompted the council to contact the police to ask for assistance with "wanton damage in the village".[616]

In April Councillor Wyeth met with Inspector Shelley to discuss the provision of a permanent police presence in Ashingdon. Inspector Shelley had doubts about the availability of funding for this, but promised to contact the Chief Constable about it.[617]

The following month Councillor Wyeth duly received a visit from a Superintendent of the Police from Brentwood, who advised that the organisation's preferred approach was to have police officers on bicycles constantly criss-crossing the local area. He added that a sergeant and constable were always available at Rochford Police Station. Councillors were happy with this and did not press the matter further.[618] Nevertheless, boys making a nuisance of themselves in the vicinity of Ashingdon Hall were still a problem in March 1938.[619]

King George VI Coronation

In October 1936 Ashingdon and South Fambridge Parish Councils held a joint meeting at Ashingdon School to plan some celebrations for the coronation of King Edward VIII.[620] Edward abdicated in December, however, so the plans had to be adapted for his successor, George VI.

The coronation of the latter took place on 12 May 1937. Ashingdon, South Fambridge and East Hawkwell residents all came together to celebrate it. The event took place on Turner's Field in Ashingdon, by kind permission of Mr. E. Turner.

---

613 ERO D/J 126/2/1
614 ERO D/J 126/1/1
615 ERO D/J 126/2/1
616 Ibid.
617 Ibid.
618 Ibid.
619 ERO D/J 126/1/1
620 ERO D/J 126/2/1

The usual public servants were at the forefront. The organising committee was chaired by Captain G.R.D. Kilner. Eric Wyeth was the vice-chairman and John Joseph Gore the secretary and treasurer. The committee comprised other members of the affected parish councils and various notable local individuals such as Mr. C.G. Ford (headmaster of Ashingdon School). South Fambridge Council's minutes from July 1937 record that the event was successful despite bad weather on the day.[621]

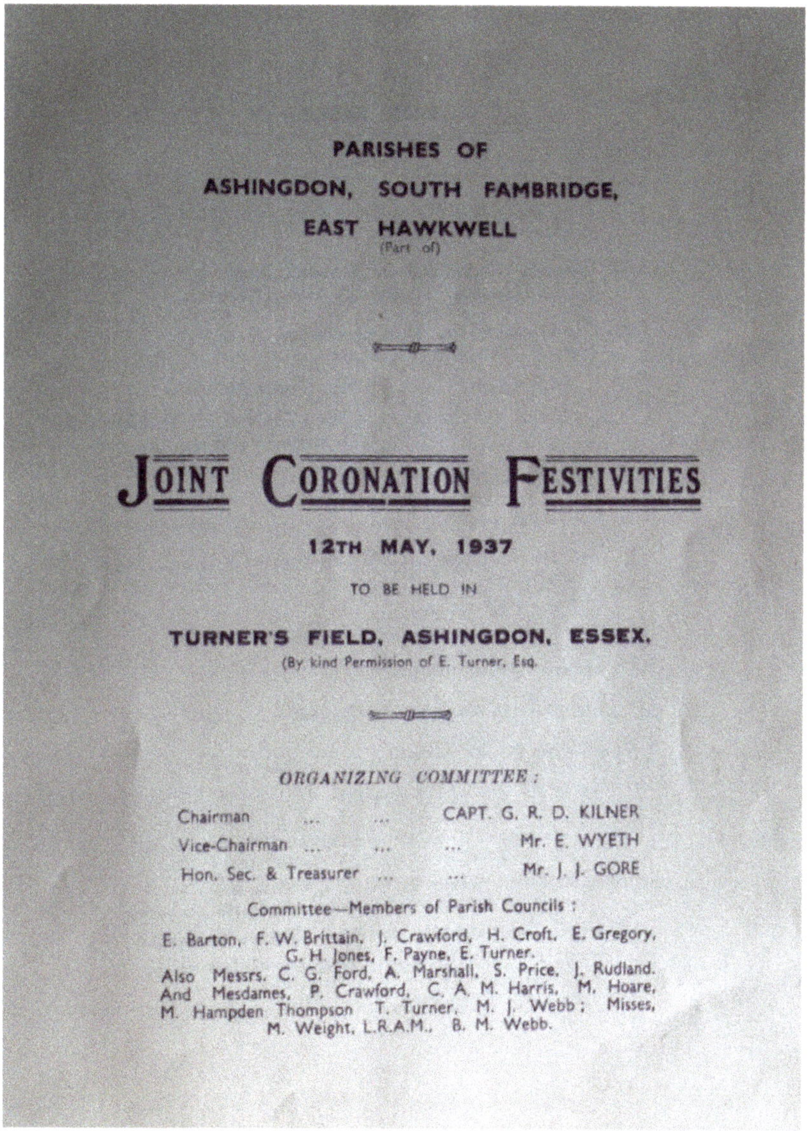

PARISHES OF
ASHINGDON, SOUTH FAMBRIDGE,
EAST HAWKWELL
(Part of)

JOINT CORONATION FESTIVITIES

12TH MAY, 1937

TO BE HELD IN

TURNER'S FIELD, ASHINGDON, ESSEX.
(By kind Permission of E. Turner, Esq.

ORGANIZING COMMITTEE:

Chairman	CAPT. G. R. D. KILNER
Vice-Chairman	Mr. E. WYETH
Hon. Sec. & Treasurer	Mr. J. J. GORE

Committee—Members of Parish Councils:
E. Barton, F. W. Brittain, J. Crawford, H. Croft, E. Gregory, G. H. Jones, F. Payne, E. Turner.
Also Messrs. C. G. Ford, A. Marshall, S. Price, J. Rudland. And Mesdames, P. Crawford, C. A. M. Harris, M. Hoare, M. Hampden Thompson T. Turner, M. J. Webb; Misses, M. Weight, L.R.A.M., B. M. Webb.

Figure 78: The title page of the Joint Coronation Festivities booklet 1937, for the parishes of Ashingdon, South Fambridge and East Hawkwell

621 ERO D/DS 313/19/1

The day's events commenced at 1pm with a procession from Ashingdon School to Turner's Field, where the opening ceremony was performed by the rector, Rev. J. Hampden Thompson. Mrs. J. Hampden Thompson was given the honour of crowning the May Queen, Miss Peggy Rollin. The latter was given her own wagon for the occasion, led by a pair of grey horses.

In the afternoon there was a fancy-dress competition and some children's sports events, followed by a tea for the children and the presentation of souvenir mugs and prizes. A tea was also held for "Old Inhabitants" of the parishes. The latter was scheduled to be held at the school and the Free Church Mission Hall if the weather turned wet.

In the evening there was a "Comic Football Match" and a concert, which would be held at St Andrew's Hall if it was too wet outside. The festivities concluded with "Dancing on the Green" and music by the "Nondescripts", again to be at St Andrew's Hall if the weather was bad. The evening's events were expected to be interrupted by the broadcasting of the King's speech.

Proceeds from the event, according to the souvenir programme for the day (which cost 3d.), were to be "donated to a fund in aid of a village hall".

Repairs were made to the tower of St Andrew's Church in 1937, possibly as part of the Coronation commemorations.[622]

The Late 1930s

In March 1937 Councillors Wyeth, Payne and Brittain were re-elected to Ashingdon Parish Council, with Councillor Wyeth being re-elected chairman. They were joined by Frank Wall, who was probably a relative of the aforementioned John Wall, a landowner and leading light in the village in the late 1920s and early 1930s, and Ernest Edward Turner, the owner of Turner's Field.[623] Frank Wall owned a coal yard on Ashingdon Road in 1939.[624] Councillor Evans, who came last in a poll of nine candidates and consequently lost his seat, was not happy and demanded a re-vote (done then by a show of hands), saying that the vote was not representative. Councillor Wyeth graciously acceded to this request and a lengthy discussion ensued. The discussion changed nothing, however, and "after some candid opinions had been expressed by parishioners" the chairman closed the meeting. Another losing candidate was Mrs. A. Thring, the first of many female candidates to stand for election to the parish council.[625]

Councillors Gore, Kilner, Crawford, Jones and Croft were all re-elected to South Fambridge Parish Council in the same month. Miss Dennington, another leading light in

---

[622] ERO A6052 Box 2
[623] ERO D/J 126/1/1
[624] ERO D/RR 2/2/2/3
[625] ERO D/J 126/1/1

the cause of female local authority representation, was one of the unsuccessful candidates, though not as unsuccessful as Mr. Ellard, who received no votes! Councillor Croft took over the role of parish clerk from Councillor Gore, who was elected vice-chairman, with Captain Kilner being re-elected as chairman. Councillors Crawford and Croft were elected as parish representatives on the Rural District Council's Rating Authority. Councillor Jones was appointed as the parish's school manager in September 1937.[626]

At the first meeting of the new Ashingdon Parish Council in April 1937, Councillors Wyeth and Wall were elected as School Managers, Councillors Payne and Brittain were elected as representatives on the district council's Rating Authority and Councillors Turner and Brittain were elected to the parish council's Lighting Committee. In September, however, members were informed by the county council that they could have only one School Manager representing the parish; Councillor Wall duly stood down.[627]

Also in November 1937, the Council received a letter from Essex County Council, asking if there were any historic buildings in the parish which were worthy of preservation. Rather surprisingly, "The clerk was instructed to reply that there were no such buildings", even though there was a potentially 917-year-old church and several ancient farmhouses.[628] South Fambridge Parish Council, on the other hand, resolved to nominate Brick House Farm and the Ferry House for this initiative.[629]

Other topics discussed by Ashingdon Parish Council in the late 1930s show that the area was slowly but surely becoming more urbanised: the need for more street lighting and better sewerage, the provision of public seats and litter bins, and the need for a doctor's surgery closer than the existing one five miles away in Rayleigh.[630]

In November 1938 the Ashingdon Parish Council chairman, Councillor Wyeth, led local opposition to a national Milk Bill, expressing the opinion that "this was another attempt to favour large combines in order to squeeze out the small man". As a shop owner himself, he would have been well aware of the challenges of keeping a small business going.[631]

A Village Hall

In March 1936 South Fambridge Parish Council discussed the question of constructing a George V "Jubilee Hall", using funding from a local fete. No action was taken but the topic was picked up again in July 1937 and again in September. Councillors resolved to contact Ashingdon Parish Council to seek their views on whether they would use such a hall if one

---

626 ER D/DS 313/19/1
627 ERO D/J 126/2/1
628 Ibid.
629 ERO D/DS 313/19/1
630 ERO D/J 126/2/1
631 Ibid.

was erected.[632]

In September 1937, Ashingdon's parish councillors discussed the need for a parish hall, which would be a community meeting place in addition to the church hall in that parish.[633] There was some doubt about whether one was needed and, if there was, who would pay for it. Following a public meeting, the council resolved in November that "in view of the lack of support of the village hall scheme" no further action should be taken.[634]

In March 1938, however, South Fambridge Parish Council received a letter from Ashingdon's Councillor Wyeth in his role as Honorary Secretary of the Village Hall Committee, asking the council to send representatives to a meeting. Councillors Gore and Jones were nominated to represent South Fambridge. A public meeting in South Fambridge the following month heard that East Hawkwell and Little Stambridge also had committee membership.[635] The Village Hall Committee was still operational in April 1939, with Councillors Wyeth and Wall representing Ashingdon Parish Council.[636]

The Fambridge Ferry

In May 1937 South Fambridge Parish Council began to receive complaints about the unreliability of the Fambridge ferry, then owned by Mr. Arnold (presumably *The Anchor* publican or a relative). More complaints followed in July and September. The Council contacted the owner without success and resolved to escalate the matter to the district council. In July 1939 it was reported that an attempt to get the district council, the county council and/or Maldon District Council to acquire the rights to the ferry had failed, with each authority rejecting the suggestion.[637]

---

632 ERO D/DS 313/19/1
633 ERO D/J 126/2/1
634 Ibid.
635 ERO D/DS 313/19/1
636 ERO D/J 126/2/1
637 ERO D/DS 313/19/1

THE SECOND WORLD WAR

The Second World War had a significant effect on the two parishes: normal business stopped and national initiatives took over. Parish council elections and the boundary review were postponed and topics such as food cultivation and allotments took centre stage.[638]

As early as October 1936 Rochford Rural District Council contacted Ashingdon Parish Council about air raid and gas precautions, seeking the latter organisation's support for their proposals on the matter. The Legion of Frontiersman attended a parish council meeting that month to provide some background.[639] Representatives of the Legion also attended a meeting of South Fambridge Parish Council and took the names of some volunteers.[640] By February 1937 the district council was actively seeking co-operation and the names of volunteers who would help out with air raids.[641]

In July 1937 a joint, well-attended meeting on air raid precautions was held between representatives from Ashingdon, South Fambridge and East Hawkwell Parish Councils and members of the public. Wing Commander C.H. Sparling, Essex County Council's nominated engineer, was in attendance to provide general information about air raids and to demonstrate equipment. This included respirators for personal use and clothing that would be worn by decontamination squads. The names were taken of several people who volunteered to help with air raids.[642]

In August 1938 it was reported that Mr. Ford, the Ashingdon School headmaster, had agreed to be Air Raid Warden for the parish. There was some concern that gas mask provision was progressing too slowly and that local people might lose interest if war preparations were not showing signs of becoming concrete. By November, however, Mr. Ford and the district council had between them successfully delivered numerous gas masks around the parish. Both were heartily thanked in writing by Ashingdon Parish Council for the excellent work that they did in this regard.[643] Mr. Taylor was appointed as Air Raid Precautions officer for South Fambridge in November 1938.[644]

In January 1939 first aid classes were provided in Ashingdon and an agreement was reached with the gas and electric companies to extinguish lights at times of national

---

638 Ibid.
639 ERO D/J 126/2/1
640 ERO D/DS 313/19/1
641 ERO D/J 126/2/1
642 Ibid.
643 Ibid.
644 ERO D/DS 313/19/1

crisis.[645] With the wartime blackout in operation locally from at least October 1939, no new lights were to be provided until after the war.[646] Ashingdon and South Fambridge had transformed fairly rapidly since the First World War from unlit, sparsely populated, rural places to lit, gradually urbanising places with increased motor traffic and numerous new incomers, especially at the former. The removal of lighting for wartime was therefore more of a challenge to the increased, and increasingly motorised, population of outsiders who were expecting it than the lack of lighting had been to the traditional farming community of native pedestrians and horse riders that had existed in the area prior to the 1920s. Street furniture such as seats were consequently being painted white by the middle of 1940. Reflective posts were also installed to warn of dangerous ditches which might be encountered.[647]

In January 1940 the topic of allotments was discussed by Ashingdon Parish Council. This topic had been discussed and dismissed locally several times over the previous decade, but by this stage national self-sufficiency was becoming increasingly important and the provision of allotment facilities was being seen as essential rather than simply desirable.[648] Similar discussions took place in South Fambridge and in June 1939 it was reported that four acres of land east of the old factory premises had been set aside for allotments if necessary. The land had previously been used as allotments by factory workers.[649]

Councillor Wyeth was re-elected as chairman of Ashingdon Parish Council in April 1940 but, by December, Councillor Wall was occupying the role in Councillor Wyeth's absence. It appears from the parish council minutes that Councillors Wyeth and Turner were both absent from Ashingdon at this period due to wartime evacuation measures and there was some discussion amongst those who remained behind as to what to do about the absentees.[650] Councillors Kilner and Jones were also absent from South Fambridge.[651]

In 1940 a salvage drive was instigated, with a van doing the rounds locally to collect wastepaper, rags, bones and metal for reclamation and reuse. Local people were also encouraged to keep pigs. The following year, timber was being requested to be stored for fuel, against the backdrop of a feared national coal shortage. By 1943, baskets had been placed along Ashingdon Road for the collection of tin cans.[652]

An Invasion Committee had been established locally by August 1941, comprising

---

645 ERO D/J 126/2/1
646 ERO D/J 126/1/1
647 ERO D/J 126/2/1
648 Ibid.
649 ERO D/DS 313/19/1
650 ERO D/J 126/2/1
651 ERO D/DS 313/19/1
652 ERO D/DS 313/19/1 & D/J 126/1/1

representatives from both parish councils, plus other organisations such as the police and the Home Guard. The latter organisation had been set up to defend the country in case of invasion, a possibility which had become of increasing concern following the British retreat from Dunkirk in May/June 1940. Early business of the committee included food distribution, rationing and the functioning of the local community as a self-contained unit if required.[653] Emergency supplies, first aid posts and the use of ponds and wells for water were also discussed, as was the ringing of church bells at St Andrew's to raise the alarm in case of invasion. Members of the public were encouraged to educate themselves about the on-going situation and to save water for reuse.[654] A photograph of members of the Ashingdon Home Guard can be seen inside the Ashingdon & East Hawkwell Memorial Hall.

The logistics of distribution and reclamation in the parishes were challenging, especially in South Fambridge. The village had historically been focused on the riverside, but now had outlying part-developed estates at Ashingdon Park, Fairview and New Hall. Each of these areas needed representatives to co-ordinate the delivery of supplies and the collection of salvage. A quick population count for the area north of Lower Road returned a figure of 96 inhabitants in March 1942.[655] Night soil (sewage) collections were also requested from Rochford Rural District Council by Ashingdon Parish Council in 1942.[656] Community buildings such as Ashingdon School were particularly important, both as a meeting place and as a distribution centre for essential goods.

Defence

At the start of the war, Rochford district was designated as a Reception Area, taking children and families from London. Ashingdon School gained extra pupils and was full to bursting as a result. This changed, however, as the South East became increasingly targeted, so pupils were soon evacuated to the Midlands.

The school was hit by two bombing raids, one in 1940 and one in 1944. Incendiary bombs fell nearby and bullets from enemy aircraft machine guns embedded themselves into the playground tarmac. The Scottish Regiment constructed a pillbox on school grounds and there was also a gun emplacement there.[657] The school building was used as a meeting place by the highly secretive British Resistance, an Auxiliary Unit set up by Winston Churchill to cause chaos to the Germans if they ever invaded, much in the way that the better-known French Resistance did in France. The local unit was led by the

---

653   ERO D/DS 313/19/1
654   ERO D/J 126/1/2
655   Ibid.
656   ERO D/J 126/1/1
657   Ibid.

school's headmaster, Captain Ford, which made the use of the school for its activities easy and unobvious. A British Resistance hideout is thought to survive underground in Trinity Wood. It is described in the memoirs of a Mr. A.E. Cocks, author of *Churchill's Secret Army 1939-45 and Other Recollections*, who was second-in-command of the Hockley Patrol Auxiliary Unit. The hideout takes the form of a 30-feet by 12-feet underground chamber, accessed by a ladder and fitted out with shelves for explosives and provisions. Because of the necessarily secretive nature of these units, very few of their hideouts have been found. The Heritage Gateway website, directly quoting military historian Fred Nash's *Survey of World War Two Defences in the District of Rochford* (2004), says of the Trinity Wood construction:

"In considering the importance of the various categories of World War Two defence sites, Auxiliary Unit (or British Resistance) hideouts are in the top layer. Every discovery should be assessed for protection as a Scheduled Monument. It is not possible to say whether the hide in Trinity Wood still survives. However, bearing in mind its robust construction, its below-ground inaccessibility and its now unknown location, it probably does. If at any time in the future it is discovered, then it should be immediately surveyed with a view to both its statutory and physical protection. Any planning application affecting Trinity Wood should be carefully considered with this in mind."

A number of other constructions from the Second World War survive in the locality. These include two pillboxes on the south bank of the River Crouch – one north of Beckney Farm, the other north of South Fambridge village – which it seems likely were there to protect the ferry crossing, and a third in a copse to the north-east of South Fambridge Hall.

Figure 79: A Second World War pillbox on the seawall at South Fambridge, showing the importance of its strategic position overlooking the River Crouch

A fourth pillbox survives in a field to the east of Highcliff Crescent, while two others exist in the fields to the south of King George's Field and at the eastern end of Canewdon View Road. These were placed here to guard against feared paratrooper/glider landings by the Germans in the flat, open fields to the east of Ashingdon. All six are of classic reinforced concrete construction and hexagonal design.

The Heritage Gateway website, again quoting Nash, records several lost Second World War sites in the locality, including a heavy anti-aircraft gun site north of Lower Road to the east of where the Riverside Garden Centre is now and two road barriers across Brays Lane and Canewdon Road. There were also two floodlights in the fields to the west of Hyde Wood Lane and to the north of South Fambridge Hall. Several other pillboxes have also been lost, including the one at Ashingdon School, one near the Ashingdon Road/Canewdon Road junction and another in St Andrew's churchyard.

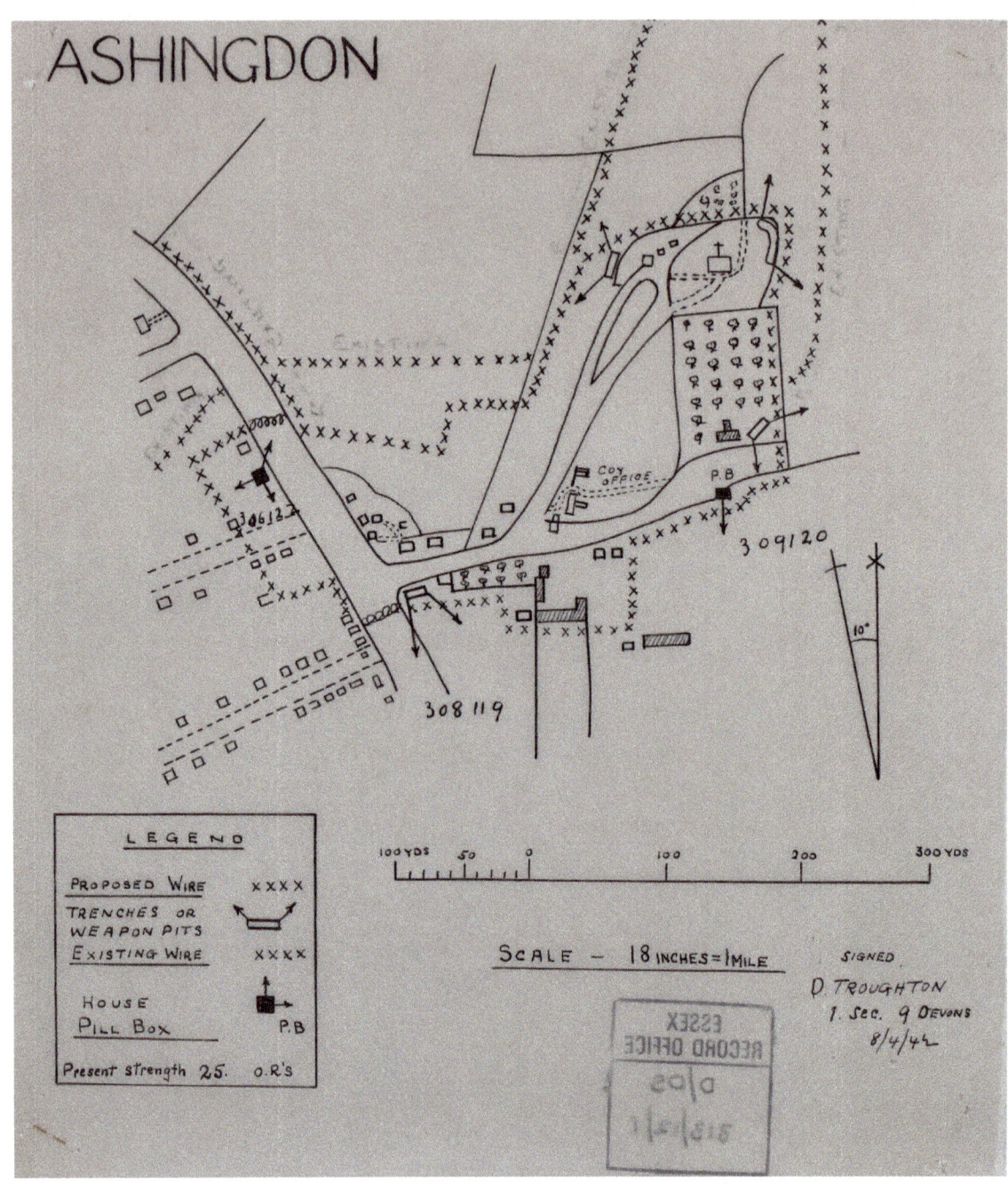

Figure 80: A sketch map of the defences on and around Ashingdon Hill in April 1942[658]

Morrison and Anderson shelters were also issued to residents across the district.[659]

---

658   ERO D/DS 313/12/1 (drawn by D. Troughton)
659   ERO D/J 126/1/1 & D/J 126/2/1

Incidents

Declassified Air Raid Precautions documents give a flavour for some of the activities that took place locally. Control Report Centre logbooks, for example, give a running, sometimes minute-by-minute, commentary on 24 hours a day of daily life under fire. A colour-coded system of air-raid warnings, ranging from white (all clear) to red (imminent danger) was in operation, with locally based volunteers manning the Air Raid Precautions station and in regular communication with the police, the army, the fire brigade, utilities companies and the Regional Control Centre for air raids in Cambridge. The logbooks also provide a flavour of the challenges of communicating promptly and accurately during wartime, with messages not always getting through, details such as addresses being vaguely given and rumours abounding. Military and first-aid exercises took place in between air raids.[660]

The period of July to September 1940 was particularly eventful, with the Battle of Britain raging in the skies, and bombs raining down across the country. On 3 September 1940 it was reported that: "One British plane crashed on sea wall Beckney Farm Rochford. Machine burnt out. Stop. Pilot baled out. Stop. Time of occurrence 11:00 hours." The message sender was asked to clarify the location and correctly responded with "South Fambridge" instead of "Rochford".[661]

At around 5:30pm on the same day, two unexploded shells fell near a pond at the rear of South Fambridge Hall and a high explosive bomb landed in a ploughed field 200 yards west of All Saints Church. Luckily, there were no casualties.[662]

On 15 September 1940 at 00:08 hours a high explosive bomb exploded on the sea wall half a mile to the rear of South Fambridge Hall. Again, there were no casualties, but Rochford Police and the Essex Rivers Catchment Board were notified.[663]

Two days later at 01:00 two more explosives fell on Marsh Field at Beckney Farm, 150 yards west of the Fambridge Ferry steps. One ignited but quickly went out; the other failed to ignite.[664]

On 17 October 1940 a high explosive bomb landed in a field on the south side of Canewdon Road in Ashingdon, half a mile east of Ashingdon School in the vicinity of Moon's Farm. Two others fell in the same locality, one just north of the church opposite Ellesmere Road and one on the marshes further to the north. Canewdon Road had to be closed until the devices had been made safe.[665]

On 23 October 1940 a high explosive bomb was dropped in a field to the rear of

---

660   ERO D/RR 1/4/2
661   ERO C/W 1/2/69
662   Ibid.
663   ERO C/W 1/2/70
664   Ibid.
665   Ibid.

Ashingdon School. There were two casualties and some damage to the nearby Free Church Mission Hall. Electricity cables were also damaged. The casualties were Grace Maud Haysman, 43, of "Lombard" in Canewdon Road, who was suffering from severe shock, and Victor Albert Haysman, 10, of the same address, presumably, her son, who was suffering from a slight head injury.[666]

Another high explosive bomb was dropped in a field to the rear of South Fambridge church on 30 October 1940 and two incendiary bombs landed in a field 350 yards north of Beckney Farm on 4 December. A high explosive landed 50 yards west of Beckney Corner (the junction of Ashingdon Road, Greensward Lane and Lower Road) on the same day, while on 27 December a parachute mine, with the parachute still attached, landed on scrub land 400 yards south of Ashingdon School.[667] Another parachute mine, presumably from the same drop, landed in the back garden of "Greenaways" in Fambridge Road, not far from the school. The owners, Bert and Gladys Greenaway, were in the house at the time but did not hear it land, as it embedded itself into their lawn.[668]

Attacks continued into 1941. On the night of 8 March in that year a high explosive was dropped without incident on "Bentall's Farm", 150 yards north-east of Ulverston Road. The following night several more bombs were dropped on the Ashingdon Park Estate and on nearby Rectory Farm. A bungalow called "Resta" in Arundel Road was damaged, along with some of the owner's furniture. A thatched barn was set alight at Rectory Farm. Fires at both places were extinguished by volunteers.[669]

On 19 April 1941 two parachute mines landed on open ground north-west of the South Fambridge pumping station without exploding. There was some slight damage to properties in the village but there were fortunately no casualties.[670]

A month later, in the early hours of 12 May 1941, about 50 incendiary bombs fell on a field to the east of South Fambridge Hall. Luckily again, there were no casualties and also no property damage.[671]

Attacks continued until virtually the end of the war, with incendiary bombs falling in South Fambridge on 29 January 1944 and Ashingdon on 22 March 1944. The Ashingdon Park Estate, Ashingdon School and Beckney Corner were all affected, with haystacks set on fire at the last of these.[672]

1944 also witnessed the arrival of a new weapon in the area, the V1 flying bomb or

---

666   Ibid.
667   ERO C/W 1/2/71
668   ERO S3013
669   ERO C/W 1/2/72
670   Ibid.
671   Ibid.
672   ERO C/W 1/2/73

doodle bug. Referred to in contemporary records as "Flies", these "revenge weapons" were fired at Great Britain from the European mainland. In June 1944 a V1 landed 200 yards north-east of South Fambridge Hall, causing damage to the farmhouse and outbuildings. In July another one fell near Moon's Farm, causing "superficial" damage to houses in Canewdon Road.[673]

Plane Crash

Ashingdon was also the location of a fatal plane crash during the war, when a United States Army Air Force Martin Marauder B26 aircraft crashed on 24 September 1944 in the fields to the north of Canewdon Road in the vicinity of Moon's Farm. The crew of the bomber, which was named "Lilly Commando", were on their way back from France to their home base at Matching Green near Harlow after a mission to Germany the previous day was aborted due to bad weather. The weather was still bad on the day of the crash and the plane was off course and running low on fuel. An eyewitness reported that it collided with some elm trees after crossing Canewdon Road from the south. Everyone on board was killed. It is believed that the crew thought that they were landing on water, as they had all removed their boots as per standard practice for a water landing and the fields on the crash site were heavily waterlogged from torrential rain. In 2009 research into the crash by the 1st Ashingdon Scout Group resulted in plaques commemorating the incident and those who lost their lives being unveiled at both Ashingdon Church Hall and the Ashingdon & East Hawkwell Memorial Hall.

---

673 ERO C/W 1/2/74

Figure 81: The plaque in the Ashingdon & East Hawkwell Memorial Hall which commemorates the crew of Lilly Commando

Victory Looms

As the war progressed, the focus of the authorities began to change.

In May 1942 the Invasion Committee discussed the plight and welfare of those who had lost their homes in bombing raids. They noted the lack of suitably-sized public buildings available in South Fambridge to house displaced people and planned to use something called a Shadow Rest Centre at All Saints church as a last resort if necessary. The committee was also concerned about the supply of emergency food rations and resolved to use South Fambridge Hall as their headquarters if an emergency occurred.[674]

There was also a canteen building on Ashingdon Hill. A meeting of Ashingdon Parish Council was held there in April 1943. This was probably supplied by a national initiative called the British Restaurant, which had a facility in Rochford and delivered to Ashingdon and South Fambridge, including to *The Victory Inn*.[675] In May 1943, however, complaints

---

674   ERO D/J 126/1/2
675   ERO D/J 126/1/1

were received by South Fambridge Parish Council about rats being present there.[676]

Local people also supported national initiatives, for example the RAF's Wings for Victory Week in 1943, when fundraising from a fete, concert or whist drive was discussed, and in March 1944 for the Army's Salute the Soldier Week. They also supported the Rochford and District War Charities Association. Conversely, Ashingdon Parish Council wrote to the Ministry of Food in February 1944 to object to the compulsory national pasteurisation of milk.[677]

In September 1943 the focus was on providing paraffin to local residents, with those on the Ashingdon Park Estate being prioritised. This was delivered to everyone's satisfaction by February 1944.[678]

In October 1943 there were complaints about a triangle of land at the junction of Ashingdon and Canewdon Roads being used as a dumping ground for all sorts of items, including tar barrels, sand and machinery. By February 1944 the tar barrels had burst open and local schoolchildren were playing with them and spreading tar all over the area. Ashingdon Parish Council resolved to ask the district council to do something about it.[679]

A regular complaint to South Fambridge Parish Council by parishioners from 1943 onwards was the damage and obstruction to a footpath leading from New Hall Road to the Fambridge Ferry as a result of farming activities taking place there by the Essex War Agricultural Committee. Apart from anything else, this led to "the isolation of the people in Vincent Road" and could well be the reason why that road was not further developed. In April 1944 the footpath was described as being closed by the military and it was noted that "nothing could be done as long as the camp remained", suggesting that there was a military camp in the vicinity as well as the agricultural activity. Even after the war, in November 1949, Mr. Jolly was criticised for ploughing up Vincent Road and was asked by a public meeting to reinstate it.[680]

In July 1944 it was suggested that the lighting of streets at night would soon be permissible again. A conference took place about this in September and it was agreed by all present that from August 1945 street lighting could be reinstated over the winter.[681]

In January 1945 a South Fambridge parish meeting discussed the national provision of "temporary" (prefabricated) houses to help those who had lost their homes. Councillor Gore had seen some examples of these and "thought that they were quite good and much superior to many of the houses on building estates in the neighbourhood". Many

---

676   ERO D/J 126/1/2
677   ERO D/J 126/1/1
678   Ibid.
679   Ibid.
680   ERO D/J 126/1/2
681   ERO D/J 126/1/1

in the audience agreed that much local housing was not of a decent standard and should be demolished. A combination of speculative land sales, piecemeal development and the coming of war in the 1930s had between them failed to deliver the complete and self-sufficient estates that the speculators had envisaged. The meeting resolved to request 25 prefabricated houses and to place them somewhere in the vicinity of the Fairview and New Hall Estates.[682] Property on the Ashingdon Park Estate had been identified as early as 1942 as becoming very dilapidated. However, Ashingdon Parish Council resolved that "as the majority of people now residing in the district were London people who would be returning [to London] at the earliest possible moment", there was no need for temporary houses. They favoured pressing the district council to provide more permanent homes.[683]

Ashingdon Parish Council's website includes some information about the military camp north of New Hall Road and some memories of local residents who witnessed V1 rockets flying over the local area in the latter stages of the war.

---

[682] ERO D/J 126/1/2
[683] ERO D/J 126/1/1

THE POST-WAR PERIOD

During the war, there were several changes to the composition of the two parish councils. Councillor Jones of South Fambridge Parish Council died in 1941 and was replaced by William Charles Shave, who was co-opted to the council pending proper elections. Councillor Croft replaced Councillor Jones as South Fambridge's School Manager representative, but tendered his resignation as voluntary parish clerk in 1943, something he said he had been planning to do in 1940. Nevertheless, he continued in the role into 1944, when he was formally appointed as a salaried clerk. He did, however, resign as a councillor; Percy Dennington of Beckney Wood House was co-opted to replace him.[684]

Long-serving chairman, Councillor Captain G.R.D. Kilner, also resigned in 1944 due to other commitments. Hector MacDonald Jolly of Rectory Farm was co-opted to replace him and Councillor James Crawford was elected as chairman.[685]

In Ashingdon, Rev. Thompson had been succeeded in 1940 as rector of St Andrew's by Rev. Alan Matheson. The latter was appointed to the living, according to Roper, by the Misses F.M. and A. Williams. He was soon co-opted onto the parish council to replace Councillor Wyeth, who resigned in July 1941.[686]

The ERO possesses a collection of correspondence belonging to Rev. Matheson which includes part of an undated letter from F.C. Ewing in which the latter assures the rector of his support and asks for his favour regarding being given authority over the churchyard. Mr. Ewing evidently felt that standards had slipped before Matheson's arrival, writing that he wanted "decent folk" involved in the church again. "I will," he writes, impressing upon Rev. Matheson his suitability for the role, "soon bring order that should be there, in a true naval fashion. These folk who have always overruled our late Rector want a lesson of discipline taught them."[687]

In 1942 Frederick William Bevan was co-opted onto the parish council to replace the absent Councillor Turner.[688] Councillor Payne replaced Mr. Wyeth as the parish's School Manager representative. Jessop Morrison, the long-serving parish clerk, tendered his resignation from the role, to be effective from October 1942. He was succeeded by Councillor Brittain.[689]

In January 1943 complaints were made to Ashingdon Parish Council about the bad state of Church Road from Ashingdon Road to "Grimwade's Farm" (presumably the former

---

684   ERO D/J 126/1/2
685   Ibid.
686   ERO D/J 126/1/1, D/J 126/2/1 & D/J 126/4/1
687   ERO A13543 Box 2
688   ERO D/J 126/1/1, D/J 126/2/1 & D/J 126/4/1
689   ERO D/J 126/2/1

Ashingdon Hall Farm).[690] The problem of farm waggons and cattle causing damage to Church Road was an issue in February 1944. Councillors consequently resolved to contact the farmers concerned.[691]

Complaints were also received in 1943 about the lack of a ferryman on the south side of the river. There should evidently have been two ferrymen because the one based on the north side was operating properly and would bring passengers across north-to-south but refused to make a special journey to the south side of the river to take people north unless he was already there.[692]

In February 1944 Ashingdon Parish Council contacted Rochford Rural District Council to ask about plans for a post-war sewerage scheme. They did the same regarding housing and factory schemes the following month.[693]

In January 1945 Councillor Payne resigned from Ashingdon Parish Council and was replaced by Sidney Price. In April Councillor Frank Wall was re-elected as chairman of the authority, with Councillor Bevan as vice-chairman. In November Councillor Price replaced ex-Councillor Payne as School Manager and Councillor Bevan replaced him as the council's representative on the Rural District Council's Rating Authority.[694] Local elections were also allowed to resume, with effect from April 1945.[695]

In October 1945 South Fambridge Parish Council began to press for greater electricity coverage in the village.[696]

A New Council

Once the war was over, the question of the review of parish boundaries and the potential merger of Ashingdon and South Fambridge Parish Councils could be reopened. This was to be handled legally via the County of Essex (Review of Rural Districts and Parishes) Order 1939, which had been created under the Local Government Act 1933 (Section 141) and had been held in abeyance since that date.[697]

South Fambridge's parish councillors were still unhappy, but they recognised that the writing was on the wall. In October 1945 they formally agreed that "there was little hope of successfully resisting the Order in view of changed circumstances brought about by the war". They did, however, want South Fambridge to be retained as a discreet ward

---

690 Ibid.
691 ERO D/J 126/1/1
692 ERO D/J 126/1/2
693 ERO D/J 126/1/1
694 ERO D/J 126/2/1
695 ERO D/J 126/1/1
696 ERO D/J 126/1/2
697 ERO D/J 126/1/1

within the newly enlarged Ashingdon Parish Council.[698]

Representatives from South Fambridge Parish Council and Essex County Council met at South Fambridge Hall on 22 October 1945 to iron out the issues. South Fambridge's councillors' principal objection to the merger was that their parish was predominantly rural whereas Ashingdon was "semi-urban". They felt that this would lead to different outlooks, some friction and their views being overruled. They also pointed out again that South Fambridge was a larger parish than Ashingdon (1574 acres compared to Ashingdon's 939). Ashingdon, however, had a higher rateable value (£3515, as compared to £1723) and population (605 compared to 224).[699]

The county representatives reassured them that their views would not be swept aside in the new authority. South Fambridge would become a ward within the new Ashingdon Parish Council area, just as they had requested, and both former parishes would continue to retain a representative on Rochford Rural District Council. The adoption of the Lighting and Watching Act 1833 would need to be approved by residents of South Fambridge, though.[700] This duly took place the following July.[701]

Councillors agreed to withdraw their objections and formally did so at a parish council meeting on 25 October 1945.[702]

Elections to the new authority were held in March 1946. South Fambridge Parish Council was formally dissolved on 1 April 1946 and the new Ashingdon Parish Council, with South Fambridge as one of its wards, came into existence.[703] The new parish covered not just the old Ashingdon and South Fambridge parishes, but also the detached part of Little Stambridge.[704] The total area covered as a result of these changes is the one that is managed by Ashingdon Parish Council today.

The new council had nine councillors elected to it, five for Ashingdon Ward (which included the former Little Stambridge part) and four for South Fambridge Ward. These were George Edward Bright, Charles William Chapel, Jessop Morrison, Sidney Price, Lilian Mary Thring (all Ashingdon) and James Crawford, John Joseph Gore, Hector MacDonald Jolly and John William Rollin (South Fambridge).[705] This was a mixture of old and new faces, some of them experienced councillors, others brand new to the role. The latter group included Councillor Mrs. Thring, the first female councillor to be elected to either

---

698 ERO D/J 126/1/2
699 Ibid.
700 Ibid.
701 ERO D/J 126/1/1
702 ERO D/J 126/1/2
703 Ibid.
704 ERO D/J 126/1/1
705 ERO D/J 126/4/1

authority, but someone who had been active in local affairs for some time.

Frank Wall, chairman of the former Ashingdon Parish Council, had decided to stand down following the merger. He was replaced as chairman of the new council by Councillor Gore, ex- of South Fambridge. Councillor Chapel was elected as vice-chairman. The long-serving South Fambridge parish clerk, Harry Croft, took a well-deserved retirement.[706]

Councillor Chapel resigned in November 1946 and was replaced by Albert Arthur Cordell. Councillor Morrison replaced him as vice-chairman. Councillor Bright resigned the following February and was replaced by Alexander George Sinclair.[707]

Plans by Southend Borough Council to extend its remit and take over administrative responsibility for the whole of the old Rochford Hundred were rebuffed c.1946-7 by Ashingdon Parish Council and many other local authorities, although Councillor Cordell was a lone voice in favour locally.[708]

In 1948 Councillor Brittain had a stroke and had to relinquish his role as parish clerk. He was replaced by Councillor Morrison, who had been in the role previously. The latter stood down as vice chairman and was replaced by Councillor Bevan in that role.[709]

In May 1949 the long-serving Councillor Gore, who had seen service on Ashingdon, South Fambridge and Rochford Rural District Councils, stood down as parish council chairman. He was replaced in the role by Councillor Bevan, who served as chairman until May 1952. Councillor Rollin replaced Councillor Bevan as vice chairman, though Rollin himself was succeeded as vice-chairman by Councillor Sinclair in July because he was having difficulty getting to meetings as he was a "rural councillor" (representing South Fambridge Ward). This was presumably due to the lack of public transport serving the village in the evenings.[710]

The decade ended with the death in November 1949 of another long-serving council member, Councillor James Crawford of South Fambridge Hall, bringing to end a father-and-son team of public service which stretched back over 50 years. A public meeting that month stood for a minute's silence in honour of the public service that James Crawford had given, "as a mark of respect to a worker who had always shown great enthusiasm in Local Government work since the days of overseers of the parish".[711] He was replaced by Councillor H. Jeffs.[712]

---

706 ERO D/J 126/2/1
707 ERO D/J 126/2/1 & D/J 126/4/1
708 ERO D/J 126/2/1
709 Ibid.
710 ERO D/J 126/1/1 & D/J 126/2/1
711 ERO D/J 126/1/2
712 ERO D/J 126/2/1

Village Life

In January 1945 it was recorded that the "top portion" of the Ashingdon playing field had been "now released" for use. This implies that it had been taken over for war purposes, perhaps for the cultivation of food, as happened at parks elsewhere in south-east Essex. Clearing up after the war by the removal of Anderson shelters and refuse dumps, and the reinstatement of ploughed-up public footpaths, is a recurring theme in council minutes in 1945-6. A sale of surplus war blankets took place in February 1947.[713]

In November 1945 Ashingdon Parish Council discussed the purchase of additional land adjoining the playing field. This land was bounded on the north by Tennis Lodge and on the south by Ashingdon House School. In April 1946 Ashingdon & District Ratepayers Association requested a meeting between the parish council and the county council to discuss the erection of a community centre there. The parish council replied that the matter was already under consideration. Discussions about this continued throughout 1946 and 1947. In April 1947 there were complaints about children playing in Ashingdon Road because the playing field was unavailable. This may have been connected to this activity.[714] A Memorial Hall Committee was formed, but its meeting in February 1948 was disrupted by "hooliganism" from members of the local youth club.[715]

One new facility which did arrive was the Elim Pentecostal Church, established in Ashingdon on 10 April 1946 on the site of the old Bethany Gospel Hall in Clifton Road.[716]

Figure 82: The predecessor of the current Elim Pentecostal Church building[717]

---

713   ERO D/J 126/1/1
714   ERO D/J 126/2/1
715   ERO D/J 126/1/2
716   Information courtesy Geoff Durham
717   ERO D/DU 1464/4, p.36 (copyright George Robinson)

Figure 83: Ashingdon Road, sometimes called "Main Road", c.1948

The war had demonstrated the benefits of quick and easy telephone communications and in April 1946 the parish council requested the installation of public telephone kiosks on the triangle of grass at the junction of Canewdon and Ashingdon Roads and outside *The Anchor* in South Fambridge. The former appears to have been installed by late 1946. There were complaints about discarded war debris there blocking its usage from then until January 1948. The South Fambridge kiosk was still not in place by November that year.[718] Councillors were irked that one had, however, been provided, with district council support, in very rural Shopland.[719] There was also a need for Nurse Thorne, "the new midwife", to have a phone and the council contacted the General Post Office about this in January 1949.[720]

In February 1947 the parish council discussed with the County of London Electricity Supply Company the old South Fambridge Parish Council's proposal to extend the local electricity supply to South Fambridge village. The company replied that it was happy to support this plan but that materials were currently in short supply due to the war. In April

---

718   ERO D/J 126/2/1 & D/J 126/1/2
719   ERO D/J 126/1/2
720   ERO D/J 126/2/1

the council discussed replacing gas with electricity throughout Ashingdon and South Fambridge.[721]

In March and April 1947 it was reported that many local cesspits were overflowing. Councillor Mrs. Thring advocated the "German system of cesspit construction" to address this, which was rather ironic so soon after the end of the war.[722]

A review of voting procedures led in July 1947 to the removal of a show of hands for local elections in favour of a secret ballot. The parish council formally resolved to use Ashingdon Primary School (as it was now called) and St Andrew's Church Hall as polling stations for future elections.[723]

In September 1947 there was a proposal to establish a clinic at Ashingdon, due to overcrowding at the existing clinic in Rochford.[724] By December there was also a proposal to establish a clinic at South Fambridge and to use the Mission Hall there for that purpose.[725]

Also in September 1947 the council recognised the "ever increasing necessity for a definite programme regarding amenities for unmade roads" in the area. This campaign would be aided by the passing of the Town & Country Planning Act 1947, which revolutionised the planning process by giving local authorities more powers and introducing the concept of planning permission for land development. Ownership of land no longer automatically included the right to develop it.[726]

In September 1948 the topic of council house provision was discussed at a public meeting.[727] Four months later the parish council contacted the district council to ask for homes to be provided for old age pensioners. The latter was not unsympathetic to this request, but replied to say that the housing need for families was greater.[728] The 1948 meeting also included agreement to the publication by the Home Publishing Company of what was almost certainly the first ever guidebook about Ashingdon.[729]

---

721 ERO D/J 126/1/1
722 ERO D/J 126/2/1
723 Ibid.
724 ERO D/J 126/1/2
725 ERO D/J 126/2/1
726 ERO D/J 126/1/2
727 Ibid.
728 ERO D/J 126/2/1
729 ERO D/J 126/1/2

Figure 84: Another view of "Main Road", Ashingdon, from the same series as the previous picture, so likely of a similar date

The regular topics of footpaths, bus shelters, public seats and the playing field continued to occupy the council until the end of the decade. Rochford Rural District Council announced its intention to purchase a changing hut for the latter in November 1948. The dumping of rubbish at the junction of Ashingdon and Canewdon Roads also cropped up regularly in the late 1940s, as did the extension to the electricity supply network and the need for more public telephone kiosks. Local residents received food parcels from abroad in the immediate post-war period.[730] In May 1949 the parish council discussed the need for chiropodists in the area.[731]

Bus services, too, were often discussed, including in September 1949 when the parish council wrote to Essex County Council to ask for a bus service for schoolchildren from South Fambridge in the early morning. This request was rejected, so the council wrote to the bus company and asked them to lay one on. Lighting discussions, too, continued to crop up regularly.[732]

---

730   ERO D/J 126/2/1 & D/J 126/1/2
731   ERO D/J 126/2/1
732   ERO D/J 126/2/1 & D/J 126/1/2

Property Ownership

In July 1944, following the death of Edgar Imray in 1942, his estates were sold at auction at the Corn Exchange in Chelmsford. His total land ownership in Ashingdon was a little over 158 acres, which was sold in seven lots: Ashingdon Hall, the neighbouring "Assandune" bungalow, another bungalow in Church Road and four lots of farmland.[733] A licensed victualler, Imray was living at *The Elms Hotel* in Leigh-on-Sea at the time of his death.[734]

Ashingdon Hall was bought by Mr. Myleton for £425. It was described in the sale particulars as being "at present in a dilapidated condition but if restored would make a delightful residence or could be utilised as a Refreshment and Tea Room". It had six bedrooms, and had main water and gas laid on. There was a bus service on the adjacent main road every half an hour.[735] The Hall was occupied by T.H. Turner in 1948, so had evidently been sold on by then. Buildings and premises there were occupied by Oliver Quincey, who lived next door at Assandune.[736]

One of the farmland areas was operated as a smallholding and was bought by its occupier, Mr. Baines. A section of mixed farmland next to it was bought by Mr. Watkin. Some pasture land at the junction of Ashingdon and Canewdon Roads was bought by E. & H. Grimwade, who were already occupying it. This was the old Chamberlain's farmland and included the site of the Wantz Barn, which had by now been demolished. The land had been marketed as being of considerable building value, but was retained as pasture. The final piece of farmland was along Canewdon Road and was described as "formerly part of Moon's". It was bought by Mr. Watkin.[737]

---

[733] ERO SALE/B5506 & D/CC 99/2
[734] ERO A13442 Box 1
[735] ERO SALE/B5506
[736] ERO D/RR 2/2/5/2
[737] ERO SALE/B5506

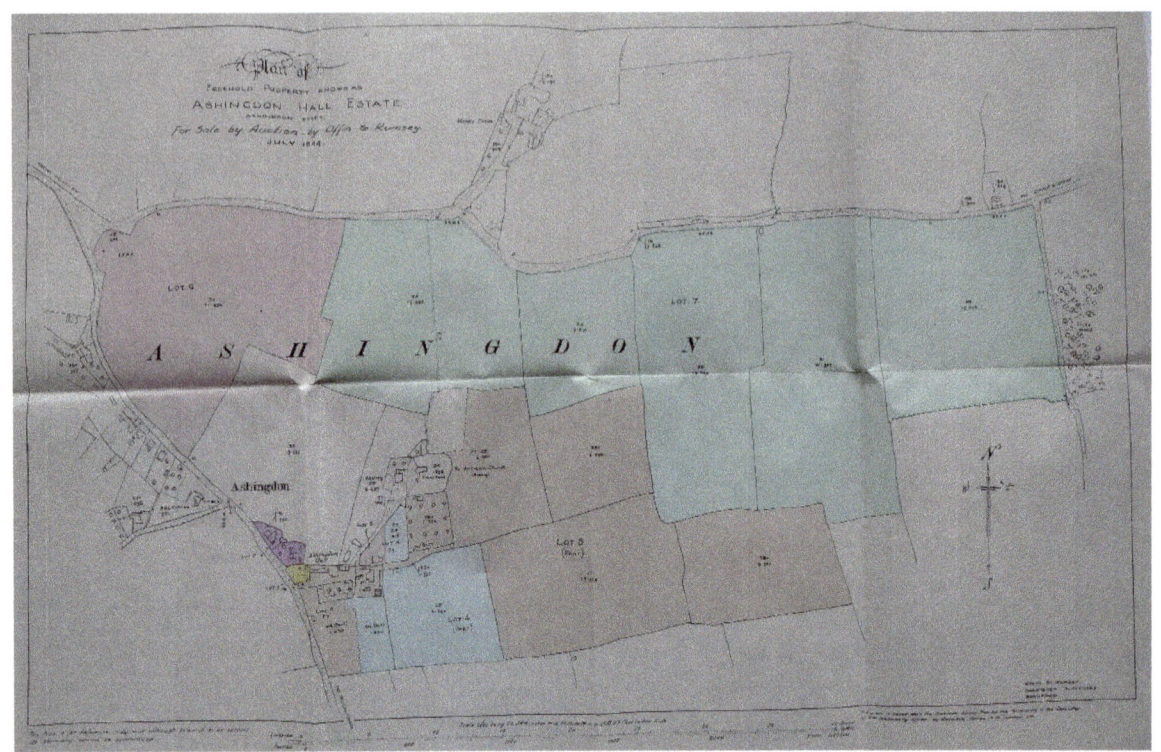

Figure 85: A map accompanying the sale of Edgar Imray's Ashingdon Hall estates in 1944[738]

    1.5 acres of Imray's land were separately sold in 1944 by his executors, Edgar Clifford Imray and George Erskine Harkness, to Rev. Alan Matheson for an extension to Ashingdon churchyard. This was no doubt required because of the increasing population in the village, which passed 1,000 for the first time in the 1940s. This churchyard extension was consecrated in 1948.[739] The boundary between the original churchyard and the new extension can still be easily made out on the ground.

---

738   ERO SALE/B5506

739   ERO D/CC 99/2; the population figure has been deduced from *Essex Chronicle* reports on the restoration of Ashingdon church on 19 January 1951 and 11 June 1951 which quote the population then as being 1100.

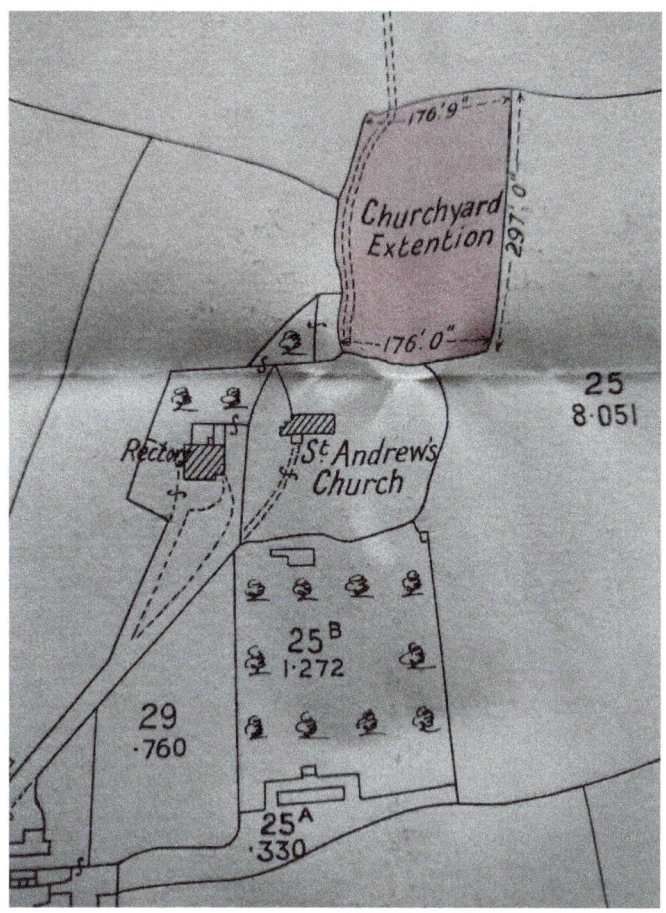

Figure 86: A plan from 1944 showing the proposed extension to Ashingdon churchyard[740]

In 1945-8 Rouncefall was still owned by Herbert Bacon. Henry Harris still owned and operated Ashingdon House School. Tennis Lodge was occupied by Mr. G. Baines. Homefield Farm was occupied by George H. Shorto. The Smith Brothers were still operating in the Crouch. Harrogate Farm was occupied by Edward Watson in 1945 but W.F. Nice in 1948. W.L. Clements was at Beehive Farm in 1945, but W. Sparke was there in 1948. Mrs. M.B. Muers was at Hockley Nurseries in 1945, with Charles Muers evidently having passed away. These were described as being in The Chase rather than in White Hart Lane, as heretofore. In 1948, however, Hockley Nurseries was listed as being in Greensward Lane and occupied by F. Brock. Leamington Road had appeared by this stage.[741]

In South Fambridge, Trinity Stores were owned by Mrs. E. Massie in 1945 and 1948. Percy Dennington was still at Beckney Wood House and Henry William Arnold was still at *The Anchor*. There was a café, run by F. Figg, next to the latter by 1948. Rectory Farm was

---

740   ERO D/CC 99/2 (author unknown)
741   ERO D/RR 2/2/2/7 & D/RR 2/2/5/2

owned by the Jolly Brothers and Brick House Farm was still owned by J.W. Rollin. Pulpits Farm was occupied by A. China in 1945 but by W.A.C. Smith in 1948. Jack Pinborough was at New Hall Farm in both years.[742] This had been occupied by Mrs. Thomas in 1942.[743] Sidney Brown was at the Ferry House in 1948, while The Old Blacksmith's in Greensward Lane was home to the Eltax Rubber Company Ltd.[744]

Education

In 1948 the headmaster, Captain Ford, left his job as headmaster of Ashingdon School for a new, rather different, role as Educational Organiser with the Board of Education in the Bahamas. Jerram-Burrows described Ford in her 1973 centenary booklet about the school as follows: "A man of many facets with the School very much at heart; a man of courage and great leadership whose devotion to duty and especially to the children in his charge, will colour forever the pages of our local history."

Ford was replaced in 1949 by Mr. L.C. (Leonard) Taylor. There were 133 pupils at the time, being taught in four classrooms – the two in the original brick block, the wooden classroom and the Free Church Mission Hall. In 1973 Mr. Taylor recalled that, when he took up the post, the entrance to the headmaster's room was through one of the original brick classrooms, so he often climbed in-and-out of the window to avoid disturbing lessons. Unsurprisingly, he soon had a separate entrance put in. The toilets were still basic when he arrived and there was only a small playground and no playing field.

A New Decade

One topic discussed by Ashingdon Parish Council in 1950-1 was the riding of horses on the pavement in Wellington Road (which does not have any pavements now) and on the footpath between New Park Road and Greensward Lane. The situation was alleviated a little by the need for a footpath map of the parish to be created under the Access to the Countryside Act 1949. Eleven footpaths were identified and confirmed in September 1951.[745]

The question of allotments once again reared its head at this period, with Rochford Rural District Council having requisitioned a plot in Golden Cross Road for these. The district council also wanted the parish council to take over responsibility for the Ashingdon playing field, but the latter was opposed to this. The question of more pillar boxes for the parish was also discussed.[746]

The perennial problems of inadequate bus services to South Fambridge and dangerous

---

742 ERO D/RR 2/2/12/9 & D/RR 2/2/5/2
743 ERO D/J 126/1/2
744 ERO D/RR 2/2/5/2
745 ERO D/J 126/1/2
746 Ibid.

footpaths and ditches continued to be discussed. The supply of electricity to domestic properties in South Fambridge was also a problem. It was recorded at a public meeting in November 1950 that the latter was going to be "a very tricky business for the ward is a very large [one] and of little rateable value". The meeting concluded that a few public street lights from Ashingdon School to *The Anchor* "will have to suffice".[747]

The question of better sewerage across the parish was also a big one in the early 1950s, with local people identifying a very urgent need for proper sewerage provision at Golden Cross Road, Canewdon View Road, Brays Lane and the Ashingdon Park Estate. Many of these places were still served by individual cesspits and there were regular complaints about blocked and overflowing ditches, the need for piping and the public nuisance caused by them. The parish council wrote to the district council about this but received the somewhat disappointing reply in September 1951 that no dates could be given when proper piped sewerage systems would be provided and, in the case of the Ashingdon Park Estate, "it will have to wait for a very long time". The parish council resolved to contact the local MP to see if he could expedite matters. In November 1952 the council also contacted the Minister of Housing and Local Government to try to force some action in respect of Golden Cross Road. Twelve months later, residents on the Ashingdon Park Estate set up a petition to press their case.[748]

Another topic which was causing issues was the lack of name plates on roads. It was reported in January 1952 that the postman was three hours late one day because he could not find all the roads he had to deliver to.[749] By 1951 houses in the main streets of Ashingdon Road and Greensward Lane had been given numbers, as had some suburban streets, such as Crouch View Crescent and the new Pulpits Close. St Thomas Road in South Fambridge had had numbers from the start. Nevertheless, most properties in the area continued to be known by a house name.[750]

In 1952 several new councillors were elected to the parish council. These included T.H. Turner of Ashingdon Hall, D.H.G. Bacon of Hill Farm (Rouncefall) and James Quincey, who quickly became chairman. They also included Bernard Crick, who would go on to become a long-serving member of both the parish and district councils.[751]

Attendance at public meetings appears to have been very patchy at this period. In April 1948 members of the public were complimented by councillors on their excellent attendance. However, in February 1951 the following was recorded at a parish meeting:

"Councillor Sinclair said the public attitude toward local affairs in Ashingdon was

---

747   Ibid.
748   Ibid.
749   Ibid.
750   ERO D/RR 2/2/5/5 & D/RR 2/2/4/1
751   ERO D/J 126/4/1

deplorable. Whatever public meeting you go to in Ashingdon you always see the same old faces and few of them at that. The people of this village have not the slightest interest in public affairs as shown by the 16 people present at this meeting."[752]

Councillor Sinclair was not re-elected in 1952, perhaps because he said that, but one suspects that the situation is probably similar now in communities the length and breadth of the country.

The Restoration of St Andrew's Church

On 11 November 1948, the advowson of the United Benefice of Ashingdon and South Fambridge was transferred to the Master, Fellows & Scholars of the College of Corpus Christi and the Blessed Virgin Mary at the University of Cambridge.[753] Their first appointment for Ashingdon and South Fambridge was Rev. Charles Evelyn-White, who took over from Rev. Matheson as incumbent in 1949. Rev. Evelyn-White oversaw a major restoration of St Andrew's Church, the fund-raising campaign for which led also to a landmark visit to Ashingdon by a delegation from Denmark.

Rev. Evelyn-White had approached the Danish Embassy for help with raising the £2,000 required for the restoration because of that country's connections with the parish through the battle of 1016. In due course St Andrew's hosted the visit of a Danish delegation, who had come to England to commemorate Denmark's links with Ashingdon and to provide financial help for the restoration of the building. It is said that Rev. Evelyn-White sat outside *The Victory Inn* collecting money in jam jars towards the restoration.[754]

The Danish visit took place on 18 January 1951. The *Essex Chronicle*, reporting on the event the following day, wrote that Ashingdon had "never known such a day", as it was "in the news for the first time since Canute won the day some 50 years before the Battle of Hastings". The church was packed with dignitaries from Essex and Denmark for a special commemoration service, whose proceedings were relayed to villagers who stood at the back of the church and outside, lining the paths. Part of the service, which included a Danish hymn, was performed by a pastor from Denmark who was described as "lending a medieval air with his stiffly starched Lutherian ruff". The principal guest was Prince Georg [sic], second cousin of King Frederick IX of Denmark, who presented a model of a Viking longship from Mr. R. Jorgsen of the Danish Embassy. Other dignitaries present included the Lord Lieutenant of Essex (Colonel Sir Francis Whitmore), Mr. Dennis Brown DL, Sir William and Lady Spens, Lady Champion of Crespigny, and the Archdeacon of Southend, the Venerable Ellis N. Gowing. The Danish media were also in attendance and the service was broadcast to Denmark. Some members of the press climbed a 30-feet high scaffolding

---

752 ERO D/J 126/1/2
753 ERO D/CP 1/13
754 'The fields that saw our barbaric past' by Dennis Morgan, *Southend Standard*, 24 April 1974

ladder inside the church, which was there as part of the on-going restoration work, to get a better view. Local schoolchildren waved the Danish flag in a show of support. The support of the Danish contingent enabled the restoration of the church to be completed by the summer.[755]

Figure 87: Rev. Evelyn-White accepting a Danish flag from Prince Georg

Prince Georg donated a Danish flag to the church and Mr. Rye Clausen donated a diptych (altarpiece), featuring scenes of Canute. These and the model of the longship can be seen on display inside the church, the latter hanging from the ceiling of the nave. Roper writes that while the roof of St Andrew's was being repaired, the church was closed and services and weddings took place in the Church Hall.

Figure 88: Repairs underway at St Andrew's in 1951

---

755   ERO A12773 Box 39, *Essex Chronicle* 19 January 1951 & 11 June 1951

For a while after Prince Georg's visit, close ties were established and maintained between Ashingdon and the town of Jelling in Denmark, which was historically the seat of various Viking monarchs. There were plans to twin the two towns, but these never came to fruition.

Structural work to the building in 1951 included the retiling of the roof, the repair and renewal of the roof timbers and the underpinning of the buttresses supporting the north wall and the parish vestry. The interior of the porch was also repaired. The electrical wiring had all been reviewed in 1948.[756]

The Great Tide

On the night of 31 January 1953 Essex suffered major flooding, as north winds combined with high seas to create a "Great Tide" which swept down the east coast of England. At South Fambridge, the seawall was breached and water flooded onto the adjacent farmland, just as had happened in the 1872 breach. The seawalls were raised afterwards, to prevent further flooding of a similar magnitude.

The 1953 Coronation

On 2 June 1953, the Coronation of Queen Elizabeth II was celebrated by local people at the King George V Playing Field. Rev. Evelyn-White was chairman of the Organising Committee for the event. The committee's other key members were Mr. O. Quincey (vice-chairman), Mr. E. Wyeth (treasurer) and Miss B. Webb (secretary). Other members included Mr. Taylor, the headmaster of Ashingdon School, and Mrs. E. Wyeth and Miss E. Wyeth, who were presumably the treasurer's wife and daughter.

---

[756] ERO A6052 Box 2

Figure 89: The cover of the local souvenir programme for Queen Elizabeth II's Coronation

The programme of events for the day began at 2pm with a procession to the playing field, using "Tractors and Trailers kindly loaned by local farmers". A "Coronation Queen" – Miss Audrey Turner – was crowned by Mr. Quincey. This was followed by the judging of a children's fancy dress and tableaux competition. Rev. Evelyn-White then conducted a short service, after which there was a programme of sports activities. Apart from traditional running races and obstacle courses, the sports activities also included "Potato peeling" for Gentlemen and "Catching the Train" (whatever that was!) for Ladies. The afternoon's events culminated in the presentation of souvenir mugs and a commemorative tea for children aged 15 and under. In the evening, there were further celebrations, with a "Grand Gymkhana" of horse-riding skills and "Dancing on the Enclosure" to the music of Fred Tracy's Quartet. The dancing lasted from 8pm to 11pm. A tea for elderly residents was also planned for a later date as part of continuing coronation celebrations.

Figure 90: Ashingdon in the early 1950s

The End of the Ferry

After centuries of regular use, followed by several years of gradual decline, the ferry service across the River Crouch came to an end. This seems to have happened in the early 1950s.

A parish meeting in September 1950 discussed the provision of a bell at South Fambridge to alert the North Fambridge ferryman to passengers waiting on the south bank. The ferry rights at the time were owned by a Mr. Maskell. Attendees resolved to get Rochford Rural District Council involved.[757]

The last ferryman appears to have been Harry Catton. His sister, Elsie, operated it during the Second World War because he was in the army. She used to row troops stationed locally across the river. It is believed that the ferry ceased to operate after the war when Harry died.[758]

The ferry is mentioned in the minutes of Ashingdon parish meetings in October and November 1954, but it is not clear from those if it was still in use at the time.[759] It must have been closed by November 1959 when Ashingdon Parish Council requested the removal

---

757 ERO D/J 126/1/2
758 John Albion, 'South Fambridge' in *East Anglian Magazine* (Vol.31, No.2, December 1971)
759 ERO D/J 126/1/2

of a sign pointing to it from outside Ashingdon School because it was misleading drivers and pedestrians alike.[760]

Roads

The question of the increasing amount of traffic on local roads continued to crop up. In November 1951 there was a suggestion to construct a roundabout "outside the school at Ashingdon Hill", presumably to resolve the issues caused by the close proximity of the Ashingdon Road/Canewdon Road and Ashingdon Road/Fambridge Road junctions.[761] Speeding along Fambridge Road was also an issue. Meanwhile, in January 1953, a lorry damaged the post box outside Ashingdon Hall.[762] In August 1953 the question of straightening Ashingdon Road near the school, to improve safety for children, was discussed.[763]

The lorries bringing men and supplies to the area to carry out repairs to the sea wall following the floods were a regular bone of contention throughout 1953. The "apathy" of Essex County Council in dealing with local road issues was minuted by the parish council, with suggestions being made in November that the county was neglecting the whole of rural south-east Essex. Councillors resolved to contact the district council's road safety committee and their elected county representative, Councillor R. Fryer.[764]

Councillor Fryer duly attended a parish meeting in December 1953, having previously met with the County Surveyor, the Ashingdon Parish Council clerk and residents from the Ashingdon Park Estate. The official County Council response to complaints about local roads and footpaths was read at the meeting and "received some caustic remarks". Nevertheless, parishioners greatly appreciated Councillor Fryer's attendance and efforts, and thanked him warmly for trying to do what he could.[765]

There were still problems in January 1954, however, when it was reported that Fambridge Road "was in constant use by 12–15-ton lorries carrying plywood", presumably either to the factory in South Fambridge village or in connection with the repairs to the sea wall. This had created numerous potholes which needed repairing.[766] In March 1954 it was said that there were 50 lorries on average operating continuously locally due to the on-going work to repair the sea wall. Councillor Fryer reassured residents that speed limits in the area were under discussion.[767]

---

760   ERO D/J 126/2/2
761   ERO D/J 126/1/2
762   ERO D/J 126/2/1
763   ERO D/J 126/1/2
764   Ibid.
765   Ibid.
766   ERO D/J 126/2/1
767   ERO D/J 126/1/2

The Mid-Fifties

Councillor Bevan was replaced as parish council chairman in May 1952 by Councillor Quincey. One of the long-running projects which the council took up under his chairmanship was the question of the provision of a Memorial Hall. The project had been initiated by the Ashingdon & District Ratepayers Association and had been running since the beginning as an independent Memorial Hall Committee, chaired by Mr. Muggleton. It appears to have been going nowhere fast, however, and in July 1952 the parish council raised the prospect of taking over the management of the project.[768] In October, however, it was reported that public enthusiasm had begun to wane and the council consequently decided to leave it with the committee.[769] Nevertheless, the question of the need for what was also described as a "Village Hall" rumbled on, including during "a very spirited discussion" about it in August 1953.[770]

That month a young boy tragically drowned at South Fambridge, apparently having been caught out by the receding tide. Councillors wrote to the district council to ask for a lifebuoy and warning notices to be provided as a result.[771]

As the 1950s wore on, more and more public streetlights were converted from gas to electricity. Development of the area continued, with houses being planned for a then agricultural site opposite Lascelles Gardens.[772]

One unusual topic of discussion in October 1953 was the realignment of the public footpath through St Andrew's churchyard. According to the parochial church council, this apparently ran at the time between the church and the rectory, although this was news to Ashingdon's parish councillors and had evidently been omitted from the public footpaths map that had been drawn up. Everyone concerned agreed that the path could be realigned to its current route to the east of the church.[773]

On 31 March 1954 the long-serving Jessop Morrison stood down as parish clerk and took a well-earned retirement. There were three applicants for his post, with interviews held for each of the candidates.[774] The successful applicant was Miss E.M. (Ethel Maud) Leggatt.[775]

The need for proper sewerage continued to be a bone of contention, as did that of the provision of a piped water supply for the Fairview Estate. In March 1954 the question of

---

768 Ibid.
769 ERO D/J 126/2/1
770 ERO D/J 126/1/2
771 ERO D/J 126/2/1
772 Ibid.
773 Ibid.
774 Ibid.
775 ERO D/J 126/1/2

charging those residents without a proper sewerage system a lower rate than those with one was discussed at a public meeting.[776]

Traffic continued to be an issue, with a suggestion in May 1954 for Fambridge Road to be widened. The parish council resolved to contact the county council about this. It was reported in August that there was a lot of heavy traffic in the road, presumably servicing the factory in South Fambridge.[777]

In May 1954 Councillor Bevan resumed his role as council chairman, following the resignation of Councillor Quincey, who was leaving the district. Councillor Crick was appointed as vice-chairman.[778]

There was clearly some frustration at this period about the speed of resolving identified issues. At a public meeting in September 1954 it was noted that the parish council's powers "were mainly limited to suggestions and recommendations which may or may not yield results". The real power for major local action on topics such as development, highways and education lay with the district and county councils.[779]

Education

The state of Ashingdon School was beginning to cause concerns in 1953, due it would seem in part to a lack of local representation on the management board.[780] The Free Church Mission Hall was still being used as an additional classroom, but this was reported in February 1954 as having a leaky roof and being too cold in the winter months. In March, overcrowding at the school was discussed and the question of better schooling provision was planned to be raised with Essex County Council and at a public meeting. A suggestion from the county that another temporary classroom should be erected was rejected by locals on the basis that this would just delay the inevitable need for more permanent school space. The parish council agreed to set up a committee to look into schooling provision.[781]

An official assessment of affairs came in March 1955 when the Ashingdon and South Fambridge County Junior and Infants' School was reviewed by Her Majesty's school inspectors. They found during their two-day visit that pupil numbers had increased from fewer than 150 to more than 200 in the previous five years, with the biggest growth spike coming in 1953. This was clearly a reflection of the on-going development of Ashingdon

---

776 Ibid.
777 Ibid.
778 ERO D/J 126/2/1
779 ERO D/J 126/1/2
780 ERO D/J 126/2/1
781 ERO D/J 126/1/2

in particular since the war.[782]

There were five classes at the school, with the top one containing pupils from a wide age range, suggesting that some reorganisation was needed. These were accommodated in four classrooms and the Mission Hall. The two classrooms in the original brick building were separated by a wood-glass partition and one of them was very small. There was also a wooden classroom which had a small brick-built kitchen attached to it and doubled as a dining hall at lunchtimes, requiring it to be cleared each day for this purpose. "The only really satisfactory classroom," wrote the inspectors, "is the new 'Medway' hut which was erected two years ago." The lack of a hall meant that no assembly or corporate religious worship could be held and there was no indoor space for sports. The headmaster, Mr. Taylor, shared a small room with his clerical assistant and it was invaded during breaks by other members of staff, as there was no staff room. The kitchen was described as being inadequate for the 120 meals-a-day that it was providing. The playing field, at least, which had evidently been improved since Mr. Taylor's arrival, was described as "Excellent".[783]

Although the premises might have been inadequate, the teaching staff received positive reviews. "All are conscientious and hardworking," wrote the inspectors, "and are on good terms with the children. This happy state of affairs owes much to the Headmaster who is devoted to his school." Mr. Taylor regularly gave up part of his holidays for the annual school camp.[784]

The children, too, were highly thought of, being described as "industrious". Most of their exercise books contained "neat careful work", their behaviour was "sensible" and "they are usually alert and responsive in class".[785]

At a parish meeting in August 1954 members of the public asked for a policeman from Rochford to be provided at the start and end of the school day to help children cross the increasingly busy road outside the school. The police agreed to monitor the situation, but had announced by November that they were not prepared to supply anyone. The parish council agreed to contact the Essex Chief Constable to try their luck with him, but by February 1955 he had also turned down their request. Teachers were voluntarily helping children to cross the road at the time, in addition to their regular duties. The parish council resolved to write to the "Chief Education Authority", presumably Essex County Council, "asking why Ashingdon was the only school without a patrol". Some parents threatened to keep their children at home until the issue was resolved. In June the parish council tried to obtain the services of a police officer who had previously acted as a safety patrolman

---

782 ERO C/DE 7/94
783 Ibid.
784 Ibid.
785 Ibid.

at Hockley school.[786]

The parish council tried again to get a school crossing patrol outside the school without success in December 1956.[787] Another attempt was made in April 1957 but was turned down in July. The council resolved to contact the local MP.[788] In October Mr. Taylor, the headmaster, announced that teachers would stop escorting children across the road with effect from 4 November.[789] This twin-pronged approach evidently paid dividends, as the Chief Constable finally authorised a school crossing patrol in November 1957.[790]

In April 1955 free school transport was available for children who lived over 1.5 miles from their school. The parish council took steps to try to get this facility made available for children who lived in South Fambridge village.[791]

Property Ownership

The renumbering of properties in Ashingdon Road and Greensward Lane affected the shops as well as the residential premises. The row of shops dominated by the Wall family was now renumbered as 444-50 Ashingdon Road. Eric Wyeth's newsagents and sweet-shop became number 428. By 1954, however, it had been taken over by A.P. Tridgell. Trinity Stores, now 308 Greensward Lane, was still being run then by Mrs. E. Massie. The shops on the Ashingdon Park Estate were not affected by the renumbering, with Mrs. L.M. Wainwright running a shop at "The Croft" in Canewdon Road in 1951 and Mr. C.N. Newland still running one at "Alma", three doors down.[792]

Mrs. F.M. Bacon had succeeded Herbert Bacon at Rouncefall by 1954, presumably following the latter's demise.[793] Mrs. P.E. (Phyllis) Crawford (née Bentall) had similarly succeeded her husband, James, at South Fambridge Hall.[794] T.H. Turner was still at Ashingdon Hall. The Jolly Brothers were still at Rectory Farm, which was occupied by H.M. Jolly. Brick House Farm was still owned by J.W. Rollin. New Hall Farm was still owned by Jack Pinborough. Beehive Farm was still owned by W. Sparke. Homefield Farm was still owned by G.H. Shorto. Pulpits Farm was still in the ownership of W.A.C. Smith. The Smith Brothers were still operating oyster layings in the Crouch.[795]

---

786 ERO D/J 126/1/2
787 ERO D/J 126/2/1
788 ERO D/J 126/1/2
789 ERO D/J 126/2/1
790 ERO D/J 126/1/2
791 ERO D/J 126/2/1
792 ERO D/RR 2/2/5/5 & D/RR 2/2/4/1
793 Ibid.
794 ERO D/RR 2/2/5/5 & D/RR 2/2/4/1 and Rochford District Community Archive: A Lost Fambridge Crawford http://www.rochforddistricthistory.org.uk/page/a_lost_fambridge_crawford
795 ERO D/RR 2/2/5/5 & D/RR 2/2/4/1

The Anchor at South Fambridge had been taken over by 1951 by A.W. Mascall. The Old Blacksmith's Shop, now 223 Greensward Lane, had been taken over by T. Fawke and was being operated as a workshop. Hyde Wood Poultry Farm had also come into existence and was owned by Mr. S.J. Harold.[796]

Constitutional Crisis

In April 1955 the usual number of nine councillors was elected to Ashingdon Parish Council, but one of those elected, Councillor Jeff, informed the council in May that he would not be taking up office. The council responded by co-opting Mr. D. Sutton. The chairman, Councillor Rollin, who had only just taken up the chairmanship the previous month, used his casting vote in a two-way tie to secure this. The process of co-option was one that had been successfully used several times in the 1940s, but the laws governing local government procedures had changed since this time and the co-option of Mr. Sutton was found to be unlawful.[797] Not only that, but he was not an Ashingdon resident.[798]

The May meeting also heard that the parish clerk, Miss Leggatt, had been elected the previous month as a councillor on Rochford Rural District Council.[799] She was also a county councillor the following year.[800] She was asked by those present what her intentions were with regard to the clerkship and she said that she planned to stay on. She was asked to leave the meeting while the councillors discussed the matter. No-one took any minutes while she was out of the room.[801]

Miss Leggett returned to the meeting after the above discussion and was asked to resign her post as clerk. Councillors stressed that they were very happy with her work, but were concerned about the potential conflict of interests. Councillor Turner even told Miss Leggatt that he had no confidence in her because she had said that she was not going to stand for election to the district council but did so anyway. No-one could find a formal record of Miss Leggatt's appointment as clerk, however, so it was difficult to see how she could resign if she had not been formally appointed. Miss Leggatt proposed that six months' notice should be given her and the councillors accepted this suggestion.[802]

The mishandling of the above two events led to a vote of no confidence in the parish council at a public meeting in June 1955, with the chairman and his vice chairman, Councillor Adams, coming in for particular criticism. There was much discussion about

---

796 Ibid.
797 ERO D/J 126/2/1
798 ERO D/J 126/1/2
799 ERO D/J 126/2/1
800 ERP D/J 126/1/2
801 ERO D/J 126/2/1
802 Ibid.

the proper procedure in both cases. The meeting passed a resolution that the council should resign en bloc. Two of the councillors voted for this. Councillor Gore asked that he not be included in the vote, as he had given 25 years' good service to Ashingdon by this stage, but all councillors appear to have been treated the same. Miss Leggatt's appointment as parish clerk was retrospectively confirmed as dating from 18 January 1954.[803]

On 18 July 1955 the eight parish councillors – minus "Councillor" Sutton – convened a meeting to try to find a way forward. It was pointed out at the start of the meeting that they could not be convening as the parish council because a motion had been passed asking them to resign. Councillor Bacon had already tendered his resignation prior to the meeting, but no-one else had done so. All agreed that they needed some definite rules – Standing Orders – by which to operate council business. It was the lack of these that had caused the issues.[804]

A letter signed by seven parishioners was read, calling for a parish meeting due to an infringement of the Local Government Act 1933 and the Representation of the People Act 1949.[805] At a public meeting on 26 July 1955, a no confidence vote in the council was passed by 69 votes to 3. There was even talk of a Public Inquiry.[806]

By August 1955 Councillor Quincey had resigned. A letter from the district council about the electoral process was read at a parish council meeting that month and it was clear that the council had breached local government rules. Councillors Bevan, Crick and Gore submitted letters of resignation at the meeting. Councillors Adams, Rollin and Turner announced their intentions to do the same afterwards.[807]

New elections were held and in October the successful candidates were announced as Councillors Bernard Banfield, Frederick Bevan, Dorothy Boothby (Mrs., only the second female councillor), Bernard Crick, Leonard Gabell, John Joseph Gore, Albert Mascall, Kenneth Pudney and Robert Thomas. Two-thirds of these were new to the council and some had been instrumental in calling the former council to account.[808] Councillor Crick was elected as chairman, with Councillor Gore as vice-chairman.[809]

A Standing Order Committee was established in October 1955 and its findings were signed off in February 1956.[810] The constitutional crisis had passed and the council could

---

803   ERO D/J 126/1/2
804   ERO D/J 126/2/1
805   Ibid.
806   ERO D/J 126/1/2
807   ERO D/J 126/2/1
808   ERO D/J 126/1/2, D/J 126/2/1 & D/J 126/4/1
809   ERO D/J 126/2/1
810   Ibid.

recommence with the management of parish business, with elections to it taking place every three years from 1955.

Development

By this stage the question of overdevelopment was becoming an issue. As early as July 1954 Mr. L. Gabell, presumably later the above councillor, asked the parish council to provide details of all building work which had taken place or was due to take place between the period 1 April-31 October that year. The fact that he made this request suggests that there was quite a lot of it.[811]

In January 1955 the question of lighting for the new "Norwegian Houses estate" arose.[812] These were built in a new road, Nansen Avenue, using money sent from Norway as a thank you for support during the war. They were designed to provide housing for people who had been made homeless by the 1953 floods and were named after one of the Norwegians, Mr. Nansen.[813] They were technically a gift to Rochford Rural District Council, which chose to erect them in Ashingdon parish. The parish council was keen to see a plaque erected to commemorate this generosity and the district council duly provided one.[814]

Figure 91: The memorial plaque on Ashingdon Road at the entrance to Nansen Avenue

---

811   Ibid.
812   Ibid.
813   Ashingdon Parish Council: Footpaths https://ashingdonparishcouncil.gov.uk/footpaths/
814   ERO D/J 126/2/1

In April 1956 it was reported that "Hall Farm" had been purchased, apparently for use as a brick field. It is unclear from the available records whether this was Ashingdon or South Fambridge Hall Farm. Pulpits Farm was also being proposed for development. There was general dissatisfaction with these developments amongst local residents, not least because of the already inadequate schooling provision. When Mrs. Thring stated during a public discussion about it that "there was too much good agricultural land already taken for building and development" this marked a shift in local attitudes. Until the early years of the 20th century, Ashingdon and South Fambridge had been entirely rural. From then until the Second World War, piecemeal development by speculative developers had led to much unregulated, creeping urbanisation. Legislation after the war had brought some order, but development had continued. Now, probably for the first time, local people were beginning to question the amount of development that was taking place.[815]

Discussions about a "new estate behind Pulpits Farm" continued until January 1956, when it was reported that Essex County Council had refused development there. There was talk in February of the matter going to a Public Inquiry, something which appears to have happened by April.[816] No doubt local residents were delighted with the resultant planning refusal, but the new environmental awareness that was demonstrated by Mrs. Thring's remark would mean that this would be just the first of many development versus environment discussions which would arise over the following decades.

The Late 1950s

Another topic that arose during 1955 was the question of Rochford Rural District Council seeking Urban status. In October 1955 Ashingdon residents were wrongly informed that this had already happened. Neither they nor the parish councillors were best pleased, as none of the parish councils within the district had been consulted. Councillors sought the attendance of a representative from the district council at a local meeting to explain what was going on. The latter's clerk, Mr. S. Harris, duly attended a public meeting in December, only to be on the receiving end of a 29-3 vote against the quest for Urban powers.[817] In November 1959 local people also opposed the planned administrative removal of any more parts of Rochford Rural District into Rayleigh Urban District, which had been formed from Rayleigh and Rawreth parishes in 1929.[818] Rochford Rural District Council never did get Urban powers.

October 1955 also witnessed a spate of discarded milk bottles around the parish. The council contacted the local milk supplier, Howard's Dairies, to find out what was going on.

---

815 ERO D/J 126/1/2
816 ERO D/J 126/2/1
817 ERO D/J 126/1/2
818 ERO D/J 126/2/2

Meanwhile, nuisances from cesspools, flooded ditches and unrepaired roads and pavements continued to trouble residents throughout the 1950s.[819]

Traffic matters also continued to be a problem, not least in Fambridge Road, where laybys were proposed in November 1955 to allow for passing places.[820] Private car ownership was increasing, which was contributing to the problems.

The provision of a pavement along Greensward Lane from Pulpits Close to Beckney Corner, first raised in March 1956, was a rolling issue for several years, including getting it extended to the school.[821] This reached a critical stage in September 1958 when a child was killed on the road in the vicinity of Pulpits Close, one of many who were forced to walk in the road due to the lack of a footpath. In November 1960 the county council informed local people that the footpath was being constructed in sections, pending negotiations with individual landowners.[822]

Meanwhile, in July 1956, the parish council resolved to try to get Ashingdon Road upgraded to a B-road. Their request, however, was rejected by the county council in December.[823]

In October 1956 a parish meeting resolved not to support a Road Safety Campaign on the grounds that no notice was taken about residents' road safety concerns, so there was no point in engaging with it. The county council instead got it in the ear the following month for the perceived deplorable state of the roads and footpaths throughout the area. It seems, though, that they could not win: in April 1961 complaints were made about a new road surface on Ashingdon Hill which was causing skidding because it was "too smooth"![824]

In February 1956 the parish council heard that Essex County Council was planning some alterations to ward boundaries which might affect Ashingdon. Parish councillors expressed their opposition to this. A Public Inquiry about it, to be held at St Andrew's Church Hall, was scheduled for June. By October it was being reported that there would be no change to existing arrangements.[825]

In March 1956, 86 acres which were "Part [of] Moon's and Chamberlain's Farm" were sold at auction at the Women's Institute Hall in Rochford. This land lay to the east of Fambridge Road. The above naming of the auction lot shows how land from two of the historic local

---

819   ERO D/J 126/1/2
820   ERO D/J 126/2/1
821   Ibid.
822   ERO D/J 126/1/2
823   ERO D/J 126/2/1
824   ERO D/J 126/1/2
825   ERO D/J 126/2/1

farms was being treated as one parcel by this stage.[826]

One unusual matter which arose in March 1956 was the activity of the local fox hunt. The parish council's minutes for that month include the following: "Mr. Gabell reported the disgraceful state in which the Triangle at Ashingdon [at the junction of Ashingdon and Canewdon Roads] had been left after the meet, and the manners of the people were objectionable. Letter to be sent to Essex Union Hunt asking for damage to be made good and an apology from them."[827]

An apology was received the following month, but no compensation was forthcoming. It was left to the county council to sort out the damage the following April.[828]

In May 1956 activity was reported at Hill Farm (Rouncefall) which seemed to parishioners to be suggesting that development might be taking place there. It was noted that there was no water supply or drainage there, which might count against development. In June it was stated at a parish meeting that the building was being damaged and action needed to be taken to resolve this. The parish council wrote in October to Eastwoods Ltd., who by now owned the property. Their response suggests that it was unoccupied and being vandalised, as the parish council considered drawing up a list of local people who could act as a caretaker for the premises.[829] The problem had evidently been resolved by 1958, by which time Rouncefall was in the ownership of Mr. L.J. Chapman.[830]

In June 1956 there were complaints about bad smells and water seepage coming from an "egg-packing" factory in Lower Road.[831] This was traced to Rodan's Poultry Company, where the wall of a cesspool had been broken and a trench dug to allow its contents to flow into a nearby ditch.[832] A Public Health Inspector from Rochford was sent to investigate and gave instructions for the situation to be remedied. The matter nevertheless rumbled on into May 1957.[833]

The process of urbanising some of the former plotland areas continued throughout the 1950s, but only gradually. It was reported in the summer of 1956 that over 20 properties on the Fairview Estate were still without a piped water supply. In September, Ashingdon people took issue with a claim from the district council that 99.8% of properties in the district had mains water. This was still an issue in October 1958, so the parish council

---

826 ERO SALE/B4517
827 ERO D/J 126/2/1
828 Ibid.
829 ERO D/J 126/1/2
830 ERO D/RR 2/2/1/2
831 ERO D/J 126/1/2
832 ERO D/J 126/2/1
833 ERO D/J 126/1/2

raised it with the local MP, Bernard Braine, the following month.[834] A water supply for the estate was finally approved by the Ministry of Housing and Local Government in April 1960.[835]

In May 1956 the parish council was asked for its views on whether Ashingdon should be included in the Green Belt, a nationwide measure aimed at controlling urban growth. Councillors resolved to seek the categorisation of all non-developed areas in the parish in this way.[836] This stance was supported by a parish meeting in July.[837]

In September 1956 it was reported that the district and county councils had passed a scheme for a "Lobster Pool" on Ferry Marsh in South Fambridge. Ashingdon residents were not happy about this. It was one of an increasing number of examples where the parish council had not been informed about decisions affecting the parish.[838] The council had already voted in July to ask the Rural District Council, the planning authority, to notify them of any proposed large-scale developments in the parish.[839]

Despite some local concerns about on-going development, the mid-1950s saw the construction of what was called the "Highams Estate", built predominantly to the east of Broadlands Road and Avenue. Although much of this area was in Ashingdon parish, it felt geographically closer to Hockley. This caused great confusion, due to the conflicting definitions of the historic parish boundaries and the modern communities which straddled them. In December 1956, for example, it was reported that some residents who lived in Ashingdon were wrongly paying their rates to Hockley Parish Council. This was because their properties were incorrectly shown on their deeds as being in Hockley, due to an error by the district council. Ashingdon Parish Council acted swiftly to try to get this resolved. The incorrect referencing of certain local streets as being in one parish when they were actually in another one regularly crops up in the parish council minutes, including in statements by some of the parish councillors.[840]

The need for a playing field for this estate arose in April 1957 and the council sought the following month to obtain the support of Hockley Parish Council for one. This support was forthcoming in July, but permission for its construction was not granted until December 1971.[841] Even then, things were not plain-sailing and there was a Compulsory Purchase

---

834   Ibid.
835   ERO D/J 126/2/2
836   ERO D/J 126/2/1
837   ERO D/J 126/1/2
838   Ibid.
839   ERO D/J 126/2/1
840   Ibid.
841   ERO D/J 126/1/2 & D/J 126/2/3

Order in 1972 and a Local Inquiry in May 1973.[842] Ultimately, the open space planned for the estate was removed from local planning altogether in February 1987 and replaced by a new one in the Malvern Road.[843]

Beaches Close, Chestnut Close, Foxfield Close, Mapleleaf Close, Southbourne Grove, Southview Road and Westbourne Close had all appeared by 1958, along with nearby Cheltenham Road.[844] Tonbridge Road had appeared by 1961.[845]

Also in April 1957 it was stated that the ditch next to the Free Church Mission Hall needed to be piped "as children were jumping in it and causing a nuisance".[846]

Sometime during the mid-1950s Hockley Nurseries moved to New Hall Farm, where it was run by Jack Pinborough. It is referred to interchangeably as "Hockley Nurseries" and "New Hall Nurseries" in local authority minutes.[847] Meanwhile, in Hyde Wood Lane in 1958 there was the Hyde Wood Poultry Farm, owned by Mr. H.V Quinton, and a mink farm, owned by the London-based New World Mink Ranches Limited.[848] Crane Court Estates Limited owned the factory in South Fambridge. The oyster layings in the Crouch were owned by the Burnham River Company Limited.[849]

In December 1957 a plan was announced to build bungalows on Moon's Farm land. The parish council was opposed to this, as was the rural district council, which refused permission for it the following month. Houses were proposed for a nearby field at the bottom of Ashingdon Hill in September 1959, but this plan did not come to fruition either.[850] The rate records for Ashingdon and South Fambridge at this period record a disproportionately high number of bungalows, as opposed to two-storey houses. This was presumably a legacy of the modern settlements' plotland origins.[851]

In May 1959 the parish council wrote to the rural district council about the provision of a local swimming baths, but heard back in July than none would be provided.[852]

In September 1960 "the Ashingdon surgery of Dr. Jones of Hockley" was raised as a topic, due to the lack of a waiting room at the premises.[853]

---

842 ERO D/J 126/2/4
843 ERO D/J 126/2/6
844 ERO D/RR 2/2/1/2
845 ERO D/RR 2/2/1/5
846 ERO D/J 126/2/1
847 Ibid.
848 ERO D/RR 2/2/1/2
849 Ibid.
850 ERO D/J 126/2/1
851 ERO D/RR 2/2/1/2
852 ERO D/J 126/1/2
853 Ibid.

More Issues/More Councillors

There were regular discussions throughout the 1950s about the frequency of parish meetings. These were held monthly, but the question of reducing the frequency often arose. In May 1957 Councillors Gabell and Gore were elected as chairman and vice-chairman respectively of Ashingdon Parish Council. At the parish meeting in November, Councillor Gabell, who had tried unsuccessfully to get their frequency reduced, announced that due to poor attendance he would not be attending unless matters of importance were brought to his notice in advance. An argument with Mrs. Way, the secretary of Ashingdon & District Ratepayers Association, quickly ensued, with the latter being asked to leave the meeting. She refused to do so and the meeting ended abruptly, apparently in chaos.[854] The matter did not end there. At the next parish council meeting Councillor Gabell sought support for his position from his councillor colleagues. This was not forthcoming, so he resigned as both chairman and a councillor and left the meeting. Councillor Thomas was elected to succeed him as chairman the following month.[855]

Mr. Gabell's post on the council was left vacant until the next set of elections in spring 1958. Mrs. Kathleen Way, with whom he had argued, was one of the incoming councillors and only the third female to be elected.[856] By this stage, the county council had agreed that due to the increasing population in Ashingdon, the parish could have 11 councillors instead of nine, seven representing Ashingdon and four representing South Fambridge.[857] This arrangement came into effect from 20 May 1958 under the County of Essex (Number of Parish Councillors) Order of that year.[858] A request was also made for a second district councillor for the growing Ashingdon ward, something which the rural district council supported.[859]

Councillor Bevan returned as parish council chairman in May 1959. Councillor Pudney, who had been on the council since 1955, resigned in that month due to other commitments and was replaced by Councillor Mrs. Boothby, who had served before but had lost her seat in 1958. In September 1959 a motion was proposed that the chairman should relinquish the chair if he wished to participate in "contentious debate", something which had evidently recently happened.[860]

In November 1959 Miss Leggatt gave six months' notice of her intention to resign as parish clerk, as she planned to stand for election as a councillor on the parish council.

---

854   ERO D/J 126/1/2 & A13442 Box 5
855   ERO D/J 126/2/1
856   ERO D/J 126/4/1
857   ERO D/J 126/1/2
858   ERO D/J 126/2/2
859   ERO D/J 126/1/2
860   ERO D/J 126/2/2

She was replaced by Mr. N.J. Coke with effect from 1 April 1960 and was duly elected as a councillor in May 1961.[861]

Increased Schooling Provision

The topic of increasing the local schooling provision regularly reoccurred in the mid-1950s. In January 1955 it was reported that there was a real need for an extra classroom at Ashingdon School.[862] In February 1956 discussions took place about the need for a new school building and an annex to the Free Church Mission Hall to help with overcrowding.[863] The latter building was owned by the county council at this stage, so its use for education rather than worship had evidently been formalised.[864] In April 1956 it was noted that many of Ashingdon's over 11s were having to go to Southend High School because there was insufficient provision for them locally.[865]

Plans for a major rebuilding of the school were discussed at a parish meeting in September 1960. The lack of proper flush toilets, an assembly hall and adequate staff and classroom accommodation were on-going concerns.[866]

New construction finally took place there during the 1960s, with the advent of a much-needed new hall and administration block with flushing toilets. Some long-serving teachers also reached the end of their careers around this time. Mrs. Colenutt, who was noted for her passion for music, taught at the school c.1922-57. Mrs. Bryan, who is remembered for her mannequin parades on open days, was deputy head 1957-67. Mrs. Edwards, who was a teacher at the school 1953-72, succeeded Mrs. Bryan as deputy head, serving in that capacity 1967-72. She is particularly remembered for her work in providing an adventure playground for pupils. Mr. Linn taught at Ashingdon from 1951 to at least 1973, with some short breaks in between. He is remembered for introducing country dancing to the school. Meanwhile, Mrs. Belchamber, a clerical assistant, reached the end of her service in that role in 1965, having taken up her post in 1948. The Parents/Teachers Association was formed in 1962.[867]

More widely, there was talk of providing more secondary schools in the district. The existing one in Rochford was badly affected by aircraft noise from Southend Airport. Representatives of the relevant authorities were invited to a specially convened Ashingdon parish meeting in September 1959 but none of them turned up. Those present

---

861   Ibid.
862   ERO D/J 126/1/2
863   ERO D/J 126/2/1
864   ERO D/RR 2/2/1/2
865   ERO D/J 126/1/2
866   Ibid.
867   L.E. Jerram-Burrows, *Ashingdon County Primary School: Centenary 1873-1973*

complained passionately – and at length – about the poor state of secondary school provision in the district, although it was reported that a new secondary school was planned for Greensward Lane on the borders of Ashingdon and Hockley, where house-building was increasing. This was duly delivered in 1960 and is now the Greensward Academy.[868] Ashingdon Parish Council held its meetings there from time to time in 1961-2. What is now Plumberow Primary Academy in Hamilton Gardens, Hockley, also took infant and junior pupils from Ashingdon when it opened in 1961.[869]

Another secondary school was believed at the above meeting to have been proposed for Oxford Road in Rochford, just outside Ashingdon parish, south of Brays Lane. This, too, was duly delivered and is now the King Edmund School. It was formed from the merger of the Rochford and Wakering Secondary Schools and opened c.1961-2.[870]

The Church

In August 1958 Rev. Evelyn-White wrote to his superiors to say that the Archdeacon (Rev. William Neville Welch, later the first Bishop of Bradwell) had suggested on a recent visit that All Saints church in South Fambridge should be demolished. This was because it had been closed for services by the Bishop in 1953, due to a dwindling congregation, and was in a poor state of repair. Most of the interior fittings had been moved to a new church in Southend.[871]

"The building is in a terrible state," wrote Rev. Evelyn-White, whose tone suggests that he was in favour of demolition, "and it would need hundreds to put it in order."[872]

The decision to classify the undeveloped land around it as Green Belt meant that there would be no nearby development forthcoming, so no new congregation for the church. It was, wrote Rev. Evelyn-White, commenting also that the churchyard was overgrown, "a white elephant".[873]

Rev. Evelyn-White's letter, which survives at the ERO, reveals that the church had previously been closed for 27 years in the early part of the 20th century, presumably due to a dwindling congregation and the cost of maintenance. It was only reopened when the then rector of Ashingdon had a priest friend come to stay with him as "it gave him something to do!"[874]

The churchwardens, Rose Wyeth and Major Sidney Cox, supported the rector's desire

---

868 ERO D/J 126/1/2
869 ERO D/J 126/2/2
870 ERO D/J 126/1/2
871 ERO D/CF 98/5
872 Ibid.
873 Ibid.
874 Ibid.

for demolition and all three signed a faculty request to that end. Approval for demolition was formally authorised in January 1959 but was never enacted.[875]

In 1960 Rev. Evelyn-White was succeeded as rector of Ashingdon and South Fambridge by Rev. Norman James Cotgrove. Rev. Cotgrove served in the post for 21 years, making him the longest-serving rector since Rev. Septimus Nottidge in the 19th century.

Shortly after taking up his post, Rev. Cotgrove was driving past All Saints when he saw the door open. He went inside and discovered four boys cleaning up there. The boys – Robert Kerslow, David Marr, Terry Wessell and Tony Wessell – had been out cycling and decided to explore. They were all aged 10-12. Rev. Cotgrove took this as a sign that the church should be reopened, and with the help of the parochial church council, numerous volunteers and excellent publicity, including on BBC television, he was able to realise this aim. Donations flooded in from across the country and the official reopening ceremony was performed, somewhat ironically, by Rev. Welch, with many other local dignitaries in attendance.[876]

A new external oak door was fitted to the reopened building as a memorial to Mr. & Mrs. Croft. The churchwardens, William Turnbull and Henry Meredith, met with others at *The Anchor Inn* to discuss the project. The door was made by a local builder and was officially dedicated by Rev. Welch.[877]

Meanwhile, at Ashingdon, a survey of St Andrew's which took place in the 1960s revealed that there was some movement of the earth beneath the building, something which had been happening regularly over the centuries. The situation had been exacerbated by a dry summer in 1959, which caused some fractures in the church structure. Some "glass tell-tales" were put in place in various parts of the building in 1962, presumably to confirm movement if they broke. The church's timber floors were renewed in 1965. In 1966 a new pulpit was designed for Ashingdon church by the architect, Brian Muggleton, whose brother ran Muggleton Building Contractors Limited and who was presumably related to the Village Hall Committee chairman. This pulpit is not in the building, so it may never have been delivered.[878] A Mr. Muggleton was present at the first Ashingdon parish council elections in 1931.[879]

The 1960s

In May 1960 Councillor Stanley George Finch, who was elected in 1958, was chosen as chairman of Ashingdon Parish Council. Meanwhile, Councillor George Leslie Smith,

---

875 Ibid.
876 Jerram-Burrows, *South Fambridge*
877 ERO A6052 Box 2
878 Ibid.
879 ERO D/J 126/1/1

another who had been elected in 1958, had failed to attend council meetings over the previous six months. His fellow councillors resolved to write to him on the assumption that he had resigned and informed him that he would consequently be replaced. This duly happened the following month with the re-election of former councillor Bernard Banfield, who had lost his seat in the 1958 election. Councillor Banfield became parish council chairman in May 1961.[880] He was also chairman in the 1970s.[881]

In April 1961 Councillor Arthur Edward Ellard, yet another of the 1958 intake, "reported that there was evidence of increasing vandalism by youth in the Parish" and "cited particularly the terrorising of children by youths riding motorcycles in the Recreation Ground, a small child receiving injuries". The council resolved to contact the police and to ask for a Police House to be established in Ashingdon.[882] Nothing happened in this regard, so a request for a police constable in the village was again submitted in December 1966.[883]

In September 1961 Phyllis Crawford decided to retire and sold South Fambridge Hall Farm to the Gibbons family, who already owned Beckney Farm.[884] Jack Pinborough still owned New Hall Nurseries in 1961, but New Hall Farm was occupied by Mr. E.W. Tate. The South Fambridge factory was owned by Mr. R.H. Reay.[885]

Thomas Hollick's old engineering factory had seen a number of uses over the years. One company manufactured wellington boots, tarpaulins and raincoats there. Others used it as storage for plywood, cars, grain and furniture. During the Second World War it had been used for children's parties and weapons weeks. After the war, a car breaking firm moved in and opened a scrapyard there.[886] This latter activity proved to be contentious and there are numerous references to it in the parish council and parish meeting minutes. In January 1961, for example, there were complaints that lorries using the site had caused damage to St Thomas Road and Fambridge Road, including to kerbs and posts. The smell and the noise from the facility were also causing issues. The activity was partly taking place in the new Green Belt area too. The parish council initially contacted the rural district council about this, but in March they wrote to the local MP, Bernard Braine. By September a Local Inquiry was planned. Discontinuance of the activity was recommended by the rural district council, but it was felt that there would probably be an appeal. Nevertheless,

---

880 ERO D/J 126/2/2
881 ERO D/J 126/2/4
882 ERO D/J 126/1/2
883 ERO D/J 126/2/3
884 Rochford District Community Archive: A Lost Fambridge Crawford
http://www.rochforddistricthistory.org.uk/page/a_lost_fambridge_crawford
885 ERO D/RR 2/2/1/5
886 Jerram-Burrows, *South Fambridge*

an Enforcement Order to cease the activity was issued in January 1962.[887] In late February or early March 1963 a Public Inquiry was held about it in Rochford. Enforcement action was taken against the owners. Another scrap metal business in Foxfield Close was also briefly problematic at this period.[888]

Vandalism was a repeated problem in the 1960s. In February 1961, for example, it was reported that the Electricity Board had asked for a tree in Church Road next to one of their lamp standards to be removed because "boys climb this tree and interfere with the lighting installation". By June, the glass in local bus shelters was being broken. In October it was public seats. In December the question of vandalism across Rochford District was being discussed. In May 1965 five newly installed streetlamps were vandalised.[889] In April 1967 it was the turn of street nameplates.[890]

One unusual type of noise complaint was also an issue. In July 1961 "A complaint was lodged by Mr. Councillor Finch [a former parish council chairman] that an ice cream vendor was causing annoyance in the district by the volume of noise emanating from his musical conveyance". A different complainant had also raised the issue with one of the neighbouring local authorities, so it must have been pretty loud![891]

Sewerage and flooding problems also regularly occurred around this time, especially in Brays Lane and at Leamington and Cheltenham Roads. In September 1961 the parish council raised the question of the provision of a proper sewerage system in South Fambridge with the Rochford Rural District Parish Councils Association. The question of who should pay for lighting on the Hawkwell side of Ashingdon Road also cropped up that month, with Ashingdon Parish Council, who were footing the bill, not unreasonably seeking some financial assistance from its Hawkwell counterpart. A third issue that month was the parking of lorries at the top of Ashingdon Hill for long periods which were blocking the road while their drivers visited a nearby tearoom.[892]

In October 1961 came an early example of something which was then rare but is now thankfully more common: a mental health awareness event, which took the form of a flag day. The latter were once popular fundraising events where members of the public gave money to charity collectors in the street and were given a flag, later a sticker, to show that they had contributed, much like a Poppy Day event now.[893]

October 1961 also saw the resignation of Councillor Thomas from Ashingdon Parish

---

887   ERO D/J 126/1/2
888   ERO D/J 126/2/2
889   Ibid.
890   ERO D/J 126/2/3
891   ERO D/J 126/2/2
892   Ibid.
893   Ibid.

Council. He was replaced by Councillor Gabell, who had previously left the council under a cloud. Councillor Thomas's role as vice-chairman was taken over by Councillor Mrs. Way, the first woman to occupy that position.[894]

It is hard now to picture an Ashingdon which was clearly in transition at this period. The village's growth had been quite rapid over the previous half-century, as it transformed from a rural community into an urban one, but the process of urbanisation was slow and piecemeal. The provision of streetlighting, sewerage works and made-up streets was made in batches over long periods of time. A quotation about Ashingdon Road from January 1962 sums this up nicely, with it being reported at a parish council meeting that month that "in places, no path exists and in other places, paths had been so damaged by traffic as to be indistinguishable from the road". It is hard now to picture the main road in the village having no kerbs or pavements! Constant efforts were made by the parish council to get this road reclassified to improve pedestrian safety and reduce accidents and congestion, including via direct communications with the Ministry of Transport, the recording of traffic censuses and the taking of photographs. A fatal accident on Ashingdon Road in 1963 was found by the coroner's jury to be in part due to "inadequate lighting". Ashingdon parish councillors were clearly spooked by this and countered that they had been trying unsuccessfully to get the road upgraded, had installed new sodium lighting and had been seeking a financial contribution to the latter from Hawkwell Parish Council. The county council announced in December that they were negotiating with landowners to try to acquire land for road-widening and the provision of paths and laybys. When asked by the district council in May 1964 for their views on dog-fouling on local footpaths, Ashingdon's councillors responded by saying that it wasn't an issue because they didn't have enough footpaths to be fouled in the first place![895] It must have been a great relief to local councillors when the responsibility for lighting the main roads was taken over by Essex County Council with effect from 1 April 1967.[896]

From December 1962 to March 1963 the UK suffered from one of its most severe winters on record. Snow fell throughout this period, with blizzards a regular occurrence and temperatures dropping to minus 20C. The sea froze, roads and railway lines were blocked and many villages were cut off. One of these was evidently South Fambridge, as Fambridge Road was reported as being blocked by snow in January 1963.[897]

By September 1963 the large Newton Hall site in Ashingdon Road had been sold for redevelopment. Newton Hall was demolished and its grounds were covered with two new

---

894 Ibid.
895 Ibid.
896 ERO D/J 126/2/3
897 ERO D/J 126/2/2

streets, Newton Hall Gardens and Assandune Close, which were completed in 1964.[898]

Figure 92: Newton Hall, whose site was developed for Newton Hall Gardens and Assandune Close[899]

In May 1964 Councillor Miss Leggatt was elected as Ashingdon Parish Council chairman, becoming the first female to occupy the role. The elections of Councillors Albert Edward Frank Ellard and Albert Edward Henry Ellard in 1964 and the co-option of Rhoda Victoria Ellard due to a vacancy in 1965 saw initially two and then three members of the same family serving on the council for the first time. Meanwhile, the clerk, Mr. Coke, tendered his resignation and was replaced by Mrs. J. Shepherd with effect from 1 July 1964. In January 1966 John Jolly, grandson of the John Jolly who had served the local community for three decades, was co-opted to fill another vacancy.[900] He remained on the council for many years and became its chairman in May 1972.[901]

In June 1965 a pile of shingle was causing problems. It had been dumped on the traffic island outside the school and children were scattering the stones far and wide. Numerous complaints were received from local residents about this. The shingle was removed the

---

898   Ibid.
899   ERO D/DU 1464/4, p.35 (copyright George Robinson)
900   ERO D/J 126/2/2
901   ERO D/J 126/2/3

following month.[902]

In November 1966 a new street, Moon's Close, was under construction. This was so named as the land there "had connections with the old farm".[903] A planned extension to it in 1973-4 caused some consternation, as the extension crossed a public access route into the King George V Playing Field from Ashingdon Road. This area was still described at the time as "land at Moon's Barn Farm" (compare the modern layout with the 1808 map above). A solution was found by retaining the right-of-way, which now extends from Ashingdon Road across the extended part of Moon's Close into the playing fields.[904]

In December 1966 there were problems with a coal depot in Church Road which appears to have expanded beyond its agreed boundaries.[905]

In April 1967 the local MP, Bernard Braine, attended a parish meeting to listen to complaints about sewerage, flooding at Hockley Secondary School, the replacement of dwellings destroyed by fire and drains in Leamington Road.[906]

By May 1967 Councillor Crick was back in the role of parish council chairman. One of the first tasks he had to deal with in July was a report that "a certain amount of rowdyism was taking place at South Fambridge, usually coinciding with 'closing time'…". It was unclear whether these two things were connected, but the police were asked to visit the village at an appropriate hour.[907]

The Memorial Hall

The question of the need for a Memorial Hall or Village Hall had rumbled on unresolved throughout the 1950s. In January 1955, for example, it was stated at a public meeting that some land had been purchased for one. Mrs. Thring impressed upon attendees the need for some definite action on the topic and the parish clerk was tasked with obtaining a plan of the proposed site the following month. In March 1955 it was reported that the Village Hall Committee had circulated some response cards to local residents to establish once-and-for-all the level of desire for such a facility.[908] Nevertheless, progress was painfully slow. The parish council discussed the topic every month from April to October in 1957 without resolution.[909] Similar discussions took place in the last few months of 1960.[910]

---

902   ERO D/J 126/2/2
903   ERO D/J 126/2/3
904   ERO D/J 126/2/4 & D/J 126/1/3
905   ERO D/J 126/2/3
906   ERO D/J 126/1/3
907   ERO D/J 126/2/3
908   ERO D/J 126/1/2
909   ERO D/J 126/2/1
910   ERO A13442 Box 5

By January 1961, however, progress appeared to be being made. Another public meeting took place, in February, and there were rolling discussions about whether the parish council should contribute to the funds already raised. The council agreed to do this and sought permission from the government to sell the stock it still had from the sale of the Rochford properties in the 1930s. Permission was granted in March and the council agreed to support the project with the £443 4s 7d that would be realised.[911] By 1962 it was being reported that "in the vicinity of the Recreation Ground, a village hall would shortly be erected".[912]

Matters dragged on until November 1966, when Councillor Davis, who had been elected during 1964, reported that "it would appear that after all these years something concrete was at last being carried out".[913] Sure enough, the Ashingdon and East Hawkwell Memorial Hall was finally constructed and was officially opened on 16 September 1967.[914] It hosted its first parish council meeting on 1 April 1968.[915]

Figure 93: The Ashingdon & East Hawkwell Memorial Hall

---

911   ERO D/J 126/1/2 & A13442 Box 5
912   ERO D/J 126/2/2
913   ERO D/J 126/2/3
914   Commemorative plaque inside the building
915   ERO D/J 126/2/3

In December 1974 the Memorial Hall Committee advised the parish council that they were in such a healthy financial position that they would not need to take up the offer of the £443, thus saving ratepayers from this expense.[916]

The Memorial Hall has been a valuable community meeting place since its construction, reducing the reliance on Ashingdon School and St Andrew's Church Hall which had hitherto between them hosted most community functions.

The End of the Decade

In December 1966 there were discussions about changes to ecclesiastical boundaries locally, with Albert, Alexandra, Clifton, Stanley and York Roads (which came under St Mary's in Hawkwell) being transferred to St Andrew's parish. This had duly taken place by April 1968 and its completion opened up again the discussion of moving these streets administratively into Ashingdon's civic parish as well. It was noted at the time that "Many people of these roads already considered themselves as residents of Ashingdon". Ashingdon Parish Council wrote to its Hawkwell counterpart to try to initiate this transfer, but was met with a lack of interest in this in June.[917]

Certain unwelcome industrial businesses continued to provide a challenge locally. In May and June 1968 there were many complaints about five-ton lorries delivering packing crates and car parts to an address in Ulverston Road. A planning application to formalise this was refused towards the end of the year.[918] Meanwhile, between November 1967 and May 1968 there were rolling complaints about a breaker's yard and the associated car parking arrangements at The Forge in Greensward Lane.[919] This cropped up again in July 1976.[920] Issues with car sales at the premises also arose in 1993.[921]

In September 1968 there were complaints about another scrapyard elsewhere in Greensward Lane. In December 1969 it was the turn of an unauthorised factory in Lower Road. All these activities demonstrated the need either for light industrial facilities in Ashingdon or for the businesses to be moved to other parts of the district. When the district council refused permission for industrial development at Beckney Wood House in June 1970 the tide began to turn.[922]

From September 1968 onwards there were suggestions of building an annex to the brand-new Memorial Hall to provide library facilities there. In September 1969, however,

---

916 ERO D/J 126/2/4
917 ERO D/J 126/2/3
918 Ibid.
919 ERO D/J 126/1/3
920 ERO D/J 126/2/4
921 ERO D/J 126/1/4
922 ERO D/J 126/2/3

Essex County Council wrote to say that it would be unlikely to be able to fund a branch library in Ashingdon.[923]

In November 1968 a parish meeting discussed, amongst other things, the status of Vincent Road, the former plotland street whose development had evidently been arrested due to wartime activities. Mr. Tuson lived there at the time and had his water provided by a standpipe.[924]

In January 1969 Hullbridge Parish Council wrote to Ashingdon Parish Council to ask for the seawall path between Hullbridge and South Fambridge to be reinstated. It had apparently been out of action since 1890! Ashingdon's councillors felt, however, that it would be too expensive to repair.[925]

The lack of a proper sewerage system (especially on the Ashingdon Park Estate and in South Fambridge) was particularly contentious at this period. A £1 million-scheme proposed by the district council in January 1969 did not include initiatives at the above locations, though residents there were expected to contribute to it through their rates. They were not likely to get any appropriate facilities either until at least 1973. Ashingdon Parish Council responded by setting up a Lower Ashingdon Sewerage Sub-Committee in February to review the whole situation.[926]

In April 1969 problems on the Ashingdon Park Estate were compounded when a firm of solicitors fenced off several unoccupied plots there. They appear to have decided to take ownership of these plots and posted notices asking their owners to come forward. Residents on the estate were threatened with violence when they tried to remove the notices and fences, and Hillsborough and Arundel Roads were closed off.[927]

The development footprint in Ashingdon continued to be consolidated. Author Marcus Crouch, who visited the area as part of a tour round the county for his book, *Essex*, which was published in 1969, wrote wryly that "Ashingdon… has 'enjoyed' much modern development" in recent years.

General problems regarding the random dumping of rubbish around the parish and the poor condition of roads, ditches and footpaths continued to occupy local councillors' time throughout the rest of the decade and into the 1970s. They at least at last got to see some of the planning applications which were passing through the district council before permission was granted or refused.[928] They strengthened their position on this in October

---

923 Ibid.
924 ERO D/J 126/1/3
925 ERO D/J 126/2/3
926 Ibid.
927 Ibid.
928 Ibid.

1973 by forming a planning committee for the first time.[929]

The Early 1970s

The year 1970 saw the 950th anniversary of St Andrew's Church celebrated with an "Ashingdon Festival Week" in September. This generated a profit of £166 9s 9d. Ashingdon Carnival is mentioned in the parish council minutes for the first time in July 1970. It may have been started in connection with the Festival. Rochford Carnival had come to the village prior to that.[930]

In June 1970 it was announced that six acres of land at the end of Leamington and Tonbridge Roads were to be developed for housing.[931] These, and Harrogate and Orchard Roads, all still needed to be made-up. Low-voltage electricity was also an issue in this part of the parish, until the Eastern Electricity Board installed a new sub-station in Pulpits Close.[932] Power cuts caused by the miners' strike in 1972 affected parts of the parish, including Ashingdon School.[933]

In October 1970 a one-way traffic system was proposed for the green outside the school at the junction of Ashingdon and Fambridge Roads.[934] This would not be delivered in full until 1987, but it would nonetheless become the parish's first-ever one-way system.[935] October 1970 also saw a road safety initiative for teenagers learning how to drive.[936]

In 1971 the South Fambridge factory was in the occupation of an engineering firm. The many lorries attending the premises then churned up some of the local roads.[937] The lobster sheds of J. Arno & Co. Ltd. were also in operation in the village, next to the long pool near the sea wall which had been created in the 1950s. Lobsters were kept in salt-water tanks there.

In January 1972 one-man buses came into operation and caused some consternation amongst local bus users who had been used to having a driver and a conductor.[938]

In February 1972 Mrs. J.M. Lowen succeeded Mrs. Shepherd as parish clerk. That month also saw an application for a toilet block at Ashingdon playing fields rejected by Essex County Council due to the perceived intrusive nature of its design. Revised plans were

---

929 ERO D/J 126/2/4
930 ERO D/J 126/2/3
931 Ibid.
932 ERO D/J 126/1/3
933 Henry, *Ashingdon*
934 ERO D/J 126/2/3
935 ERO D/J 126/2/4 & D/J 126/2/6
936 ERO D/J 126/2/3
937 Jerram-Burrows, *South Fambridge*
938 ERO D/J 126/2/3

passed in May, however.[939]

Problems at the scrapyard in South Fambridge continued throughout 1972, despite the issuing of an Enforcement Order many years earlier. A second Enforcement Order was issued in July 1973. The district council took ownership of the problem and sought another more suitable site. Meanwhile, in May 1973 a car repair business in New Park Road was causing a nuisance.[940]

In July 1973 residents in Ashingdon and elsewhere encountered the unpleasant phenomenon of "worms" in the water supply. These were chironomid larvae which were largely removed by the investment of £85,000 in a micro-strainer in October. Nevertheless, a chemical was applied to the water in September 1974 as an additional precaution. Complaints were received at this time about poor water quality and low water pressure locally.[941]

The clash of traditional agriculture and modern development still showed itself in the parish at times, such as in October 1973 when some pigs from "Mr. Kirby's field" wandered into the garden of a house in Greensward Lane.[942]

Maplin Airport

In 1968 the Roskill Commission was established to investigate sites for a new third airport for London in addition to Heathrow and Gatwick. One of the sites being looked at was just off Foulness Island and came to be known as "Maplin Airport". The provision of access to any new airport in that vicinity would include new road and rail routes through Rochford District and have potential noise and pollution implications, as well as adversely affecting wildlife. In March 1969 residents at an Ashingdon parish meeting expressed their opposition to this proposal.[943]

By 1971 Maplin was looking to be a strong candidate for a new airport site. A "Defenders of Essex Association" was set up locally to oppose this and its chairman, Derrick Wood (a long-time district councillor), attended a public meeting in November to explain to Ashingdon residents what it was all about.[944] Ashingdon Parish Council joined the Defenders of Essex the following month.[945]

In October 1973 the parish council convened a public meeting about the issue, having invited Friends of the Earth and Enoch Powell MP to attend. This meeting took place in

---

939   Ibid.
940   ERO D/J 126/1/3
941   ERO D/J 126/1/3; the author lived in Leigh-on-Sea at the time and encountered a similar thing there
942   ERO D/J 126/2/4
943   ERO D/J 126/1/3
944   Ibid.
945   ERO D/J 126/2/3

October. Its attendees passed a resolution describing the airport scheme as "unnecessary, irrelevant and irresponsible".[946]

After much consultation, the Conservative government favoured Maplin as the site for the third London airport, but the scheme was abandoned in 1974 when Labour came to power, largely because of the astronomical expense involved.

Nevertheless, it seems that ideas for some aspects of the scheme rumbled on. In November 1975, for example, the parish council considered the question of a seaport at Maplin. They opposed it on various grounds, including overdevelopment, the expected increase in traffic and the lack of jobs for women in the scheme.[947] This, too, never went ahead.

The parish council minutes of March 1983 record the hope that "this year should kill the Maplin Airport project once and for all time". Two years later it was noted that the Defenders of Essex organisation had run its course.[948] The threat of Maplin was over.

School Centenary

On 26 May 1973 Ashingdon School celebrated its 100th anniversary, with a pageant, a cricket match, music and Morris dancing.[949] By then there were 300 children on the register in nine classes and there was no longer any need to use the Free Church Mission Hall. The school had a good reputation and happy pupils, as testimonies from many ex-pupils in Jerram-Burrows' commemorative book about it reveal. Mr. Taylor was still the headmaster, but there had been some other staff changes by 1973: Mrs. Joy Ralph had taken up post as Deputy Head in October 1972 and Mr. Porter had completed 15 years of service as school caretaker. Councillor Miss Leggatt was Chairman of the School Managers and the school had a Parent-Teacher Association, which provided and built a swimming pool with financial assistance from Essex County Council. The temporary wooden classroom was still in use, however.[950] In 1974, at the height of IRA activity nationally, there was a bomb hoax at the school. In March 1975, some new classrooms were added.[951]

Mr. Taylor retired in April 1976, after 27 years as headmaster. He was replaced in January 1977 by Brian C. Baldry. Mrs. Ralph served as Acting Head for the intervening period. There were 290 children on the register when Mr. Baldry joined.[952]

---

946 ERO D/J 126/2/4
947 ERO D/J 126/2/4
948 ERO D/J 126/2/5
949 Henry, *Ashingdon*
950 Jerram-Burrows, *Ashingdon*
951 Henry, *Ashingdon*
952 Ibid.

Local Government Reorganisation

In March 1970 Ashingdon Parish Council was notified about a White Paper for the reorganisation of Local Government in England. This would in due course lead to the merger of Rochford Rural District Council and Rayleigh Urban District Council with effect from 1 April 1974. Ashingdon parish was not greatly affected by this and the parish council was happy to support these plans as early as December 1971.[953]

One unforeseen benefit was that the Local Government Act 1972, which legislated for this change, also allowed parish council chairmen and -women to claim for expenses, giving them at least some recompense for their own outlay.[954]

The Mid-1970s

The introduction of the Heavy Commercial Vehicles (Control & Regulations) Act 1973 was welcomed locally, as increasingly heavy lorries had been rumbling more regularly by this stage through what were essentially slightly widened, historic country lanes. In February 1974 the parish council even provided feedback in response to this in favour of using barges on the River Crouch to move freight and thus reduce the pressure on the road network. The diversion of lorries along Brays Lane instead of Canewdon Road in February 1976 was not, however, welcomed, as the road was lacking pavements and was thought to be too narrow, so in October complaints were received about heavy lorries using Hyde Wood Lane.[955]

The problem of inadequate sewerage provision, especially on the Ashingdon Park Estate and at "the Hamlet of South Fambridge" had rumbled on throughout the opening years of the 1970s.[956] Councillor Miss Leggatt had met with the MP Bernard Braine – Sir Bernard with effect from the 1972 honours list – to discuss it again in September 1971.[957] A "sewerage embargo" was in place in May 1973, possibly because the Anglian Water Authority was set up in 1974 under the Water Act 1973 which reorganised water, sewerage and river management in England and Wales.[958] Delays to sewerage provision in South Fambridge were certainly caused by this in June 1974 as the new authority was still determining its budgetary arrangements. Neighbouring Stambridge parish managed to get a new sewerage works in that year, but probably because it had already been approved under previous arrangements.[959] Perhaps the most surprising development in all this was

---

953   ERO D/J 126/2/3
954   ERO D/J 126/2/4
955   Ibid.
956   ERO D/J 126/1/3
957   ERO D/J 126/2/3
958   ERO D/J 126/1/3
959   ERO D/J 126/2/4

that residents on the Ashingdon Park Estate wrote to Essex County Council in May or June 1974 to object to the making-up of roads and the installation of a modern sewerage system on their estate. Presumably, they were happy with the un-urbanised nature of the area. Nevertheless, a public meeting in September voted 18-6 in favour of improving sewerage arrangements in Ashingdon generally.[960]

In July 1974 complaints were made to the parish council about a nuisance caused by what appears to have been a car business operating from premises almost opposite *The Victory Inn*. The District Council took enforcement action in January 1975 to try get this stopped, but it recurred throughout the rest of the decade.[961]

In October 1974 it was reported that the old Ferry House in South Fambridge was deteriorating. The council took steps to stop this happening. The same month also saw vandals shooting out lights in Ellesmere and Lower Roads. In April 1975 Councillor Flowers, who had been elected to the council the previous year, generously offered prizes to children at Ashingdon School for essays about vandalism, in an effort to make the next generation aware of the need to look after their local area. The winner, Steven Vince, was announced in November.[962]

In November 1974 planning permission was granted for the construction of 62 detached houses with garages at Harrogate Farm. This was on the six-acre site north of Tonbridge Road. A small play area was included at the north-western corner of the site.[963] The new street in which the houses were built was given the name "Malvern Road" in November 1975.[964] The play area had originally been planned for the Broadlands Estate but was officially reassigned to this one in February 1988.[965] It was still recorded as "proposed", however, at a parish meeting in April 1993, so was presumably delivered after that.[966]

The question of a Sunday market in the area also arose in November 1974, but the council was opposed to this. Another unwelcome arrival was the practice of not giving change on buses, which did not go down well with local bus users when it was introduced in January 1975. A legal challenge was mounted against this, but it was found in February 1976, in Queen's Counsel opinion, not to be unlawful.[967]

In March 1975 the stretch of road outside Ashingdon School, which had until then been named as part of "Lower Road", was renamed as part of "Ashingdon Road". In April

---

960 ERO D/J 126/1/3
961 ERO D/J 126/2/4
962 Ibid.
963 ERO D/J 126/1/3
964 ERO D/J 126/2/4
965 ERO D/J 126/2/6
966 ERO D/J 126/1/4
967 ERO D/J 126/2/4

1976 the parish council asked for flashing lights to be installed here to warn drivers of children potentially crossing the road. This request was agreed to by the county council in September 1977.[968]

March 1975 also saw an appeal for a zebra crossing outside the Memorial Hall, the driver for this being the number of schoolchildren crossing the road there to get to buses. Essex County Council turned the request down in May on the grounds that providing a zebra crossing specifically for children did not meet their criteria.[969] A public meeting in July 1975 called for a pelican crossing to be installed there instead. Hawkwell Parish Council was also in favour of a crossing at this site.[970] The question of a zebra crossing was raised again in January 1978.[971] A 70-person petition for a crossing was created in November 1979 but had no effect.[972]

On 21 August 1975 there were five accidents in one day at the bend outside Lowlands Farm in Lower Road. The county council was asked to improve the signage there. The following year a series of accidents in Fambridge Road led for renewed calls to take preventative measures there too.[973]

In September 1975 the licence for *The Anchor* was transferred to E.G. Griffin and N.J. Lindsell. This in turn led to the submission and approval of a late-night music and dancing licence. An extension to this in March 1978 was opposed by local people, though it evidently went ahead because in April 1979 it was reported that there were often disturbances outside the pub at 2-3am.[974] In July 1980 the parish council submitted a request for the licence holders to reside on the premises, something that was evidently not happening. The venue was beginning to struggle for custom by this stage: signage pointing people to its "remote" location was installed at the Ashingdon Road-end of Fambridge Road in December 1981 to try to encourage more visitors.[975]

In October 1975 an apparently inaccurate report in the *Evening Echo* newspaper about horses prompted Councillor Banfield, the Ashingdon Parish Council chairman, to take a tape recorder to the council's monthly meeting. He made his point and received an apology from the *Echo* the following month.[976]

In November 1975 concerns were expressed about the fencing off of public land in

---

968 Ibid.
969 Ibid.
970 ERO D/J 126/1/3
971 ERO D/J 126/2/4
972 ERO D/J 126/2/5
973 ERO D/J 126/2/4
974 Ibid.
975 ERO D/J 126/2/5
976 ERO D/J 126/2/4

the Beckney Wood area, where a Clearance Order had been issued in 1970. This was one of a number of examples of what was referred to as "land grabbing" in the semi-urban plotland parts of the parish, where residents there, who were unencumbered by neighbours or made-up roads, seemed to be taking it into their own hands to acquire vacant and unattended land adjacent to their own. In January 1976 a mound of earth blocking the junction of Woodside and Grenville Roads was another example of this apparent lawlessness. In July 1979 unauthorised activities were reported in both New Park Road and in the Woodside Road/Clarendon Road area. Local residents were threatened with physical violence at the latter when trying to intervene to get the situation regularised.[977] Allegations of land grabbing were also made against some individuals on the Ashingdon Park Estate in October 1979.[978] Land-grabbing and road-blocking were a rolling problem in most of the former plotland areas into the late 1980s.[979]

Figure 94: Woodside Road, viewed from its western end

Meanwhile, infilling of the more developed areas continued, for example with the construction of bungalows in Ashingdon Road, approximately opposite Albert Road, in

---

977   Ibid.
978   ERO D/J 126/1/3
979   ERO D/J 126/2/5, D/J 126/2/6 & D/J 126/1/4

1976, and the development of land in Church Road the following year, both built by the local firm of Muggleton Building Contractors. Two new streets on land south of Church Road were named in October 1978 as Highcliff Crescent and Arnolds Way.[980]

Many of the barns from Ashingdon Hall Farm survived in Church Road into the late 1970s. These were referred to as "The Black Barns". At least one was in use as a garage for the servicing and repair of motor vehicles. The company operating the business specialised in Jaguars and other good quality marques. One small barn survives today, opposite the southern end of the Parish Hall car park.[981]

In September 1976, a new Roach Valley Conservation Zone was proposed, which would give some protection to the landscape around Ashingdon and South Fambridge.[982]

In December 1977 Ashingdon Parish Council objected to the provision of a residential caravan at Ashingdon Riding School in Canewdon Road "on the grounds that spasmodic forms of development such as this should not be repeated as this would go on all the time".[983]

Queen Elizabeth II Silver Jubilee

1977 saw celebrations across the country to mark The Queen's Silver Jubilee. Ashingdon Parish Council and St Andrew's Parochial Church Council worked together on the event, along with Hawkwell Parish Council. A ball was held at the Memorial Hall in April and street parties were held in numerous local streets, including Alexandra Road, Assandune Close, Stanley Road and York Road. The parish council also decided to pay for a seat half-way up Ashingdon Hill as a permanent reminder of the event.[984]

---

980 ERO D/J 126/2/4
981 Ashingdon Parish Council: History http://www.ashingdonparishcouncil.gov.uk/history/
982 ERO D/J 126/2/4
983 Ibid.
984 ERO D/J 126/2/4 and the Ashingdon Village News and Local Information Facebook group

Figure 95: The 1977 Silver Jubilee seat on Ashingdon Hill, with The Chase in the background

On 18 June 1977 there was a procession from the King George Playing Fields to Ashingdon School. This included the Rochford carnival queen and her court and was led by a shire horse. There were also games and races for children.[985] Infant pupils at the school were each given a Jubilee Crown. Sports events and a picnic were also held there, despite somewhat inclement weather.[986]

A Radical Plan

The late 1970s saw much discussion locally about the Essex Structure Plan, which set out the county strategy for the coming years on topics such as housing development, service provision and the Green Belt. The Plan was controversial locally, not least in proposing that the Ashingdon Park Estate should be developed, something which was opposed by the residents.[987] This led to a revival of the Ashingdon Park Residents' Association in July 1977 and a public meeting in September to oppose the plan. Already frayed tempers were not calmed by a petition sent to Rochford District Council somehow ending up in Rayleigh and by Councillor Mrs. Boothby taking a different line from the residents the

---

985   ERO A13543 Box 2
986   Henry, *Ashingdon*
987   ERO D/J 126/2/4

following year.[988]

Even more controversial than that, though, was a radical plan put forward in 1978 to develop 143 acres of Green Belt land on Rectory Farm by building 700 houses to the west of Fambridge Road. This would be accessed by a feeder road from a new roundabout west of the school in Ashingdon Road. This plan was proposed by Trinity College, Cambridge, who had bought the land *c.*1972/3. The scheme, which was to be developed by Rush & Tompkins Homes Ltd., who had recently built 1,000 homes at Chelmer Village in Chelmsford, also featured public open space, a recreation centre and a car park to the south of All Saints church.[989]

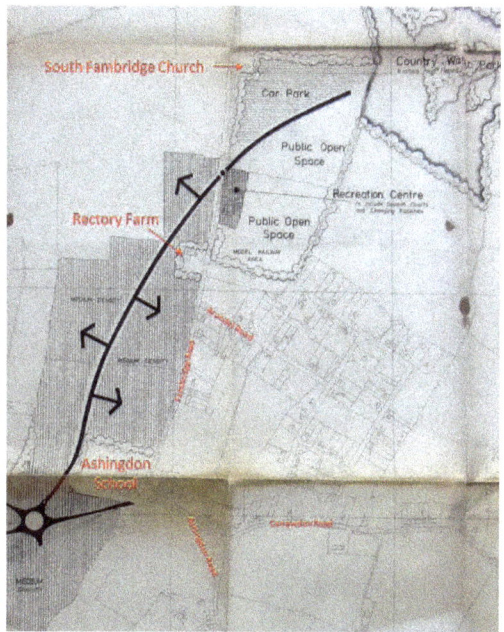

Figure 96: A plan of the proposed 1978 development around Fambridge Road, annotated in red by the author to help the reader orient him/herself

However, the applicants rather shot themselves in the foot by applying for planning permission while the Essex Structure Plan discussions were going on. Councillor Cyril Pohl, who had been elected to Ashingdon Parish Council in 1972, was quoted at the time as saying that "It is against the Essex Structure Plan which was designed to protect the countryside".[990]

The parish council informed Rochford District Council that it would seek a Public

---

988   ERO D/J 126/1/3
989   ERO D/J 126/2/4 & D/DS 190/3
990   ERO D/DS 190/3

Inquiry if the latter approved the scheme. Another opponent was the Federation of South-East Essex Amenity Societies, whose members included the Rochford Hundred Amenity Society, the South End Conservation Society and the Leigh Society. A leading spokesperson for this group was Beryl Webb, who would go on to be elected to the parish council in 1983. Key reasons for objection included the loss of Green Belt and the expected increase in traffic and pressure on local services.[991]

In October 1979 a delegation from Ashingdon Parish Council met on-site with one led by Dr. Bradfield, the bursar of Trinity College. A public meeting in December unanimously opposed any development of the site, fearing that it would change the character of the district and that more development would follow. In January 1980 Rochford District Councillor Derrick Wood, one of the founders of the anti-Maplin Defenders of Essex group, attended a specially convened meeting in Ashingdon and spoke out against the Rectory Farm plans.[992]

In the event, the district council failed to reach a decision within the legal time limit, so the applicants took their application to appeal. This protracted process led in 1980 to the Public Inquiry threatened by the parish council. This ran for 13 days in June and July and the Planning Inspector's findings were then sent to the Secretary of State for the Environment, Michael Heseltine, to make the ultimate decision. While the decision was being awaited, the legal department of Rochford District Council, who did also oppose the scheme, wrote to Ashingdon to say that "the Inspector cannot fail to have been impressed by the professional and convincing manner in which local residents put their case". This professionalism and conviction duly won the day and the scheme was rejected.[993]

The Wildlife and Countryside Act 1981 and increased coastal protection policies introduced by Essex County Council would both later contribute to the on-going preservation of the local landscape. In February and March 1973 the comparatively modern topic of coastal ecology had already been discussed by the parish council.[994] The Essex Structure Plan was formally signed-off in May 1982.[995]

The Late 1970s/Early 1980s

In May 1978 the position of parish council chairman was unusually decided by the toss of a coin, as two candidates could not be separated by voting. Councillor Thomas Wilkins,

---

991 ERO D/DS 190/3 & D/DS 126/4/1
992 ERO D/J 126/1/3
993 ERO D/DS 190/3
994 ERO D/J 126/2/4
995 ERO D/J 126/2/5

who had been elected in 1972, won out over Councillor Arthur Thorne (1973).[996]

In March 1979 the question of inadequate premises at the school rose its head once more, with an additional classroom being required. Essex County Council informed the parish council the following month that it was on their radar but there were other schools with more pressing needs.[997]

May 1979 saw the arrival of a new parish clerk for Ashingdon: Mrs. L.H. Shelley of Crouch View Crescent being appointed.[998]

A clinic and library were both operating in the Memorial Hall in 1980.[999]

In September 1980 plans were put forward for a harbour and some mooring pontoons at South Fambridge. Ashingdon Parish Council was opposed to this development.[1000] The scheme, which was proposed by a company called Lymington Yacht Haven, was withdrawn the following month.[1001]

Christmas Eve 1980 saw the sad passing of Councillor Ethel Leggatt, a long-time public servant in Ashingdon. The parish council stood for a minute's silence at its January 1981 meeting to honour her service. She was described as "a very sincere, hard-working and knowledgeable councillor who will be missed by many people". A memorial service was held for Miss Leggatt at the Memorial Hall in March and a public collection was raised which resulted in the purchase of a trophy in her name which was given to Ashingdon School to present to worthy pupils, a place with which she had had a long association. A commemorative seat for Miss Leggatt was unveiled at St Andrew's in July 1983, a plaque on it paying tribute to her long public service as parish clerk 1954-60, district councillor 1955-76 and parish councillor 1961-80.[1002] Betty Whittingham succeeded Miss Leggatt as chairman of the school governors in February 1981. Wendy Cordess was the first winner of "The Ethel Leggatt Trophy" in July.[1003]

Rev. Simon Hankey took over from Rev. Cotgrove as rector of both Ashingdon and South Fambridge in January 1981.[1004] The two ecclesiastical parishes were formally united into one in 1984, though each parish, unusually, continued to have its own parochial church council, perhaps in recognition of the two parishes' independent historic statuses.[1005]

---

996   ERO D/J 126/2/4
997   Ibid.
998   Ibid.
999   ERO D/J 126/2/5
1000 Ibid.
1001 ERO D/J 126/1/4
1002 ERO D/J 126/2/5 & D/J 126/1/4
1003 Henry, *Ashingdon*
1004 ERO D/J 126/2/5
1005 Jerram-Burrows, *South Fambridge*

The question of motorcyclists riding on footways on the Ashingdon Park Estate proved a challenging one to resolve throughout 1981, due in part because they were riding on "footways" not "footpaths". The former had a vague legal status and it was difficult to take enforcement action in respect of them, especially when they ran next to unmade or unadopted roads such as existed on the estate. Ashingdon at least had its own police constable, PC McNamara, by this stage, but there was little he could do without the backing of the law.[1006]

The unmade and private nature of the roads on this estate caused some unexpected problems, such as an ambulance not being able to get through Lyndhurst Road from the Fambridge Road end because it had been made impassable. In January 1983 it was reported that a Mr. Appleton had blocked the road with a fence and had refused to remove it until the county council stated officially that the road had highway status. The county council formally responded in October 1984, saying that it was unable to do this, because all the roads on the Ashingdon Park Estate were private streets, not public highways, so presumably the fence remained. The section of Lyndhurst Road west of Ellesmere Road is certainly impossible to drive along today.[1007]

Figure 97: The western end of Lyndhurst Road

There were also on-going issues with sewerage and drainage on the Ashingdon Park Estate, including in May 1983 when one elderly couple had eight or nine inches of floodwater in their home. The following month there was flooding in Arundel Road

---

1006   ERO D/J 126/2/5
1007   Ibid.

and four inches of water were found beneath the floor of another home in Canewdon Road.[1008] Sandbags were issued to the estate's residents in September in preparation for the expected winter rainfall. Nevertheless, as late as December 1989 it was reported that residents on the Ashingdon Park Estate were opposed to improvements to drainage in the area, as they were afraid it would lead to full-scale development there.[1009]

1981 also saw the realignment of Canewdon Road, which until then joined Ashingdon Road in two places, either side of a grassy area known as "The Triangle". The northern access, near Hillsborough Road, was permanently closed off and survives today as a feeder road for the houses there. The southern access, closer to the bottom of Ashingdon Hill, was realigned to create more of a perpendicular T-junction. A new bus stop and shelter were included in the scheme. The following year, Councillor Norman Drayton-Thomas, who had been elected in 1976 and would become parish council chairman for the first of many occasions in 1983, was quoted as saying that "he recalled that some years ago the fence on the right-hand side of Canewdon Road, at the new road alignment, used to be behind the pond and willows and this is now completely fenced in". This area is still fenced in. The pond was probably a legacy from the old Chamberlain's Farm days.[1010] Councillor Drayton-Thomas was still serving on the council in 2003.[1011]

Figure 98: The junction of Canewdon and Ashingdon Roads, showing the closed-off section

---

1008   Ibid.
1009   ERO D/J 126/1/4
1010   ERO D/J 126/2/5
1011   ERO D/J 126/4/2

In June 1982 Ashingdon Parish Council was informed by the Department of the Environment that the latter was looking at alternatives to the existing domestic rating system, which was based on property values and was used to fund local government activities. In due course, this would lead to the unpopular Community Charge or Poll Tax and associated rioting in London.[1012]

In July 1982 poor passenger numbers on buses into South Fambridge set the scene for the eventual removal of the service.[1013] Heather Glynn, later a district councillor and a Hawkwell Parish councillor, took over the running of the local Girl Guides in 1982.[1014]

Conflict between horse riders and other road users was a recurring issue at this period, perhaps a legacy of the creeping urbanisation of Ashingdon against a backdrop of being a traditionally rural area. Ashingdon Riding School is regularly mentioned in the parish council minutes at this period, either being on the end of criticism or through its efforts to work with the council to improve the situation, for example by ensuring that all of its riders had a coloured band on their jackets to show which riding school they came from. In January 1983 it was reported that a car had been damaged by a horse. Stray horses, the presence of horse manure on pavements and the damage caused by horses to grass verges all led to calls for better regulation, including, from the horse-riding lobby, repeated calls for better bridleways in the area.[1015]

In January 1983 Ashingdon was awarded a "Well-Kept Village" certificate. This was framed and placed on a wall in the Memorial Hall.[1016]

The 1983 parish council elections resulted in many new faces joining the council and a lot of the old guard either retiring or losing their seats. The new faces included Councillor Beryl Webb, who had been a leading opponent of the Rectory Farm scheme.[1017] She also served on the parochial church council at St Andrew's.[1018]

Stubble burning by farmers, something which had been noted before, was a topic which appeared to come to a head in late 1983. The fire brigade provided statistics to the parish council about the numbers of fires to buildings, vehicles and hedges which had been caused by this activity, as well as for the number of false alarms which had been raised.[1019] Stubble burning was effectively outlawed in 1993 by the Crop Residues (Burning) Regulations, so ceased to be a problem after that.

[1012]   ERO D/J 126/2/5
[1013]   ERO D/J 126/1/4
[1014]   ERO A13543 Box 2
[1015]   ERO D/J 126/2/5 & D/J 126/1/4
[1016]   ERO D/J 126/2/5
[1017]   ERO D/J 126/4/1
[1018]   ERO D/J 126/2/8
[1019]   ERO D/J 126/2/5

Another development in 1983 was the submission of planning permission to convert Ashingdon Hall into a private nursing home. This was duly granted in December.[1020]

In 1984 plans were drawn up to remodel Ashingdon School. The temporary classrooms were in poor condition and the various extensions which had been added gave the feeling that there was no proper entrance to the building. Internal circulation was poor, with no inside access to the administration block and with staff and pupils having to pass through classrooms to get to other areas in the building. The remodelling sought to address these issues, by removing all the temporary buildings and constructing some additional permanent extensions.[1021] The parish council initially favoured retaining the wooden buildings, as there was talk of using them for a nursery school.[1022] This duly came into effect that year. Three new classrooms at the back of the school were delivered in March 1986, with improvements to the foyer/office area taking place that August.[1023]

In October 1984 six people were arrested on the River Crouch and a large consignment of drugs was seized during a joint police and Customs operation. Officers from both organisations were based at Ashingdon School during the day of the arrests.[1024]

Also in October 1984 plans were put forward for some reorganisation at Pulpit's Farm, which was to include a new doctor's surgery and the relocation of some farm buildings. By this stage the population of Ashingdon had risen to over 2,500, so additional services of all kinds were needed, including the provision of a larger mailbox outside the Post Office in February 1985. The Pulpit's Farm scheme proved to be contentious in scale and was ultimately rejected in June 1985 by the Department of Environment, who stated that they would accept the principle of a surgery but not the large-scale redevelopment. There was a doctor's surgery at 99 Greensward Lane at the time. The relocation of this was tied in with the Pulpit's Farm plan. The outcome of this aspect of the scheme was the Greensward Surgery which now stands next to Pulpit's.[1025]

Running Pulpit's Farm was evidently a challenge at this stage for the owner, Miss Hilary Smith, who had bought it in 1984 but had lived there since 1947. In January 1987 there were dilapidated buildings on the site and in June 1988 Miss Smith attended a parish council meeting to explain her plight. She stated that the farmhouse needed £150,000 spent on it and as she had not got the money for that she had been trying to come up with ways to obtain it. The above proposal encompassing the doctor's surgery was one of these schemes. Another was to sell the land off in plots, which neither she nor the parish

---

1020 Ibid.
1021 ERO C/DA 1/32
1022 ERO D/J 126/2/5
1023 Henry, *Ashingdon*
1024 Ibid.
1025 ERO D/J 126/2/5

council were keen to do, due to the unsightly appearance of the area that was likely to result. A compromise was reached where a bungalow for agricultural workers could be constructed on the property. Nevertheless, a plan was submitted for a detached house on the site in February 1990 and the parish council opposed this on the grounds that it could set a precedent for development there. Councillors also opposed a plan to extend and refurbish the Pulpit's farmhouse on the grounds that the resulting roofline would be higher than the original building.[1026]

In 1983 Mr. Steward became the owner of Beckney Woods. By November 1984 Mr Kingston was the owner of New Hall Nursery. He submitted a plan to increase the number of buildings on the site in January 1985. In February 1985 Mr. Chapman was the owner of Rouncefall.[1027] In 1985 Frank and Peggy Jeff were living at Brick House Farm, while the Old Ferry House was occupied by John and Hazel Nicholls and their family.[1028] Frank Jeff was Ashingdon Parish Council's go-to person in 1981 for information about the local history of the area. Glazebrook Farm in Canewdon Road had appeared by July 1985.[1029] Mr. Himfen is mentioned as being the owner in December 1986.[1030]

In October 1984 Councillor Crick was pleasantly surprised to receive congratulations at a public meeting for his 60th birthday and the thanks of attendees for the service he had given to date to Ashingdon as a parish councillor (31 years) and district councillor (22 years).[1031]

The District Plan

In November 1984 a public discussion about a new Rochford District Plan included an announcement that 59 acres of land between Canewdon View Road and Nelson Road had been identified as suitable for development with 70 houses. Councillor Crick went through the details and informed attendees at the meeting that he had already requested the number of houses to be reduced and the building line to be brought in.[1032]

The Plan also included the official recognition of a strip of land between Pulpit's Farm and Hockley as public open space, essentially checking the north-eastwards development of the Hockley urban area any further into Ashingdon parish. Councillor Crick said he would like to have seen better facilities for horse riders included in the plan, as this activity had grown out of all proportion, as well as better access to the river at South

---

1026 ERO D/J 126/2/6
1027 ERO D/J 126/2/5
1028 Jerram-Burrows, *South Fambridge*
1029 ERO D/J 126/2/5
1030 ERO D/J 126/2/6
1031 ERO D/J 126/1/4
1032 Ibid.

Fambridge.[1033] In February 1989 there were reports of cars being driven to the sea wall down the private track to the old ferry steps and a request was made for the access gate to be locked to prevent this.[1034]

South Fambridge Village Plan

South Fambridge was a key site in the District Plan and many felt that it warranted a plan of its own.[1035] Issues with the former factory site there had continued to recur in the first half of the 1980s, not least because of the number and size of the lorries that were servicing the site.[1036] There were also complaints about oil pollution from a leaking tank.[1037]

It had long been clear that modern industry was not appropriate for the early-20th-century factory site and thoughts began to turn to making the site residential. As early as January/February 1979 "a small development of houses" had been proposed in the village, but this had been opposed by local residents and was refused by Rochford District Council in March that year.[1038] By 1981, however, the residential option was looking preferable and "a detailed discussion" took place about this at a public meeting in February that year. Cranes and engines were reported in September to be in use on the site from 6am to after 10pm seven days a week. Enforcement action had reduced the number of heavy vehicles visiting the site, but there were still said by an eyewitness to be up to 15 lorries a day entering and leaving it.[1039] In March 1986 complaints were received about bonfires at the old factory site and the activities of a skip hire company which was operating there.[1040]

Parking problems were also an issue in South Fambridge. In November 1982 a proposal for a 54-space car park at the junction of Fambridge and St Thomas Roads was discussed, a location which would be handy for customers of *The Anchor*. Local residents felt this to be too many spaces and expressed concerns about pub users slamming doors outside their houses late at night. They proposed instead a strip of parking in Fambridge Road which would accommodate around 20-24 cars. The original scheme was abandoned in February 1984. The Fambridge Road strip is in operation, albeit on rough ground, so that evidently went ahead.[1041]

1033 Ibid.
1034 ERO D/J 126/2/6
1035 ERO D/J 126/1/4
1036 ERO D/J 126/1/3
1037 ERO D/J 126/2/5
1038 ERO D/J 126/2/4 & D/J 126/1/3
1039 ERO D/J 126/1/4
1040 ERO D/J 126/2/5
1041 Ibid.

The District Plan of 1984 formally identified South Fambridge as a rural area and earmarked it only for "limited and suitable additional development". This seemed to mark a turning point in resolving the long-standing issues with the factory site and in 1988 a planning application was submitted for the development of the site with 50 houses. This was felt at a public meeting in March to be overdevelopment and to need better lighting and drainage. By May, the number of planned properties had been reduced to 27, though it was noted that even on this scale it would double the village's population.[1042] By June residents were calling for a public meeting about residential development in South Fambridge.[1043] In July the number of properties was further reduced to a more manageable 18 and there was talk of a proper South Fambridge Village Plan. The settlement still had a distinct, historic, rural character and it was felt by many that it was important to protect this.[1044]

In November 1989 it was announced that a new sewage treatment plant would be constructed as part of the factory site redevelopment. This would have benefits, not just to the owners of the proposed new homes, but to other villagers as well.[1045]

In 1994, planning permission was sought – and refused on appeal the following year – for a development of 30 houses on the old factory site. Objections included the lack of employment opportunities in South Fambridge and the expected increase in traffic on the already busy, pavement-less Fambridge Road.[1046] In September 1998 the plans were scaled back to 18 houses once again and this was indeed the number that was built.[1047] The street that served these properties was duly named "Pemberton Field" in honour of Noel Pemberton Billing who had pioneered early aviation on the site.

[1042] ERO D/J 126/1/4
[1043] ERO D/J 126/2/6
[1044] ERO D/J 126/1/4
[1045] ERO D/J 126/2/6
[1046] ERO D/J 126/2/7
[1047] ERO D/J 126/2/8

Figure 99: Pemberton Field in South Fambridge

In October 1988 a smaller-scale plan for nine houses with integral garages next to *The Anchor* was discussed.[1048] By February 1990 this had been revised down to four semi-detached and three detached houses with integral garages.[1049] In October 1995 a new scheme for six detached properties of this latter type was proposed. This was to be the one that was finally delivered there.[1050]

Jerram-Burrows described South Fambridge in her 1985 book about it as "a truly rural Essex village".

Ashingdon Youth Club

Vandalism continued to be a problem, including frequently to bus shelters, and in December 1981 there were issues with youths shooting woodpeckers in Beckney Woods. Numerous steps were taken to address this behaviour. A Friday night youth club at the United Free Church in 1982 had some success at keeping teenagers – the main culprits – off the streets, but it was quickly closed down due to complaints about loud music. In

---

1048   ERO D/J 126/1/4
1049   ERO D/J 126/2/6
1050   ERO D/J 126/2/7

December 1982 "The clerk reported that the bottle banks sited at the Memorial Hall had been set alight by vandals and burnt to a cinder". The police were informed, and Les Noad, who was employed by the parish council to fix bus shelters and install public seats, even gave up his own time to monitor the situation at night.[1051]

In June 1983 a Mr. Holt set up a welcome replacement youth club at the Church Hall. By March 1984 this had morphed into a War Games Club, so a new home for a new youth club had to be sought. The logical place for it was the Memorial Hall, but the parish council, who were keen to get the situation resolved, experienced some kick-back from the Memorial Hall Management Committee. Neither could the hall be booked on the desired evening of a Friday because of irregular bookings taking place on those evenings.[1052]

While discussions were going on, the problems continued. In May 1984 it was reported that there had been vandalism at the Memorial Hall, plus arson attacks on seats, hedges and rubbish heaps. On one occasion refuse was set on fire and put through the letter-boxes of nearby houses. The local police officer, WPC Blake, was appointed to monitor the situation and in June 1984, during a parish meeting at the Memorial Hall, Councillor Maureen Stevens, who had been elected the previous year and would become parish council chairman in 1987, left the room to speak to some youths who were hanging around outside the building. It transpired that all they wanted was a place to meet their friends, drink some coffee and play some records.[1053] Councillor Stevens regularly served as parish council chairman until she stood down from the council in 1995. She donated a gavel as a farewell gift.[1054]

In October 1984 three boys presented a 50-signature petition to the parish council in support of creating a BMX track in Ashingdon, something that councillors were happy to support, as they hoped it could be tied in with their on-going youth club project. Unfortunately, however, the King George V Field had a byelaw banning cycling on it and there was a general reluctance to change this, as it might open the whole field up to cycling. Councillors explored a common land site in New Park Road before accepting a proposal from Rochford District Council to place the track in a park off Magnolia Road (in Hawkwell parish).[1055]

In March 1985 it was suggested that Ashingdon youngsters could be driven by minibus to a youth club in Rochford, but there were fears that some apparent bad blood between the two groups could cause issues. Two months later a group of parents and children attended a parish council meeting to present a petition for the establishment

---

1051 ERO D/J 126/2/5
1052 Ibid.
1053 ERO D/J 126/2/5 & D/J 126/2/6
1054 ERO D/J 126/1/4
1055 ERO D/J 126/2/5

of a youth club in Ashingdon. WPC Blake supported this and Essex County Council promised to provide two wardens for it. After some discussion, the meeting concluded that the district council should be approached to request the use of the pavilion at the King George V Field. It was also agreed that a strongly worded letter should be sent to the Memorial Hall Management Committee – who were described during a parish council discussion as "totally inflexible and uncooperative towards a youth club" – to ask them to be more flexible with their bookings and to make a regular night available for Ashingdon youngsters. There was even talk of voting in a new committee. The parish council, for its part, agreed to provide some funding towards the venture.[1056]

In June the district council agreed that the pavilion could be made available on Tuesdays and a "very successful" disco was held in the interim at the Church Hall. The youth club was duly formed the following month and proved to be very successful as well, under the leadership of Trevor Ashton.[1057] In April 1988 some girls from the club won a national disco dancing competition at Tots nightclub in Southend and progressed to the international stage of the competition in Belgium.[1058]

Sadly, the summer of 1989 was to see a relapse, and the youth club was closed for several weeks from May onwards due to vandalism, with two youths being banned from the club. WPC Blake's replacement, PC Aldridge, had been transferred to Westcliff and no-one had replaced him. The lack of a phone in the pavilion to telephone for assistance when any was available was also an issue. Chris Cook took over from Trevor Ashton in July, following the latter's appointment to a new role in Great Wakering, and she began reopening the club one hour at a time as an experiment. Things were not plain sailing though: in September a motorbike was set alight at the Memorial Hall and in February 1990 there were complaints from local residents about youngsters playing football at midnight behind the building. There had already been requests for better lighting to be installed there to prevent anti-social activities. There were also discussions at this period about locking the car park at night, although again there was tension between the parish council and the Memorial Hall Management Committee about who should be responsible for this.[1059] The latter were also unhappy that the parish council wanted the car park to be closed overnight.[1060]

Thankfully, a concerted effort by all concerned meant that by December 1990 the corner had been turned and the club was up-and-running successfully again.[1061] New

---

1056   Ibid.
1057   Ibid.
1058   ERO D/J 126/2/6
1059   ERO D/J 126/2/6 & D/J 126/1/4
1060   ERO D/J 126/2/4
1061   ERO D/J 126/2/6

lighting behind the Memorial Hall was proven to have reduced crime there and a new police officer, PC Rae Hill, was working hard to build up a good rapport with youth club members.[1062]

Boundary Changes

In July 1985 it was reported that Hockley Parish Council was interested in taking Leamington, Harrogate, Tonbridge and Malvern Roads, and the streets in the Broadlands Road and Avenue area, into their parish. This prompted discussion again about the potential transfer of the streets between Albert and Stanley Roads into Ashingdon parish from Hawkwell. The backdrop was a review of parish boundaries by a government-appointed Boundary Commission, which held an exhibition at the Freight House in Rochford in December. In February 1986 it was noted that land to the west of the Albert/Stanley Roads area was in Ashingdon, but was wanted by Hawkwell Parish Council because development of it was looking likely. This would in due course become the northern section of Rectory Avenue.[1063]

In July 1988 Ashingdon's parish councillors proposed an extension to their parish which would incorporate not just the Albert/Stanley Roads area of Hawkwell parish but the whole of the west side of Ashingdon Road as far south as Rectory Road and westwards from there to the railway bridge. This had echoes of Eric Wyeth's proposal in 1934. It also led to some tension between the two parish councils.[1064]

On 13 July 1989 a meeting was held between Ashingdon, Hawkwell, Hockley and Rochford Parish Councils and Rochford District Council to talk through the options and issues. Ashingdon's councillors do not appear to have been very happy about how the meeting was minuted, saying later that it did not accurately reflect some of their views. They seem to have revised their ambitions a little too regarding taking parts of Hawkwell into the parish, giving Doric Avenue now as the southern boundary of their proposed intake. They were happy though for the Leamington/Harrogate/Broadlands areas to be transferred into Hockley.[1065]

There were clearly still practical issues with these roads being in Ashingdon parish but the Hockley urban area. In April 1990 a newly hired litter collector, Mr. Allen, asked for clarification about where the Ashingdon parish boundary ended in Greensward Lane. In February 1990 the Hockley Ratepayers Association wrote to Ashingdon Parish Council to ask for funding towards making up "the unmade portion of Broadlands Road, Hockley". The parish council noted that "this is a significant part of Ashingdon", but did not have

---

[1062] ERO D/J 126/1/4
[1063] ERO D/J 126/2/5
[1064] ERO D/J 126/2/6
[1065] Ibid.

the money to assist with it. In May the parish council sought financial assistance from those whose properties were in that street, but most were not prepared to help.[1066] The cost of making-up the road was estimated to be £35,000. Sixty percent of this would be provided by the county council and 10% by Hockley Parish Council. Ashingdon Parish Council made provisions towards the remainder in their budget for the next financial year.[1067] The making-up of the road duly went ahead in 1992.[1068]

By September 1991 the Boundary Commission was talking about completing a Partial Parish Review, focusing on the above areas.[1069] Their final report was released in August 1992. This confirmed their intention to transfer the Broadlands and Leamington/Harrogate areas into Hockley. What it did not do, however, was recommend the transfer of the Albert/Stanley roads into Ashingdon. Ashingdon's councillors had been very fair in agreeing to the transfer of the relevant streets to Hockley and had expected to be treated fairly in return by receiving the latter streets from Hawkwell. They were therefore not best pleased that they would potentially be losing some streets – and their residents – but not gaining any in return. The parish clerk calculated that Ashingdon parish would lose 37.63% of its population in this transfer (putting the population at 2259 prior to transfer). This was not just a matter of losing streets and people, it also meant losing income from taxation which was used to fund local services. Councillors submitted a long list of reasons why they were dissatisfied with this proposal and, somewhat surprisingly, they were ultimately successful, with the Boundary Commission announcing in December 1993 that no streets would be transferred either way.[1070]

This would, however, not be the end of the matter and some of these streets were, in fact, later transferred into Hockley parish.

1066 Ibid.
1067 ERO D/J 126/1/4
1068 ERO D/J 126/2/7
1069 ERO D/J 126/2/6
1070 ERO D/J 126/2/7

Figure 100: Harrogate Road, on the border of Ashingdon and Hockley

A Bypass for Ashingdon

In September 1986 two elderly people were tragically killed in Ashingdon Road, which led unsurprisingly to yet more calls for improvements to pedestrian safety there, including by the reduction in the numbers of heavy lorries, many of which were described as having loads which overhung the pavement.[1071] The question of a zebra crossing, which had been on the requirements list since 1975, raised its head once again. The county council advised the parish council that it would be at least three years before one was provided.[1072] At a parish meeting in December, Mr. Holt, who had been knocked off his bicycle by traffic a few days earlier, suggested a footbridge over Ashingdon Road, "but this seemed unlikely to be forthcoming".[1073]

In October 1986 there were reports of numerous lorries taking refuse to South Fambridge.[1074] This was due to a new scheme using rubbish to build up and infill the sea

---

1071   ERO D/J 126/2/5
1072   ERO D/J 126/2/6
1073   ERO D/J 126/1/4
1074   ERO D/J 126/2/5

wall and was scheduled to run until March 1992.[1075] It was stated by officials at a public meeting in Ashingdon in February 1987 that 99% of Rochford District refuse would be going into the wall over a stretch of 3.2km in a five-year period. There would be 50 lorry movements per day and access to the wall would be via South Fambridge Hall. Fences had been erected to prevent refuse from blowing around the neighbourhood. The completion of the one-way system outside Ashingdon School that year was a key plank in the delivery of this scheme, as it would slow traffic down and be safer for children. Mr. Allen informed a parish meeting in March 1990 that he was collecting litter from one side of Fambridge Road only because he was finding the other side too dangerous.[1076]

Another major scheme which first raised its head in 1986 and which was outside the parish but would affect it, was the proposed development of Baltic Wharf on Wallasea Island.[1077] This went to a Public Inquiry in December.[1078] Councillors expressed fears about yet more heavy vehicles using local roads, including Brays Lane.[1079] The scheme was cancelled, however, in November 1987, when it was withdrawn by its promoters, Bambergers.[1080]

As a result of all this activity, a clamour arose for a bypass to be built around Ashingdon, although it was recognised that this was unlikely to happen until well into the 1990s.[1081] Councillor Pohl produced a rough draft of a potential bypass at a parish council meeting in April 1987. He acknowledged in doing this that much of it of necessity would have to pass through Green Belt, something which the council was jealously guarding.[1082]

A wider activity, the South-East Essex Traffic Study, took place in 1988.[1083] This also included consideration of a bypass. The parish clerk was asked in February that year to submit feedback to the study about the "intolerable state of traffic at peak periods" in Ashingdon. In November, Councillor Stevens, the Ashingdon Parish Council chairman, attended an exhibition about the Study at the Freight House in Rochford.[1084]

The parish council had always been protective of Green Belt land in Ashingdon and by 1991 it was clear that this was taking precedence over the provision of a new road. At a parish council meeting in May that year it was reported that, following a public meeting

---

1075 ERO D/J 126/2/6
1076 ERO D/J 126/1/4
1077 ERO D/J 126/2/5
1078 ERO D/J 126/2/6 & D/J 126/1/4
1079 ERO D/J 126/2/5
1080 ERO D/J 126/1/4
1081 Ibid.
1082 ERO D/J 126/2/6
1083 ERO D/DS 523/18
1084 ERO D/J 126/2/6

about the matter, "The majority favoured no bypass but an improvement in the existing road network".[1085]

A bypass for Ashingdon has yet to materialise. Nevertheless, as Southend and Rochford continue to grow, there is a strong probability that, without a reduction in population numbers or vehicle usage, one will make an appearance at some stage.

The Late 1980s

In January 1985 local people played their part in a significant international event, raising money for Ethiopian Famine Relief, a cause championed by former Boomtown Rat, Bob Geldof, which culminated in the Live Aid concerts in London and Philadelphia that summer.[1086]

A local activity in October 1985 was the commemoration of the death of King Canute, who died 950 years earlier. Various activities took place at St Andrew's church for this, including a visit by the Danish Ambassador and the presentation of a watercolour of St Andrew's to a Danish church. This renewed connection with Denmark led again to talk of Ashingdon being twinned with Jelling, although no formal twinning ever took place. A Viking exhibition was held at St Andrew's in October 1986.[1087]

Also in November 1985 it was announced that International Stores, then a large supermarket chain, was interested in purchasing a large plot of land at the junction of Ashingdon and Rectory Roads (in Hawkwell parish) which was used as public open space.[1088] Planning permission for this went to appeal in January 1988.[1089] Permission was ultimately granted and an International supermarket and other shops were established on the site, which became known as the Golden Cross Shopping Parade. International morphed into Gateway and then Somerfield. The last of these was taken over by the Co-operative, now the current occupant of the site, in 2008.

In September 1986 improvement work was on-going at Ashingdon School. By March 1989 there was talk of acquiring adjacent land for a car park.[1090] The parish council agreed to contribute some funding towards this in July and planning permission for it was submitted by November 1990.[1091] By December 1991 construction for it was under way.[1092] It was formally opened as the "Betty Whittingham Car Park" in May 1992, named after the chairman of the school governors, and it helped greatly to reduce traffic congestion in

---

1085　Ibid.
1086　ERO D/J 126/2/5
1087　Ibid.
1088　Ibid.
1089　ERO D/J 126/2/6
1090　ERO D/J 126/2/5
1091　ERO D/J 126/2/6
1092　ERO D/J 126/2/7

the area at the beginning and end of the school day. A new demountable classroom was also provided at the school, in 1989.[1093]

1987 witnessed two striking weather phenomena: heavy snow at the beginning of the year and a hurricane in October.[1094] Ashingdon School was closed for 10 days due to the snow, as many local roads were impassable and damage was caused to the school's sewerage system.[1095] The hurricane caused power cuts throughout Ashingdon and damage to a streetlight.[1096] The school was again forced to close, this time due to a lack of electricity. The school building lost some roof tiles and a tree was also blown over there.[1097]

A class from Ashingdon School appeared live on the BBC's *Saturday Superstore* programme in March 1987 in conjunction with an entertainment project that they were working on.[1098]

Also in March Rochford District Council notified the parish council that they were thinking of installing a putting green at the King George V Field.[1099] This had been delivered by October 1988 but there were complaints that it was too small and not adequately managed.[1100]

Despite the fact that proper golf had been banned on King George's Field in late 1975, someone hit a golf ball through a window of a house adjacent to it in September 1987. The culprit was identified the following month and threatened with prosecution. The flying of model aircraft had also been banned there in spring 1976.[1101]

Woodview Kennels, operated by the Simpkin family, had appeared by May 1987. Ferry House Fisheries was operating at South Fambridge in April 1989.[1102]

In July 1987 there were issues with a clay pigeon-shooting facility at Moon's Farm which was causing annoyance to residents on the Ashingdon Park Estate. One of the parish councillors attended in October to review the situation and reported that the event was well-run. Mr. Fennel was the owner there. Nevertheless, there was evidently some contravention of permissions going on, as notice was served on the activity in December. Clay-pigeon shooting also took place on land in New Park Road that month.[1103]

1093   Henry, *Ashingdon*
1094   ERO D/J 126/2/6
1095   Henry, *Ashingdon*
1096   ERO D/J 126/2/6
1097   Henry, *Ashingdon*
1098   Ibid.
1099   ERO D/J 126/2/6
1100   ERO D/J 126/1/4
1101   ERO D/J 126/2/4 & D/J 126/2/6
1102   ERO D/J 126/2/6
1103   Ibid.

Also in July 1987 a petition was raised locally about the poor service being received from the mobile library.[1104] This led in November to members of the library service attending a public meeting, listening to feedback and promising to make improvements.[1105]

In July 1987 there were also issues with customers at *The Anchor* parking their cars across the main road. It was discovered that the highway ran officially through the pub's car park, which was why it was getting blocked.[1106]

The following month the parish clerk reported that "a person unknown stole a road-roller which had been left in close proximity, connected with road repairs, and drove it through the back of the shelter at Ashingdon School". Extensive damage was caused and the police were informed.[1107]

In 1989 villagers in South Fambridge held a May Day Fair to raise funds for the making-up of St Thomas Road. Through this and subsequent efforts they raised £4,967 by July 1990.[1108]

Also in May a large, tracked vehicle was reported as having shaken properties when being driven along Fambridge Road. It should have been on a transporter.[1109]

In June 1989 the Carnival Committee resigned en masse and a new Ashingdon Fair Committee was set up to replace it.[1110]

In October 1989 Chief Inspector John Brown attended an Ashingdon Parish Council meeting with some of his officers to report on crime rates in the area. He reported that there had been a 64% increase in crime in Ashingdon in the year to date over the 1988 figures. He also reported the arrest of six people who were known to frequent the Memorial Hall car park regularly. Between them, they had admitted to 65 crimes. Chief Inspector Brown also offered the services of his officers in monitoring discos at the troubled youth club. Thankfully, the crime figures had dropped by at least 23% by September 1990.[1111] Chief Inspector Brown sadly died unexpectedly in 1994.[1112]

The late 1980s also saw Ashingdon affected by wider initiatives, including the Local Government (Access to Information) Act 1985. In 1988 there was the national salmonella-in-eggs scare, caused by remarks made by Edwina Currie MP, and the Fire Over Essex commemorations celebrating 400 years since the defeat of the Spanish Armada. In 1989

1104   Ibid.
1105   ERO D/J 126/1/4
1106   ERO D/J 126/2/6
1107   Ibid.
1108   Ibid.
1109   Ibid.
1110   ERO D/J 126/1/4
1111   ERO D/J 126/2/6
1112   ERO D/J 126/2/7

there were county-wide celebrations for Essex Heritage Year and discussions took place about a national review of the Sunday-trading laws, which were ultimately revamped.[1113]

Village Signs

In April 1989 the parish council discussed erecting a village sign. Councillor Drayton-Thomas produced two sketches of potential designs for this. Councillor Mrs. Joyce Baker, who had been elected to the parish council in 1988, built on what Councillor Drayton-Thomas had done and took a leading role in the design for a village sign during 1990, researching the local history of the area and producing some sketches for signs in both Ashingdon and South Fambridge based on her findings. For Ashingdon she chose images of a Viking ship, St Andrew's church and a Viking warrior, with the main panel to be coloured and the surround left in wood. For South Fambridge, the design was to be of unpainted, carved wood, featuring a sea plane, a boat, a wader and a chimney. Gary Bines of Aero Lodge in South Fambridge also helped with the signs' designs.[1114]

The 1990s

By October 1988 plans had been approved for the redevelopment of the Free Church Mission Hall with a new building and car park.[1115] The congregation had been in decline since the Second World War but by the mid-1980s it was beginning to bounce back. The building, however, was showing its age. The decision was made by those running the facility that it should be demolished and replaced with a new one. The old building was knocked down in January 1994, with the new one being erected in phases from 1992 to 1999.

1113 ERO D/J 126/2/6
1114 Ibid.
1115 Ibid.

Figure 101: Ashingdon United Free Church

Mrs. Shelley stepped down as Ashingdon parish clerk in December 1989 and was replaced by Mrs. Joan Tully. Mrs. Tully was in the role only until April 1990, citing other commitments as the reason for stepping down, although the fact that she lived in Wickford may have been a contributing factor.[1116] She was replaced with effect from 30 July by Mr. Peter Murray, a retiring local police officer who wanted to continue to serve the public.[1117] Ashingdon gained a new Neighbourhood Beat Officer in November 1990, in the person of PC Cousins.[1118]

Outside the parish, the planned closure of Rochford Hospital was announced in 1990. Local people were opposed to this.[1119] In October 1990 a 10,000-signature petition was presented against the hospital's closure, with the procession to deliver it being led by a piper.[1120] The petition was in vain, however, and the hospital closed in the 1990s, with all

---

1116   Ibid.
1117   ERO D/J 126/1/4
1118   ERO D/J 126/2/6
1119   Ibid.
1120   ERO D/J 126/1/4

the main services transferring to Southend.[1121]

In March 1990 there was talk of providing mains drainage in The Chase.[1122] Meanwhile, in October, it was reported that the residents there had made-up the road themselves. There was a suggestion that they should be entitled to some financial compensation for this.[1123]

In October 1990 Ashingdon Parish Council was approached to take part in Essex Euro Week, during which it was hoped to match 12 parishes to 12 countries. The council immediately asked to be paired with Denmark, due to the long-standing connections with that country. Celebrations took place in April 1991, with a historical drama by Southend College and music from Rayleigh Brass Band both adding some external colour to the occasion. They were also attended by the Mayor of Jelling.[1124] The Ashingdon village sign was unveiled as part of these activities.[1125]

In November 1990 some speed repeater signs were requested for Ashingdon Hill. These are fairly common now but were a new invention then.[1126] The case for their installation was hampered by the results of a county council survey of speeding there in December 1989, using special equipment, when "unfortunately only a bicycle had come by".[1127] This must have been an extremely quiet day because the parish council and parish meeting minutes are full of issues regarding traffic speed and volume on the main road around this time.

Throughout 1989 and 1990 the Post Office arrangements in Ashingdon were revised, with residents temporarily having to use the facilities at Golden Cross. In March 1990, however, a new Sub Post Office was approved for opening in Mr. Patten's hardware shop with effect from 30 April. Residents were encouraged to use it or lose it.[1128]

In February 1991 there were complaints about sewage overflowing onto fields in South Fambridge. The Anglian Water Authority (AWA) was soon on the case.[1129] The matter continued into 1992, however, with several residents refusing to pay their rates to the AWA because they had had to resolved sewage issues themselves, for example by unblocking waste pipes. This led to an impasse which required several extraordinary parish meetings

---

1121 Rochford District History: Rochford Hospital
http://www.rochforddistricthistory.org.uk/page/rochford_hospital
1122 ERO D/J 126/1/4
1123 ERO D/J 126/2/6
1124 Ibid.
1125 Henry, *Ashingdon*
1126 ERO D/J 126/2/6
1127 ERO D/J 126/1/4
1128 Ibid.
1129 Ibid.

that year, attended by representatives from the AWA. Local residents had taken a video of some of the issues to support their case and legal proceedings were threatened. Messrs. Eastman and Marshall, from the AWA, explained their position and proposed the installation of a new pumping and piping scheme to connect South Fambridge to mains drainage at Ashingdon. This was estimated to take 18 months to deliver and would be very expensive. Planning permission was sought for it in May 1992.[1130]

The design of the above scheme enabled residents on the Ashingdon Park Estate to be connected to it at a later date if required.[1131] The latter initially remained resolutely against modern sewerage provision, stating in April 1991 that they wanted to remain on cesspool arrangements because if mains drainage was installed it would lead to more houses being built on the estate. The parish council appeared to offer some support for this position, stating that they were "interested in keeping the area free from development".[1132] However, the residents' stance appears to have mellowed by February 1995, when it was recorded that there was "more support from residents than at any other time" for a mains sewerage system on the estate. The AWA hosted a roadshow, showcasing their planned scheme, at Ashingdon School in the autumn.[1133] By February 1996 it was being reported that the scheme would be complete within five-to-six weeks.[1134] There were also signs of progress at The Chase, where the AWA was working with Rochford District Council in the early 1990s to agree a scheme for the provision of mains drainage there.[1135]

In April 1991 Essex County Council informed Ashingdon Parish Council that the requested pedestrian crossing outside the Memorial Hall was 31st on their crossings priority list. The matter had been rumbling on for 16 years by this stage and in October local people submitted another petition about it.[1136] In November 1992, however, the county council reported that the crossing had slipped to 42nd on their list and was consequently now so low down that they had taken it off the list altogether! They did, however, agree to install a pedestrian refuge in the 1993/4 financial year, as a compromise.[1137] After a few more years of to-ing and fro-ing, it must have come as a great relief in October 1998 when the clerk was finally able to inform a parish council meeting that "a zebra crossing will be installed in Ashingdon Road".[1138]

1130   ERO D/J 126/2/7
1131   Ibid.
1132   ERO D/J 126/1/4
1133   ERO D/J 126/2/7
1134   ERO D/J 126/2/8
1135   ERO D/J 126/1/4
1136   ERO D/J 126/2/6
1137   ERO D/J 126/2/7
1138   ERO D/J 126/2/8

In September 1991 a public meeting heard that planning permission had been sought for the provision of a hot-food takeaway at 519-21 Ashingdon Road. Attendees were opposed to this on the grounds of parking issues, noise and late-night disturbances. Perhaps somewhat surprisingly now, in the fast-food/home delivery world of the early 21st century, it was stated that "There is a takeaway at Golden Cross and it was not considered necessary to have another in this area". The plan was refused by the district council the following month.[1139] A similar plan at 452 Ashingdon Road in April 1992 was also opposed by local residents.[1140] This, too, was refused.[1141] A third plan, for a bistro at 450 Ashingdon Road, met with a similar fate in 1995.[1142] This latter premises was converted into residential use in 1998.[1143]

In October 1992 planning permission was submitted for a telecommunications tower to be installed near Rouncefall, at the highest spot in Ashingdon parish.[1144] This was duly erected as a transmitter aerial, standing 102 feet (31 metres) tall. It was used initially for mobile phones, but since 2011 has been used as a digital television relay station as well.[1145]

Figure 102: The Rouncefall transmitter tower

1139 ERO D/J 126/1/4
1140 ERO D/J 126/2/7
1141 ERO D/J 126/1/4
1142 ERO D/J 126/2/7
1143 ERO D/J 126/2/8
1144 ERO D/J 126/2/7
1145 Rouncefall transmitter information: http://tx.mb21.co.uk/gallery/gallerypage.php?txid=1827

Throughout the early 1990s there were regularly accidents at the Greensward Lane/Lower Road junction.[1146] This was initially addressed by making changes to the chevrons there.[1147] In 1996, however, with accidents still continuing and the extant signage evidently inadequate, "yet larger signs" were installed.[1148]

In 1993 Rev. Frederick W.B. Kenny succeeded Rev. Hankey as rector of Ashingdon and South Fambridge, following the latter's death. Councillors at a parish council meeting in February observed a minute's silence as a mark of respect for the service that Rev. Hankey had given.[1149] Rev. Kenny occupied the role for only five years, being succeeded in 1998 by Rev. Mary West, who became the first female minister of either parish under a revised job title of "Priest-in-Charge".

Anti-social behaviour at the Memorial Hall continued to be a problem. In June 1994 there were reports of vandalism there, while in February 1995 cars were seen driving wildly around the car park late at night and using it as a "skid pan". The car problems continued into June, when youths kicking footballs against closed shutters were also causing unacceptable noise and nuisance to local residents.[1150] In September 1996 some of the windows at the Memorial Hall were broken and there was also damage at St Andrew's. Glue sniffing and other anti-social activities were reported in Golden Cross Road.[1151]

In September 1994 there were fears that the commercial centre on Ashingdon Road was at risk, as a number of local shops were closing. The parish council tried unsuccessfully to entice Sainsbury's into opening a small outlet there to address this. By June 1996 the shops opposite *The Victory Inn* were "vacant and becoming an eyesore". The Nutan Pharmacy, which now occupies some premises here, was in operation by July 1997, so had evidently moved in by then and begun to redress the balance.[1152]

In October 1994 Councillor George Dawson passed away. He had been a councillor for 27 years and, amongst other things, was a great supporter of youth activities in Ashingdon. It was suggested at a parish meeting that a "George Dawson Trophy" should be awarded for youth work in the parish.[1153] 1994 was also the year that Terry Cutmore was first elected to the parish council.[1154] Councillor Cutmore would go on to become

---

1146 ERO D/J 126/2/7
1147 ERO D/J 126/1/4
1148 ERO D/J 126/2/8
1149 ERO D/J 126/2/7
1150 ERO D/J 126/1/2
1151 ERO D/J 126/1/4
1152 Ibid.
1153 Ibid.
1154 ERO D/J 126/4/1

parish council chairman in 1999.[1155] He was also chairman of Rochford District Council from 2004 to 2019 and served for seven years as councillor for Rochford North on Essex County Council.[1156]

In January 1995 it was suggested that a small car parking area could be created on the site of an orchard in St Thomas Road, South Fambridge. This would accommodate up to seven cars.[1157] It was delivered in early 1998.[1158] Some initial issues experienced in April 2000, such as cars being dumped there and children climbing trees to look into neighbouring gardens, appear to have been mercifully short-lived.[1159]

In 1995 it was announced that the parish council would sponsor a local rugby team. This investment duly paid off when the team won a trophy which was displayed at a parish meeting in April 1996.[1160]

Also in April 1996 the parish council sent a letter of condolence to the residents of Dunblane in Scotland who had lost loved ones during a school shooting there in March.[1161]

By January 1997 a speed camera had been installed in Ashingdon Road, outside Norfolk Court. The camera sign was quickly painted with "a pink substance" by someone who evidently opposed this development. The substance was removed, but by June 1998 red paint had been put on the camera itself.[1162]

At a scheduled meeting of Ashingdon Parish Council on 1 September 1997 councillors observed a minute's silence in remembrance of Diana, Princess of Wales, who had been killed in a car crash the previous day. There were rolling issues with local highways at this period and Councillor Tracey Chapman from Essex County Council was coincidentally in attendance at the meeting to listen to feedback about them.[1163]

Ashingdon's parish clerk, Peter Murray, was instrumental in helping establish parish councils at Great Burstead & South Green and Ramsden Crays at this period. Ashingdon's councillors agreed to loan both his time and some of their facilities towards this endeavour.[1164]

At the November 1997 meeting of the parish council it was reported that the long-serving parish and district councillor, Bernard Crick, had died unexpectedly, while still in

---

1155 ERO D/J 126/4/2
1156 *Echo* newspaper: Terry Cutmore
https://www.echo-news.co.uk/news/18353902.coronavirus-rochford-council-veteran-terry-cutmore-dies/
1157 ERO D/J 126/2/7
1158 ERO D/J 126/1/4
1159 ERO D/J 126/2/8
1160 Ibid.
1161 Ibid.
1162 ERO D/J 126/1/4
1163 ERO D/J 126/2/8
1164 Ibid.

service. Councillor Crick had first been elected in 1952 and had given decades of service to the local community.[1165] He was also the only member of Rochford District Council ever to have been awarded the title of "Honorary Alderman of the District of Rochford" up to this point.[1166]

In July 1999 the parish council indicated its approval of plans to convert the former shellfish packing station at South Fambridge, which had evolved out of the 1950s lobster sheds, into a boatyard.[1167]

In November 1999 Roger Spink was co-opted onto the parish council. He quickly became chairman and served in that capacity continuously for six years from May 2001.[1168]

Ashingdon School

The 125th anniversary of the school was celebrated on Saturday 6th June 1998. A memorial seat for the late Councillor Crick was one of the attractions on view at there.[1169]

By this stage, Mr. Baldry had been headmaster at the school for 21 years and he recorded in the introduction to Colin Henry's 125th anniversary book about the school that he had seen numerous significant changes in his time there. These included the advent of the National Curriculum (NC), Key Stages (KS), the Local Management of Schools (LMS), the school having its own budget, the introduction of computers, the Office for Standards in Education (OFSTED) inspections, Grant Maintained Status (GMS), league tables and the large car park for parents. The NC, KS, LMS and GMS were all introduced by the Education Reform Act 1988, the most important piece of education legislation since the war. The KS initiative, which was structured around pupil age groups, brought with it the Standard Assessment Tests (SATs), which also became a new part of school life. The LMS initiative gave more administrative and financial control to the school rather than to the relevant education authority. OFSTED, a new national system for school inspection, was introduced under the Education (Schools) Act 1992. GMS meant that a school could opt out of local education authority control and receive funding direct from the government instead. Ashingdon sought this from 1992 onwards and duly achieved GMS with effect from 1 January 1994.[1170] This development ended the long-standing practice of one of the parish councillors automatically being on the school's board of governors, something which had been happening in one way or another since its founding in 1873. The last

---

1165 Ibid.
1166 ERO A13442 Box 1 (Correspondence)
1167 ERO D/J 126/2/8
1168 ERO D/J 126/4/2 & D/J 126/2/8
1169 ERO D/J 126/1/4
1170 Henry, *Ashingdon*

parish councillor to serve in this capacity was Councillor Beryl Webb.[1171] By 1996 there were 321 pupils on the school register, probably the highest number ever up to that point and a reflection of the increasing residential development in the area.[1172]

"Can you imagine," mused Mr. Baldry in 1998, looking back 25 years to the school centenary in 1973, "the Ashingdon of 2023?".[1173]

Residential Development

In September 1987 there was a hint of some significant development which was to come at the northern end of Rectory Avenue and at Ashingdon Heights, when Mrs. Chapman of Rouncefall told a public meeting that a 500-year-old hedge at the edge of her property should be protected because building was due to take place post-1990 in the adjoining field.[1174]

In November 1989 Ashingdon Parish Council discussed a plan to build seven houses with garages on land adjacent to The Chase and Stanley Road. The planning application for this went to a Public Inquiry in December and was dismissed in February 1990.[1175]

In September 1990 a planning application was submitted for seven houses and four bungalows in what would become the top end of Rectory Avenue. The parish council was happy with the houses but felt that the number of bungalows should be reduced to three.[1176] Some work in this vicinity had evidently taken place by June 1991 because local residents complained to a public meeting that month that developers had left Clifton and Stanley Roads in a bad state.[1177] In May 1992 planning permission was submitted for a further nine detached houses in Rectory Avenue.[1178]

In November 1994 The Chase Residents' Association expressed concerns about plans to build houses in the fields near the top end of that road: the future site of Ashingdon Heights.[1179] At a parish meeting in October 1995 "Councillor Webb stated that the land at the end of Rectory Avenue had several outline permissions going on".[1180] In 1996 planning permission was granted for residential development at the end of Clifton and York Roads.[1181] Further planning permission on land at the end of Clifton Road was opposed by

---

1171 ERO D/J 126/2/7
1172 Henry, *Ashingdon*
1173 Ibid.
1174 ERO D/J 126/1/4
1175 ERO D/J 126/2/6
1176 Ibid.
1177 ERO D/J 126/1/4
1178 ERO D/J 126/2/7
1179 Ibid.
1180 ERO D/J 126/1/4
1181 ERO D/J 126/2/8

those at a parish meeting in May 1997 on the grounds of the resultant loss of Green Belt, wildlife habitats and leisure facilities, plus an increase in traffic and the likely additional burden on local schools.[1182] Edward Close was in existence here by September 1997. The Clifton Road site went to a Public Inquiry in April 1998.[1183] Houses were ultimately built at Ashingdon Heights and went on sale in the period 1999-2003.[1184]

Figure 103: The Ashingdon Heights estate

Housing development across the district was also beginning to affect Ashingdon, especially in Rochford, where the redevelopment of the Matchbox site at Lesney Gardens had already led to increased traffic on Ashingdon Road. The Essex Replacement County Structure Plan of 1998 proposed a further 2,800 homes in the area, something which Ashingdon Parish Council opposed on the grounds of a shortage of employment opportunities, inadequate infrastructure and threats to the Green Belt. A suggestion was made to locate homes and workplaces closer to one another to reduce the need for commuting. Meanwhile, in South Fambridge, a proposal to build a detached residence in the grounds of the Old Ferry House was opposed by the parish council for various reasons. Councillors had mellowed their position by March 1999, however, and a dwelling was duly constructed there, alongside the new properties in Pemberton Field.[1185]

1182 ERO D/J 126/1/4
1183 ERO D/J 126/2/8
1184 Rightmove www.rightmove.co.uk sale prices/dates
1185 ERO D/J 126/2/8

Another contentious housing scheme at this time was a plan to build houses on land behind Golden Cross Road, a site that had been identified for building on in the 1984 District Plan. A public meeting was held in Ashingdon about this in April 1999, with two district council officers present to explain the proposal, which was for 73 houses, with garages, a pond and a public open space. Objections were made by local people about housing density, the likely increase in traffic and the question of access. Attendees were encouraged to object to the scheme. Rochford and Hawkwell Parish Councils advised the following month that they would also be opposing it.[1186]

Figure 104: The bungalow (left) in Golden Cross Road which was demolished to provide access to the new housing site; the entrance to Victory Lane now occupies this spot[1187]

The scheme made national headlines in spring 2000 when a demonstration march was held by local residents and "eco-warriors". The latter included teenager, Christiana Tugwell, who had recently become famous for leading an environmental protest against house-building in Etheldore Avenue, Hockley.[1188] Treehouses had been constructed on the Golden Cross site in March by some of the protesters. They stayed there until May, when they were forcibly evicted by up to 100 police and security personnel.[1189] Planning permission for the housing scheme went to appeal and was ultimately granted. The road put in to serve it opened in 2001 and was named Victory Lane. A proliferation of sale

---

1186   Ibid.
1187   This photograph has been taken from Belinda M.J. Daly's PhD thesis, 'Direct Action Environmental Protest in Britain: A Critique of Radical Environmentalism and Environmental Ethics' (2005)
1188   Gazette News: https://www.gazette-news.co.uk/news/5513936.ashingdon-demo-over-homes-bid/
1189   Gazette News:
https://www.gazette-news.co.uk/news/5511996.ashingdon-bailiffs-move-on-to-golden-cross-site/

boards there, despite a previous agreement not to have them, caused some additional contention in March 2001.[1190]

By 1999, as a result of these and other developments, the combined population of Ashingdon and South Fambridge had reached 2,433.[1191]

1190 ERO D/J 126/2/8
1191 ERO A13442 Box 5 (Boundaries)

THE 21ST CENTURY

The Millennium was marked, as elsewhere, with significant celebrations. A permanent memorial was provided in the form of a commemorative seat on the green at South Fambridge, in front of the parish sign.[1192]

Figure 105: The Millennium seat on the green at South Fambridge

In April 2000 planning permission was sought for a property in Fambridge Road for the unusual activity of keeping monkeys there. The parish council had no objection to this.[1193]

Also in 2000, a small but visually prominent site on the south side of the junction of Church Road with Ashingdon Road was revamped in memory of Councillors Crick and Dawson. This "Triangle Rest Area", as it was known at the time, was constructed on a site which had long consisted of a single horse chestnut tree and a homemade information board. That is until George Wall, the last survivor of one of the old Ashingdon families, offered to pay for a public seat in remembrance of his family and the parish council chose this location as the place to install it. The area was paved, turfed and provided with brick

---

1192   ERO D/J 126/2/8
1193   Ibid.

planters. A second seat, commemorating Councillor Dawson, was installed, along with a proper noticeboard, commemorating Councillor Crick. The area was formally dedicated in September 2000 by Rev. West and it received a Highly Commended Heritage Award in April 2001 (presented the following month). The parish clerk, Peter Murray, had liaised secretly with Rochford District Council about the award, so that it would come as a nice surprise to the parish councillors.[1194] Rev. West was succeeded in 2002 by Rev. Timothy Clay, who became Priest-in-Charge of Ashingdon and South Fambridge.

Figure 106: The Triangle Rest Area, showing in the foreground the seat donated by George Wall

In 2005 planning permission was granted to demolish *The Anchor* in South Fambridge and replace it with the Maritime Mews flats. The pub had been struggling for business and was no longer viable.[1195] As early as October 1972 its owner, Mr. Mascall, had proposed its redevelopment.[1196] South Fambridge had had a pub for centuries, however, and its value as a public meeting place was important. It was therefore a condition of the residential

---

1194   ERO D/J 126/2/8 & A13442 Box 1 (Correspondence)
1195   Save South Fambridge blog http://savesouthfambridge.blogspot.com/p/mews-bar-change.html and Companies House:
https://find-and-update.company-information.service.gov.uk/company/06779753/filing-history?page=1
1196   ERO D/J 126/2/3

redevelopment that a bar should be included. This was duly delivered as the *Mews Bar*, a bar/café on a much smaller scale. It was initially run commercially, but in 2008 it was taken over by a locally run Community Interest Company. This too, struggled, and was dissolved in 2013.[1197] The bar has since been converted into residential premises. The presence of a public house in the village, stretching back to at least the 1670s, in the form of the predecessor of the Old Ferry House, had finally come to an end.

In May 2007 Councillor Margaret (Peggy) Shaw, a long-serving member of the parish council, was elected as chairman. She served continuously in that role for three years until being succeeded in May 2010 by Councillor Debra Constable. John Dyke was appointed as parish clerk in May 2007.[1198]

In 2008 26-year-old Lieutenant Aaron Lewis, a local man, was killed while on active service during military operations in Afghanistan. He is commemorated on a plaque inside the Memorial Hall. The Aaron Lewis Foundation was set up in his honour.[1199]

Things were on-the-up at this period for the Ashingdon United Free Church, which experienced some growth in the early part of the 21st century. On 1 April 2018 it merged with the Community Church in Rochford to form the Life Community Church, which is the institution which is now on the site of the original Free Church Mission Hall. Meanwhile, at St Andrew's, Rev. Ernie Guest succeeded Rev. Tim Clay the following year.

In October 2018 a tree was planted in memory of long-serving former parish councillor, Norman Drayton-Thomas, who died in March 2017. Councillor T. Flowers was parish council chairman 2017-21, with Councillor D. Catchpole succeeding him in the last of these years. John Dyke was succeeded as parish clerk by Kelly Holland and then, in January 2019, by Karen Boyce.[1200]

An extension to the play area at King George's Field was opened in November 2018 and a community defibrillator was installed at the Memorial Hall in December 2021.[1201]

By mid-2019 the population estimate for Ashingdon and South Fambridge was 3,590, an increase of more than 1,000 in the previous 20 years.[1202]

Like the rest of the world, Ashingdon and South Fambridge entered 2020 with the

---

1197 Save South Fambridge blog http://savesouthfambridge.blogspot.com/p/mews-bar-change.html and Companies House: https://find-and-update.company-information.service.gov.uk/company/06779753/filing-history?page=1
1198 ERO D/J 126/4/2
1199 Aaron Lewis Foundation: http://www.aaronlewisfoundation.org.uk/about-us/
1200 Ashingdon Parish Council: Minutes https://ashingdonparishcouncil.gov.uk/council-meetings-2018-19/
1201 Ibid.
1202 Office for National Statistics: https://www.ons.gov.uk/peoplepopulationandcommunity/populationandmigration/populationestimates/adhocs/12324parishpopulationestimatesformid2001tomid2019basedonbestfittingofoutputareastoparishes

COVID-19 pandemic making the headlines. In March the first of several national lockdowns took place. Some local businesses struggled, church services were cancelled and many people turned to online meetings for professional and social activities.

Figure 107: Ashingdon thanks NHS staff for their hard work during the COVID pandemic in spring 2020

By this stage solar farming – the use of solar panels to harvest the sun's energy – had come to some of the former agricultural fields in South Fambridge. Plans are currently afoot to expand solar farming provision in the area, the flat fields of which seem to be ideal for this activity.[1203]

In February 2022 Anglian Water announced a £1.5 million investment in a new sewerage system in Ashingdon, allowing some residents to connect to mains sewerage for the first time. Ashingdon and Canewdon Roads were briefly closed, but the bulk of the work took place on adjacent fields.[1204]

1203   Grasslands Solar Farm: https://www.grasslandssolarfarm.co.uk/
1204   Anglian Water: https://www.anglianwater.co.uk/news/first-time-sewage-system-in-ashingdon-begins-this-month/

Figure 108: Work under way for the new sewerage scheme, at the bottom of Ashingdon Hill in March 2022

According to straw poll in the "Ashingdon Village Local News and Information" Facebook group, conducted by the author in August 2022, the main issues in the area since the millennium have been an increase in residential development, the resultant loss of green space and increase in traffic (especially on Ashingdon Road), and the resultant increase due to the latter in potholes and temporary roadworks. Inadequate bus services and clashes between cyclists and pedestrians were also cited. Other topics included a lack of community activities, especially for teenagers, the need for improvements to facilities at King George's Field, the closure of shops and banks, the lack of a regularly visible police presence and problems with getting doctor's appointments. Ashingdon residents also remain dependent on services outside the parish, such as secondary schools, supermarkets and hospitals.

The previous chapters in this book have shown that virtually all of the above have cropped up in the council minutes over the decades, following the creeping urbanisation of Ashingdon, especially since the war. More widely, feedback from other communities across the UK suggests that these are also likely to be amongst the main topics elsewhere. Until the country is ready to have a serious conversation about population growth, and the increased amount of house-building and road-building which results from it, it is difficult to see how these can be addressed. A plan by Bloor Homes to build 662 houses in Rochford, east of Ashingdon Road and north of Rochford Garden Way, which was approved in March 2022, will surely only compound some of the above issues.[1205]

One outstanding local issue is the long-planned replacement of the Church Hall. As early as February 1998 plans were presented to a parish meeting "on the proposed new Ashingdon Community Hall which would replace the existing Church Hall".[1206] In March £5,000 was allocated in readiness for its construction, but it has still to be built.[1207]

On the national stage, the Internet, mobile phones, social media, satellite navigation systems, smart TVs and numerous other modern communications technologies have all come to play a significant part in day-to-day lives locally since the Millennium. Electric cars and climate change are also regularly in the news. 2022 saw the death of Queen Elizabeth II, the country's longest-serving monarch, who had recently celebrated an incredible 70 years as head of state. The next phase of Ashingdon life will take place under the reign of King Charles III.

1205   *Echo* News: Bloor Homes https://www.echo-news.co.uk/news/19980299.ashingdon-road-bloor-homes-wins-battle-662-huge-housing-plan/
1206   ERO D/J 126/1/4
1207   ERO D/J 126/2/8

CONCLUSION

The administrative boundaries of Ashingdon and South Fambridge have in some ways made the intertwined history of the two parishes quite complex. The winding, intricate nature of the original boundary of the main part of the historic Ashingdon parish, its two detached parts, the parish's interweaving with South Fambridge and the manorial landholdings that crossed the boundaries between Ashingdon and South Fambridge and into neighbouring Hockley, Hawkwell and Little Stambridge, all demonstrate that landownership in the area was historically very complex indeed. In many ways it is appropriate that most of these landholdings have come together in the modern era to comprise the Ashingdon parish of today.

There are, however, some modern anomalies, occasioned by the abuttal of the Hawkwell streets between Albert and Stanley Roads onto what is commonly thought of as the centre of Ashingdon village, and the urban growth of Hockley into the southwestern corner of the parish. These have been described by Ashingdon Parish Council as "Hawkwell in Ashingdon" and "Ashingdon in Hockley" respectively.[1208]

Ashingdon's presumed role in the 1016 Battle of Assandun and South Fambridge's location as the site of Britain's first airfield in 1909 have both served to put these comparatively small and out-of-the way parishes onto the national stage. Meanwhile, generations of locals – from medieval agricultural labourers to 21st-century commuters – have lived, loved and laughed in the two villages, brought up families and enjoyed the combination of community, history and countryside that the area brings.

Ashingdon was already one of my favourite places before I started researching this book. The research and the writing of its history has cemented its place in my heart.

1208   Ashingdon Parish Council: Boundaries https://ashingdonparishcouncil.gov.uk/boundaries/

BIBLIOGRAPHY

Documentary Sources

Albion, John, 'South Fambridge' in *East Anglian Magazine* (Vol.31, No.2, December 1971)

Beer, Noel, *Health Care in Early 19th-century Rayleigh* (HTR Publications, 2001)

Benton, Philip, *The History of the Rochford Hundred, Vol. I* (A. Harrington, 1867 (Unicorn Press folio edition, 1991))

Board, Beryl A., 'The Fambridge Colony: an experiment in land reclamation by unemployed Londoners 1906-7' in *Essex Archaeology & History (Transactions)*, 3rd Series, volume xviii (1987)

Brewer, David, *Know St Andrew's Ashingdon* (Ashingdon Parish News, undated but early 21st-century)

Brown, A.F.J., *English History from Essex Sources 1750-1900* (Essex County Council, 1952)

Burne, Lt. Col. Alfred H., *More Battlefields of England* (Methuen & Co. Ltd., 1952)

Camden, William, *Britannia* (George Bishop & Joannes Norton, 1586)

Campbell, Alistair (Ed.), *Encomium Emmae Reginae* (Cambridge University Press, 2004 Digital Printing Edition)

Caton, Peter, *East Coast Walk* (Matador, 2009)

Chapman, John & André, Peter, *Map of Essex* (1777 (Essex County Council edition, 1950))

Clark, Dr. Michael, *Rochford Hall: The History of a Tudor House* (Alan Sutton Publishing Ltd., 1990)

Clarke, Vernon, *Walking the Seawalls of Essex* (self-published, 1983)

Cocks, A.E., *Churchill's Secret Army 1939-45 and Other Recollections* (The Book Guild Ltd., 1992)

Coller, Duffield William, *The People's History of Essex* (Meggy & Chalk, 1861)

Crouch, Marcus, *Essex* (B.T. Batsford Ltd., 1969)

Daly, Belinda M.J., 'Direct Action Environmental Protest in Britain: A Critique of Radical Environmentalism and Environmental Ethics' (PhD thesis, 2005)

Davids, T.W., *Annals of Evangelical nonconformity in the county of Essex* (Alpha Editions, 2019)

Digest of Parochial Returns, Select Committee on Education of the Poor (UK Government, 1818)

East Anglian Magazine (Vol.31, No.2, December 1971)

Englander, David, *Poverty & Poor Law Reform in 19th Century Britain, 1834-1914: From Chadwick to Booth* (Addison Wesley Longman Ltd., 1998)

Essex Chronicle – Prince Georg of Denmark visit (19 January 1951 & 11 June 1951)

Ferguson, Catherine, Thornton, Christopher & Wareham, Andrew (Eds.), *Essex Hearth Tax Return Michaelmas 1670* (The British Record Society, 2012)

Fowler, Robert & Ratcliff, Sidney, *Feet of Fines for Essex, Vol. III* (The Essex Archaeological Society, 1929-1949)

Freeman, Prof. E.A., *The History of the Norman Conquest of England, Vol. I* (Clarendon Press, 1867)

Helliwell, Leonard, *South-east Essex in the Saxon Period* (County Borough of Southend-on-Sea, 1971)

Henry, Colin, *125 Years of Ashingdon School: The Story of an Essex village school 1873-98* (Ashingdon School Publishing, 1998)

History, Gazetteer & Directory of the County of Essex (William White, 1848)

History, Gazetteer & Directory of the County of Essex (William White, 1863)

House of Commons papers, Volume 41, Abstract of Education Returns (UK Government, 1833)

Jerram-Burrows, L.E., *Ashingdon County Primary School: Centenary 1873-1973* (Ashingdon County Primary School, 1973)

Jerram-Burrows, L.E., *Smugglers' Moon: An Anthology of the Rochford Hundred* (The Rochford Hundred Historical Society, 1993)

Jerram-Burrows, L.E., *The History of South Fambridge in the County of Essex* (self-published, 1985)

Kelly's Directory (Kelly's Directories Ltd., 1882)

Medlycott, Maria, *Ashingdon: Historic Settlement Assessment* (Essex County Council, 2003)

Mingay, G.E., *Rural Life in Victorian England* (Stroud, 1990 (illustrated edition of 1976 original))

Morant, Philip, *The History & Antiquities of the County of Essex, Vol. I* (1768 (EP Publishing edition, 1978))

Morgan, Dennis, 'The fields that saw our barbaric past', *Southend Standard* (24 April 1974)

Nash, Fred, *Survey of World War Two Defences in the District of Rochford* (Essex County Council, 2004)

Neale, Kenneth, 'Historians of Essex' in the *Saffron Walden Historical Journal* (No. 12, Autumn 2006)

Neale, Kenneth, *Essex in History* (Phillimore & Co. Ltd., 1977)

Newcourt, Richard, *Repertorium Ecclesiasticum Parochiale Londinense, Vol. II* (Benjamin Motte, 1710)

Newton, K.C., *Medieval Essex* (Essex County Council, 1976)

Ordnance Survey (OS Historical series), *Roman Britain* (Ordnance Survey Limited, 2016 reprint of 2010 edition)

Page, William (Ed.), *The Victoria History of the Counties of England: A History of Essex, Volume II* (Archibald Constable & Co. Ltd., 1907)

Pevsner, Sir Nikolaus, *The Buildings of England – Essex* (Penguin, 1954 (1988 reprint))

Pewsey, Stephen & Brooks, Andrew, *East Saxon Heritage: An Essex Gazetteer* (Alan Sutton Publishing Ltd., 1993)

Pollitt, William, *Southend Before the Norman Conquest* (Southend-on-Sea Borough Council, 1953)

Pooley, Colin G. & Whyte, Ian D. (editors), *Migrants, Emigrants and Immigrants in a Social History of Migration* (London, 1981)

Post Office Directory of Essex (Kelly & Co., 1874)

Pugh, R.B. (Ed.), *The Victoria History of the Counties of England: A History of Essex, Volume III* (Oxford University Press, 1963)

Rackham, Oliver, *The Woods of South-East Essex* (Rochford District Council, 1986)

Reaney, Dr. P.H., *The Place-names of Essex* (Cambridge University Press, 1969)

Roper, Anne, *The Minster at Ashingdon* (Messrs. Geering, 1951)

Royal Commission on Historic Monuments – Essex, Vol. IV (Her Majesty's Stationery Office, 1923)

Savage, Anne, *The Anglo-Saxon Chronicles* (London, 1988)

Smith, Graham, *Essex and its Race for the Skies* (Countryside Books, 2007)

Smith, J.R., *The Speckled Monster* (Essex County Council, 1987)

Southend Museums Service, *A Short History of Prittlewell Priory* (Southend Museums Service, 2013)

Southend Standard (21 April 1904 and 24 April 1974)

The Anglo-Saxon Chronicle (Red & Black Publishers' 2009 edition)

The Illustrated Sporting & Dramatic News (17 April 1936)

Vingoe, Lesley, *Hockley, Hawkwell & Hullbridge Past* (Phillimore & Co. Ltd., 1999)

Wilkinson T.J. & Murphy, Peter, 'Archaeology of the Essex Coast, Volume I: The Hullbridge Survey', *East Anglian Archaeology, No. 71* (East Anglian Archaeology, 1995)

Wilkinson, T.J. and Murphy, Peter, *The Hullbridge Basin Survey - Interim Report Nos. 1 & 2* (Publisher unknown, 1982 & 1983 respectively)

Wright, Thomas, *The History & Topography of the County of Essex, Vol. II* (George Virtue, 1835)

Yearsley, Ian, *Hadleigh Past* (Phillimore & Co. Ltd., 1998)

Yearsley, Ian, *Rayleigh: A History* (Phillimore & Co. Ltd., 2005)

Yearsley, Ian, *The Battle of Ashingdon (1016)* (self-published, 2006)

Yearsley, Ian, with illustrations by Larwood, Graham, *The Battle of 'Assandun' (1016) – 1,000th Anniversary Commemorative Booklet* (Ashingdon Parish Council, 2016)

The minutes of Ashingdon Parish Council and its Ashingdon and South Fambridge predecessors, along with the minutes of public meetings held in the two parishes, were invaluable in helping to tell the story of the two settlements throughout the 20th and 21st centuries. Essex Record Office documents, as referenced in the text, have been essential throughout.

Websites

A History of Littleton and Harestock Show: https://www.lhshow.org.uk/show-history

Aaron Lewis Foundation: http://www.aaronlewisfoundation.org.uk/about-us/

Anglian Water (First time sewerage system in Ashingdon begins this month): https://www.anglianwater.co.uk/news/first-time-sewage-system-in-ashingdon-begins-this-month/

Ashingdon Hall: http://ashingdonhall.com/

Ashingdon Parish Council: http://www.ashingdonparishcouncil.gov.uk/

Ashingdon Through The Years: http://www.ashingdon.net/history/

Ashingdon United Free Church history: http://www.curiousfox.com/uk/mbprof2.lasso?eid=30192&-nothing

Ashingdon Village Local News and Information: https://www.facebook.com/groups/855872487839281

Basildon History website: http://www.basildon.com/history/chronology/19201929.html

British Listed Buildings: https://britishlistedbuildings.co.uk/england/ashingdon-rochford-essex#.XVkn20d7mUk

Companies House (*Mews Bar* CIC): https://find-and-update.company-information.service.gov.uk/company/06779753/filing-history?page=1

Essex Archives Online: https://www.essexarchivesonline.co.uk/ [individual documents consulted are referenced in the footnotes]

Echo News (Battle of Assandun): https://www.echo-news.co.uk/news/14488146.a-thousand-years-later-villagers-will-come-together-to-remember-battle-which-led-to-danish-conquest-of-england/

Echo News (Second World War plane crash): https://www.echo-news.co.uk/news/4674708.1st-ashingdon-scouts-unearth-bombers-history/ and https://www.echo-news.co.uk/news/local_news/4690856.shirley-remembers-the-bomber-crash/

Echo News (Terry Cutmore): https://www.echo-news.co.uk/news/18353902.coronavirus-rochford-council-veteran-terry-cutmore-dies/

Echo News (Bloor Homes development): https://www.echo-news.co.uk/news/19980299.ashingdon-road-bloor-homes-wins-battle-662-huge-housing-plan/

Gazette News: https://www.gazette-news.co.uk/news/5513936.ashingdon-demo-over-homes-bid/ (Ashingdon: Demo over homes bid) and https://www.gazette-news.co.uk/news/5511996.ashingdon-bailiffs-move-on-to-golden-cross-site/ (Ashingdon: Bailiffs move onto Golden Cross site)

Heritage Gateway: https://www.heritagegateway.org.uk/Gateway/

History House for Ashingdon: https://historyhouse.co.uk/placeA/essexa12.html

History House for Great Tey: https://historyhouse.co.uk/placeG/essexg29a.html

History House for South Fambridge: https://historyhouse.co.uk/placeS/essexs11.html

History of Parliament (re: Robert Darcy): https://www.historyofparliamentonline.org/volume/1386-1421/member/darcy-robert-1448

Imperial War Museum (B26 Marauder crash): https://www.iwm.org.uk/memorials/item/memorial/87050

Keith Briggs' computational maps website on Roman roads: http://keithbriggs.info/Roman_road_maps.html

Luminarium: https://www.luminarium.org/encyclopedia/richardrich.htm

Mendola, Luigi, 'Odo of Bayeux' in *Best of Sicily* magazine (2012): http://www.bestofsicily.com/mag/art418.htm

National Library of Scotland Ordnance Survey Maps: https://maps.nls.uk/view/102342005, https://maps.nls.uk/view/101455982 and https://maps.nls.uk/view/101457131

Open Domesday: https://opendomesday.org/place/TQ8693/ashingdon/ and https://opendomesday.org/place/TQ8695/south-fambridge/

Prosopography of Anglo-Saxon England: http://www.pase.ac.uk/jsp/DisplayPerson.jsp?personKey=-20221&pr2=1#pr2

Pub Wiki (*The Victory Inn*): https://pubwiki.co.uk/EssexPubs/Ashingdon/victory.shtml

Rightmove (house sale dates and prices): www.rightmove.co.uk

Rippon, Stephen, 'Stonebridge: An Initial Assessment of its Historic Landscape Character': http://humanities.exeter.ac.uk/archaeology/research/projects/stonebridge/

Rochford District Community Archive (Canewdon View Road): http://www.rochforddistricthistory.org.uk/page_id__337.aspx and http://www.rochforddistricthistory.org.uk/page/canewdon_view_road_-_ashingdon

Rochford District Community Archive (Crawford family): http://www.rochforddistricthistory.org.uk/page/a_lost_fambridge and http://www.rochforddistricthistory.org.uk/page/a_lost_fambridge_crawford

Rochford District Community Archive (Rochford Hospital): http://www.rochforddistricthistory.org.uk/page/rochford_hospital

Rochford District Council Local Development Framework Local List Supplementary Planning Document 2013: https://www.rochford.gov.uk/sites/default/files/planning_localist_adopted_1_0.pdf

Rochford District Historic Environment Characterisation Project: https://www.rochford.gov.uk/sites/default/files/planning_historic_environment_project.pdf

Rochford District Listed Buildings: https://www.rochford.gov.uk/sites/default/files/Listed%20Buildings%20in%20Rochford%20District_0.pdf

Rouncefall transmitter: http://tx.mb21.co.uk/gallery/gallerypage.php?txid=1827

Salzman, L.F. (Ed.), *The Victoria County History of the County of Cambridgeshire and The Isle of Ely, Volume II* (1948): https://www.british-history.ac.uk/vch/cambs/vol2/pp199-210

Save South Fambridge (*Mews Bar*): http://savesouthfambridge.blogspot.com/p/mews-bar-change.html

South Essex District Cricket Board (1953 – Umpires Bribed at Ashingdon): http://www.sedcb.org.uk/yesterdays-our-timeline/1953-ashingdon

Southend Timeline (Chester Moor Hall): https://www.southendtimeline.co.uk/2/southend-timeline-chester-moor-hall-history-of-southend-on-sea.html

Survey of London, Vol. XVIII (1937): https://www.british-history.ac.uk/survey-london/vol18/pt2/pp1-9

The Clergy Database: https://theclergydatabase.org.uk/jsp/locations/DisplayLocation.jsp?locKey=11120

The Coggeshall Family: http://www.coggeshallmuseum.org.uk/coggesfamily.htm

The Essex Society for Archaeology & History: https://www.esah1852.org.uk/publications/transactions

The Hull Project: http://www.domesdaybook.net/home

The Portable Antiquities Scheme: https://finds.org.uk/

Utopia Britannica: http://www.utopia-britannica.org.uk/pages/ESSEX.htm

Films

The films and accompanying reminiscences of Ashingdon barber and artist, John V. Chambers

INDEX

Albert Close, 175

Albert Road, 175-6, 187, 262

Alexandra Road, 175, 187, 193, 254, 263

Anarchy, 139-140, 183

Anchor Inn, 115-6, 122, 132, 152, 153, 157, 163, 167, 184, 200, 218, 223, 225, 236, 247, 261, 273, 275, 284, 198

Arnolds Way, 263

Arundel Road, 165, 172, 183, 208, 255, 268

Ashingdon Carnival, 256, 284

Ashingdon Church (St Andrew), 6, 14, 19-20, 38-43, 47, 49, 58-9, 61, 79, 83, 86, 91, 95, 105, 109, 125, 130, 133, 151, 159, 174, 175, 181, 198, 203, 205, 213, 226-8, 232, 247, 254, 256, 263, 267, 270, 282, 285, 290, 299

Ashingdon Church Hall, 76, 105, 181-2, 200, 209, 219, 227, 240, 254, 276-7, 302

Ashingdon Fete, 177-9

Ashingdon Hall Estate, 175-7, 188

Ashingdon Hall, 34-5, 40, 79, 81, 82, 97-100, 105-6, 110, 114-5, 118-9, 129, 130-1, 132, 136, 140, 148, 159, 161-2, 175-6, 196, 214, 221-2, 225, 231, 235, 263, 271

Ashingdon Park Estate, 165-7, 172, 181, 185, 188, 208, 211-2, 225, 231, 235, 255, 259-60, 262, 264, 268-9, 283, 288

Ashingdon Rectory, 59, 77-9, 105, 109, 118-9, 125, 133, 149, 177-9, 232

Ashingdon Road, 9, 12, 14, 34, 65, 68, 77, 79, 81, 82-3, 104-6, 111, 113, 120, 145, 148-9, 150, 158, 162, 165, 167, 169, 171, 175-6, 180, 186, 187, 192, 198, 202, 205, 208, 213, 217-8, 220, 225, 231, 235, 238, 240, 249-50, 252, 256, 260-2, 265, 269, 278, 280, 288-91, 294, 297, 301-2

Ashingdon Youth Club, 217, 275-8, 284

Assandune Close, 251, 263

Battle of Assandun, 6-7, 14-21, 42, 66, 112, 187, 226, 303

Beaches Close, 243

Beckney Wood House, 179, 192, 213, 223, 254

Beckney Wood, 31-2, 65, 85, 89, 101, 103, 111, 114, 122-4, 148, 161, 262, 272, 275

Beckney, 24, 28-9, 31, 35, 37, 43, 50, 64-5, 68, 74, 76, 84-5, 86, 87, 95, 98-101, 103, 110-1, 113, 114, 118-9, 122-4, 128-9, 131, 133, 135, 148-9, 161, 187, 204, 207-8, 248

Boundaries, 8-9, 12, 28, 31-2, 67, 76-7, 81-3, 85, 86, 88, 101, 112, 116, 118, 145, 175, 186-8, 191, 201, 214, 222, 240, 242, 252, 254, 278-9, 303

Brays Lane, 9, 65, 81-2, 105-6, 113, 149, 162, 187, 192, 205, 225, 246, 249, 259, 281

Brick House Farm (aka Forsters), 64, 71-3, 86, 98, 110, 112, 113, 115, 118-9, 122-3, 128, 161, 163, 173, 199, 224, 235, 272

Broadlands Avenue, 242, 278-9

Broadlands Road, 242, 278-9

Bypass, 280-2

Canewdon Road, 65, 67, 77, 83, 145, 158, 165, 167, 169, 187, 194, 205, 207-9, 211, 220, 221, 231, 235, 241, 259, 263, 269, 272, 300

Canewdon View Road, 145, 162, 169, 179, 205, 225, 272

Cavendish Road, 172, 179

Chamberlain's Farm, 79-81, 85, 97-101, 103-4, 107, 110, 112, 114-5, 117, 123, 128, 131, 133, 135, 145, 149, 158, 160, 165, 221, 240, 269

Chestnut Close, 243

Church Road, 34, 78, 104-6, 137, 169, 174, 213-4, 221, 249, 252, 263, 297

Clarendon Road, 172, 262

Clifton Road, 175-6, 217, 254, 293-4

Coronations, 156, 196-8, 228-9

Crane Court Drive, 138, 151

Crawford family, 36, 135, 147, 149, 150-1, 163, 173, 184-5, 198-9, 213, 215-6, 235, 248

Crick, Bernard, 225, 233, 237, 252, 272, 291-2, 297-8

Crouch View Crescent, 108, 172, 225, 267

Cycling, 179, 195-6, 247, 276, 280, 287, 301

Domesday Book, 22-5, 28, 29, 31, 80

Edward Close, 294

Ellesmere Road, 162, 165, 207, 260, 268

Ethelbert Road, 165

Fairview Estate, 172, 191, 203, 212, 232, 241

Fambridge Colony, 151-2, 157

Fambridge Road, 14, 35, 65, 68, 77, 83, 111-2, 120, 130-1, 150, 157, 158, 165, 167, 192, 208, 231, 233, 240, 248, 250, 256, 261, 265, 268, 273-4, 281, 284, 297

Ferry House/Ferry Inn, 64, 73-4, 96, 107, 109, 115, 118-9, 122, 124, 128, 157, 163-4, 186, 199, 224, 260, 272, 283, 294, 299

Ferry, 9, 44, 48, 50, 52-3, 55, 56, 62, 64, 74, 86, 96, 113, 115, 118-9, 128, 147, 184, 200, 204, 207, 211, 214, 230-1, 273

Fire protection, 182, 193-4, 207, 270

First World War, 155, 158-9, 202

Flooding, 113, 122, 125, 181, 228, 231, 238, 240, 249, 252, 268-9

Flying Fleas, 194-5

Forsters – see Brick House Farm

Foxfield Close, 243, 249

Free Church Mission Hall, 150-1, 158, 167, 170, 180, 198, 208, 224, 233-4, 243, 245, 258, 285, 299

Golden Cross, 55, 81-2, 100, 114, 124, 145, 282, 287, 289

Golden Cross Road, 145, 172, 224-5, 290, 295

Gore, John Joseph, 183, 184-6, 197, 198-200, 211, 215-6, 237, 244

Granville Road, 172

Great Brays Farm, 82, 99-100, 106, 115

Greensward Lane, 65, 85, 86, 88, 96, 103, 108, 112, 118, 124-5, 129, 131, 133, 145, 169, 171, 174, 186, 187, 192, 196, 208, 223-4, 225, 235-6, 240, 246, 254, 257, 271, 278, 290

Harrogate Drive, 65, 103, 172

Harrogate Estate, 145-6

Harrogate Farm, 161, 174, 223, 260

Harrogate Road, 145, 172, 256, 278-80

Highams Estate, 242

Highcliff Crescent, 105, 205, 263

Hill Farm – see Rouncefall

Hillsborough Road, 147, 165, 255, 269

Hollick, Thomas, 137-8, 147, 149, 162

Hollick's Engineering Factory, 137-8, 139, 141, 147, 149, 151, 157, 163, 185, 248

Holloucks Farm, 85-6

Hyde Wood Lane, 65, 81-3, 187, 194, 205, 236, 243, 259

Hyde Wood, 18, 65, 81, 83

Jolly family, 126-7, 132, 135, 147-9, 150, 160, 163-4, 173, 189, 211, 213, 215, 224, 235, 251

Jubilees, 188-9, 199, 263-4

Keyes family, 61, 65, 83, 85, 90, 91-3, 95, 97-101, 103-5, 108, 109-10, 112, 114-5, 117-9, 122-3, 125, 129, 130

Lascelles Gardens, 68, 81, 191, 232

Leamington Road, 223, 249, 252, 256, 278-9

Leggatt, Ethel Maud, 232, 236-7, 244, 251, 258, 259, 267

Little Brays Farm, 82

Lower Road, 35, 65, 86, 87, 108, 111, 147, 160, 186, 187, 192, 203, 205, 208, 241, 254, 260, 261, 290

Lyndhurst Road, 147, 165, 268

Magnolia Road, 276

Malvern Road, 65, 103, 243, 260, 278

Manors & manor houses, 22, 25-31, 34-7, 68, 72, 74, 80, 97, 109, 173, 303

Mapleleaf Close, 243

Maplin Airport, 257-8

Memorial Hall, 159, 169, 203, 209-10, 217, 232, 252-4, 261, 263, 267, 270, 276-8, 284, 288, 290, 299

Moon's Cottage(s), 83-4, 85, 87, 105, 112, 133, 160

Moon's Farm, 64, 67-8, 76, 81, 83, 98-101, 105, 109-10, 112, 114-5, 118-9, 123, 126-8, 131, 135, 148, 150, 160, 162, 194, 207, 209, 221, 240, 243, 252, 283

Moons Close, 81

Nansen Avenue, 81, 238

Nelson Road, 172, 272

New Hall Estate, 146, 160, 186, 191, 212

New Hall Road, 172, 211-2

New Hall, 87, 94, 115, 122, 128-9, 132, 146, 147, 160, 163-4, 186, 191, 203, 212, 224, 235, 243, 248, 272

New Park Road, 172, 224, 257, 262, 276, 283

Newton Hall, 149, 189, 250-1

Newton Hall Gardens, 149, 179, 251

Nottidge family, 27, 60, 70, 78-9, 92-3, 99-100, 102, 104-5, 109-10, 115, 118-9, 122, 125-6, 130, 247

Pemberton Field, 155, 274-5, 294

Playing fields, 179, 182, 185, 189-90, 217, 220, 224, 228-9, 234, 242, 252, 256, 264

Police, 181, 196, 203, 207, 234, 248, 252, 268, 271, 276, 278, 284, 286, 295, 301

Population, 48, 71, 75, 96, 120, 134, 139, 140-4, 148, 169, 172, 174, 177, 180, 185, 190, 202, 203, 215, 222, 244, 271, 274, 279, 282, 296, 299, 301

Potash, 112-3

Potter family, 44, 65, 71, 90, 93-6, 98-101, 107, 109, 113, 114-6, 118-9, 122-3, 125, 130

Pulpits Close, 88, 225, 240, 256

Pulpits Farm, 87-9, 97-100, 104, 108, 109-10, 114, 118-9, 123-4, 128, 148, 161, 224, 235, 239, 271-2

Radnor Road, 165

Railways, 69, 97, 110-2, 134, 135-6, 147, 187-8, 250, 278

Rectory Avenue, 176, 278, 293

Rectory Farm, 68, 117, 127-8, 132, 135, 163-4, 173, 208, 213, 223, 235, 265-6, 270

Rectory Lane/Road, 187

River Crouch, 9-10, 11, 13, 14, 16-8, 34, 35, 48, 55, 63, 74, 86, 96, 97, 107, 111, 115, 124, 137, 146-7, 149, 151-2, 153, 156, 157, 185, 187, 191-2, 203, 204-5, 214, 230, 243, 259, 271, 272

Rouncefall, 65-6, 76, 81, 88, 89, 92, 95, 97-101, 104, 111, 114-5, 125, 128-9, 131-2, 148, 162, 223, 225, 235, 241, 272, 289, 293

Schools & education, 106, 115, 119-21, 122, 132, 135, 140, 147, 148, 149, 150-1, 157-8, 165, 170, 173, 180, 181-3, 184-5, 187, 189, 191, 192, 196-8, 199, 201, 203-5, 207-8, 211, 213-4, 217, 219, 220, 223, 224, 225, 227, 228, 231, 233-5, 239, 240, 245-6, 251, 252, 254, 256, 258, 260-1, 264, 265, 267, 271, 281, 282-3, 284, 288, 291, 292-3, 294, 301

Second World War, 138, 155, 164, 188, 191, 201-12, 230, 239, 248, 285

Shops, 85, 98-100, 103-4, 108, 114, 118-9, 149, 160, 163-4, 169-72, 175, 181, 199, 223, 235-6, 282, 287, 290, 301

Smith's Farm, 65, 76-7, 79, 81, 83, 85, 88, 97-101, 103-4, 110, 112, 114, 117, 123, 128, 131, 133, 135, 145, 148, 150, 161, 165

South Fambridge Airfield, 153-6, 157, 303

South Fambridge church (All Saints), 43-7, 86, 107, 109, 112, 127, 130, 135, 137, 161, 163, 207, 210, 246-7, 265

South Fambridge Hall, 35-7, 56, 81, 83, 86, 87, 94, 98, 100, 107, 109-10, 112, 118-9, 122, 126, 128-9, 135, 147, 163, 204-5, 207-9, 210, 215, 216, 235, 239, 248, 281

South Fambridge New Town, 116, 138

South Fambridge Parsonage, 64, 68-70, 83, 86, 94, 98, 100, 107, 110-2, 117

Southbourne Grove, 88, 243

Southview Road, 88, 243

Speeding, 192-3, 231, 287, 291

St Thomas Road, 137-8, 139, 153, 163-4, 167, 186, 225, 248, 273, 284, 291

Stanley Garage, 169

Stanley Road, 175-6, 187, 254, 263, 278-9, 293, 303

Street lights, 181, 190-1, 199, 201-2, 211, 215, 220, 225, 232, 238, 249-50, 260, 274, 277-8, 283

The Chase, 32, 65-6, 135, 139, 148, 165-7, 175, 181-2, 189, 191, 196, 223, 264, 287-8, 293

Tonbridge Road, 243, 256, 260, 278

Trinity Wood Road, 32-3, 85, 171-2

Trinity Wood, 32-3, 65, 86, 111, 146, 160, 196, 204

Victory Inn, 169, 176-7, 210, 226, 260, 290

Victory Lane, 295

Village Hall – see Memorial Hall

Village signs, 21, 156, 285, 287

Vincent Road, 172, 211, 255

Wellington Road, 172, 224

Westbourne Close, 243

White Hart Lane, 149, 223

Witchcraft, 62-3

Woodside Road, 262

Wyeth family, 140, 149, 150, 161-2, 169, 181-3, 186-7, 190, 193, 196-7, 198-9, 200, 202, 213, 228, 235, 246, 278

York Road, 175, 187, 254, 263, 293

www.ingramcontent.com/pod-product-compliance
Lightning Source LLC
Chambersburg PA
CBHW061747290426
44108CB00028B/2914